The New Intergovernmentalism

ρ 4−5+16+39

The New Intergovernmentalism

States and Supranational Actors in the Post-Maastricht Era

Edited by
Christopher J. Bickerton, Dermot Hodson,
and Uwe Puetter

OXFORD
UNIVERSITY PRESS

OXFORD
UNIVERSITY PRESS

Great Clarendon Street, Oxford, OX2 6DP,
United Kingdom

Oxford University Press is a department of the University of Oxford.
It furthers the University's objective of excellence in research, scholarship,
and education by publishing worldwide. Oxford is a registered trade mark of
Oxford University Press in the UK and in certain other countries

First Edition published in 2015
Impression: 1

Published in the United States of America by Oxford University Press
198 Madison Avenue, New York, NY 10016, United States of America

British Library Cataloguing in Publication Data
Data available

Library of Congress Control Number: 2014960024

ISBN 978–0–19–870361–7

Printed and bound by
CPI Group (UK) Ltd, Croydon, CR0 4YY

For our partners and families

Preface

Generally speaking, students of politics can be divided into those who are interested in stability and those who seek to understand change. This book has a foot in both camps. It is, above all, an investigation into the changing dynamics of European integration since the Maastricht Treaty was signed in 1992. In the two decades since this milestone, the European Union (EU) has witnessed a dramatic increase in the scope of its activities in areas such as economic governance, foreign policy, justice and home affairs, and, most recently, financial supervision. And yet, in spite of such change, the basic constitutional settlement agreed at Maastricht remains remarkably stable. In 1992, the member states of the embryonic EU agreed that new areas of policy-making would not empower supranational institutions along classic lines and so, by and large, it has remained.

Under the traditional Community method, the European Commission is involved at key stages of policy initiation, implementation, and monitoring and it falls to the Court of Justice of the EU to uphold the rule of law. Since 1992, national governments have tended to sidestep such delegation in favour of deliberation in settings such as the European Council, the Eurogroup, and the Euro Summit. Delegation, where it has taken place, has tended to involve the creation and empowerment of *de novo* bodies. The launch of the European Central Bank in 1998 and the extension of its powers from monetary to financial matters in 2013 is one manifestation of this trend. The creation of the European External Action Service, a new diplomatic corps, Frontex, a new EU border agency, and the European Stability Mechanism, a new financial rescue fund, are others.

Existing theoretical approaches struggle to explain this paradoxical tendency towards integration without supranational policy-making. Since the mid-1990s, governance scholars have accumulated a wealth of empirical detail on new modes of policy-making but they have tended to see such developments as a deviation from the norm rather than what they really are: the new normal. Research in the governance tradition also shies away from thinking about the current and future direction of the EU as a whole. Theories of European integration are more comfortable with this subject matter but there has been a lack of innovation in this field since the debates between intergovernmentalism and supranationalism in the late 1990s and early 2000s. This is testament to the robustness of these earlier theories but also to their tendency to downplay the importance of European integration in the post-Maastricht period. In a sense, supranationalists await the second coming of the Community method, while intergovernmentalists date the end of European history to *c.*1992.

This book offers a novel take on this post-Maastricht integration paradox. Its point of departure is that EU policy-making since 1992 can be understood as an instance of new intergovernmentalism. In this kind of integration, EU policy-makers remain willing to pursue collective solutions to shared policy problems but they have become more reluctant to delegate new powers to supranational institutions along traditional lines. This reluctance, we argue, reflects tensions within traditional processes of national preference formation owing to changes in the post-Maastricht political economy and a crisis of representation among political parties and pressure groups. As a result of these shifts, we argue, national governments are drawn more than ever into the EU policy-making arena but they are either disinclined to delegate further powers to the Commission and the Court of Justice or unwilling to make the case for such transfers. Far from resisting this tendency, the Commission, the Court of Justice and the European Parliament have been largely supportive of it, which is indicative of the fact that supranational institutions are no longer hard-wired for the pursuit of ever closer union.

Contemporary theories of European integration tend towards a sanguine view about the political challenges facing the EU. For supranationalists, crises are a catalyst for deeper integration while for intergovernmentalists they serve as a distraction from the EU's essential legitimacy via its accountability to democratically elected national governments. The new intergovernmentalism takes a different view. Crises of trust and confidence are a perennial feature of European integration, as are periods of intense institutional change, we contend, but the post-Maastricht period is unique in seeing both occur in tandem. In the 1970s, the stagnation in European integration coincided with increased scepticism among the general public about the benefits of being in the European Economic Community. In the 1980s, conversely, efforts to complete the single market took place at a time of increasingly favourable public opinion concerning the European project. The 1990s and 2000s, in stark contrast, saw the EU extend its reach amid public disenchantment about the benefits of European integration. These challenges have been plain to see during the euro crisis, which has deepened integration among some member states while widening political dissent over the pursuit of ever closer union. Such challenges reflect a trend towards integration without legitimation over the last twenty years and the fact that the EU now exists in a profound state of disequilibrium. A key question that emerges from the research presented in this book is whether the EU can survive in its current form if policy-makers and the public continue to part ways.

As with so many intellectual investigations before it, this book began life in a Budapest coffee house. The occasion was a breakfast meeting between the three editors following a workshop on methods of integration organized by Uwe Puetter at the Central European University in July 2012. This workshop brought together a group of scholars from across Europe to discuss their current research interests. What emerged from this discussion was a sense that scholarship on the EU had drifted away from the kinds of questions that motivated earlier generations with good reason, perhaps, but in ways that created uncertainty about the dynamics of integration at a moment of high crisis for the EU. Puetter's concept of the new intergovernmentalism provided a basis for further reflection of this topic and in November 2013, a second workshop was convened in Budapest, once again, to discuss a tentative theoretical chapter written by Puetter, Christopher J. Bickerton, and Dermot Hodson and a series of empirical papers reacting to this piece.

At this point, the editors had developed the argument on new intergovernmentalism further and for the first time presented a set of hypotheses for discussion among the group of colleagues who subsequently became the contributors to this volume. The links between the six hypotheses of the new intergovernmentalism and the previous work of the editors are clear. However, their collaboration has taken them far beyond their respective starting points. The main intellectual stimulus for the new intergovernmentalism as a broad analytical framework for the study of post-Maastricht integration came from the fusing of ideas which were generated in very different research projects completed around the same time. Bickerton's work on the transformation of the European nation-state provided a macro-level perspective which helped to explain the political and societal context for a set of institutional choices also studied by Hodson and Puetter, but with a greater focus on micro-institutional dynamics. Though originally starting from different ends of the EU's institutional spectrum, the links between Hodson's work on supranational actors and *de novo* bodies—notably the European Central Bank and the Commission—and Puetter's research on the changing roles of the European Council and the Council of Ministers as intergovernmental forums were quickly discovered. In both cases, research findings challenged conventional beliefs on the role and position within the EU's institutional politics of these institutions. This volume is the product of this exchange among the editors and the contributors of the individual case study chapters, as well as several other rounds of revision and discussion in various venues. The contributors to this project have been chosen not because they subscribe to the new intergovernmentalism but rather because they have the expertise and experience to challenge it. As such, we think of what follows as an exercise in theoretical stress-testing rather than a single statement of account from scholars working within an existing intellectual paradigm.

Our thanks go to the fourteen other contributors to this book—Paul James Cardwell, Thomas Christiansen, Marie-Pierre Granger, Tamara Hervey, Marzena Kloka, David Howarth, John Peterson, Johannes Pollak, Lucia Quaglia, Susanne K. Schmidt, Peter Slominski, Michael E. Smith, Sarah Wolff, and our 'critic-in-chief', Simon Bulmer—for encouraging us to sharpen our claims about the changing dynamics of European integration post-Maastricht. All colleagues displayed a very high degree of professionalism in writing and rewriting their draft chapters and taking on board editorial feedback that ranged from extensive to excessive. The Central European University and its Center for European Union Research was a generous host for both workshops, and Birkbeck College provided a contribution to the second. Both these institutions and the University of Cambridge provided intellectual and financial support to complete this project, which we duly acknowledge here.

Although we did not realize it at the time, this book has been many years in the making and it would be remiss therefore not to mention the teachers, colleagues, and students who have encouraged us to think afresh about EU politics and European integration. The editors would like to thank, in particular, Jenny Anderson, Brian Ardy, Kenneth Armstrong, Iain Begg, Stijn Billiet, Michelle Cini, Deirdre Curtin, Servaas Deroose, Kenneth Dyson, Erik O. Eriksen, Bob Hancké, Colin Hay, David Howarth, Erik Jones, Markus Jachtenfuchs, Christian Joerges, Joost Kuhlmann, Patrick Le Galès, Christopher Lord, Ivo Maes, Imelda Maher, David Mayes, Louis Pauly, John Peterson, Mark Pollack, Jim Rollo, Lucia Quaglia, Sabine Saurugger, Waltraud Schelkle, Marco Scipioni, Helena Sjursen, Wolfgang Streeck, Amy Verdun, Helen Wallace, Antje Wiener, Alasdair Young, and Jonathan Zeitlin for inspiring ideas that have borne fruit in this volume. Uwe would like to thank the students of his EU integration seminars at the Central European University for being among the first to 'test' the new intergovernmentalism. Together we thank Dominic Byatt, Olivia Wells, and their colleagues at Oxford University Press for their support and hard work in getting this book to the finishing line. Any errors that remain in the book are ours alone. This book is dedicated to our partners and families for making a politically challenging period for the EU such a personally fulfilling one for us.

CB

DH

UP

Cambridge, London, and Budapest,
September 2014

Contents

Contents

Part III. EU Institutions in the Post-Maastricht Period

Part IV. Critique and Conclusions

List of Table and Figures

Table

Figures

List of Abbreviations

ACER	Agency for the Cooperation of Energy Regulators
ACTA	Anti-Counterfeiting Trade Agreement
AFSJ	Area of Freedom, Security and Justice
ALDE	Alliance of Liberals and Democrats for Europe
AMIS	African Union Mission in Sudan
ASEAN	Association of Southeast Asian Nations
AU	African Union
BEREC	Body of European Regulators for Electronic Communications
BiH	Bosnia-Hercegovina
BRR	Bank Recovery and Resolution
CAP	Common Agricultural Policy
CCBM	Correspondent Central Banking Model
CDU	Christian Democratic Union
CEPOL	European Police College
CFSP	Common Foreign and Security Policy
CMPD	Crisis Management and Planning Directorate
CPCC	Civilian Planning and Conduct Capability
CRD	Capital Requirements Directive
CSDP	Common Security and Defence Policy
DG	Directorate General
DG-E	Directorate General for External and Political/Military Affairs
DGS	Deposit Guarantee Scheme
DRC	Democratic Republic of Congo
DRI	Digital Rights Ireland
EASO	European Asylum Support Office
EAW	European Arrest Warrant
EBA	European Banking Authority
ECB	European Central Bank

ECDC	European Centre for Disease Prevention and Control
ECHA	European Chemicals Agency
ECHR	European Convention on Human Rights
ECP	Enhanced Cooperation Procedure
ECtHR	European Court of Human Rights
EDA	European Defence Agency
EEAS	European External Action Service
EFC	Economic and Financial Committee
EFSA	European Food Safety Authority
EFSF	European Financial Stability Facility
EIOPA	European Insurance and Occupational Pension Authority
EMA	European Medicines Agency
EMU	Economic and Monetary Union
EP	European Parliament
EPC	European Political Cooperation
EPP	European People's Party
ERA	European regulatory agencies
ERTA	European Road Transport Agreement
ESDP	European Security and Defence Policy
ESM	European Stability Mechanism
ESMA	European Securities and Markets Authority
ESRB	European Systemic Risk Board
ESS	European Security Strategy
EU	European Union
EUFOR	European Union Force
EUMC	European Union Military Committee
EUMS	European Union Military Staff
EUNAVFOR	European Union Naval Force
EUPM	European Union Police Mission
EUROJUST	European Union's Judicial Co-operation Unit
EUROPOL	European Police Office
FRA	European Union Fundamental Rights Agency
Frontex	European Agency for the Management of Operational Cooperation at the External Borders of the Member States of the European Union
FSAP	Financial Services Action Plan
FYROM	Former Yugoslav Republic of Macedonia

G20	Group of 20
G7	Group of 7
GP	general practitioner
Greens/EFA	Greens/European Free Alliance
GUE/NGL	European United Left/Nordic Green Left
HR	High Representative of the Union for Foreign Affairs and Security Policy
IFS	Instrument for Stability
IGC	Intergovernmental Conference
IIA	Inter-institutional agreement
IMF	International Monetary Fund
IR	International Relations
JHA	Justice and Home Affairs
LIBE	Civil Liberties, Justice and Home Affairs
LMA	Lessons Management Application
MEP	Member of the European Parliament
MLG	Multi-level governance
NATO	North Atlantic Treaty Organization
NHS	National Health Service
OLAF	European Anti-fraud Office
PNR	Passenger Name Records
PSC	Political and Security Committee
QMV	Qualified majority voting
RCA	Central African Republic
RTGS	Real-time Gross Settlement system
S&D	Progressive Alliance of Socialists and Democrats
SEA	Single European Act
SEPA	Single European Payments Area
Sitcen	European Union Joint Situation Centre
SRM	Single Resolution Mechanism
SSM	Single Supervisory Mechanism
SWIFT	Society for Worldwide Interbank Financial Telecommunication
TARGET	Trans-European Automated Real-time Gross settlement Express Transfer system
TCN	Third-Country National
TEU	Treaty on European Union

List of Abbreviations

TFEU	Treaty on the Functioning of the European Union
TTIP	Transatlantic Trade and Investment Partnership
UCITS	Undertakings for Collective Investment in Transferable Securities
WEU	Western European Union
WTO	World Trade Organization

List of Contributors

Christopher J. Bickerton is University Lecturer, Department of Politics and International Studies, University of Cambridge, and a Fellow of Queens' College, Cambridge.

Simon Bulmer is Professor of European Politics at the Department of Politics, University of Sheffield.

Paul James Cardwell is Reader in EU External Relations Law at the School of Law, University of Sheffield.

Thomas Christiansen is Jean Monnet Professor of European Institutional Politics and Co-Director of the Maastricht Centre for European Governance at Maastricht University.

Marie-Pierre Granger is Associate Professor at the Central European University.

Tamara Hervey is Jean Monnet Professor of European Union Law at the School of Law, University of Sheffield.

Dermot Hodson is Reader in Political Economy, Birkbeck College, University of London.

David Howarth is Professor of Political Economy at the University of Luxembourg.

Marzena Kloka recently graduated with a PhD from the Institute of Political Science at the University of Bremen and now works for a business association in Germany.

John Peterson is Professor of International Politics in the Department of Politics and International Relations and a member of the Europa Institute, University of Edinburgh.

Johannes Pollak is Head of Department of Political Science at the Institute for Advanced Studies in Vienna, and University Professor of Political Science at the International Relations Department at Webster University Vienna.

Uwe Puetter is Professor in Public Policy at the Central European University (CEU), Budapest and Director of the CEU Center for European Union Research.

Lucia Quaglia is Professor of Political Science at the Department of Politics, University of York.

Susanne K. Schmidt is Professor of Political Science, Institute of Political Science, University of Bremen.

Peter Slominski is Assistant Professor at the University of Vienna/Institute for European Integration Research.

Michael E. Smith is Professor of International Relations in the Department of Politics and International Relations at the University of Aberdeen.

Sarah Wolff is Lecturer in the School of Politics and International Relations, Queen Mary College, University of London.

1

The New Intergovernmentalism and the Study of European Integration

Christopher J. Bickerton, Dermot Hodson, and Uwe Puetter

The European Union (EU) has undergone a remarkable transformation since the Maastricht Treaty was signed in 1992. In the two decades that followed this historic event, the EU not only increased its size from 12 to 28 member states, it also significantly increased the scope of its activities. Macroeconomic policy, financial supervision, labour market reforms, migration, police and judicial cooperation, and foreign affairs are just some of the areas in which the EU extended its reach during this period. In consequence, there are now few areas of public policy and political life in which the EU is not actively involved. In spite of this intensification of European integration, the basic constitutional features of the EU, which were decided in 1992, have remained stable. At Maastricht, it was agreed that major new areas of EU activity—such as economic governance, foreign policy, or justice and home affairs (JHA) cooperation—would be cast outside the traditional supranational decision-making regime. Integration in these areas would not involve further delegation of competences from national authorities to supranational institutions like the European Commission or the Court of Justice of the EU. This principle was, by and large, reaffirmed in all subsequent treaties, from Amsterdam through to Nice and then Lisbon, resulting in what Sergio Fabbrini has called the EU's 'dual constitution' (Fabbrini 2013).

This tendency towards European integration without supranationalism since Maastricht has been predicated on an increasingly deliberative and consensual approach to EU decision-making. This approach is not new—the EU has long been considered a consensus-generating machine par excellence (Menon 2008: 109; Bickerton 2012: 21–50)—but it has traditionally been viewed as a conduit for negotiations over competence transfers to supranational institutions. National actors, particularly at the executive level, were assumed to pursue clearly defined national strategies. The European Council was the place where the alignment of these strategies occurred through regular summits of the heads of state or government taking place two or three times per year. The 1984 Fontainebleau summit, for instance, was heralded as the moment where France, Germany, and the UK resolved their differences over the British budget rebate and set in motion plans to complete the single market that significantly strengthened the power of the Commission (Wall 2008: 18–40; Short 2013).

What is striking about post-Maastricht integration is that deliberation and consensus have become dominant behavioural norms. The emergence of the European Council as a centre for governing major new areas of EU activity and crisis management is one manifestation of this trend (Puetter 2014; see also chapter 8 by Puetter in this volume). In the period 2008–12, EU and/or Euro area heads of state or government met on average seven times per year in sessions that were often convened at short notice; while the Commission was involved in such deliberations it was rarely empowered as a result (Hodson and Puetter 2013). This deliberative turn is by no means confined to the European Council but rather permeates all levels of collective EU decision-making, notably those directed at new areas of EU activity. The relevant formations of the Council of Ministers,[1] the Eurogroup and a plethora of dedicated expert committees are at the heart of this process. In his work on the 'field' and 'habitus' of security and defence policy, for instance, Frédéric Mérand has observed that professionals across Europe relate to one another as shared members of an increasingly 'cosmopolitan-minded' military community (see also Howorth 2010; Cross Davis 2011).

It would be wrong to suggest that no conflicts occur within these deliberative and consensus-seeking settings. One only needs to think of divisions over Iraq in 2003 or the disagreements over the terms of emergency loans to Greece in 2010 to see that conflicts exist. The decision to appoint Jean-Claude Juncker as President of the Commission in 2014 was also divisive, with the British Prime Minister David Cameron eventually pushing for a vote in the European Council. What was striking about the latter example is how unusual it was. Conflict would also appear to lie behind another important feature of the EU, namely its growing differentiation (Holzinger and Schimmelfennig 2012; Leuffen, Rittberger, and Schimmelfennig 2012). Observers have often seen in this development the formalization of divisions between member states: principled disagreements over border control or on the merits of monetary union have resulted in a more fragmented and divided Union. In fact, as Rebecca Adler-Nissen has argued at length, the supposed trade-off between

[1] Here and elsewhere, we use the term Council of Ministers rather than the Council or the Council of the European Union.

integration and autonomy exists more in theory than it does in practice (2014: 40). Countries with opt-outs are still able to exert influence on policy areas of which they are not formally a part, and this is often the case because of the powerful desire of national officials to remain part of the EU policy-making process.

Along with a preference for deliberation and consensus-seeking, the delegation of powers has taken a new form in the post-Maastricht period. Instead of delegating to traditional supranational institutions such as the Commission and the Court of Justice as under the Community method, delegation has by and large been to *de novo* bodies.[2] Generally speaking, we think of *de novo* institutions as newly created bodies that often enjoy considerable autonomy by way of executive or legislative power and have a degree of control over their own resources. As a rule, they fulfil functions that could have been delegated to the Commission and tend to contain mechanisms for member state representation as a part of their governance structure. Some *de novo* institutions, such as the European External Action Service (EEAS) are familiar and have elicited considerable scholarly and public discussion (Batora 2013; Duke 2013; Smith 2013). Others, such as the European Food Safety Authority, the EU Agency for Fundamental Rights and the European Banking Authority, are less well known. *De novo* bodies are often based outside Brussels and are involved in information gathering and in the provision of technical expertise. A few, with the European Stability Mechanism being a case in point, have more substantive policy-making powers. Renaud Dehousse reports that while only two semi-autonomous agencies existed prior to the 1990s, by 2013 there were 35 in total. Thirteen such agencies were created during the Prodi Commission alone (Dehousse 2013: 15–16). More than just a series of chance occurrences, 'a phenomenon of such magnitude and regularity is likely to be a response to structural constraints' (Dehousse 2013: 16).

Even though it is true that EU member states have been ready to delegate new powers to the Commission in the field of JHA, as one of the major new areas of EU activity, in so doing they have deviated in important respects from the traditional Community method. Emek Uçarer refers to JHA as still an 'intrinsically intergovernmental' policy area (2013: 293), which is reflected in the special oversight powers of the European Council in this area and the fact that the Commission's right of initiative has been curtailed in relation to certain sensitive policy issues. Maylis Labayle observes that member states

---

[2] Scholars differ in their definitions of the Community method. We follow the European Commission's White Paper on European Governance (Commission 2001a: 8) in emphasizing: (a) the Commission's right to initiate policy and legislation; (b) the responsibility of the Council of Ministers and the European Parliament to adopt legislative and budgetary acts; (c) the role of the Commission and/or member states in policy implementation; and the Court of Justice's defence of the rule of EU law.

remain 'the real leaders in the field' of JHA (2013: 230). The European Parliament (EP) has, of course, gained enormously in power and in prestige in the course of the post-Maastricht period (Hix and Høyland 2013). Its precise contribution to the evolution of the EU and its decision-making procedures, however, is highly ambivalent. The EP's impact on the Community method has been to make it a more hybrid and complex legislative process. In its interactions with the Council of Ministers and the European Council in particular, the Parliament has tended to favour a style of decision-making which, in many ways, emulates the Council of Ministers (Burns et al. 2013: 948; see also Costa 2014).

Taken together, these developments in the post-Maastricht period represent an *integration paradox*: member states have pursued integration in this period at an unprecedented rate and yet have stubbornly resisted further significant and lasting transfers of ultimate decision-making power to the supranational level along traditional lines (Puetter 2012: 168). This paradox poses a challenge to scholars of European integration, who in spite of their differences over the economic and political drivers of integration rely on a shared definition of integration as involving a transfer of competences to supranational institutions (compare, for example, Haas 1964 and Moravcsik 1999a). Because of this definition, scholarship on European integration after Maastricht has tended to miss or misinterpret important changes in the character of European integration. It has also struggled to make sense of popular discontent over European integration, as expressed through a string of failed referendums on European issues since 1992, rising levels of distrust in the EU, and the emergence of Euro-sceptic parties in many member states (Usherwood and Startin 2013). Governance scholars are more alive to these concerns, but they tend to eschew big questions about the overall direction of the EU in favour of fine-grained analysis of policy-making in specific policy fields (see Kohler-Koch and Rittberger 2006).

The starting point for this book is that the post-Maastricht period is not a temporary deviation from a supranational norm. Rather, it is a new phase in European integration that has become gradually more entrenched and systematic since the signing of the Maastricht Treaty in 1992. In order to give this period the underlying unity which we think it has, we call this form of integration the *new intergovernmentalism*. This approach shares with its intergovernmental antecedents the analytical focus on the role of member state governments as drivers of European integration. Where the new intergovernmentalism as an analytical approach differs from these earlier accounts is in its challenge to conventional assumptions about the practice of intergovernmental relations, what member states and supranational institutions want, and where the dividing line between high and low politics is located. Simply put, the new intergovernmentalism sees the tendency towards integration without traditional forms of delegation since Maastricht as a choice by national governments that remain committed to cooperative solutions, but deeply reluctant to cede further powers to the Commission and Court of Justice even in domains that have traditionally been seen as technocratic. Supranational institutions have been complicit in this shift rather than resistant to it, the new intergovernmentalism contends, but the significant increase in the scope of EU activity since 1992 rests uneasily with public opinion. National governments' reticence about empowering Community institutions can be seen as a concession in this context but it is a partial one at best given policy-makers' determination to press ahead with integration through other means. This tension within the process of national preference formation goes right to the heart of the integration paradox, we argue, as well as pointing to profound tensions to come if policy-makers and the public continue to part ways over the European project.

In the remainder of the chapter, we take up this term new intergovernmentalism in detail and seek to define it more precisely. We explore the differences between the pre- and post-Maastricht period in order to highlight the novelty of the latter (section 1.1) and we provide a selected overview of existing scholarship on European integration since 1992 (section 1.2). We go on to providing a contextualized explanation for why this particular form of integration has emerged since 1992 (section 1.3). We then elaborate six hypotheses of the new intergovernmentalism that serve to structure the subsequent chapters of this volume (section 1.4) and which we hope will serve as the basis for future debate and research within the field of EU studies. By way of conclusion, we return to the issue of what is 'new' about the new intergovernmentalism followed by a plan of the volume as a whole (sections 1.5 and 1.6).

1.1 European Integration Before and After Maastricht

European integration, as historians have often remarked, is a non-linear phenomenon that does not lend itself easily to neat periodization of the kind favoured by political scientists (Kaiser 2008; Van Middelaar 2013: 40). This caveat notwithstanding, scholars usually speak of two key turning points in the history of the European project. The first occurred in the mid-1960s, which saw the initial flurry of activity to establish a customs union, a common market, and a common agricultural policy give way to a period of 'Eurosclerosis'. The second took place in the mid-1980s, which saw the re-launch of European integration through plans to complete the single market and move towards economic and monetary union (EMU). Although some challenge this portrayal of the 1970s as a lost decade for Europe (Awesti 2009), successful integrationist initiatives in this period were few and far between.

Plans for EMU were adopted in 1972, but they were soon abandoned as member states failed to forge a common response to the international economic crisis. Deliberations over political union were even less successful. Belgian Prime Minister Leo Tindeman may have sought to strike a pragmatic note in his high-level report on 'European Union' in 1975, but the institutional reforms he proposed proved far too idealistic for other heads of state or government (Tindemans 1976). Some integrationist initiatives did take hold during this period, including the establishment of the European Regional Development Fund, the European Political Cooperation and the Trevi Group. However, these schemes were limited in their scope and modest in their ambition.

The launch of the European Monetary System in 1979 marked the beginning of the end for Euro-sclerosis as member states signalled their willingness to cede a degree of sovereignty in a highly sensitive policy domain. Much more significant was the Single European Act in 1986 as a first major treaty amendment following the original Rome Treaty to introduce qualified majority voting on a range of single market issues and give the EP a greater say over legislation. The Single European Act also gave the Commission new powers in the fields of social and environmental policy and bolstered the EU's judicial system through the creation of the Court of First Instance.

The Single European Act is an important event when it comes to understanding the nature of supranationalism in Europe. The Treaty is thought of by some scholars as 'the zenith of the Community method' (Majone 2005: 51). The core institutional framework of Western European integration and the respective roles of the Commission, the Court of Justice, the Council of Ministers, and the EP, as a slowly emerging fourth component of the original institutional triangle, were established by the Rome Treaty. Yet, at the time of signing the Single European Act, the political implications of Community method decision-making were much more clearly understood by member state governments. Notably, the case law of the Court of Justice which had emerged during the 1960s, 1970s, and early 1980s had led to the establishment of core legal doctrines such as supremacy and direct effect. This case law involved non-trivial cases which had far-reaching consequences for the socio-economic policies of the member states (Scharpf 1999). European citizens and economic actors invoked their rights and previously established patterns of state intervention were challenged. The Single European Act's emphasis on decision-making rules as the key instrument of institutional engineering—as evident in the expanded use of the qualified majority voting rule—was also consistent with the Community method.

The Single European Act included only a symbolic reference to EMU but by 1989 member states had agreed to embark on a three-stage plan towards the realization of this goal. This plan was codified in the Maastricht Treaty in

1991. The envisaged transition towards a single European currency implied a major transfer of policy-making powers to the EU. This dimension of the Maastricht Treaty was further underlined by the extension of the EP's legislative role through the introduction of the co-decision procedure which recognized the growing need for further legitimation of EU legislative decision-making. The Maastricht Treaty's social policy dimension is relevant here too. Though highly contested by the UK, which had also been granted an opt-out from the single currency, most EU member states agreed on expanded legislative competences for the Union in this domain by signing the so-called Social Protocol and Social Agreement.

At first glance, the Maastricht Treaty appears as another powerful endorsement of the Community method. Moreover, the Maastricht Treaty provided for an unprecedented expansion of the scope of the EU's activities. Next to the single currency and the Social Protocol the new areas of EU activity included economic policy coordination in the framework of EMU, industrial policy, education, vocational training, and youth policy. The Maastricht Treaty also included two new 'pillars' on 'European Union' which comprised a Common Foreign and Security Policy (CFSP) and cooperation in the sphere of JHA.

Whilst rightly remembered as being a major step forward for European integration, the Maastricht Treaty is everything but an unequivocal endorsement of supranationalism. Not least, it empowered existing supranational institutions to only a limited degree. The Commission under Jacques Delors may have been a vocal champion of EMU but it won few new powers in relation to this project (Hodson 2011a). The EU executive was given an agenda-setting role in relation to economic and fiscal surveillance but member states retained the first and final say over the formulation and implementation of their economic policies under EMU. Control over monetary policy, meanwhile, was delegated to the European Central Bank (ECB), a *de novo* institution with a high degree of independence from the Commission and the Court of Justice. Indeed, rather than think of powers over monetary policy as simply being transferred from the national to the supranational level, the real change was in the minimization of discretionary political power in this area. This was an instance of depoliticization rather than supranationalization as such (Majone 2009: 13). Resistance to further supranationalism was also evident in the Maastricht Treaty's provisions on industrial policy, education, vocational training, and youth policy, which allowed the Commission to encourage coordination between member states but stopped well short of a common policy in the traditional sense. It should also not be forgotten that the Maastricht Treaty was the moment when subsidiarity was made a general principle of Community law. As observers at the time noted, this principle was a response by the Commission's critics to what they saw as an excessive expansion in its competences under the Single European Act (Bermann 1994: 146).

In the new areas of EU activity, the Maastricht Treaty favoured close policy coordination between member state governments rather than delegation. Instead of the Commission and the Court of Justice, it empowered the European Council and the Council of Ministers as the central political decision-making bodies.[3] In relation to economic governance, CFSP, and JHA, the Treaty obliged member states to regard domestic policy decisions within sensitive areas of national sovereignty as matters of common concern. These commitments were matched by new Treaty provisions that kept the Commission and the Court of Justice at arm's length and as such they embodied a decentralized conception of EU policy-making. Cooperation in these fields was based on a central political role of the Council of Ministers as an initiator and implementing body of policy coordination. The Court of Justice was not granted jurisdiction over substantive policy decisions. Under the so-called second pillar on CFSP, it was agreed that the Commission would be associated with the coordination of member states' foreign policies. The Commission was also given the right, alongside member states, to issue proposals in this field. Yet, the Council of Ministers was not bound by these proposals and the European Council obtained an overall oversight responsibility for this policy field. The third pillar introduced a broadly similar set of arrangements for JHA. The Commission had to share its right of initiative with the Council of Ministers, whereas the latter remained the ultimate decision-maker. Even in the field of economic governance, within which the Commission was granted the role of independent watchdog in the context of the multilateral surveillance of economic policies and the excessive deficit procedure, its traditional right of initiative was clipped. Instead of formal proposals the Commission was only granted the right to issue 'recommendations', which could be overturned easily by the Council of Ministers within the context of the most frequently used decision-making procedures.

It is also noteworthy that in the social policy domain—where Maastricht had, indeed, led to an expansion of the EU's legislative powers—these new legislative powers did not inform successful major social policy initiatives later on, with the exception of a few measures immediately following the entry into force of the Treaty. Thus, Maastricht should be seen as 'the peak and end of legislative activism' as a method to bring about further integration (Puetter 2014: 10–17). It confirmed the EU's institutional framework and the existing domains of Community method decision-making in the context of single market integration and yet, at the same time, it marked a watershed in European integration by institutionalizing policy coordination as a decisively different method of integration. Remarking on the length and complexity of

---

[3] For an in-depth account on the roles of the European Council and the Council of Ministers as the key venues for EU policy coordination in the post-Maastricht era see Puetter (2014).

the Maastricht Treaty, Andrew Glencross observes how member states sought 'to tie themselves to very precise policy procedures and objectives, not allowing much latitude for controversial policies to emerge from the ordinary supranational political system'. Such detail was intended to 'diminish the likelihood that supranational decision-making could result in inconvenient outcomes for member states' (Glencross 2014: 70).

The mood surrounding European integration had changed by the time that Maastricht was ratified in June 1993. Speaking to the EP in February 1993 at the beginning of his third term as President of the Commission, Jacques Delors argued that European integration had 'run out of steam' and that member states no longer saw 'eye to eye on the fundamental question of where Europe is headed' (Delors 1993). Delors' pessimism reflected the painful process of ratifying the Maastricht Treaty, which was rejected by Danish voters at the first time of asking and only narrowly approved by the French electorate. In spite of this pessimism, the two decades that followed saw a significant increase in the scope of the EU's activities. In 1997, the Amsterdam Treaty gave the EU a more prominent role in the coordination of employment policies and a new role in anti-discrimination. In 2000, the Nice Treaty included new provisions on the coordination of social protection policy. The signature of the Stability and Growth Pact in 1997, meanwhile, gave the EU a more prominent role in fiscal policy coordination. In the foreign policy sphere, the Amsterdam Treaty increased the EU's visibility in international affairs by creating the High Representative of the EU. The Nice Treaty went further still, in Cologne in 1999, by codifying leaders' commitment to a European Security and Defence Policy with the capacity for autonomous action in response to international crises. The Nice Treaty also enhanced the institutional infrastructure for policy coordination by setting up the Political and Security Committee. The Lisbon Treaty developed further the defence policy component—now referred to as the Common Security and Defence Policy (CSDP) and created a European Defence Agency. It upgraded the post of High Representative, who is now also the chair of the Foreign Affairs Council and commands the EU's new diplomatic resource: the EEAS.

The EU's competences in JHA were gradually extended too during the period following the Maastricht Treaty. At Amsterdam, it was agreed that asylum, immigration, and judicial cooperation in civilian matters would be transferred to the first pillar. The Nice Treaty introduced qualified majority voting for some of these areas before the Lisbon Treaty abolished the EU's three pillar structure altogether with the result that most aspects of the JHA portfolio can now be decided under Community method decision-making rules. Yet, these new legislative powers come with an important modification of the standard legislative procedure. The European Council assumed overall agenda-setting powers in relation to all JHA decision-making in general and the direction taken by the Council of Ministers and the Commission in particular.

Significant though these changes were, they did not constitute a radical break from the constitutional settlement agreed in 1992. The Lisbon Treaty rather confirmed this settlement. At Maastricht, it was accepted that major new areas of EU activity would not entail significant new policy-making powers for the Commission and Court of Justice but instead would be governed through novel policy coordination procedures, and so it has remained since then. In most of the new areas of EU activity, there has been little or no significant delegation to the traditional engines of European integration in the past two decades. The Stability and Growth Pact was signed to speed up and clarify the enforcement of the Maastricht Treaty's rules on government borrowing and multilateral surveillance rather than to seek new policy-making power for the Commission in this domain. The Lisbon Treaty also codified the central role of informal policy coordination in the context of euro area governance by formally recognizing the Eurogroup, which until this point lacked a Treaty basis. The Amsterdam Treaty's provisions on employment policy coordination, likewise, relied on deliberation between member states rather than delegation of ultimate decision-making powers to supranational institutions.

In foreign policy, the Commission emerged as an actor working with, rather than instead, of national governments, the former having few policy-making powers of its own in this field. Member states' reluctance to delegate to the Commission along traditional lines is exemplified by the upgrading of the High Representative post at Lisbon. By combining the High Representative role with the old external relations portfolio of the Commission, the Lisbon Treaty acknowledges the significance of the Commission's external affairs resources but aligns the political command structure closely with decision-making in the Foreign Affairs Council and the European Council. This is also reflected in the rules for hiring and firing the High Representative, who is an appointee of the European Council. This arrangement is at odds with the conventional principle of Commission collegiality. Similarly, the EEAS effectively replaced the Commission's Directorate General for External Affairs with a new diplomatic corps that operates at one remove from the EU executive and which also is staffed by former Council Secretariat officials and a significant number of seconded member state officials.

JHA is, as noted, a complicated case here. Although some scholars speak of cooperation in this field as having been communitarized, others stress that the institutional arrangements remain 'intrinsically intergovernmental' (Uçarer 2013: 293). The latter assessment can be supported by the above reference to the special oversight powers of the European Council and the modified right of initiative. These governance arrangements depart from the traditional

Community method in several key respects. Significant is the fact that areas such as family law and police cooperation retained a special status. Moreover, there is a clear tendency towards empowering *de novo* institutions such as Frontex and Eurojust rather than strengthening the Commission's powers in this domain yet further.

With the signing of the Lisbon Treaty in October 2007, member states' appetite for institutional innovation appeared to have waned.[4] It soon recovered, however, as member states responded to the devastating effects of the 2007–8 global financial crisis on Europe with a further round of reforms. Taken as a whole, these measures illustrate, once again, member states' reticence about delegation to the traditional engines of European integration (Hodson and Puetter 2013). This can be seen in relation to the European Stability Mechanism (ESM), a €500 billion fund created in 2012 to provide loans to member states facing financial distress. Although the Treaty was amended to allow for the creation of this fund, its statutes are set out in an intergovernmental treaty between the participating member states. In this treaty, finance ministers are assigned a key role but the Commission is involved in an observer capacity only. A similar story can be told about European Banking Union, which has given the ECB important new powers in relation to financial supervision and the Commission a curtailed role in relation to bank resolution. In the case of the former, the ECB has assumed overall responsibility for the supervision of more than 6,000 banks. In the case of the latter, the member states that share the single currency agreed to create a single fund to deal with failing banks. The Commission has been given a key role to play here deciding how support to such banks will be provided but the question of whether such financing is needed will fall to either the ECB or a *de novo* Bank Resolution Board that includes representatives of the Commission and national governments.

In short, although the EU has significantly increased the scope of its activities since 1992 these changes remain in keeping with the spirit of the Maastricht Treaty. For this reason, we use the term post-Maastricht period to refer to the course of European integration since 1992. Any attempt at clearly delineating one phase from another is, of course, a difficult exercise. From a strictly historical perspective, one can always trace the roots of one era or phase in an earlier period raising the question of how 'new' is the new intergovernmentalism. Framing the new intergovernmentalism as a post-Maastricht phenomenon also begs the question of how effective legal junctures, such as a treaty signing, can be for denoting more fundamental shifts in

---

[4] Illustrative of the fact is EU heads of state or government's instruction to the so-called Gonzales Group in December 2007 to reflect on long-term challenges for the Union 'within the framework set out in the Lisbon Treaty' (European Council 2007: para. 9).

politics and society. The marker of 1992 is by no means perfect but we feel that it functions as an effective and clear boundary denoting the beginning of a shift towards a new phase in the European project.

1.2 Theorizing European Integration

A key claim of this book is that European integration in the post-Maastricht period represents an important paradox, for the discipline of EU studies as a whole. Before looking systematically at how existing theories of integration and other, so-called post-integration theories (Rosamond 2013) struggle to make sense of this paradox, it is worth reflecting upon why this paradox and puzzle has not been much discussed by scholars.

One explanation is simply that the 'methods of integration' debate has fallen out of fashion in recent years. While European studies used to be preoccupied with the 'nature of the beast' (Puchala 1971), this approach has given way to a more pragmatic one that accepts the EU as simply 'out there', and seeks to investigate particular parts of it rather than reflect upon it as a whole. As Jean Leca has put it, commenting on the present-day state of the EU studies field, 'the proof of the elephant is that we want it with us, whatever we think it is' (Leca 2009: 312). Another explanation, alluded to by Leca, is that there is a marked reluctance within the field of EU studies to explore the 'methods of integration' debate too deeply in case something is found that challenges the field's broad normative commitment to further EU integration. In his discussion of this issue, Giandomenico Majone considers why scholars 'have been reluctant to examine the operational code of EU decision-makers . . . preferring instead to limit their investigations to legal, economic or institutional technicalities' (2009: 2). His answer is that EU scholars, rather like scholars in fields such as environmental or gender studies, tend to have a strong sympathy with their object of study. To find, therefore, that the expansion in EU activity in the post-Maastricht period is not associated with further supranationalism may be a conclusion that meets strong normative resistance among scholars within the EU studies field.

A third possibility is that the disinterest in 'methods of integration' debates is driven less by a normative commitment to further integration than by a theoretical conviction that these 'ontological' debates about the 'nature of the beast' have all been answered. Why investigate first principles when everyone is well aware of what they are? This seems to be the answer given by Walter Mattli and Alec Stone Sweet in their overview of fifty years of European integration scholarship. Arguing strongly for a comparative study of integration, they suggest that scholars today take it as self-evident that the EU can be considered an 'autonomous, quasi-federal political system in its own right'

(Mattli and Stone Sweet 2012: 3) and that the move towards comparative research on regional integration is underpinned by the knowledge that the EU can be treated as a stand-alone polity alongside national polities.

A message that emerges from this book is that, on the contrary, some of these foundational assumptions about the nature of the EU integration process have been challenged by the direction taken by integration in the post-Maastricht period. The new intergovernmentalism, as a way of understanding the last twenty-five years of European integration, stresses that a number of comparisons that refer to the EU as a quasi-federal polity often involve questionable assumptions about what kind of polity the EU actually is.[5] As we shall see from the following overview of EU integration theories, there is more need than ever before to renew the 'methods of integration' debate and to look at some of the foundational assumptions made by EU scholars today. Far from confirming these assumptions, the events of the post-Maastricht period challenge them. Not to do so is to risk missing many of the key trends and developments that will help us understand the contemporary EU and its future development.

1.2.1 'Grand Theories' of European Integration

Integration theory was the first attempt to think systematically about the surge in cooperation between six Western European countries after the Second World War. The first grand theory of integration, neo-functionalism, was developed by Ernst Haas in his pioneering book on the European Coal and Steel Community (Haas 1958), followed by a seminal series of studies on the early European Economic Community (Haas 1961, 1964, 1968). In its original formulation, neo-functionalism saw integration as being driven by a combination of spill-over and loyalty transference. Frequent reworking of these terms has left them without a stable meaning, but in essence spill-over describes a self-reinforcing centralization of decision-making structures, while loyalty transference refers to a process whereby political elites and interest groups shift their allegiance from national governments to the supranational level and thereby add to the pressure for centralized policy solutions. Supranational institutions played a key role for Haas (1964), who described the early Commission's efforts to 'upgrade the common interest' by brokering solutions between states that saw the former's competences increase at the expense of the latter's.

---

[5] This is not to deny the possibility of comparing the EU with other forms of regional integration and/or national polities; it simply questions the sanguine assumptions about the nature of the EU that often underpin such comparisons.

Neo-functionalism provided a plausible, if not completely convincing, account of the six founding member states' rapid transition from sector-specific cooperation to customs union and to common market policies but they struggled to account for the slowdown in European integration in the mid-1960s. Haas's initial response to the political impasse that followed the empty chair crisis was to defend his theoretical approach (Haas 1968) but it was not long before he declared neo-functionalism obsolescent (Haas 1975). Haas had no monopoly on neo-functionalism, of course, and a number of gifted scholars sought to rework its insights into a more robust theory of integration in the 1970s (Lindberg and Scheingold 1970, 1971; Schmitter 1971). This research programme soon faded out and most of its proponents moved on to other areas of study. Despite periodic attempts to revive neo-functionalism (Haas 2004; Sandholtz and Stone Sweet 2012) there have been few applications of this approach to the post-Maastricht period. Arne Niemann is among those to have swum against this intellectual tide, although his revised neo-functionalist accounts of European integration since 1992 focus either on pre-existing areas of cooperation, such as trade (Niemann 2006) or those rare cases in which traditional supranational actors gained new powers, such as justice and home affairs (Niemann 2013).

Neo-functionalism falls short as a theory of post-Maastricht integration for several reasons but Phillipe Schmitter (2003) puts his finger on an important one. A key neo-functionalist premise, he suggests, is that 'successive spillovers will accrue to the same regional institution', an expectation that is plainly at odds with member states' reluctance to empower the Commission since 1992. Schmitter's neo-neo-functionalism seeks to make amends here by allowing for the possibility that member states will assign new tasks to 'independent regional agencies', but this theoretical approach still struggles to make sense of the integration paradox. One reason is that Schmitter sees the involvement of such agencies as something less than integration. What that something is or might become is the real research question behind neo-neo-functionalism, which puts forward neologisms such as *consortio* and *condominio* in the attempt to conceptualize alternatives to integration.

Another important attempt to rework neo-functionalism is the so-called supranationalist school. At the core of this research programme (see Sandholtz and Stone Sweet 1998; Stone Sweet, Sandholtz, and Fligstein 2001; and Sandholtz and Stone Sweet 2012) is the distinction between intergovernmental and supranational politics. Whereas states reign supreme in the first of these categories, the second is one in which supranational institutions and trans-national actors can exert a significant degree of influence and where the institutionalization of policy-making helps to drive integration forward. Illuminating though it is, the supranationalist school struggles to make sense of the post-Maastricht integration paradox. One reason is that this approach is primarily interested in explaining those instances in which the EU has centralized policy-making powers in the hands of traditional supranational institutions. While this lends itself to compelling case studies of EU regulation in areas such as telecommunications (Sandholtz 1998) and trade policy (Stone Sweet and Caporaso 1998), it has less to say in those instances in which supranational institutions have not been empowered along traditional lines. To its credit, the supranational school does not shy away from difficult case studies but it still struggles to deal with them. A case in point is Michael E. Smith's cogent analysis of cooperation in the field of foreign and security policy. Having looked to the possibility of supranational governance in this domain in the first of the supranational school's edited volumes (Smith 1998), he found no shortage of policy activity but no compelling evidence of supranational decision-making in the second in spite of the institutionalization of cooperation in this domain and functional pressures for change (Smith 2001).

Intergovernmentalism began as a critique of neo-functionalism in the early 1960s. Its chief proponent was Stanley Hoffmann, who saw concepts such as spill-over and loyalty transfer as downplaying the importance of states and states' interests in the integration process and as overlooking the distinction between high and low politics. In the absence of a fully fledged theory of integration, the high–low politics distinction did much of the heavy lifting for Hoffmann's intergovernmentalism, although what he meant by it changed over time. The original intention behind the distinction was not to grant special status to some policy areas over others, though Hoffmann had given this impression in his earlier writing. Writing later, Hoffmann clarified that what qualified as 'high' and 'low' politics varied over time, the determining factor being an issue area's 'momentary salience' (1995: 218). Here Hoffmann had in mind the rapid politicization of seemingly uncontroversial issues of 'low' politics, such as economic growth and welfare in the Golden Age of post-war European capitalism, following the economic crisis of the 1970s. With this clarification, Hoffmann offers a sense of why EU member states may be reluctant to empower traditional supranational institutions in the post-Maastricht period but he does not tell us why cooperation in these domains carries on through other means. Such hesitancy can be seen in Hoffmann's analysis of EU foreign policy cooperation after Maastricht (Hoffmann 2000). Hoffmann is at his most lucid here in showing how the European Security and Defence Policy (ESDP) was produced by a convergence in national interests among key EU member states and the United States after the Cold War. He is more elusive, however, in discussing the institutional arrangements behind ESDP. As with neo-neofunctionalism, Hoffmann is more interested in offering a view on where European integration might lead to than on where it has arrived.

The 1980s and 1990s saw a series of efforts to develop more systematic accounts of the then existing reality of Community integration following Hoffmann's intergovernmental critique of neo-functionalism. In the vanguard of these efforts was Simon Bulmer, who was among the first scholars to incorporate a theory of domestic politics into the study of European integration. Bulmer's (1983) critique of integration theory in the early 1980s was two-fold. First, scholars were preoccupied with the effects of European integration on institutions, whereas it was the latter that shaped the former. Second, existing institutional analysis placed too much emphasis on the Community level and so overlooked the importance of national polities in shaping the course of European integration. By the term *national polities*, he refers to the institutional site in which national governments, interest groups, parliamentary bodies, and political parties battle for influence and legitimacy. Applied to the integration paradox, Bulmer's approach redirects our attention towards the domestic level but it does not tell us what we might find there. That no self-respecting student of European integration would overlook the importance of national polities today is testament to Bulmer's influence but his insights invite further reflection as to how precisely these polities matter.

There is another complementary aspect of Bulmer's work which deserves attention here: his interest in the European Council and the Council of Ministers in the late 1980s and early 1990s. Bulmer (1996) conceives of these intergovernmental forums for collective decision-making among member state governments as 'shapers of a European confederation'. Bulmer and Wessels, in their seminal study of the European Council, stress that the ability of member state representatives to engage in 'shared problem-solving' (Bulmer and Wessels 1987: 134–5) rather than stubborn defence of the national interest is a pre-condition for successful supranationalism. As such, the roles of the European Council and the Council of Ministers as institutions that can seek out agreement should not be underestimated. Though Bulmer's argument about the European Council and the Council of Ministers helps to reconsider previously held notions of the relative importance of individual Community bodies, it was not meant to diagnose a change in European integration. Rather, it was intended to clarify the respective roles of the core Community institutions in the process of single market integration. The European Council and the Council of Ministers were seen to enable supranationalism rather than to replace it, as has increasingly been the case in the post-Maastricht period.

Another major innovator during this period was Andrew Moravcsik. In a series of seminal articles in the 1990s followed by his landmark 1998 book, Moravcsik (1991, 1993, 1997, 1998) set out a theory of liberal intergovernmentalism that seeks to explain European integration in three steps. Similar to

Bulmer, the first step focuses on domestic politics, although Moravcsik narrows his focus here to national governments and socio-economic interest groups as well as making stronger assumptions about how the interests of these parties are aggregated through a process of national preference formation. The second step focuses on bargaining between national governments under conditions of asymmetric interdependence. The first of these assumptions describes the tendency of states with strong preferences for cooperation to make significant concessions to those that do not. The second challenges the idea that individual actors can systematically exploit asymmetries between bargaining positions. The final step in liberal intergovernmentalism focuses on institutional choice, with the delegation of policy-making powers to supranational institutions designed to enhance the credibility of cooperation commitments. While supranational institutions may gain powers they are unlikely to influence the future course of European integration because of the difficulties of mobilizing information and ideas on integrationist initiatives more rapidly than national governments (Moravcsik 1999a).

According to Moravcsik, liberal intergovernmentalism has become a 'baseline theory' in the study of regional integration, due to its 'theoretical soundness, empirical power and utility as a foundation for synthesis with other explanations' (Moravcsik and Schimmelfennig 2009: 67). Notwithstanding these claims, liberal intergovernmentalism's ability to make sense of the post-Maastricht period is problematic and tensions exist in its analysis of the 1990s and 2000s. Chief among these is the question of whether the post-Maastricht period can be characterized by stability or change and whether changing approaches to European integration in this period are at all meaningful. On the first of these points, Moravcsik appears to be in two minds as to whether the changes contained within the Amsterdam Treaty, for example, are constitutionally significant (Moravcsik and Nicolaïdis 1999) or not (Moravcsik 2002). On the second, Moravcsik agrees, in principle, that member states may wish to coordinate activities among themselves (Moravcsik and Schimmelfennig 2009: 72) but he is scathing of such efforts in practice (Moravcsik 2010). Faced with these tensions, liberal intergovernmentalism arrives at the view that the EU is tending towards a 'stable institutional equilibrium' after Maastricht. Yet, this conclusion is difficult to square with the significant increase in the scope of EU activity since 1992 and the shifts in the relative roles of core EU institutions within these processes. By focusing on instances in which intergovernmental negotiations lead to limited transfers of power to supranational institutions, liberal intergovernmentalism, it would seem, is predominantly a theory of supranationalism. This may explain why it has so far not acquired a prominent role in contemporary research on intergovernmental decision-making within the new areas of EU activity.

1.2.2 'Post-integration' Theories of EU Policymaking

It should not be surprising that theories of European integration warrant reconsideration in view of developments in the post-Maastricht period. European integration is a live experiment that has always given theorists pause for thought about the economic and political dynamics behind the pooling of sovereignty. What is surprising is how quickly debates about integration fell out of favour in the 1990s in spite of the significant changes that the EU was undergoing during this period. As Markus Jachtenfuchs (2001) concluded at the beginning of the new millennium: 'The old battles of the past between grand theories such as neofunctionalism and intergovernmentalism still continue, but they have lost their structuring force because they are of interest to only a small fraction of those studying the EU.' What caught scholars' imaginations from the mid-1990s onwards was not the changing dynamics of European integration but the changing character of EU policy-making. This development can trace its origins to the 'policymaking turn' of Wallace, Wallace and Webb (1977). Reflecting the growing complexity of the European Community at the time, it was argued that abstract generalizations about the nature of integration should give way to specialized studies of the European Community's individual policy areas, each of which are political in their own right and have considerable impact on the daily life of European citizens (Wallace 1977: 302; Bickerton 2012: 10–12).

This argument proved even more compelling in the post-Maastricht period as the EU moved further and further away from the traditional Community method of policy-making. The result was a sizeable body of work on different areas of EU policy-making, ranging through social inclusion (Armstrong 2010), social welfare (Heidenreich 2009), immigration and asylum (Fletcher 2003), public health (Farrell 2005), macroeconomic policy (Hodson 2011), tax competition (Radaelli 2003), and external relations (Lavenex 2004), which can be subsumed under the heading of the governance approach. Several of those contributions were focused on the three most dynamic new areas of EU activity in the late 1990s and early 2000s—economic governance, CFSP and social and employment policy coordination under the Open Method of Coordination—and they featured a distinctive empirical and theoretical focus on new micro-institutional contexts which were developing as part of new governance structures. Decision-making in these contexts was found to differ substantially in terms of prevailing practices and behavioural attitudes. Most importantly, the focus on intergovernmental policy coordination as opposed to traditional Community method decision-making was reflected in the proliferation of a whole range of new bodies for collective decision-making both at the level of ministers and senior civil servants who were representing the member state governments. The Eurogroup, the Economic and Financial

Committee (EFC), and EMU economic governance (Puetter 2006), the Political and Security Committee (PSC), Council working groups and Common Foreign and Security Policy (CFSP) coordination (Howorth 2004, 2011; Juncos and Pomorska 2006; Juncos and Reynolds 2007; Cross 2011), and the Employment Committee and the mechanism of employment policy coordination (Borrás and Jacobsson 2004; De la Porte and Nanz 2004; De la Porte and Pochet 2004; Jacobsson 2004; Trubek and Mosher 2003) were all institutional contexts which not only provoked renewed interest in the empirical study of EU decision-making but also shifted the conceptual focus to inner-institutional dynamics such as socialization, consensus-seeking, learning, deliberation, informal agreement, and confidentiality. These mechanisms were considered essential in enabling EU member states to change policy or develop new EU policy approaches in the absence of legally binding mechanisms for the implementation of formally stated EU policy objectives.

This governance approach has a number of important advantages over traditional integration theories when it comes to understanding the integration paradox. A key advantage is that the former is built on a much less stylized understanding of how the EU works and so it is much less wedded than traditional theories of European integration to supranational decision-making. The policy-making approach is more sensitive to the periodic political crises facing the EU since 1992 as concerns over accountability, transparency, and participation permeate this literature. Research under the heading 'new governance' has, in particular, been directed at the new areas of EU activity and has highlighted the differences between new governance arrangements and those decision-making mechanisms traditionally associated with the Community method. A key limitation of these approaches, however, is that they are less well suited to thinking about the overall direction of EU integration. This is partly for practical reasons. Sectoral or institutional-specific analyses have dominated the field; because of their narrow focus, they have been necessarily less sensitive to systemic level changes. When one works at the micro-level, it is very difficult to differentiate mere functional adaptation from wider systemic transformation (Streeck 2009: 16) and this may go some way to explaining the fragmentation and over-specialization that has come to characterize much of contemporary EU studies (Bickerton 2012: introduction). It is also the case that some of the new governance approaches treat decentralized, non-hierarchical and soft law modes of decision-making as an 'experimental' (Sabel and Zeitlin 2008) deviation from the EU's standard operating procedures, rather than considering them as the new norm for EU policy-making.

What may have further complicated the evolution of a broader perspective on post-Maastricht integration was the fact that many EU scholars were focusing on a different question altogether, namely one which is closely tied to the notion of the traditional Community method as a mechanism that reshapes domestic public policies through European rules and norms. This rapidly expanding Europeanization literature focused on how supranational rules and norms are implemented at the domestic level and how they alter national institutions and policy trajectories (Cowles, Caporaso, and Risse 2001). Despite the fact that with Maastricht new forms of integration were already beginning to emerge, the concrete implications of extending the Community method by means of the Single European Act were only just beginning to capture the attention of scholars. As with the governance turn in EU studies, the research agenda of the diverse Europeanization literature was guided by the overarching idea that European integration had become a highly complex process requiring new forms of detailed and comparative analysis. Notably, the consequences of EU integration implied policy change and the adjustment of established practices at all levels of domestic policy-making. These processes involved a complex web of mutually influential dynamics of hierarchical (top-down) and decentralized (bottom-up) processes of policy implementation, alteration, and contestation. Moreover, the litera-ture on Europeanization expanded at pace, not least because of the unprece-dented scale of EU enlargement witnessed in the 2000s. For many students of EU integration and, indeed, for the new member states themselves which were at the receiving end of this process of Europeanization, enlargement consti-tuted the heyday of supranationalism, with the Commission serving as the main actor overseeing compliance with the wealth of provisions and regula-tions referred to as the EU acquis (Schimmelfennig and Sedelmeier 2005).

Increasingly tired and wary of the ontological questions posed by 'grand theories' of European integration, heavily influenced by the emphasis on multi-level diversity pushed by the governance agenda, and still operating under the Community method influence by virtue of the empirical terrain being exploited by Europeanization scholars, it is little wonder that the contours of post-Maastricht integration highlighted by the new intergovern-mentalism were missed by scholars. As an analytical approach the new inter-governmentalism seeks to benefit from the detailed empirical contribution provided by the post-integration scholarship of the governance school in particular, and its sensitivity to the dynamism of integration activity outside of the Community method. Yet, the new intergovernmentalism combines this focus with an interest in institutional, social, and political changes that go beyond incremental modifications to the status quo and touch on the deeper questions dear to earlier integration theorists: namely, what is the nature of the EU and what sort of actor has it become? The ambition is to combine recent empirical advances in EU studies with a renewed interest in the con-cerns that gave earlier EU theory its scope, ambition, and range. By developing the idea of 'new intergovernmentalism', this book aims to bring together policy and institution-specific work with an interest in historical and systemic change that has often been missing in EU studies. It also aims to re-engage with some of the more foundational theoretical questions concerning the nature of the EU polity and its normative implications for the practice of politics in contemporary Europe.

1.3 The Politics of the Post-Maastricht Period

In seeking to go beyond existing theoretical approaches, we begin with two developments that are key to understanding the EU's tendency towards integration without supranational policy-making post-Maastricht: changes in Europe's political economy and transformations in the process of preference formation within European states. Formally speaking, we are focusing here on middle range causal variables that put the emphasis on the domestic and endogenous pressures for change that lie behind the new intergovernmentalism. Exogenous change has been a feature of the post-Maastricht period, of course: from the acceleration of globalization and the perceived rise of neoliberalism to the enlargement of the EU after the collapse of the Berlin Wall (Zielonka 2006; Harvey 2007; Kriesi et al. 2008). Our own focus is not intended to dismiss this broader context but rather to recognize that as causal variables these exogenous forces have indeterminate institutional effects.

Neoliberalism, for instance, is a popular concept to invoke when studying the post-Maastricht period of European integration and it has become central to explanations provided by the critical political economy school of EU scholars (e.g. van Apeldoorn 2000; Cafruny and Ryner 2009). The term itself, however, is open to multiple interpretations: some view it purely as a set of market-enhancing economic processes, others as a political project. Some even integrate the term into a holistic account of transformations within modernity itself. 'Neoliberal governmentality', for instance, conjoins the term to a Foucauldian analysis of society and has been used to study the EU's new governance agenda (Parker 2013). The problem with such explanations is that they are indeterminate: neoliberalism can work as an explanation for both *more* supranationalism in the manner of van Apeldoorn's focus on the transnationalization of capital (Apeldoorn 2000; see also Mandel 1967; Cocks 1980) and as an account of *less* supranationalism in the name of more assertive national capital, what some have called the return of 'economic patriotism' (Clift and Woll 2013). A similar indeterminacy affects globalization and the geopolitical changes associated with the collapse of the Iron Curtain. Predictions based on such causal variables have repeatedly been found wanting (e.g. Mearsheimer 1995; see Howorth and Menon 2009 discussing the predictions of International Relations (IR) theory on European defence policy).

In order to be able to pinpoint precisely why European integration has developed along new intergovernmentalist lines, we need to go beyond large macro-historical explanations and focus on the internal dynamics of European polities and societies. In so doing, we seek to understand *how* domestic politics matter, a question that has long preoccupied intergovernmentalism. Liberal intergovernmentalism has focused on domestic interest groups and has attempted to systematize the role played by interest groups, individual leaders, and political ideology (Moravcsik 1998). Our understanding of domestic politics, and its relevance for understanding European integration, is broader and—like Simon Bulmer's use of the term 'national polity' discussed above—it includes problems of legitimacy and authority. Moreover, rather than simply studying the ideological content of preferences (e.g. more 'social Europe' v. more market liberalization) we also see the preference formation process itself as an input into institutional change at the EU level. That is to say, the manner in which parties behave, their relationship to the state, tensions between a party base and its elite, attitudes towards the representative process as a whole, challenges to parliamentary politics from non-party movements—all these dynamic aspects of interest representation play a role in shaping the European integration process. Seen in this way, preference formation and EU integration are not neatly separated in space and time, with the former occurring first at the national level and the latter following on in the form of strategic bargaining between member state governments. Rather, EU integration has become increasingly shaped by pressures occurring within the processes of preference formation, creating a more dynamic and unstable set of relationships between domestic constituencies, member state governments, and EU policies and institutions.

1.3.1 *The Political Economy of Post-Maastricht Integration*

Our starting point for explaining why so much forward movement in integration was possible from Maastricht onwards is the convergence in member state government preferences around the need for a specific set of policies as a solution to prevailing economic and political problems. This convergence can trace its origins to the early 1980s. Having been the solution to problems of growth and social peace in the late 1940s, the post-war corporatist compromise between business and labour was now seen as part of the problem. The impetus behind EMU, in one sense, was François Mitterrand's abandonment of the 'Keynesianism in one country' platform, upon which he had been elected in 1981 in favour of a policy of *rigeur* based on a domestic commitment to low inflation reinforced by European constraints. Mitterrand's conversion to the cause of macroeconomic stability was complemented by a belief in reinvigorating French firms by completing the single market, a project that found favour with Helmut Kohl and Margaret Thatcher. As one French journalist has put it, during his second term, Mitterrand swapped socialism for 'Europe', knowing that the former would never be compatible with a market economy (Durand 2013).

This abandonment of the post-war economic consensus was by no means even and governments adopted different national strategies in their attempt to preserve the fragile balance between growth and social protection. In his study of national responses to the crisis, Peter Gourevitch observed of the 1970s and early 1980s: 'as policy debate appears to have broadened, so has the range of policy shifts'—from Mitterrand's brand of 'socialism in one country' to Thatcher's free market revolution, from the return of Swedish social democrats in 1982 to the weakening of social democratic majorities in Denmark and Norway (Gourevitch 1986: 181–217). Neo-corporatism, in fact, as both a policy approach and as a scholarly concept, was developed as a distinctive response to the economic pressures of the early 1970s. The qualifying prefix of 'neo' pointed to the fact that pioneers in neo-corporatism were often those countries whose experience with traditional corporatism had been relatively limited, such as the UK (Schmitter 1974; Crouch 1993: 8). Academic observers in the 1980s often argued that this particular response, rather than the structural changes advocated by the Reganite or Thatcherite right, was far more likely to succeed and pointed to Western Europe as evidence of success. Indeed, in John Goldthorpe's view, a modified Keynesianism was far more likely to achieve the goal of social peace in a turbulent Europe than the alternative of what he called 'the new laissez faire' (Goldthorpe 1987: 397–401; see also Scharpf 1987: 256). By the beginning of the 1990s, this argument was no longer as convincing. Instead, a certain ideational uniformity prevailed among political elites in Western Europe regarding the supremacy of price stability, the limits of government intervention, and the superiority of markets over planners as the pillars of societal organization.

Robert Keohane and Stanley Hoffmann wrote about the Single European Act that, 'like the Treaty of Rome, [the Act's] ratification resulted less from a coherent burst of idealism than from a convergence of national interests around the new pattern of policymaking: not the Keynesian synthesis of the 1950s and 1960s but the neoliberal, deregulatory programme of the 1980s' (Keohane and Hoffmann 1991: 23). In fact, this ideational uniformity pointed to more than a convergence of policy goals. It signalled a broader and deeper restructuring of the European state itself, where key post-war institutions and their corresponding policy frameworks were dismantled (Bickerton 2012: 90–109). That is not to say that institutions disappeared overnight or that institutional change proceeded at an even pace across all member states. Quite the contrary. In some cases, such as the UK, the institutional determinations of neo-corporatism were firmly set aside. In others, such as in Germany or in the Benelux countries, corporatist practices remained key to the governing and conduct of industrial relations. However, the balance of power had shifted against organized labour and the goals set for these practices had changed (Katzenstein 1997; Streeck 2009; Becker 2011). Central to these changes was a growing recognition among national elites—from Mitterrand in France to Papandreou in Greece—regarding the limits of national strategies. Hitherto, governments would pursue their goals via wider European frameworks and the rigid state-society ties that had conditioned government responses in the post-war period gave way to a looser set of relations that were significantly less national in scope. This was the moment when the planning and big government instincts of the post-war period were finally jettisoned. Nation-states in Europe had become member states (Bickerton 2012).

This uniform acceptance of the limits of national solutions did not eliminate national differences as such, which is why the 'varieties of capitalism' literature has proved so popular. Whether one looks at the role of the state in the economy, industrial policy, taxation regimes, regulation, labour relations or training practices, differences remain that have made EU-level deliberative practices all the more essential (Hall and Soskice 2001: 56; Crouch 2004; Schmidt 2009: 310). As Uwe Puetter has argued, a key aspiration of the Eurogroup among finance ministers has been to overcome national resistance to reform (Puetter 2004: 863). This has also been true of the Maastricht convergence criteria, the Stability and Growth Pact and the so-called Six-Pack of institutional reforms, which was introduced as part of the EU's responses to the economic and financial crisis. However, institutional diversity across member states is not the same as competition between entities tightly integrated through national compacts between business and labour. Whilst such diversity is an on-going feature of Europe's political economy, convergence has taken place at the underlying level of capitalist social relations (Streeck 2009: 2014). Policy coordination at the EU level is propelled forward by the latter whilst intended to manage the challenges posed by the former. For member state governments, the absence of such social compacts has made it increasingly difficult for them to discipline domestic constituencies. In this regard, the EU's institutional settings represent a valuable source of political authority and for this reason such transnational networks have become critical for national governments. Participation in them is today a constitutive feature of statehood (Kahler and Lake 2009).

This shift was already apparent as Jacques Delors entered his third term as Commission president. A key architect of French *rigeur* in the early 1980s, Delors nonetheless started out with a Keynesian vision of monetary union in which the establishment of a common monetary policy necessitated the establishment of a fiscal federation to cushion the effects of country-specific economic shocks in the absence of national monetary autonomy. By the time the Delors Commission published its White Paper on Growth Competitiveness and Employment in 1993, such thinking had been shelved in favour of a de-regulatory agenda that acknowledged the importance of a 'decentralized economy' in an era of increasing international competition. The post-Maastricht expansion of EU economic policy to the domain of macroeconomic policies including fiscal policy, wage and employment policy, and the question of the future of (national) social security systems exacerbated this trend further. Thus, with the 2000 Lisbon Strategy—the broadest ever EU economic policy strategy—member states preferred peer pressure and the exchange of best practices under the Open Method of Coordination to the codification of reform commitments under the Community method. Liberalization in general is thus consistent with institutional diversity at the national level. Even in policy frameworks that seem to adopt a 'one size fits all' approach, such as EMU, we find a preference for government-to-government deliberation within the 'Eurogroup' that reflects the importance of such fora for bolstering domestic level reform efforts (Puetter 2004: 863). The institutional settings of the new intergovernmentalism are thus clearly intended as ways of achieving collective goals but in a context of entrenched national specificities that cannot be eliminated by legally binding supranational rules.

1.3.2 The End of the Permissive Consensus and Europe's Crisis of Political Representation

Another critical shift that marks out the post-Maastricht period is the politicization of European integration. The integration paradox is partly the result of political economy changes propelling national elites forward in their integration activities. However, it is also the result of new constraints and challenges faced by these same elites as a result of a much-changed political environment. It is this peculiar mix of dynamism and constraint that helps explain the form taken by European integration in the post-Maastricht period.

The early decades of European integration had benefited from a 'permissive consensus': domestic populations did not challenge national governments' responsibility for integration-related decisions (Lindberg and Scheingold 1970) and when they were solicited for their opinions they generally followed the recommendations of their elites. In his diaries, the theatre director and critic Kenneth Tynan noted that when asked why he thought a majority had voted in favour of remaining in the Common Market in 1975, Labour politician Roy Jenkins answered that they had taken the advice of those they were used to following (Lahr 2002: 248; cited also in Mair 2007: 2, fn. 2). Scholarship on the EU has come to recognize that much has changed in the post-Maastricht period. Euro-scepticism is increasingly seen as an enduring feature of contemporary European integration. Simon Usherwood and Nick Startin describe it as an 'embedded and persistent phenomenon within the integration process' (2013: 12). The term 'politicization' has also become increasingly popular, leading to the founding of a mini sub-field within EU studies where the term itself is framed in multiple ways (for a conceptual overview, see de Wilde 2011; see also de Wilde and Zürn 2012).

Although there is no shortage of scholarship on how European integration is contested (Marks and Steenbergen 2004), less attention has been paid to the question of whether such contestation has reshaped integration itself. In those instances where the connection between politicization and integration has been made, it has generally been assumed that there is an inverse relationship between the two. Liesbet Hooghe and Gary Marks, for instance, in their 'postfunctionalist' theory of European integration, make much of what they call the 'constraining dissensus' around the EU (Hooghe and Marks 2008: 5). While their stress on domestic conflicts, politicization, and growing Euro-sceptic sentiment is a welcome addition to EU integration theory, they argue that these developments will result in *less* integration than in the past: as European issues are politicized, so will the 'scope of agreement' between governments shrink, making advances in European integration less likely (Hooghe and Marks 2008: 14). This is not what the post-Maastricht period tells us, where an unprecedented expansion in EU activity has occurred alongside growth in domestic contestation and dissatisfaction with the EU.[6]

European politics in the post-Maastricht period have shaped European integration in a number of ways. Most importantly, the preference formation process at the national level has succumbed to both difficulties in the articulation of interests and to a more generalized crisis of representative politics (Mair 2008; Papadopoulos 2013). Difficulties in preference formation stem from what Schmitter has referred to as the 'generalized loosening of the links between interests and organizations' (2008: 208), meaning the unravelling of those interests forged out of the grand cleavages of religion and class and mediated by the Christian, social democratic, and communist parties (Lipset and Rokkan 1967). In their place has arisen a volatile and indeterminate sort of politics, where individuals seek direction and guidance from a range of actors, many of whom do not last long on the political scene. Anger and frustration coexist alongside more traditional organized interests, the legitimacy of which is increasingly contested by domestic publics. Though the trajectory of post-communist states has been different, a similar frustration and

---

[6] According to the Eurobarometer, the percentage of respondents who, generally speaking, see their country's membership of the EU as a good thing fell from 71 per cent in March 1991 to 47 per cent in May 2011 (source: Eurobarometer interactive search system).

anger at the political establishment characterizes many, if not all, these societies (Ost 2005; Krastev 2007).

The impact of this crisis of representation on European integration has been contradictory. On the one hand, it has strengthened the commitment of national executives to European policy-making, thus pushing the EU towards what Jürgen Habermas called a system of 'executive federalism' (Habermas 2011; see also Crum 2013). On the other hand, the evident decline in the permissive consensus on the EU and concern about democratic representation has made member state governments wary about their involvement in pan-European policy-making. Europeanized governments find themselves embedded within non-Europeanized polities. This was the phrase used by David Allen (2005) to describe the particular case of the UK but it also describes well the situation faced by many governments across Europe.

These political developments have profoundly affected state–society relations across Europe, resulting in a restricting of the state itself. What has emerged is a marked separation between politics and policy-making, with the latter dominated by European cooperation and the former obstinately national in form (Schmidt 2006). Indeed, the lack of correspondence between national political theatres and pan-European policy-making has become a common theme in EU studies. In their study of Euro-sceptic parties and their impact on government policy towards the EU, Paul Taggart and Aleks Szczerbiak found that as minor parties moved closer towards the exercise of power (i.e. the sphere of policy-making proper) they lost much of their Euro-sceptic fire. For larger governing parties, Euro-sceptic rhetoric tended to coexist with pro-European policies. In the cases of both smaller and larger parties, participation in government often led to bifurcated party machines, with activists on the ground more sceptical and the party's elite far closer to the pro-European mainstream. In a striking reflection on the inability of political parties to bridge the gap between pro-European elites and hostile publics, Taggart and Szczerbiak conclude that, 'whatever the overall nature of recent changes in the European integration process, the power of Europe is still predominantly to reinforce a permissive consensus onto parties of government' (2013: 33). Here, we can see more precisely how the decline in the 'permissive consensus' has pushed integration forward rather than backwards, though also ushering it in new directions in comparison with the past.

Committed to further rounds of policy coordination but having also to manage domestic disillusionment with representative politics, member state governments have struggled to find any real equilibrium. At the European level, they have favoured more informal and 'secluded' modes of decision-making, a move the EP has supported owing to the benefits it can reap from exercising its co-decision powers via the relative obscurity of inter-institutional agreements (Reh et al. 2013). As a result of this unravelling in the relationship between interests and organizations, and the impact upon the preference formation process at the domestic level, national executives in Europe often seem to identify more with one another than with their own populations. We saw this in the treaty negotiations of the 1990s and 2000s, in particular the French 'petit oui' of 1992 and the 'grand non' of 2005. Also, the outcome of the 2014 European parliamentary elections could be understood in this way. The results of this contest were significant for the strong showing made by many Euro-sceptic parties and movements, from the National Front in France, the UK Independence Party in the UK, and the Five Star Movement in Italy. Governments responded by agreeing that Europe 'had to change' but there was no direct correspondence in the short term between electoral outcomes and institutional reform. Public discontent and elite commitment to EU policy-making coexist with one another but without ever connecting in a direct fashion.

These problems of political representation and the conflicts between governments and their own domestic publics have become structuring elements of the European integration process, alongside the more typical conflicts between member states themselves. Spatially, we can say that to the vertical divisions between national polities familiar to students of European integration has been added a horizontal dimension, where governing parties and political elites combine in their outlooks at the European level, and together confront from above their own domestic constituents whose frustration and anger appear to them as something they must contain rather than engage with or represent.

1.4 The Six Hypotheses

The above introduction to the politics of the post-Maastricht period allows us to formulate a more precise set of expectations concerning the new intergovernmentalism. Our conceptual point of departure—the integration paradox— serves as both an observation and a challenge to existing theories. The new intergovernmentalism, as we see it, is not just an assemblage of simultaneously occurring phenomena but involves concrete institutional choices by states and supranational actors, which can be linked to each other and the underlying political and economic context in which post-Maastricht integration evolves. The above review of this particular context for integration thus enables us to formulate more precisely what we expect the major institutional choices to be and what political repercussions they might have. The overarching aim of this book is to shed light and stimulate further debate on how and why these choices tended towards integration but away from supranational modes of policy-making since 1992 and to what end. In this section we put forward six hypotheses which together seek to elucidate, explain, and understand the institutional and normative implications of the integration paradox.[7] Some of these hypotheses are couched in more general terms than others; such generality is a conscious choice, as we are keen to avoid framing our research question in either explicitly rational choice or constructivist terms. Ontological debates over how best to study the EU have dominated scholarship in the post-Maastricht period (see, for example, Moravcsik 1999b). Important though these debates are, they tend to overstate the differences between rationalist and constructivist approaches to the study of the EU and they have had a divisive effect on an area of study that was once celebrated for its inter-disciplinarity and methodological pluralism. All of our hypotheses are open to empirical testing, however such testing is defined. They serve not only as a focal point for the remaining chapters in this volume but, we hope, as a basis for further research on the changing dynamics of European integration.

Hypothesis 1: Deliberation and consensus have become the guiding norms of day-to-day decision making at all levels

A key claim of the new intergovernmentalism is that deliberation and consensus have become ends in themselves in the post-Maastricht period rather than, as they have traditionally been, a means to building supranational policy-making competences. This is especially so in the European Council and the Council of Ministers, as captured by Puetter's concept of 'deliberative intergovernmentalism' (2012, 2014). Many other examples exist of the spread of these behavioural norms in relation to new areas of EU activity. In specialized foreign and security policy committees, for instance, such as the PSC, the relevant Council working groups on external affairs and the EU Military Committee or the Civilian Crisis Management Committee, the epistemic dimension and a principled commitment to coordination has grown in importance. This has made deliberation over collective policy responses, rather than hard bargaining over supranational solutions, the default group norm (Juncos and Pomorska 2006; Juncos and Reynolds 2007; Cross Davis 2011). Deliberation and consensus-seeking have become institutionally uncoupled from supranationalist dynamics since 1992, we argue, and have as a result taken their place at the heart of EU policy-making. They are the defining feature of governance mechanisms within the new areas of EU activity. Moreover, throughout the post-Maastricht period we see evidence of institutional engineering which is aimed at enhancing the consensus-generation capacity of forums for intergovernmental policy coordination

---

[7] In so doing we follow Brady and Collier (2010) in thinking about a hypothesis as a 'tentative answer to a research question' (2010: 331).

(Puetter 2014). EU policy-makers' preferences among member states for informal working methods, face-to-face debate, confidentiality and routines that are aimed at socializing new members into existing decision-making routines speak to this point.

As integration has followed the new intergovernmentalist path, the responsibility for policy-making also lies more squarely on member states. This means that they have become more involved in day-to-day policy-making and collective agreement is required on a more immediate basis than in the past. If we take the intensive involvement of the European Council in the minutiae of justice and home affairs policy as an example, or its role in supervising policy coordination under the Stability and Growth Pact, the Lisbon agenda, or in the context of the global economic and financial crisis, then we can see how deliberation and consensus-seeking have become the operative norms of daily EU governance.

This is not to say that deliberation and consensus did not play a crucial role in European Council and Council of Ministers decision-making during earlier periods of European integration, as Simon Bulmer (1996) has highlighted. For example, both forums played a key role in establishing what Ole Elgström and Christer Jönsson referred to as the 'normative consensus around the European common market' (2000: 701). Yet, the growing importance of deliberation and consensus in post-Maastricht EU decision-making is, we argue, a consequence of the decentralized character of decision-making in the new areas of EU activity and is therefore not limited to long-term agreement on underlying policy norms and the related empowerment of supranational institutions. It is precisely because of this decentralization that deliberation and consensus are so important in the post-Maastricht period: they are the only means through which collective action is possible.

In this context it is also worth noting that, as regards the domain of legislative decision-making under the traditional Community method, scholars have observed that the emergence of qualified majority voting as the default decision-making rule of the post-Maastricht period has not prevented the emphasis on consensus as a behavioural norm. The achievement of consensus is upheld even in cases where this consensus is what Stephanie Novak (2013) has referred to as 'apparent consensus'—a situation in which individual member states refrain from stating differences in opinion unless a broader group of critics exists. The gap between how one might expect qualified majority voting to work in a setting such as the Council of Ministers and how it works in practice is a testimony to the power and the reach of deliberation and consensus-seeking as guiding norms in post-Maastricht EU decision-making in general.

Hypothesis 2: Supranational institutions are not hard-wired to seek ever closer union

Another key claim of the new intergovernmentalism is that supranational institutions, far from resisting the turn towards more decentralized modes of decision-making since 1992, have in some cases been complicit in it. Our argument here is not that supranational institutions have been devoid of ambition since Maastricht but that their ambition has been directed elsewhere at projects that did not entail a transfer of significant new powers to the supranational level. In the case of the Commission, for instance, the post-Maastricht period has seen successive presidents focus their energies on projects such as economic reform (Jacques Delors and José Manuel Barroso), institutional reform (Jacques Santer), and enlargement (Romano Prodi), which entailed few new powers for the EU executive. This hypothesis is at odds with much of the literature on European integration, which assumes that supranational institutions are hard-wired for the support of supranational decision-making. This assumption originated with neo-functionalists (Haas 1964; Lindberg 1965) and is shared by supranationalists (Stone Sweet and Sandholtz 1998) but it also resonates with scholars working in the intergovernmentalist tradition. Moravcsik (1999a), for instance, sees the Commission as a supranational entrepreneur that mobilizes information and ideas in support of further integration, albeit with limited success because of the predominance of interstate bargains in decisions over the future direction of the EU. It also underpins rational choice institutionalist accounts of European integration, with both Mark Pollack (2003) and Jonas Tallberg (2004), for instance, treating the Commission as an agent that has more intensive preferences for supranational decision-making than member state principals.

Building on Dermot Hodson's work on the European Commission, we consider two overarching reasons why supranational institutions may be less positively disposed towards the pursuit of ever closer union than was previously thought to be the case (Hodson 2013). The first appeals to the idea of strategic entrepreneurship by seeing supranational institutions as reluctant to make the case for a transfer of competences to the EU level where such proposals stand little chance of success. The second allows for the possibility that supranational institutions are motivated by preferences other than the pursuit of ever closer union. In the case of the Commission, the tendency since Maastricht to choose presidents from the ranks of the former heads of state or government may have made a difference here. So too may a shift in preferences among the officials who work in the Commission (Kassim et al. 2013).

Other EU institutions, bodies, and agencies, we conjecture, may have been equally cautious about seeking new competences for themselves or making the case for supranational decision-making more generally. The Court of Justice, for one, appears to be cautious about challenging national governments' authority in new areas of EU activity. Even the EP, for all its expanding powers, may not be a special case. Partisan preferences tend to trump integrationist inclinations in the EU legislature, Simon Hix, Abdul Noury, and Gerard Roland (2006) suggest. So too may be a preference for securing a role for the Parliament in areas of EU cooperation that operate at one remove from the traditional Community method.

Hypothesis 3: Where delegation occurs, governments and traditional supranational actors support the creation and empowerment of de novo *institutions*

Though in general member states have resisted the delegation of substantial decision-making powers to traditional supranational actors, the post-Maastricht period is not free from examples of delegation. Yet, it is important to inspect these instances of delegation more closely and note the difference between pre- and post-Maastricht institutional choices. *De novo* institutions tend to diverge in their institutional design in several respects. They often have an intergovernmental strand to their governance structure that is more conducive to member state control. The management board of the EU border agency, Frontex, for example includes representatives of each EU member state, as does the Board of Governors of the ESM, and the EEAS blends the elements of a supranational diplomatic service with those of a bureaucratic infrastructure for intergovernmental policy coordination. *De novo* bodies, in other words, are not supranational institutions in the traditional sense of the term and it is this difference that helps to explain the former's appeal to member states.

How do we explain the creation of *de novo* institutions in the post-Maastricht period? On one level, we see this development as being driven by a reluctance on the part of EU member states to empower the Commission along traditional lines. Such reluctance reflects problems of public justification; given rising levels of public distrust in the EU, member states are reluctant to be seen to delegate further powers to an institution that has come to personify the pursuit of ever closer union. While the interests of member states are key for understanding this tendency towards the creation of *de novo* bodies it would be wrong to reduce this phenomenon to a power struggle between national and supranational actors. Since the vast majority of *de novo* bodies derive their legal status from secondary EU law, this means that the Commission is complicit in the creation of such agencies. Traditionally, the EU executive has defended the so-called Merconi doctrine, which states that EU agencies should not be given discretionary powers in cases where such powers are not provided for under the Treaty (Kelemen and Majone 2012). There are signs in the post-Maastricht period that the Commission's commitment to this doctrine is a qualified one, as evidenced by its tacit support for the creation of bodies such as the ESM and the EEAS. Such support may be pragmatic but it speaks to the idea that supranational institutions are less committed to the pursuit of ever closer union than was once thought to be the case. The Court of Justice's openness to *de novo* institutions in the *Pringle*[8] also resonates with this line of reasoning.

Hypothesis 4: Problems in domestic preference formation have become stand-alone inputs into the European integration process

The new intergovernmentalism provides an alternative perspective on the role played by domestic preference formation processes in determining EU policy-making. To think of preference formation primarily in terms of the role of sectoral interests in shaping government positions, as liberal inter-governmentalism does, is to present a very ahistorical and surprisingly apolitical account of how interests are represented in society and how those interests affect EU policy-making. As well as the views of producer groups or other influential lobbies, we need to consider ruling ideologies, the nature and substance of contestation in any given period, the changing patterns of state-society relationships, and their correspondence to a set of institutional forms that may or may not derive from actually existing social and political relations. Preference formation in Europe in the post-Maastricht period has thus become inseparable from a growing frustration with procedural issues and scepticism towards the idea of majoritarian-based representative democracy. *How* interests are identified and represented has become as much of an issue as has that of what those interests are. Populist parties and movements mobilize on a basis that is partly ideological (anti-immigrant, for instance) but also one that is procedural where the target is the political establishment as a whole. We also see the rise of movements and parties whose interest is in changing the processes of government more than the actual exercise of power itself, such as the Pirate parties in Germany and Sweden. The politicization of data access issues evident in the WikiLeaks and Snowden cases also rests upon a desire to recalibrate the relationship between citizens and the state. As seen with the 'Indignados' in Spain, anger and frustration have become a self-sufficient basis for mobilization. In Germany, the word of the year in 2010 was 'Wutbürger' (angry citizen) (Kaldor and Selchow 2013). In Eastern Europe, corruption of the political class has become a key political concern, discrediting many post-1989 political parties and institutions (Krastev 2007).

A key feature about political contestation in the post-Maastricht period is therefore its growing orientation towards problems associated with the political process itself. This hypothesis points to the fact that we should expect this to have a considerable effect on the European integration process. In short, the

---

[8] Case C-370/12 *Pringle* [2012] ECR I-756.

claim is that as the dynamics of preference formation change at the domestic level, so will those changes, to a considerable degree, shape the EU's policy-making dynamics. The obvious transmission belts are national executives, whose role within the European Council and the Council of Ministers will express as much their own particular ideological preferences as it will their broader concerns about the nature of their authority and their legitimacy. Another transmission belt is the EP. Though ostensibly an antidote to problems of democratic representation in the EU, the Parliament has not by any means been immune from the crisis of political representation prevailing across Europe as a whole. Indeed, though its institutional power has undoubtedly grown, the EP has not become a popular institution. Confident of its hold on the EU decision-making process, but less sure of its representative capacity vis-à-vis European citizens at large, the Parliament has opted for a collaborative style of policy-making that maximizes its influence over policy at the expense of publicity and transparency. Far from bridging the divide between politics and policy-making, the Parliament has ended up contributing to it.

Member states are therefore not only conduits for sectoral interests; they are also embodiments of a set of social and political conflicts that today increasingly centre upon the dysfunctional nature of representative government. Instead of encouraging people to organize themselves and thus take on entrenched interests, as occurred in earlier periods of popular mobilization, today distrust itself has become the basis around which political life is organizing itself. The idea of 'credible commitment', key to liberal intergovernmentalist theory, comes from a critique of partisanship and of political discretion (Kydland and Prescott 1977). This stems from public choice theory, the roots of which lie in a reaction against the expanding and interventionist state of the 1950s and 1960s. The new intergovernmentalism holds that only a broad, historical, and contextualized account of preference formation can grasp the role this crisis of representation has played in transforming the direction and nature of European integration in the post-Maastricht period.

Hypothesis 5: The differences between high and low politics have become blurred

The new intergovernmentalism also holds that post-Maastricht integration has further distorted the distinction between high and low politics. Today EU policy-making rarely triggers threats of ultimate withdrawal from European integration or serious attempts to fully isolate a given domain of domestic decision-making from EU influence. Yet, member state governments are equally eager to closely monitor EU decision-making and are wary of the independent powers of traditional supranational actors, which they see as potentially encroaching on sensitive domains of national decision-making. The fact that the European Council itself once found it necessary to discuss the results of a Working Group on the Output Gap speaks to this point.[9] In other words, it has become difficult to say what constitutes an issue of heightened national concern and what may be considered a purely technocratic issue which could be left to expert decision-making.

To be clear, we are not simply referring here to the fact that what constitutes high or low politics is variable and can change from one period to the next. This has been commented on extensively (e.g. Christensen 1981) and it has led to a revision of the argument as made by traditional intergovernmentalists. The differences between Hoffmann's account and the contemporary blurring between high and low politics in the post-Maastricht period derive in part from what he thinks determines why an issue assumes momentary salience. For Hoffmann, what is crucial is that an issue appears as being of an *existential nature* for a national government. In his words, what matters is 'how essential it appears to the government for the survival of the nation or for its own survival' (1995: 218).

Considering what those issues of an existential nature for governments in the post-Maastricht period are, it would appear that being isolated or left out of EU policy-making is more important than the desire to isolate oneself. In other words, existential concerns are raised by withdrawal from the logic of European integration, not from participation. What lies behind Hoffmann's understanding of the high/low politics distinction is a fundamental trade-off between national survival and participation in European integration. What marks out the post-Maastricht period is the fact that survival is ensured through—not against or outside of—the EU. As already remarked with respect to the phenomenon of differentiation in the EU, it is striking how even formal opt-outs do not constitute a demarcation between high and low politics. When John Major negotiated the UK's opt-outs at the time of Maastricht, the impression given was that they were of an existential importance for the UK. In fact, subsequent governments have repeatedly sought to exercise influence in this policy area despite the UK being formally excluded from it. The concern felt about closer integration in the euro area is similar: non-euro area members do not necessarily want to join the currency regime, but they worry about being left out. Finally, the opposition shown by David Cameron to the nomination of Jean-Claude Juncker as President of the Commission in 2014 appeared at various points to touch upon the special domain of high politics and Cameron suggested that this was an issue touching the core of British membership of the EU. Soon after the nomination, however, the British premier was seeking to build bridges with the new Commission President.

---

[9] The output gap measures the differences between actual and potential economic output. Its construction is a technical matter but it is one that has high political stakes when it comes to determining compliance with the stability and growth pact.

Another difference comes from the implications of the above hypothesis on preference formation and the crisis of political representation in Europe. Hoffmann assumed a degree of correspondence between popular and elite sentiment; indeed, the notion of an issue having existential importance suggests the mobilization of an entire society around a particular problem or policy. As already emphasized, under conditions of considerable disaffection by publics regarding the views of politicians, and scepticism about their ability to represent, such correspondence is often absent. Take the case of François Hollande's election in 2012 and his promise to renegotiate the Fiscal Compact. Evidently, this was an important aspect of his electoral platform and in so far as Europe was discussed during the campaign, it focused on this single issue of pushing the EU towards more pro-growth policies and fewer austerity measures. Not long after his election, however, and in a definitive way at the beginning of 2013, Hollande jettisoned his growth rhetoric and supported Angela Merkel instead. Far from commanding popular support for this policy shift, Hollande found himself increasingly isolated: after the departure of popular left-wing ministers from his government, he enjoyed only a very slim majority in the national assembly and even that depended on his political opponents within his own party voting in his government's favour. Evidently, his commitment to a pro-growth agenda at the EU level was not an existential matter for Hollande, in spite of the prominence of the issue in the 2012 election. For the French public, it was also unclear whether this agenda belonged to the realm of high or low politics: salient enough to sink Hollande's presidency, but not salient enough to question France's participation in the euro area and in EU economic governance.

Hypothesis 6: The EU is in a state of disequilibrium

The new intergovernmentalism puts the accent on the specific features of the post-Maastricht period and tries to characterize European integration since 1992 as a distinctive development, related to, but not merely an extension of, earlier periods of regional cooperation. In its explanation of what makes this period distinctive, this chapter has highlighted the importance of Europe's continued movement away from the post-war economic consensus, the loosening of state–market ties which this entailed and the sharpening of institutional differences between national societies which liberalization has also produced. It has argued that political developments, particularly in the growing disorganization of societal interests and the associated demise of the 'permissive consensus', have come to fundamentally reshape the European integration process.

Put together, these factors suggest that the current EU is in a state of disequilibrium. It expresses an uneasy and potentially unstable combination of socio-economic transformation and political development. In particular, it encapsulates a growing tension between governments and their own societies, where the latter have converged upon a pro-integration consensus that has had to be institutionally shielded from growing public disenchantment with public policy outcomes. Clearly, the new intergovernmentalism does not simply postulate that the EU is in crisis today; by some measures it always has been. Our point is rather that the post-Maastricht period has revealed the extent to which European integration is in a profound state of disequilibrium rather than existing in a steady state or being on a smooth adjustment path to one.

Such framing of integration as both unstable and contradictory breaks with a strong scholarly preference for focusing on stability and expressing optimism vis-à-vis the future of the European project. Our analysis of the genesis of the post-Maastricht integration leaves us sceptical about the claim that by (re)introducing patterns of pre-Maastricht integration practices we can (re)balance the relationship between governments and their societies. Contemporary theories of European integration are surprisingly sanguine about the crises that have characterized the post-Maastricht era. Haas agonized about the periodic crises facing European integration between the 1950s and 1990s—to the detriment of neo-functionalism as a theory, it could be argued—but supranationalists do not appear to have lost much sleep about the state of the EU in the 1990s and 2000s. References to crises in the seminal supranationalist analysis of Wayne Sandholtz and Alec Stone Sweet (1998) are few and where they do arise, as in the contribution of Neil Fligstein and Jason McNichol (1998), they tend to focus on the pre-Maastricht period. While the authors acknowledge the end of the permissive consensus they see public support for policy integration among EU member states as favourable on the whole. Stone Sweet, Sandholtz, and Fligstein (2001) are more open to the possibility of crisis in the European project although their prediction that 'the people of Europe' could tire of having so much decision-making ceded to the 'Brussels complex' gave no indication that this scenario had already come to pass at the time of writing.

Supranationalists' sense of optimism about the European project was seemingly undiminished by events in the 2000s. Writing before the global financial crisis, Fligstein (2008: 34), for example, acknowledges that 'the process [of European integration] has been fraught with difficulties, ambiguities and crises' but he sees them as mere milestones on the road to further integration: '[t]he remarkable thing is that at every crisis the governments have found ways to overcome their differences and push forward their cooperative efforts'. Writing after the onset of the sovereign debt and banking crisis, Mattli and Stone Sweet (2012: 14) describe the economic and financial turmoil facing the EU as 'revealing the striking absence of what Europe needs most: strong political leadership capable of forging a more federal EU'. They are cautiously optimistic about this outcome, noting that 'the [European] regime has proved to be remarkably resilient in the face of past crises' even though 'regional integration constitutes a deeply political project'. As an aside here it is worth noting that neo-functionalists such as Leon Lindberg and Stuart Scheingold (1970) offered a more subtle reading of crises. They could serve as catalysts for European integration in some cases, they argued, but in other cases national governments could close ranks against supranational institutions during periods of economic and political turmoil (see Lefkofridi and Schmitter 2014).

Liberal intergovernmentalism has been equally upbeat about the state of the EU in the post-Maastricht period. Nowhere is this more so than in Moravcsik (2002), which offers an impassioned defence of the EU against charges that it suffers from a democratic deficit. Here Moravcsik situates his liberal intergovernmentalism within a wider liberal institutionalist framework in which the representatives of states possess a high degree of indirect legitimacy in the international arena, by virtue of their accountability to domestic constituents, while supranational institutions and non-governmental actors with their more amorphous claims to accountability do not. There is nothing here to suggest that representative political institutions at the national level are in any way suffering from legitimacy deficits of their own. Thereafter, Moravcsik has been quick to call for calm during moments of perceived crisis for the European project. Confronted with the collapse of the European Constitution in 2004, Moravcsik (2006) argued that the project was a misplaced attempt at participatory legitimacy that, through its failure, confirmed the primacy of national governments in EU decision-making. A similar defence was mounted in the light of the global financial crisis, with Moravcsik (2012) viewing macroeconomic imbalances as problematic for the smooth functioning of EMU but seeing policy responses to the crisis as more or less effective and, more importantly, illustrative of the fact that 'Europeans should trust in the essentially democratic nature of the EU'. In general, liberal intergovernmentalists place too much faith in the ability of national governments to legitimate decision-making beyond the state. National governments may face few credible rivals in the international political system but they do face significant challenges in the domestic arena.

Thus, the new intergovernmentalism is far more ambivalent about the state of the Union in the post-Maastricht period and the prospects for the European project thereafter. The fact that the EU survived successive crises since 1992 and lived to tell the tale is not in itself proof of its good health. Rather, it calls for an examination of the EU's 'lifestyle choices' to understand why it is so prone to crises as well as an understanding of environmental factors, chief among them being that the European project in its current reform is an embodiment of many of the economic, political, and social problems faced by Europe since the early 1990s. All of this poses the question of whether the

EU can survive in the coming years without finding new and imaginative ways to address mounting concerns over its effectiveness and legitimacy.

1.5 What's 'New' in the 'New Intergovernmentalism'?

Taking the limitations of existing theoretical approaches as its point of departure, this book puts forward the new intergovernmentalism as a way of thinking through the dynamics of European integration after Maastricht. The term 'new' occupies a controversial place in the scholarly lexicon. While some scholars have a tendency to dress up old ideas in new clothes, others have a habit of dressing down those who seek new ways of thinking about a familiar phenomenon. For this reason, a few words are warranted on the subject of what is new about the new intergovernmentalism.

As proponents of an intergovernmental approach to European integration we naturally look to national governments as key players in European integration. As such, we explain the tendency towards integration without supranationalization post-Maastricht as the product of political choices made by national governments motivated by a sense of self-interest because they do want to limit the further expansion of powers of the Commission and the Court of Justice. Traditional intergovernmentalists would see this situation as a loss for supranational institutions, which are assumed to be hard-wired for the pursuit of ever closer union and so in search of further powers for themselves in most cases. The new intergovernmentalism challenges this view by suggesting that supranational institutions have, for a variety of reasons, become more circumspect about the pursuit of ever closer union in the post-Maastricht period. Thus, the new intergovernmentalism does not neglect the role of supranational institutions but rather seeks to recast it in a new mould. Moreover, the new intergovernmentalism does not ignore the vast powers that the Commission and the Court of Justice have accumulated under the Community method over time. Yet, it argues that we cannot conceptualize the role of these bodies in the post-Maastricht period simply in terms of a series of (often unsuccessful) attempts to convert the new areas of EU activity eventually into domains of classic Community method decision-making.

The new intergovernmentalism also sheds new light on the role and actions of the Council of Ministers and European Council in post-Maastricht integration and thus acknowledges and builds on the findings of scholars of new governance. Instead of understanding them as forums for legislative decision-making and hard-bargaining, it also emphasizes their role in forging consensus around common policy objectives which require the coordinated use of decentralized policy resources. The reliance of policy implementation on decentralized resources, which are predominantly located at the member

39

state level and cannot be made subject to legally binding EU decisions, is a key feature of the new areas of EU activity. Thus, both with regard to supranational and intergovernmental EU decision-making bodies, the new intergovernmentalism encourages the combined analysis of micro-institutional processes of EU decision-making and underlying integration dynamics. Here, the new intergovernmentalism differs clearly from liberal intergovernmentalism, which as an approach attached relatively little importance to the analysis of dynamics within institutions. We hold that both supranational and intergovernmental institutions in the EU undergo significant institutional change themselves because of the evolving constitutional basis of European integration. These processes cannot be ignored if one wants to understand the patterns of contemporary EU policy-making.

Crucially, as noted earlier, the new intergovernmentalism challenges the notion of intergovernmentalism as a synonym for a standstill or rollback of integration. This has been implicit in early notions of intergovernmentalism in European integration and it may have prevented scholars from being more open-minded towards the prospect of an expansion in EU activity. In this context we also stress that the new intergovernmentalism is not considered to be a normative theory about where integration *should* lead to. It is an analytical approach aimed at understanding European integration in a particular historical and constitutional context. The new intergovernmentalism is conscious about the instability of the existing institutional arrangements. Though it emphasizes the structural implications of the integration paradox underlying post-Maastricht integration, the new intergovernmentalism accepts that the course and character of European integration may change fundamentally or that the existing institutional framework may fall victim to the self-destructive tendencies which it undoubtedly contains. We believe that the challenge of contemporary EU studies is to consider these aspects together. In other words, it is to make sense of the duality of instability and uncertainty, on the one hand, and the continuous expansion of the scope of integration and the predisposition towards consensual policy solutions and intergovernmental policy deliberation on the other. For too long, EU studies has been marked by a crypto-normativism celebrating further supranationalism as a progressive development in human affairs. This has blinded it to the possibility of integration taking place in the absence of further transfers of powers to supranational institutions and to the internal contradictions manifest in post-Maastricht European integration.

Intergovernmentalism is interested in opening up the black box of statehood to understand why national governments choose to support or oppose European integration. In keeping with this tradition, the new intergovernmentalism looks to national polities to understand member states' preferences for integration without supranationalization since 1992. That national governments continue to take their cue from interest groups when it comes to supporting or opposing integration in particular domains, we do not dispute. Where we do depart from earlier intergovernmentalist approaches, however, is in seeing national preference formation as a process containing its own structural difficulties and problems. A key premise of earlier intergovernmental theories is that states form their preferences towards integration for functional reasons that are particular to the policy domain in question and have little to do with attitudes towards European integration in general. This line of reasoning chimes with the pre-Maastricht period, with the UK, for instance, being supportive of projects such as the single market and EMU for economic reasons in spite of the ruling Conservative Party's political reticence concerning the European project. This separation between economics and politics is no longer tenable in the post-Maastricht period, we argue, because public opinion over European integration has become so much more polarized. That the permissive consensus has come to an end since 1992 is well documented but what is not so well understood is how European integration has continued apace. Our approach to this puzzle is to see declining public support for European integration as symptomatic of the more general crisis of representation in which political parties and organized interests in general are less powerful. The impact of this changing state of affairs on preference formation is three-fold. First, a lack of popular support for European integration has made national governments deeply reluctant to be seen to delegate authority to the Commission and the Court of Justice even in those cases where there are functional reasons for doing so. Second, the crisis of representation has provided national governments with room for manoeuvre to pursue European integration through other means in spite of public unease. Third, these developments have further blurred the line between high and low politics by creating uncertainty about what the national interest really is on a given issue at a particular moment in time.

The problem of preference formation can help us to understand the context in which national governments have chosen to extend the scope of EU activity since 1992 but it does not fully explain why delegation to *de novo* institutions and deliberative forms of policy-making has proved more politically palatable than traditional forms of integration. Deliberation has always been central to EU policy-making but a striking feature of the post-Maastricht period, we argue, is how consensus building in informal settings such as the European Council, the Eurogroup and the Euro Summit has become an end it itself rather than a means to a more ambitious agreement. This shift, we argue, has not taken place at the expense of intergovernmental bargaining between national governments over the future of European integration. Hard-headed negotiations, side payments, and concessions were all a feature of the EU's response to the global financial crisis, for instance. What has changed rather is the character of intergovernmental politics in settings where voting is rare, the exercise of vetoes even less so, and where consensus has become the standard by which negotiations are judged (cf. Puetter 2014). The reasons for this shift from hard bargaining to deliberative intergovernmentalism in the post-Maastricht period are complex. For one thing, sharing sovereignty in an 'intergovernmental' setting such as the European Council is easier to sell than ceding sovereignty at a time of declining public support for European integration. Informality can also be seen as a means to work around the constraints of formal decision-making in an EU where member states are more numerous and the EP more powerful.

A similar set of reasons can explain member states' preferences for delegating policy-making powers to *de novo* institutions. A key reason is that the Commission, whether fairly or not, came to embody popular concerns about the European project, thus making it more difficult for member states to justify a further expansion of its competences. The creation of *de novo* institutions can also be seen as a response to perennial concerns over holding supranational institutions to account. A key expectation of the new intergovernmentalism, in this sense, is that the governance structures underpinning these bodies will allow for a higher degree of member state control than is the case with established supranational institutions. Another is that the Commission and Court of Justice are likely to be more predisposed towards the creation of such bodies than was once thought to be the case.

It is worth noting at this juncture that our use of the term 'intergovernmental', and the associated argument about integration in the absence of 'supranationalism', raises the question of what these two terms mean. We recognize that these terms are often contested in the EU studies field but in using them we hope to achieve some conceptual clarity. There are at least two reasons why intergovernmentalism and supranationalism, though popular terms in the EU studies lexicon, are often misunderstood. One reason is that the same terms can refer to different objects, with scholars often not specifying which object they are referring to. The other reason is that the post-Maastricht period itself has been a source of new developments that do not easily fit into the traditional conceptual categories. Each of these points is explored below.

First, in terms of the different objects to which they refer, we can say that on the one hand, these terms denote specific decision-making regimes, namely integration through formal acts and integration through voluntary cooperation (Fabbrini 2013; Puetter 2014: 40–4). Institutionally speaking, we can differentiate these two regimes and in doing so we find, as Fabbrini has argued, that both are present within the EU's treaties. Indeed, their uneasy coexistence is even formalized in the Lisbon Treaty. What makes this definition of the terms difficult is that even understood purely in institutional terms, and as different ways of making decisions collectively, there is an overlap and inter-connection between supranational and intergovernmental decision-making. The traditional Community method, for instance, is associated with the creation of autonomous decision-making powers beyond the immediate influence of member state governments. That said, this method has a critical intergovernmental component centred on legislative decision-making in the Council of Ministers. This body has long acted as the prime political institution authorizing the transfer of competences from the national to the European level. Intergovernmentalism here is associated with member states that bargain about the conditions of competence delegation and seek to address the trade-offs associated with such delegation.

Second, the terms intergovernmentalism and supranationalism are also defined in a much broader sense as contrasting theories of European integration. From this perspective, supranationalism is associated with a more general shift in political life from the national to the pan-European level. More than just an account of decision-making, it also refers to behavioural norms and practices and to matters touching upon individual and collective identities. Crucially, it presumes a weakening of the hold of the nation-state. As Paul Magnette put it, European integration is all about 'taming the sovereign' (Magnette 2000). Intergovernmentalism, in contrast, and by way of an opposite movement, is understood as the continued supremacy of nation-states. To the question of who remains in charge in Europe, the answer is its member states. Given the strong normative bias that, historically at least, EU studies has had in favour of more supranationalism (Majone 2009; Van Middelaar 2013: 5–6), intergovernmentalism has gained something of a negative connotation. It is taken to denote less integration, or simply renationalization.

As competing theories of European integration, the terms supranationalism and intergovernmentalism have become two poles in a debate about the place of the nation-state in European integration.[10] Mapped onto this theoretical debate has been a set of behavioural norms that are expected to prevail within either supranational or intergovernmental settings. As mentioned,

---

[10] In Hoffmann's formulation, states are either 'obstinately' as central as they have ever been; or they are slowly becoming 'obsolete', transcended by a thickening of pan-European political ties, loyalties and identities (Hoffmann 1995). Interestingly, in Ben Rosamond's account (2013) of theories that take us *beyond* European integration, we see clearly that attitudes towards the nation-state remain divisive. Governance scholars, for instance, emphasize the decreasing relevance of the state as the organizational framework of European politics and power, preferring to emphasize sub-national units such as the region or the city and take multi-level governance as their analytical starting point. Critical neo-Gramscian theories prefer to analyse the EU in terms of a developing neoliberal regime and thus also discount the state. International relations (IR) approaches take a different view while comparative politics scholars often treat the EU as, at the very least, a government in its own right and thus elide the question of its 'stateness' (see Rosamond 2013: 88). In Luuk Van Middelaar's distinction between a Europe of offices, states, and citizens, one's attitude towards the nation-state is central. Similarly, in his division of Europe between the outer, inner, and intermediate sphere, the deciding factor is the role given to the nation-state (Van Middelaar 2013).

deliberation and consensus are typically viewed as the behavioural styles belonging to supranational decision-making. A more conflict-laden and hard-nosed set of norms, built around the need for compromise in an environment dominated by strategic bargaining, is associated with intergovernmentalism. On this view, the terms are also tied to a set of historical events and phases. Supranationalism is associated with the early aspirational years of Schumann and Monnet, the creation of the European Coal and Steel Community and the signing of the Treaty of Rome. Intergovernmentalism had its heyday in the mid-1960s with de Gaulle's refusal to let the British enter the European Economic Community and his battle with the Commission, which led to the 'empty chair crisis' and then to the Luxembourg compromise. The 1970s is deemed a gloomy period of 'Euro-sclerosis' while the mid-1980s onwards is taken as a re-launching of Europe, cheered on by the Delors Commission, and made possible by the actions of member states within the Council of Ministers.

Separating out these different meanings given to supranationalism and intergovernmentalism helps us to achieve some clarity in our own account of the new intergovernmentalism. By tying together the unprecedented expansion in the new domains of EU activity in the post-Maastricht period with a strong preference for policy coordination between national actors, we seek to firmly undo the link between intergovernmentalism and renationalization. Our understanding of the post-Maastricht period is that it is one of unparalleled dynamism in the EU integration process.

However, in terms of decision-making regimes, this dynamism cannot be associated with 'integration through law' or the traditional Community method. We cannot overlook or wish away the fact that from Maastricht onwards, member state governments have shown great reluctance to add to the list of legislative competences of the EU. In our account of the new intergovernmentalism, Hoffmann's dichotomy of an 'obstinate' or 'obsolete' nation-state has itself become obsolete. What we see in the post-Maastricht period are the actions of national executives and of national officials, who are consistently in favour of closer cooperation at the European level, existing alongside currents of opinion within domestic societies that run in very different directions. To be 'for' or 'against' the nation-state, as much of the theoretical discussion in EU integration theory has been in the past, makes little sense in a context where societal preferences and elite or governmental preferences fail to unite within the overarching framework of the national state. It makes more sense to place the process of state transformation at the heart of our analytical approach to European integration (Bickerton 2012: 12–15).

Finally, the new intergovernmentalism serves to highlight the importance of uncoupling the associated behavioural norms of supranationalism and intergovernmentalism from any determinate institutional setting. Following Haas, for whom the term supranationality referred to a 'style of politics' as much as to any particular decision-making regime (Haas 2004: 59, 525–6), we find that in the post-Maastricht period many of the norms associated with supranationalism have become institutionally deracinated and recast as norms governing interactions between national actors in intergovernmental settings as well. The continued centrality of member states to the European integration process, and their concerted efforts to avoid delegating further powers to traditional supranational institutions, is what pushes us to deploy the term intergovernmentalism. However, given that the traditional role of nation-states in the integration process has been replaced by a more complex and indeterminate mode of articulating societal and elite interests, and owing to the fact that national actors and officials have increasingly adopted behavioural norms more typically associated with supranational settings, we have added the prefix 'new' to refer to this distinctive phase in European integration that has come to characterize the post-Maastricht period.

Having said what the new intergovernmentalism is, it is important to make clear what it is not. First, it does not claim to be a new grand theory of regional integration. The emphasis in this volume is on European integration after a specific point in time. No claims are made here about the applicability of this approach to the pre-Maastricht era and the question of whether the new intergovernmentalism extends beyond the EU is addressed only briefly in the conclusion. Second, the new intergovernmentalism offers new insights on European integration post-Maastricht but it does not offer a new way of studying them. Our claims, as we see them, are compatible with a variety of ontologies and methodologies associated with the study of European integration and policy-making. Lastly, this volume does not claim that the new intergovernmentalism is the finished article. Theory-building, as is clear from the review of existing scholarship in this chapter, requires patience, time, and constructive criticism. What follows is designed to stimulate debate rather than to settle it.

1.6 Plan of the book

This volume brings together a group of EU scholars from different intellectual traditions to consider whether and how the new intergovernmentalism can make sense of European integration since Maastricht. This introductory chapter has set out the key claims of the new intergovernmentalism and contextualized them within the empirical and theoretical field of EU studies as a whole. The six hypotheses set out above have been taken up by the contributors of this volume and explored in a variety of different ways. Not all chapters engage with all hypotheses but taken as a whole the contributions to this book provide ample evidence for a preliminary assessment of the new intergovernmentalism.

The first part of this volume focuses on changing conceptions of politics and law in the post-Maastricht period. Christopher J. Bickerton (chapter 2) reflects on the role and place of states in European integration. At the centre of his analysis is the idea that European integration is now driven not by nation-states in the traditional sense of the term but by member states in which the relationship between national governments and civil society is in flux. This process of state transformation began in the 1970s, he argues, but its effects intensified in the post-Maastricht period as policy-making in the EU was decoupled from domestic politics, as traditionally conceived. This decoupling helps to explain how and why national governments have exerted such a tight grip over EU policy-making since 1992 but in ways that render European integration inherently unstable. Paul James Cardwell and Tamara Hervey (chapter 3) explore the changing role of law in the post-Maastricht period. The course of European integration since 1992 cannot be characterized as a retreat from law, they insist, but it has seen a shift from one conception of EU law to another. The era of integration through legislation and new legal principles has faded and in its place the post-Maastricht period has seen a greater emphasis on EU law as a means of promoting procedural legitimacy and managing differences across member states and policy domains. Thomas Christiansen (chapter 4) looks at the process of EU treaty reform, taking it as a microcosm of the integration paradox. His chapter advances an institutional-ist perspective on treaty reform and, in doing so, provides support for two key arguments underpinning the new intergovernmentalism: the persistence of a disequilibrium within the European construction and the impossibility of distinguishing between 'high' and 'low' politics in EU decision-making.

The second part of this volume takes a closer look at the evolution of selected EU policy domains since 1992. Michael E. Smith (chapter 5) returns to debates about EU cooperation in the area of security and defence in the post-Maastricht period. Integration in this domain has progressed to a more significant degree than expected, he suggests, but it remains rooted in inter-governmental cooperation. A degree of experiential learning is discernible but EU operations remain in a state of political disequilibrium due to political-economy factors at home and an uncertain security environment abroad. Sarah Wolff (chapter 6) discusses EU cooperation since Maastricht in the area of justice and home affairs. Policy-making in this field has been 'commu-nitarized' by successive treaty changes since 1992 but only partially so. Key exceptions consistent with the new intergovernmentalism include the limits on the Commission's right of initiative in especially sensitive policy areas, the extensive use of opt-outs for the UK and other countries, the hands-on role played by the European Council and the preference for empowering *de novo* institutions such as Frontex and Eurojust. David Howarth and Lucia Quaglia (chapter 7) offer a different view in their analysis of financial regulation before and after the global financial crisis. This area of EU activity can be traced back to the Single European Act but integration had stalled by the mid-1990s after member states encountered the limits of regulation in a field made up of distinct models of financial capitalism. EMU provided a catalyst for change here, as did the shortcomings exposed by the global financial crisis, they argue, but in neither case did member states or supranational institutions push for delegation to supranational institutions along traditional lines. Instead a series of *de novo* institutional structures was created to facilitate cooperation between member states, culminating in a more centralized but still highly decentralized set of governance structures for European Banking Union.

The third part of the book looks at the role of individual EU institutions in post-Maastricht integration. Uwe Puetter (chapter 8) examines the emergence of the European Council as the engine room of the new intergovernmentalism and a venue for high-level policy deliberation. Summits of EU heads of state or government have been a feature of intergovernmental politics since the mid-1970s but the focus of these meetings has shifted since 1992, he argues. Whereas the European Council's agenda was once taken up with advancing major steps in EU integration, Puetter presents evidence of a reorientation since Maastricht towards involvement in the day-to-day management of the new areas of EU activity. This reflects the further blurring of the high–low politics distinction, he suggests, as well as political tensions within national politics, such that the heads of state or government must be seen to be in the lead no matter how complex the policy issue under discussion may be. John Peterson (chapter 9) rejects the idea that the Commission is in decline since Maastricht and instead sees it as having modest ambitions for a combination of external and internal reasons. As regards the former, he sees enlargement, in particular, as having complicated the task of policy formulation by creating a political system that is economically and politically more diverse. Internal changes also help to explain the Commission's reluctance to seek new powers for itself since Maastricht. Here Peterson highlights the Commission's more pragmatic approach to the creation of *de novo* institutions in cases where the EU executive stood neither to gain nor lose powers of its own. He also presents evidence of changing beliefs among Commission officials, who have become more intergovernmental in their outlook over time. Marie-Pierre Granger (chapter 10) arrives at a similar conclusion in her analysis of the Court of Justice. Through a review of EU case law since 1992, she shows that the Court is neither the supranational entrepreneur nor the intergovernmental anomaly of earlier integration theory. Instead, the Court can be understood as a self-interested actor by no means wedded to the supranational style, providing its pre-existing role in EU policy-making is protected. Marzena Kloka and Susanne Schmidt (chapter 11) shift the focus to a traditional domain of Community method decision-making and explore the legislative and judicial politics between the Council of Ministers, Commission, and Court of Justice in the regulation of patient mobility in the 1990s and 2000s. On the surface, this is an area in which the Commission has sought new powers that the Council of Ministers showed itself willing to grant through new EU legislation. The Council of Ministers had its room for manoeuvre seriously curtailed here, they suggest, in so far as legislation was seen as preferable to the case law driven by the Court of Justice. Kloka and Schmidt identify a pattern of subtle interaction between supranationalist and intergovernmentalist dynamics ,which suggests that traditional domains of Community method decision-making remain largely intact within the post-Maastricht era. Johannes Pollack and Peter Slominski (chapter 12) review the EP as a problematic case for the new intergovernmentalism because of national governments' willingness to cede new powers to this body in successive treaty changes since Maastricht. That said, their analysis lends weight to the view that the Parliament's preferences are more complex than previously thought. There can be little doubt, Pollack and Slominski suggest, that the EP acted as a competence maximizer in the post-Maastricht period but it was equivocal in its support for a supranational style of policy-making. Dermot Hodson (chapter 13) looks at the emergence of the ECB as a *de novo* institution with important policy-making powers under EMU. The ECB, he shows, pushed for a more centralized approach to financial supervision during EMU's first decade but it took a hard line against integrationist initiatives in the macroeconomic sphere and on wider political questions. A concern that further integration might be detrimental to central bank independence and the pursuit of price stability appears to explain this ambivalence.

The fourth part of this volume is dedicated to critique and conclusions. Simon Bulmer (chapter 14) offers an outside perspective on this volume's attempt to understand European integration in the post-Maastricht period. In so doing, he compares the new intergovernmentalism as an analytical perspective and the contributions to this book with existing explanations that focus on the role of domestic politics, classic intergovernmental bargaining, delegation to supranational actors, and supranational entrepreneurship. In the concluding chapter, Christopher J. Bickerton, Dermot Hodson, and Uwe Puetter (chapter 15) summarize the key findings of this volume and consider the conditions under which the post-Maastricht period might come to an end. The chapter concludes by asking whether the concept of new intergovernmentalism has currency beyond the study of European politics by considering its application to other regional and international organizations.

Part I

Changing Conceptions of Law and Politics Post-Maastricht

2

A Union of Member States

State Transformation and the New Intergovernmentalism

Christopher J. Bickerton

One of the key insights of traditional intergovernmentalist theory was to conceptually uncouple European integration from supranationalism. Whether it was defined as a set of institutional procedures known as the 'Community method', or more normatively as a commitment to ever closer union, supranationalism was for a long time taken as synonymous with the project of European integration.[1] In the work of the revisionist historian Alan Milward, and then in the political science scholarship of Andrew Moravcsik, European integration was presented instead as a process driven by states and often one that strengthened rather than weakened the state (Milward 1992; Moravcsik 1998). The integration paradox, identified in this book as a key feature of the post-Maastricht period (see chapter 1 of this volume), builds upon this original intergovernmentalist insight. It highlights the way in which, from the early 1990s onwards, European integration has developed at an unprecedented pace but without leading to significant transfers of power from national capitals to supranational institutions: integration, in other words, but in the absence of supranationalism.

This book uses the term the 'new intergovernmentalism' to describe European integration in the post-Maastricht period because of a number of

[1] On the different meanings of supranationalism, see Haas (2004: 59 and 525–6) and Keohane and Hoffmann (1991: 15). Haas in particular was keen to stress that supranationalism referred as much to the behaviour of individuals as it did to any particular institutional procedure. See also the discussion of the normative dimension to writing European integration history in Kaiser (2007: introduction).

features of integration that do not correspond to traditional intergovernmentalist assumptions. Those domains incorporated into pan-European policy-making, for instance, do not respect the distinction between high and low politics or the idea that some areas are 'off-limits' to European integration. On the contrary, areas such as security and defence, policing, and even fiscal policy have been some of the most dynamic areas of integration over the last two decades. Intergovernmental settings, from comitology up to the European Council, have been characterized by deliberative and consensus-seeking behaviour rather than hard bargaining and a narrow defence of national interests (Brandsma 2013; Puetter 2012). Delegation to supranational institutions has given way to the creation of *de novo* institutions such as the European External Action Service and the European Stability Mechanism. Finally, in lieu of a constitutional plateau expected by those who saw in the European Union (EU) a stable regulatory polity (e.g. Moravcsik 2005), the EU has been marked by continued contestation and instability.

The argument of this chapter is that we can explain some of these particular features of integration in the post-Maastricht period by revisiting in detail our understanding of the state in Europe and the role and place of states in the European integration process. More specifically, this chapter claims that European integration in the post-Maastricht era should be understood as process driven not by nation-states in the conventional sense but by the actions of *member states.* The EU is thus best characterized as a *union of member states* rather than as a federal state, intergovernmental regime or neo-medieval empire. The chapter seeks to demonstrate that changes in state-society relations in Europe are what can explain why national authority is increasingly exercised through—and indeed has become reliant upon—participation within transnational networks of governance, of the sort which have proliferated at the EU level in the post-Maastricht period. The hope is that in developing this argument the chapter will help us to go beyond the spatial dichotomies that have tended to dominate European integration theory, such as the national versus the supranational or the nation-state versus the EU; dichotomies that were reinforced by the 'great' debate between supranationalist and intergovernmentalist EU integration theories. This chapter also suggests that rather than focusing on national governments or sectoral interest groups as the main agents in determining state actions, as traditional intergovernmentalist theory has done, we should look at the *relationship* between the state and civil society and the actors and institutions that mediate this relationship. It is at this level that we can grasp the dynamics that have seen European states go from being nation-states to member states and the process of European integration corresponding to this shift.

2.1 The Concept of Member Statehood

This chapter outlines an approach to thinking about European integration in the post-Maastricht period that focuses on the process of state transformation as the key driver of integration (Bickerton 2012). This argument raises a number of different issues which are dealt with in turn in this section. One concerns the nature of the state itself and where this argument positions itself vis-à-vis the voluminous literature on the state that is scattered across the social sciences. The other issues are the definition of the concept of member statehood, its observable empirical features, and how it differs from other forms of state.

2.1.1 *From the Bricks to the Mortar*

For much of the post-war period, English-language political science paid scant regard to the study of the state (Nettl 1968). Scholars were far more interested in systems of government and in interest group politics.[2] Those who were interested tended to approach the state from a Marxist perspective, seeing in the modern state an expression of determinate class interests. Exceptions existed, particularly in non-English language scholarship, but until the early 1980s the concept of the state as such had dropped out of analytical focus for many scholars of politics and society.[3] A renewed interest in the state was undertaken by US-based historical sociologists, with figures such as Theda Skocpol and Charles Tilly leading the way. Their perspective was explicitly neo-Weberian and they argued that pluralist and Marxist accounts of the state were both reductive in their own ways: pluralists reduced the state to the play of interest groups, Marxists to class power. For these neo-Weberians, what was needed was a proper appreciation of the autonomy of the state, of its bureaucratic and administrative power, of its ability to shape policy according to its own rationales and its relative independence from class forces or private interest groups (Evans et al. 1985: 3–43). The state should be considered not merely as a dependent variable in political and social analysis, it should also be thought of as an independent variable of its own, able to impact in sometimes decisive ways on the socio-economic and political trajectory of national societies. A focus on the autonomy of state elites and their formative practices was also central to the French school of neo-Weberians whose interest in the construction of elite cadres reflected a national preoccupation with the power

---

[2] For a comprehensive theoretical and historical account, see Pizzorno (1981). For an introduction to pluralist theories of the state, see Dunleavy and O'Leary (1987: 13–71).

[3] For an exception, see Foucault and his work on power and rethinking dominant conceptions of the state (1980).

and identity of state elites that continues to this day (Birnbaum 1977; Badie and Birnbaum 1979; more recently, see Genieys 2008, 2010, 2011).

This renewed interest in the administrative power and autonomy of the state was a useful corrective to earlier reductionist accounts. However, as Migdal and others observed, there was a danger in carrying this argument too far (Migdal 1988: 1997). By focusing on the autonomy of the state from society, one risked ignoring the centrality of state–society relations in constituting and reproducing state authority and power. One also risked exaggerating the role of violence at the expense of other ways in which states secure their rule, rather as Tilly and Poggi did by focusing on the figures of the warrior and the bandit as metaphors for state rule (Tilly 1985; Poggi 1990). Metaphorically, we can observe that as a construction, the state is composed of both bricks *and* mortar: state–society relations, as well as a monopoly of the legitimate exercise of violence, are what give the state its power and authority. Without these relations, the bricks alone are unable to withstand the elements for very long. This makes sense when we think of the many state forms that have prevailed over time. The terms we use consistently refer in their qualifying adjectives to the nature of the state–society relations that underpin a state's authority and legitimacy: the *absolutist* state, the *nation*-state, the *corporatist* state, the *social democratic* state. States and the regimes that form the basis of their power are often inseparable from one another.

2.1.2 *The Concept of Member State*

If we take state–society relations as the starting point for our thinking about the transition from one form of state to another, we can now introduce our definition of member statehood as a distinctive and stand-alone form of state (Sbragia 1994; Bickerton 2012). Typically, the term 'member state'—which is one of the most common in political, legal, and social studies—is understood juridically. A country that joins a regional or global body goes from being a nation-state to a member state. Were a country to leave—the UK, for instance, after a pro-exit vote in a referendum—it would revert back to being a simple nation-state. The term refers to a legal title, one that can be given and taken away. It is also often the case that countries enjoy multiple memberships: Russia, though ostracized from the G8 because of its annexation of the Crimea, remains a member of the WTO, the Council of Europe, and the UN.

If we think of it as a form of state, member statehood becomes something far more extensive and significant than merely a legal title. It refers to a form of state where power and authority is constituted horizontally rather than vertically, through the participation by national governments in transnational networks of rule. Political authority is 'denationalized' in so far as it is not legitimized purely, or even principally, in terms of 'the nation' or the 'people' (Le Galés 2013). In fact, the vertical ways of constructing state–society relations, where states present a simplified image of their citizenry to the outside world, are relativized as only one source of authority for states alongside others. In some instances, these other sources may even trump the role of the nation or the people in legitimizing state action. We saw this in the actions of governments after the unsuccessful referenda on the European Constitution in 2005 (France, Netherlands) and 2008 (Ireland): the need to strike agreements with other European governments, and to honour commitments made, was given as a reason to ratify a new treaty arrangement that was essentially the same as the one that had been rejected by popular vote.

Why we stress state *transformation* rather than transcendence is that whilst the legitimizing discourses of states have increasingly come to rely upon the logic of coordinated action and collective agreement, the actual authority and ability to act remains national. For instance, in the field of legitimized violence, very little by way of statutory powers has been transferred to regional or global bodies. However, both in the field of the police and the military, the uses to which these tools are put and the justification given for their use have become transnational in scope, to the point where individual actors themselves—soldiers, police officers—take on dominant identities that are professionally rather than nationally defined (Jachtenfuchs 2005: 50; Mérand 2008; see also chapter 5 in this volume). In the field of macroeconomic policy, the policies pursued by national governments—from convergence with the Maastricht criteria through to labour market reform—are justified in terms of European obligations. In Italy, this practice became so common in the 1990s that a term applying to relations between the North and the Mezzogiorno—the *vincolo esterno*—was used to characterize the Italian government's relationship to Europe (Dyson and Featherstone 1996). In Eastern Europe, the habit of presenting reforms as necessary requirements of EU membership became so ubiquitous as a style of rule that some styled post-communist democracy as 'voice without choice' (Ost 2005; Krastev 2007: 59).

This practice is not merely a clever state management strategy pursued by far-sighted elites. It goes beyond mere buck-passing, blame avoidance, or the pursuit of credible commitment strategies (Hood 2013; Moravcsik 1998). It is also more prevalent and less intentional than the 'strategies of scale-shifting' identified by political geographers as key to understanding processes of state transformation (Hameiri 2013; Gough 2004). These external frameworks of rule function as constitutive elements of what it means to be a European state today and they are increasingly relied upon as central pillars of national political legitimacy. To rule authoritatively is to rule through transnational networks of governance; state-society relations have, as a result, become mediated by institutional settings *external to the state*. These new settings

55

contrast with traditional mediating institutions such as estates, professional guilds, political parties, trade unions, and employer associations that were national in character and scope. Many did have a transnational component to them, as Wolfram Kaiser argued with regards to post-war Christian democracy, but they were organized within vertical structures of power and authority (Kaiser 2007). We find an exemplary case of contemporary member statehood in the referendum campaign for Scottish independence. Scottish nationalists have pressed the European Commission very hard to obtain a firm commitment about Scotland's future within the EU. In the Scottish Nationalist Party's flagship document, *Scotland's Future*, the party argues that '[w]ith independence, Scotland will take its proper place as a full member within the structures of the EU, giving us the ability to effectively represent Scottish interests within the EU' (SNP 2014: 216). Far from being a constraint upon an independent Scotland, membership of the EU appears as its guarantor.

The great mystery of post-Maastricht European integration is thus not to explain why states are giving up their sovereignty to European institutions but why these institutions have become so important to the sovereignty and power of European states. Or put slightly differently, the challenge is to determine not whether nation-states or the EU rule in Europe today; we should ask instead why the continued reproduction of state power depends so heavily upon the existence of regional institutions of governance.

In order to operationalize the concept of member statehood, we can highlight three observable and characteristic features: their legitimizing discourses; their organizational arrangements; and the modes of political conflict within member states. Each of these three are considered in detail. A final section considers how member states differ from other forms of state.

2.1.3 *Legitimizing Discourses*

Whether one locates the source of legitimate authority in the people or in the nation, the authority of the nation-state is constituted vertically in a relationship forged between a state and its own society. The secularization of political power associated with the rise of the nation-state made it clear that the ability of a state's ruler to command authority required that it command the will of its own population. Formulated initially as a relationship of absolute power in the work of Bodin and Hobbes, this became the basis for our thinking about the nature of democratic authority after 1789. The importance of these vertical relationships for international politics cannot be over-exaggerated. Concepts such as the national interest, positive international law, and even institutions such as multilateralism all rest upon an understanding of state power and its relationship to democratic authority that derive from events of the late eighteenth century (Reus-Smit 1999). Particularly within the liberal tradition, these legitimizing discourses have often made reference to sources of authority other than the pure will of the majority. This is the case of constitutions and supreme courts, for instance. However, even in these instances, legitimacy remains internal to the political system itself. As explained in *The Federalist Papers*, the legitimacy of institutional limits to majoritarian rule derive from the principle of popular sovereignty itself, not from anything outside it (Wood 1998; Ball 2003; Bickerton 2011b).

Member states, in contrast, legitimize their authority horizontally. The authority that comes from external frameworks of rule is the borrowed authority of the wider community of action. As a result, when prime ministers or heads of state find themselves marginalized at the end of negotiations (viz. David Cameron over the Fiscal Compact or the nomination of Jean-Claude Juncker as President of the Commission, Vaclav Klaus on the Lisbon Treaty), this is interpreted as a failure of diplomacy rather than as a triumph of principle over compromise.[4] Certain modes of policy-making within the EU, such as the Open Method of Coordination or the dialogue between finance ministers within the Eurogroup, are designed to provide benchmarks with which to compare reform processes in member states and to bolster flagging domestic reform programmes when need be. What is most important in these horizontally structured discourses of legitimacy is that authority rests not simply upon action in concert with others but also that decisions are made at a distance from partisan politics. Ruling through external frameworks thus refers in part to territorial externality but also to decisions that are beyond the reach of representative politics as such. In this respect, member statehood overlaps with what Shahar Hameiri, describing a prevalent form of post-developmental state in Southeast Asia, has called 'regulatory states' (Hameiri 2013: 323). This form of state finds its legitimacy in depoliticized policy-making and in the declared virtues of independent policy rules (Elster 1977; Offe 1996). The key point here is that the sources of authority for member states, reflected in their legitimizing discourses, lie *outside traditional organized interests*, both parliamentary and para-parliamentary. For member states, obligations to other member states as set out in treaties can outweigh obligations to domestic publics depending on the circumstances.

---

[4] The UK case is a little more complicated. In his first address to the House of Commons after his unsuccessful campaign against Jean-Claude Juncker's nomination, Prime Minister David Cameron was greeted with cheers by his Euro-sceptic backbench Members of Parliament. This was not, however, a sentiment shared by much of the press or the British public, for whom the campaign against Juncker was considered more of an ill-judged act symptomatic of Britain's declining influence within Europe.

2.1.4 *Organizational Arrangements*

Member states can also be distinguished by their internal organizational arrangements. It has become commonplace to note that the participation in transnational networks of governance reinforces the power of national executives (Putnam 1988; Moravcsik 1994). In the case of member states, we observe a more specific uncoupling of policy-making from the national political sphere, which signals a drifting apart of politics and bureaucracy after a period of fusion in the nation-state model (for a discussion, see Bickerton 2011a: 182–6; see also Schmidt 2006). The modern state was rarely theorized as a purely political or administrative phenomenon. On the contrary, the state was seen to rest upon an ineradicable tension between government and governance, between the 'government of men', and the 'administration of things' (Runciman 2006: 15). Studies of the modern state have taken up this tension in a number of ways. For Foucault, 'governmentality' pointed to a slow expansion in the bureaucratic authority of the state that aimed not only to coerce citizens but also to constitute them as subjects (Foucault 1991: 103). For classical social theorists, the struggle was between bureaucracy and democracy (Beetham 1987). Weber identified the clash between bureaucratic domination and plebiscitary democracy as the central dynamic of modern social systems, a conflict that some Marxists—concerned at the rise of Stalinism—felt had already been lost, in the Soviet Union at least.

Within member states, we see a curious drifting apart of politics and bureaucracy, to the point that this particular tension no longer plays a creative role in the reproduction of the state. Policymaking processes, especially at the European level, involve the close interaction of many different sets of actors, many of them national. Often located physically in Brussels, these officials repeatedly interact with one another in a setting oriented towards problem-solving, deliberation, and consensus-seeking. Few government ministries in European states today have no European office or some formalized body responsible for negotiations with other European partners. National governments differ greatly in how they manage their relations with Brussels-based institutions and how they coordinate European positions across different departments.[5] However, whether the model is one of centralized or much looser forms of coordination, cooperation with officials from other member states has entered into the core activity of national bureaucracies. In his discussion of the British policy-making process, Stephen Wall argued that this had become so integrated into wider European dynamics that Europe was now the sea in which national officials swim (Bickerton 2008; Wall

---

[5] For a comprehensive account covering all of the member states of the EU, see Bulmer and Lequesne (2013).

2008). David Allen pinpointed the British dilemma more precisely by describing the UK as a 'Europeanized government in a non-Europeanized polity' (Allen 2005).

The political sphere, in contrast, remains national both in scope and outlook. Even European political procedures, most noticeably the European elections to the European Parliament, remain trapped within national outlooks. More often than not, these debates are scrutinized for the evidence that they can shed on future voting intentions in *national* elections, as is the case today with the UK Independence Party (UKIP) in the UK, the National Front in France and the Five Star Movement in Italy. The European elections themselves remain of a second order. For all the discussion of the *Spitzenkandidaten* in the European parliamentary elections of May 2014, it is worth remembering that the German Christian Democratic Union (CDU) opted to put Angela Merkel on all of their European election posters; Jean-Claude Juncker, their nominated candidate for the presidency of the Commission, did not appear on any of them (Streeck 2014).

Even when European themes are pressing upon national concerns, as was the case during the euro-crisis, Europe falls out of domestic election campaigns. In 2012 in France, at the height of the financial and economic crisis, the contest between François Hollande and Nicolas Sarkozy rarely touched upon Europe at all, bar a vague promise made by the Socialist candidate that he would 'renegotiate' the Fiscal Compact signed in late 2011. And yet, as soon as Hollande was elected he disappeared into a maelstrom of international and European commitments that took him to the United States, to Berlin, and to Brussels. It is also striking that so little popular mobilization during the euro area crisis directly engaged with the issues of EU or euro area reform. In an empirical study of mobilization across Europe, what Mary Kaldor et al. called the 'bubbling up of subterranean politics', they observed that 'among groups and individuals engaged in subterranean politics, what was remarkable was the invisibility of Europe; the absence, by and large, of any mention of Europe, let alone debates, initiatives and campaigns' (Kaldor et al. 2012: 2).

2.1.5 *Modes of Political Conflict*

Different modes of political conflict also point to an important contrast between nation-states and member states. Corresponding to nation-states are conflicts over who should be represented and conflicts over how wealth in a society should be distributed. This fits with the vertical structure of authority and legitimacy: citizens contest the actions of governments and governments pursue policies based on preferences formed among groups of citizens. The key drivers of political conflict here are thus democratization (expanding the franchise) and redistribution. Looking at the history of political party formation in Europe, we see both these axes of conflict at work. Mass parties formed often in opposition to a restricted franchise and argued for the vote. They also reflected important socio-economic and religious cleavages. Elite factions within parliamentary assemblies transformed themselves into parties in order to undercut the radical claims of outsiders (Duverger 1951; Lipset and Rokkan 1967). This unfolding of political conflict and its steady institutionalization within the folds of parliamentary democracy was part of the overarching framework of the state and its relations to civil society.

In the case of member states, other sorts of political conflict enter, and render the above picture more complex. In particular, the political system and its presumed inability to respond to citizen concerns becomes a central factor in political life itself. Rather than making demands through political procedures, or demanding that one be included in the existing system, political mobilization in member states is oriented towards contesting the political system and its rules. However, rather than being anti-systemic in the manner of far Left or far Right movements of the inter-war period, this sort of contestation is without its own utopia or alternative. The driving force of political conflict is disenchantment with politics and scepticism about the ability of the political system to meet the demands being placed upon it. It is striking, for instance, that the labels given to political protests in recent years have not referred to their position on an ideological spectrum but rather to sentiments of anger and frustration. We have the 'indignados' in Spain for instance, or the term 'wutbuerger' (angry citizen) in Germany which was nominated new word of the year in 2010 (Kaldor et al. 2012). It is also noteworthy that the goals of many of these new movements are focused on processes rather than outcomes. Accountability and transparency are the slogans of choice and movements such as the Pirate Parties in Germany and Sweden tend to mobilize around themes such as freedom of information.

Anti-politics has thus become an active input into the political process and even manages to organize itself into populist parties that position themselves as challengers to the political establishment. These parties, of course, face the intractable problem of how to behave once they enter into governing coalitions or find themselves with some sort of political power. Evidence suggests that they tend to moderate their positions and move towards the political centre, something which opens up room for a new round of anti-political mobilization (Rooduijn et al. 2012).[6] The severing of the ties between state and civil society is mirrored at the elite level, where alternatives to

---

[6] Rooduijn, de Lange, and Van de Brug have found that 'populist parties become less populist when they have been successful in previous elections' (212: 569). There is thus an inverse relationship between a party's populism and its electoral success.

representative sources of authority are sought by participating in trans-national networks of governance. Justifications given for this tend to be in the opaque and fatalistic language of interdependence and functional necessity, which further fuels populist rejections of representative politics. Member statehood as a form of state, resting as it does upon a hollowing out of vertical forms of authority, is consistent with a redrawing of the landscape of political conflict. Conflict between projects for government (left v. right) have become interlaced and occasionally superseded by conflict between populist and technocratic justifications for ruling outside of representative democratic procedures.

2.1.6 *Old v. New*

Member states do not exist in a vacuum and the concept itself represents an exercise in simplification. In the manner of Weber's ideal-types, the concept of member state serves heuristically to emphasize some key characteristics of contemporary states in Europe. It is unlikely that any state will entirely supplant its vertical sources of legitimacy with horizontal ones; more likely are what John Loughlin has called 'hybrid states' that combine both forms of legitimacy at the same time (Loughlin 2009). Indeed, it is partly in the tensions between these different sources of legitimacy that we observe the pertinence of the member statehood concept. Between nation-state and member state, we also find more transitional forms of state, such as the post-war Keynesian state of the 'embedded liberalism' era (Bickerton 2012: 74–109) out of which member statehood emerged.

Claims of novelty are often contested and the invention of new concepts is often met with the objection that existing concepts are quite adequate to capture new developments (Keating 2013: 13–15). It is certainly true that European nation-states in the early nineteenth century were members of the Concert of Europe and derived some of their authority and legitimacy from that body. It is also true that the international system, or what Hedley Bull called the 'international society', has often been seen as constitutive of states themselves (Bull 1977). International legal doctrine appears to make this explicit in its formulation of a 'constitutive' theory of state recognition—the idea that a state exists only when it is recognized by other states within the framework of international law (Crawford 2006; Fabry 2010). Aspects of ontological dependence by nation-states on the wider international system have existed, much in the way that our concept of individuality depends upon our having a notion of society against which it can struggle and thus define itself (Hegel 1991: 367). However, until recently, states tended to be treated as ontologically prior to the international system or society. As Poggi put it, the states made the system, not the system the states (1990: 23–4). Even in constitutive theories of state recognition, states are supposed to exist in some prior sense. As Jens Bartelson has argued, constitutive theories rest upon positivist accounts of international law, where what matters above all is that states consent to law (2013: 115). In contrast, the concept of member statehood proposes a more fundamental change in the relationship between state power and the procedures of democratic rule located within domestic politics. The shift from vertical to horizontal sources of power challenges the idea that states present to the outside world the workings of their own domestic political processes.

2.2 From Nation-States to Member States: Drivers of State Transformation

Having defined member statehood and having considered its most significant observable features, we can now turn to the process of state transformation itself. How were nation-states transformed into member states? What forces and actors were responsible for this transition and where in space and time did it take place exactly? Work on causes of state transformation is extensive, if albeit far more limited than the work done on state formation and on the origins of the modern state. A feature of the work on transformation is the evocation of large macro-scale processes, such as globalization, internationalization, the rise of neoliberalism, and technological change (Wright and Cassese 1996; Harvey 2007; Cerny 2010). There is little doubt that such processes have been at work in the shift from nation-states to member states in Europe. However, it is difficult to establish precise causal connections when the dynamics of change are so general in nature. It is also difficult to account for why change takes the precise form that it does (i.e. the new intergovernmentalism). The impact of economic internationalization on the state, for instance, is indeterminate: in the late nineteenth century it consolidated the role of the state in the national economy and pushed states to expand their empires; in the late twentieth and early twenty-first centuries its affect was widely viewed as contributing to the weakening or 'shrinking' of the state. Neoliberalism is also rather indeterminate as a driver of change: commonly assumed to undermine the state, Andrew Gamble reminded us some time ago that free markets need strong states (Gamble 1988, 2014). What factors can explain such different effects on the state?

In order to provide a more precise account of the dynamics responsible for the shift from nation-state to member state and for the rise of the specific form of regional integration found in post-Maastricht Europe, the chapter will focus on mechanisms of interest representation, or domestic preference formation as it is more formally referred to in the political science literature. As Charles

Maier has argued, all such systems represent ways of channelling the conflicts associated with the uneven development of capitalist economic competition into relatively stable systems of political rule (Maier 1981). One way of thinking about different state forms is that they evolve as a function of precise modes of interest representation: from nationalism through to corporatism and welfarism. In member states, interest representation occurs through channels that are external to the state. This reflects a destructuring and reconfiguration of state–society relations and an incorporation of external frameworks of rule into the heart of the state–society relationship. We need to ask: why were domestic systems of interest representation dismantled in this way and why was this particular response chosen by governments to the problem in the 1970s of 'overloaded democracy'? Similar problems of overload occurred in the latter third of the nineteenth century but the response was to expand and deepen interest groups and political parties, not to circumvent them. We also need to inquire into how strategies undertaken in response to this crisis of post-war social democracy evolved over time into distinctive forms of statehood and whether or not such a process occurred evenly across different national societies in Europe.

Section 2.2.1 looks first at what it calls the 'age of organized interests', that is, the thickening of state–society relations and the proliferation of interest groups that characterized the period from 1860 through to the 1970s. The section then turns to the 'age of disorganized capitalism',[7] the period from the crisis of the 1970s to the present, where many of these systems of interest representation were dismantled or marginalized. Finally, it explains this shift from state management strategies to forms of statehood by considering the role played by political parties. It argues that as parties were transformed from mass parties to cartel parties, so they became active agents of depoliticization. The changed relationship between parties, the state and civil society thus became an active ingredient in the transformation of states in Europe, helping us understand how regional integration became such a key component in the reproduction of state authority.

2.2.1 The Age of Organized Interests

As argued, the democratic revolutions of 1776 and 1789 established for the first time in an unequivocal way the idea that state authority and power rested upon a vertical relationship of representation between civil society and the state. Horizontal understandings of state legitimacy that rested upon dynastic and religious ideas of authority gave way to a secular view of politics as the

---

[7] The term is both Offe's (1985) and Lash and Urry's (1987).

pursuit of individual and collective aspirations to freedom and liberty. However, this vertical relationship was only notional: in practice, political rule was still dominated by aristocratic elites whose power rested on specific bargains made with royal authority about the balance between parliamentary and monarchical power. These bargains began to change as aspiring bourgeois interests asserted their right to rule. Mid-nineteenth century liberalism was the highpoint of parliamentary accommodation of aristocratic and bourgeois interests. As Maier notes, in France, post-1848 Bonapartism was already a plebiscitarian nod to the coming corporatism, but elsewhere this was the apogee of liberalism, where a small number of individuals successfully took on the role of representing wider societal interests (Maier 1981: 40).[8]

By the 1860s, and certainly after the beginning of the economic downturn in the 1870s, this relatively thin liberal relationship of state to society began to thicken. It did so defensively, with agricultural and urban professional interests seeking state protection from the pinch of economic depression and heightened international competition. As the organization of interests proceeded apace, liberalism gave way to a more complex set of ties between society and the state. As Maier put it, 'the unified Victorian vision...of public opinion gave way to a more fragmented politics of partial interests—and patriotic passions' (1981: 42). By the time George Dangerfield wrote about the 'strange death' of liberalism in England, an overloaded liberal politics had given way to an incipient corporatism and an increasingly vibrant set of mass political parties representing organized labour (Dangerfield 1935). By 1914, with the coming of the First World War, 'the associations and conflicts of economic and social life were overflowing the juridical categories of the 19th century state' (Maier 1981: 43)—the liberal state was transforming itself into the twentieth century national corporatist party state. The inter-war period represented multiple variations on this theme: from the unstable conflict between the Right and Left in Spain through to Mussolini's Fascist syndicalism in Italy. Both democratic and authoritarian regimes had in common the rapid thickening of state–society ties, such that by the time peace returned to Europe in 1945 the societal bargain had been firmly struck: state power would be directed at social democratic goals, on condition that the market and property as such were preserved as the institutional foundations for capital accumulation. This bargain formed the political vertebrae structuring Western European societies from 1945 until the early 1970s. It was as this age of organization gave way to something else that the shift towards member statehood began.

---

[8] For a more theoretical account of these developments, see Manin (1997). For a more general historical account, see Hobsbawm (1975, 1987).

2.2.2 *Disorganized Capitalism*

The challenge facing Western European governments in the 1970s was how to manage the expectations of their populations, built up over the boom years of the post-war era, at a time when growth had stalled and when the cooperative business-labour arrangement forged in the aftermath of the Second World War had given way to a highly politicized and zero-sum relationship whose effects were felt in double-digit inflation figures (Gourevitch 1986; Goldthorpe 1987; Scharpf 1987; Mazower 1998).[9] The idea that the associative relations of the post-war era, in particular corporatism and other para-parliamentary forms of interest representation, were to blame came only later in the 1970s. Initially, governments sought to discipline their societies and manage expectations through existing institutions. Indeed, in some cases, as in the UK, neo-corporatism was identified as a possible solution. Social actors were thus empowered rather than marginalized, the goal being to preserve the core of the post-war consensus rather than to reject it wholesale.

The best example of this approach was perhaps the Netherlands: the 1982 Wassenaar accord saw Dutch unions accept wage moderation as part of a package of reforms intended to boost growth. Some years earlier in France, Prime Minister Jacques Chirac stymied his President Giscard D'Estaing's reform efforts by following his own Keynesian demand management strategy. In Italy, a system was introduced—the *scala mobile*—where wages were linked to prices in order to avoid real wage cuts. For all the variety in national responses, the common theme across Western Europe was the radicalization of existing tools and existing measures. The state–society relations of the post-war era were used as a means by which the crisis could be solved. By the latter half of the decade, however, from the 'winter of discontent' in the UK to the collapse of the Barre plan in France, this radicalized corporatist strategy had failed. Attention subsequently turned to dismantling existing associative structures altogether.

While this shift in focus was driven by a pragmatic desire to tackle the problems of high unemployment and rampant inflation, a more subtle change was taking place in the way societal interests were being viewed and understood. Maier is right to note that at some level interest groups have always been treated with some suspicion. As he puts it:

> Viewed in historical perspective, all forms of corporate representation and party delegation have awakened distrust in their formative stages...The line between conspiracy and the legitimate representation of a partial interest remains a sensitive one. (Maier 1981: 29)[10]

---

[9] For a more detailed account of this, see Bickerton (2012: 96–109).

[10] Hostility to organized interests, including political parties in particular, has a long history. Madison's critique of 'factions' is a famous example. However, by the mid-twentieth century there was a strong consensus around the association between majoritarian democracy and party

However, at this time, a sentiment was developing that organized interests of all kinds were no more than special interest groups seeking to improve their own lot. Trade unions were seen as selfish and self-regarding rather than as progressive vehicles for societal self-improvement. In Mancur Olson's influential work, this idea was theorized in the rationalist language of free-riding (Olson 1982). For Olson, corporatism in particular had the effect of allowing unions to negotiate wage increases for their own benefit but at a cost to society. The effect of partisanship in political decision-making also came under much criticism. Rather than being accepted as 'the legitimation of the partial good' (Maier 1981: 29), parties were also seen as selfish and self-interested.[11] In order to rid policy-making of the effects of both free riding and self-regarding partisan legislators, it became increasingly popular to constrain decision-making via independent rules or to delegate the decisions to bodies that were independent of political influence. At work here was an ideological shift in Western European societies, where the legitimacy of represented interests that had built up since the latter third of the nineteenth century was being eroded. The complex tapestry of interests that had comprised state–society relations in Western Europe was to be unpicked in order that decisions be made in the 'general interest', free from the narrower interests of parliamentary or para-parliamentary actors.

In practice, this shift in ideas led to a growing interest in transferring national government authority to institutional settings and bodies external to the political process, and often external to the state altogether. In the course of the 1980s, many Western European governments followed this path. Perhaps what made this ideological move against the organization of interests so powerful is that it developed in line with a growing disenchantment with the state as a collective agent. Across Western Europe in the 1980s, governments abandoned national programmes in favour of regional programmes intended to discipline governments in their reform efforts. In France, Mitterrand famously gave up his 'Keynesianism in one county' policy for one of preserving the franc within the European Monetary System, using the commitment to Europe as an ideological alternative to his earlier Keynesianism (Short, 2013). A very similar development occurred in Greece at around the same time, where the PASOK government led by Andreas Papandreou abandoned its own Keynesian platform. Indeed, in countries across the southern Mediterranean, from Greece through to Spain and Portugal, in this period EC membership became *the* key growth strategy for governing parties (Streeck 2011).

---

democracy. As Schattschneider wrote in 1942, 'modern democracy is unthinkable save in terms of the parties' (cited in Stokes 1999: 243). It is this consensus which was unravelling from the 1970s onwards.

[11] Most evident in the public choice critique of parties.

This was particularly important in Spain where Felipe Gonzalez's Socialists needed to find some framework—other than socialism itself which the party had given up—to present to voters. In the 1980s in Belgium, a commitment to an external currency peg was also used as a disciplining strategy for organized labour with the government vesting its authority in the wider EC framework. Wages were frozen in Belgium for much of the 1980s and only in 1993, after the introduction of a three-year wage freeze plan and extensive cuts to welfare provision, a general strike was called. By this time, the secular decline in labour militancy was firmly in place and Belgian corporatism had lost much of its vitality. Something similar occurred in Sweden after a radicalization of Swedish labour in the 1970s. Though the form of Swedish social democracy did not change radically, its content did (Blyth 2001). In the Netherlands, corporatist decision-making was not dismantled as such but rather its purpose was reoriented towards a new set of policy goals: low inflation, monetary stability, and a strong currency. These were very different from the emphasis on full employment and rising wages that had characterized post-war corporatism and corporatist actors were much more firmly aligned with the macroeconomic policies collectively set at the European level. National corporatist structures had been transformed into a means to implement pan-European commitments rather than a separate and nationally oriented set of state–society relations.

2.2.3 Agents of Disorganization: Cartel Parties and the Rise of Member States

From the above account, we see how internal contradictions within Western Europe's post-war political economy were tackled in the course of the 1970s and 1980s by taking on corporatist and partisan interests within which governments had hitherto been firmly embedded. In place of these domestic constraints, governments committed themselves to pan-European policy frameworks, particularly in the field of macroeconomics, and in so doing sought their authority in external frameworks of rule. At this stage, these amounted to strategies of re-scaling that aimed to liberate executives from domestic pressures. What still needs to be explained is how such strategies evolved over time into enduring forms of statehood.

The tale of the institutionalization of these strategies is really one of the changing nature of political parties. As key agents in domestic preference formation, and as critical intermediaries between the state and civil society, political parties can have a significant impact upon the nature of the state itself. As already noted, many would consider the modern state of the twentieth century to be above all a party state, what Hans Kelsen called the *Parteienstaat* (Manin 1997: 196, fn 6). The claim made here is that the shift from mass parties towards 'cartel parties' created pressure towards depoliticization from within national political systems themselves. This pressure coincided with the crisis of post-war social democracy, and the widely felt failure of the state and of national strategies, creating a powerful preference for regionalized policy-making among national political elites. The transformation of parties introduced a systemic aspect to what initially first emerged as an ad hoc series of responses to the crisis of post-war social democracy.

To speak of a crisis of parties has become commonplace. Across Western Europe, trust in parties has plummeted along with membership. However, as Katz and Mair (1995) argued, the language of crisis is misleading given that parties have persisted as the central governing agents in Western democracies. Rather than speak of crisis, Katz and Mair preferred the idea of party system change and party transformation. The connection with the shift from nation-state to member state comes with Katz and Mair's notion of the cartel party, a type of party they contrast with earlier types of parties such as mass parties and catch-all parties. Mass parties were defined by their sociological embeddedness in the structures of modern industrial society and they drew their authority from their ability to mobilize core groups of voters (Duverger 1951; Lipset and Rokkan 1967). Catch-all parties, a term coined by Otto Kirchheimer to describe post-Second World War parties in Western Europe were far less reliant upon a core constituency of voters (Kirchheimer 1966). As societies became more fluid, so parties had to become more creative in mobilizing voters and more open in terms of whom they could target. Catch-all parties became identifiable from the way in which they would create new identities and new cleavages around which they tried to win votes. For all their fluidity and doctrinal pragmatism, catch-all parties remain, in Katz and Mair's analysis, as 'competing brokers between civil society and the state' (1995: 18), meaning that they still played the crucial mediating role.

In their work on cartel parties, Katz and Mair argued that mainstream governing parties had increasingly lost many of their ties to civil society, particularly as a result of class dealignment trends and the rise of new social movements that drew individuals away from political parties. This left them reliant upon the state to survive and, as such, they tried to limit the costs of being out of power. Katz and Mair suggest that, in so far as cartel parties no longer directly represent societal interests, so their attitudes towards political competition have changed. Far from encouraging competition, cartel parties see dramatic and ideologically charged statements as likely to raise the costs of losing power. Rather than seek ideological polarization, they will actively work towards depoliticizing issues (Katz and Mair 2009: 758). By delegating authority to non-majoritarian institutions, or by concentrating policy-making processes at the EU level, domestic political competition is narrowed and the strength of the political cartel reinforced.

This mid-range theoretical focus on party transformation helps us better understand the precise way in which state transformation has occurred in Europe and its relationship to regional integration. Though the cartel party thesis has been much discussed (e.g. Kitschelt 2000; Detterbeck 2005; Aucante and Dézé 2008; Krouwel 2012) and its emphasis on state-party ties contested, the broader point Katz and Mair make about the estrangement of political parties from society remains compelling. Macro-level trends, such as enhanced international competition, and the common radicalization of organized labour in the 1960s and 1970s, encouraged governments to increase their autonomy vis-à-vis social actors such as unions. However, it is attenuation in the representativeness and mediating nature of political parties that has created for the mainstream political class a chronic problem of declining authority. Without being able to rely upon the thick associative relations of post-war European corporatism, governing parties looked outside politics and outside the state for alternative sources of authority. The fact that these external pressures coincided with a systematic internal transformation of domestic political systems has meant that over time a new form of state emerged out of these dynamics, one whose authority was constituted in the external frameworks via which national governments sought to rule authoritatively over their own societies.

2.3 Member Statehood and the New Intergovernmentalism

How exactly does this analysis of state transformation help us explain the specific features of the new intergovernmentalism? Looking at the individual hypotheses of this theory, the idea of member statehood and of the EU as a union of member states helps us explain them in a variety of ways.

The claim that deliberation and consensus-seeking have become ends in themselves rather than means to a nationally strategic end can be understood as an outcome of the transformation of the state in Europe outlined. In particular, the uncoupling of politics from policy-making helps us see how the bureaucratic perspective—a focus on expertise and professionalism, an orientation towards consensus and problem-solving—can prevail in what are, institutionally speaking, a set of intergovernmental relations. The fact that political life remains national in scope means that national outlooks are also oriented towards internal consumption, hence the national quality of electoral campaigns in Europe. At the pan-European policy-making level, however, it is the bureaucratic component of the state that is mobilized. Political actors are not immune from this and are active participants in this deliberative and problem-solving activity. The prominence given to this pattern of behaviour is a reflection of the bureaucratization of the state in Europe and the weakness of political spheres in directing and structuring the behaviour of state bureaucracies.

The hypothesis about the ambivalent preferences of supranational institutions and the preference for *de novo* bodies rather than delegation to supranational institutions make sense when we consider where the dynamic for further integration has come from. Rather than assuming it comes from supranational 'engines of integration', as much EU integration theory does, the focus on state transformation helps us identify the roots of the preference for further integration within government. As argued, the growing cartelization of political parties means that they have an active incentive to limit political competition; expanding the realm of pan-European policy-making is an obvious way of doing this. At the same time, this particular incentive puts elites at odds with their own domestic constituencies. Indeed, in some cases we see that domestic societies are still profoundly shaped by the expectations of the post-war social democratic era, which explains the reliance on private debt to finance access to property, education, and other goods that were once provided by the state (Crouch 2009). This division between governments and their own societies means that the preference for integration is accompanied by a strong reluctance to empower supranational institutions through public transfers of statutory powers from national capitals to Brussels. Indeed, if the goal is to reduce political competition then such transfers of competences and the associated need for accountability and transparency would be the opposite of what cartelized parties would wish. Instead, the institutional arrangements of the new intergovernmentalism—a powerful European Council, expanded comitology procedures, a European Parliament (EP) whose power is exercised in secluded decision-making settings—fit much more closely with this particular understanding of integration in the post-Maastricht period.

The blurring of the line between high and low politics reflects the importance of external frameworks of rule for the constitution of the state in Europe. The original distinction between high and low politics pointed to the shifting nature of politicization and salience: at times, one policy area would seem more salient than another and high politics was defined in terms of whatever was considered, at that time, as critical for the national interest and for national survival. If national survival becomes conditional upon the continued participation in transnational governance networks, then there can be no moment where such survival is opposed to these networks. On the contrary, as the Scottish example showed, national survival is viewed rather as conditional upon the continued participation in regional integration processes. The very idea of high or low politics has given way to the overriding priority of continued membership in regional institutions.

Finally, the hypothesis about the EU being in a state of disequilibrium is directly tied to the member-state perspective. The new intergovernmentalism does not treat disequilibrium as an occasional and productive input into EU integration, as much writing on the relationship between crises and integration do. Rather, it views disequilibrium as a systemic feature of post-Maastricht integration. This derives from the internal contradictions of member states themselves. As Vincent Della Sala put it with regard to the Italian state, member states are 'hard but hollow': hard in the sense that they are well insulated from societal mobilization but hollow in that the horizontal structures of legitimation that they rely upon fare very badly when pitted against the traditional vertical structures of popular sovereignty and nationalism (Della Salla 1997). Elites are thus both powerful and weak at the same time: shielded from pressures but subject to repeated crises of authority. This introduces into European integration a systemic source of disequilibrium: mobilization against the growing unrepresentativeness of domestic political rule is evident in Euro-sceptic and populist movements where anti-elite sentiment has become a key ingredient of political discourse. At the same time, the elite resistance to greater politicization at the European level is strong, resulting in a preference for more limited technocratic advances, as witnessed in the creation of ever greater numbers of new bodies, the supervision of which falls to member states. Constrained from below, but also lacking the creative imagination to pursue genuinely political integration from above, the EU is—in Offe's words—'entrapped' and thus stuck in its own repeated cycles of instability and disequilibrium (Offe 2013).

Conclusion

This chapter has taken as its starting point the integration paradox identified in chapter 1. It has argued that in order to explain this paradox we need to revisit our understanding of the state and its role in European integration. The paradox points towards a distinctive feature of contemporary European states, namely their reliance upon external frameworks of rule as sources of political authority and legitimacy.

The chapter has claimed that this feature of European state is not merely a passing fad or an opportunistic strategy adopted by political elites keen to shirk responsibility for domestic political developments. Rather, this signals the arrival of a distinctive form of state, the member state, that differs from nation-states precisely in the horizontal manner in which governments constitute their authority to rule. The chapter has differentiated member states from nation-states along three lines: the legitimizing discourses, the internal organizational arrangements, and the modes of political conflict that correspond to each form of state. By identifying the ways in which transnational networks of governance form the basis for the exercise of political power by contemporary national elites in Europe today, this chapter has sought to unravel the mystery of the integration paradox. Presenting integration as a shift of power from national capitals to supranational institutions in Brussels, as many commentators and journalists do, leaves us with the puzzle of explaining why so much integration has coincided with so little supranationalism. By thinking of integration in terms of state transformation, we are able to explain why regional integration in Europe has become a constitutive feature of statehood in Europe. Far from signalling the transcendence of the state, EU integration in the post-Maastricht period expresses the consolidation of a distinctive and stand-alone form of state in Europe, that of the member state.

In its account of the dynamics behind the development of member states, the chapter has emphasized the role played by the economic and political crisis of the 1970s. Signalling the exhaustion of the post-war Keynesian compromise between business and labour, national governments sought to liberate themselves from domestic constraints and did so by weakening or undoing altogether the post-war mechanisms of interest representation, most notably corporatism. This attack on organized interests gained traction partly from a growing ideological opposition to the idea of governing through coordination with societal interest groups and partly also as a result of a transformation in political parties. As parties became more closely tied to the state, and less embedded in civil society, so their authority and representative quality waned. Successive governments responded by seeking legitimacy in horizontal frameworks of policy-making at the European level. Member statehood is the outcome of this thinning of state–society relations. The form and content of the present-day EU corresponds to these societal and political changes.

In so far as the new intergovernmentalism is underpinned by these broader transformations in European politics and society, it is unlikely that these features of the post-Maastricht period will disappear quickly. Contemporary crises—from the euro area sovereign debt crisis to the rise of anti-EU populist parties—will tend rather to consolidate these more secular trends and exacerbate some of the internal contradictions of member statehood that give to the EU its fragile mixture of institutional continuity and widespread public disenchantment.

3

The Roles of Law in a New Intergovernmentalist European Union

Paul James Cardwell and Tamara Hervey

What are the roles of law in European integration?[1] Of course, this is not a new question. But it is a question that deserves to be revisited by successive generations of EU scholars, and not only in light of major Treaty changes to formal legal structures. Legal approaches to the EU have traditionally—and correctly—focused on the central importance of the 'Community method' as a means to pursue European integration. But as early in the post-Maastricht period as 1995, some legal scholars were already identifying 'new legal dynamics' (Shaw and More 1995), beyond Court-focused scholarship, or singular accounts of the role of law in the integration process. Legal scholars have increasingly looked towards alternative methods and processes of EU integration, including their 'law-like' qualities, as the EU has moved into new law and policy-making areas. Some political scientists have also considered the role of law, but often a rather 'thin' notion of 'law-ness', focused only upon 'command and control' and not upon law's other qualities, modes or interactions with 'non-law-like' means of integration.

[1] We are grateful to the participants at the workshops on *The Methods of European Integration*, Central University Budapest, June 2012; the panel on *Methods of Integration* at the University Association for Contemporary European Studies (UACES) Annual Conference, Passau, September 2012; and the workshops *Exploring the Legal in Socio-Legal Studies*, LSE, September 2012; *Theorising Integration and Governance after the Lisbon Treaty and During Crisis*, Sheffield, July 2013; *The New Intergovernmentalism*, Budapest, November 2013, at which versions of this paper were delivered, especially Chris Bickerton, Simon Bulmer, Dave Cowan, Dermot Hodson, and Uwe Puetter. We are also grateful to Nina Boeger, Pablo Castillo Ortiz, Jo Hunt, Jo Shaw, Niamh Nic Shuibhne, and Francesca Strumia for their useful comments and suggestions and to Charlotte Page for research assistance.

If the assumption that the Community method is less central to the European integration project in the post-Maastricht period than it used to be is correct, then three inferences may be drawn. The first is that the role of law—as traditionally understood—is largely redundant in terms of the integration project since the member states are no longer prepared to pool sovereignty to the EU law-making institutions, and—by analogy—that legal scholars' input into our understanding of the EU should be skewed towards issues such as the EU's involvement in trade disputes at the World Trade Organization (WTO), or the enforcement of existing EU law, such as competition law, that is to say areas where there still remains 'hard' law occupying the field. The second is that 'EU law' needs to include decentralized forms of law which are neither the Community method as traditionally understood, nor variants of it. The third is that the conceptual frameworks for understanding 'EU law' need to reach beyond the traditional constitutionalist frameworks that have dominated EU legal scholarship for decades, and draw on other legal conceptual frameworks, such as comparative constitutional law, and both public and private international law. For legal scholars, this implies a shift in understanding as to what matters in the discipline. For non-legal scholars, it implies taking account of what lawyers can bring to the debates in terms of the underlying importance of rules and the legitimacy grounded in them.

In this chapter, we largely agree with the claim that the EU has moved on from the Community method. However, we do not go so far as to say the Community method is so redundant as to be irrelevant. Rather, we examine the place of law within the new intergovernmentalism and make the claim that developments in EU law and our understanding of it do not represent a simple 'retreat' from law and replacement by political, consensus-based decision-making driven by governments and instrumentalized through *de novo* bodies. Instead, we see EU law in the post-Maastricht era as a heady blend of such a 'retreat' alongside newer forms of 'hyperlegalism', reliance on the procedural legitimacy afforded by law, differentiated forms of law, novel applications of legal principles, and increased significance of legal reasoning. None of the features of the post-Maastricht EU necessarily mean a decline in the importance of law. These novel legal forms may even be better suited to the political economy challenges in the post-Maastricht period. It will be obvious that we are relying upon an assumption that 'law' is distinct from 'politics'—a view that is shared by most legal scholars, but not by all EU scholars. The implication of our overall argument in this chapter is not only that law plays a role in the new intergovernmentalist EU, but also that legal scholarship has important contributions to make to the continued debate over what the EU is, what it stands for, and how it works.

3.1 The Changing Roles of Law in the Post-Maastricht Period

The question of the roles of law in European integration is one which provokes sharp divisions within the discipline—ranging stereotypically from the extreme ('Herren der Verträge')[2] notion that the law is there only as a (dispensable) servant of the political desires of the governments of the member states (a view most often associated with political science scholars such as the early work of Andrew Moravcsik (Moravcsik 1991, 1993), or Alan Milward (Milward 1992)) to the view that law is the single explanatory factor that determines the success (however defined) of the integration process. The latter view is implicit in any scholarship that assumes that more law is a 'good thing' for the EU. In part, the question is important because what distinguishes (or at least has distinguished) the EU from many (if not all) organizations or regional integration schemes is not only the 'breadth' of legal rules of which the EU is author, but also the 'depth' of interpenetration between its own legal norms and the legal norms and institutions of its member states (see, e.g. Zürn and Joerges 2005). Think, in particular, of the deep respect of national courts for the rulings of the Court of Justice of the European Union (EU), including (though, of course, there are exceptions), national constitutional courts (Chalmers et al. 2010; Craig and De Búrca 2011). Think also of the willingness of national courts to apply EU law in situations that, to all appearances, are governed only by national law (Lefevre 2004), either with the encouragement of the Court of Justice under the preliminary reference procedure,[3] or without reference to the Court of Justice at all (e.g. large areas of commercial law, consumer law, employment law, and other areas where EU law is followed *de facto*). To this we can also add the willingness of national administrative authorities to defer to EU law in such areas as competition policy, agricultural and fisheries policy, pharmaceuticals regulation, health and safety regulation, chemicals regulation, food regulation, social security coordination, and doubtless a host of others.

The question is important because the answer tells us something about what we understand the EU and its legal system to *be*—and this is certainly a worthwhile exercise in reflecting back on the EU's recent history and pursuit of an 'ever closer Union' (Article 1 TEU). If we understand the process of integration up to Maastricht to have reached a stage where we could talk of the EU in *constitutional* terms (Weiler and Wind 2003; Kumm 2006; Maduro 2010) or 'the most advanced institutional embodiment of taking constitutionalism beyond

---

[2] *Gauweiler* v *Treaty of Lisbon* 2 BvE 2/08 30 June 2009.
[3] For example, Case 166/84 *Thomasdünger* ECLI:EU:C:1985:373, Cases C-297/88 and 197/89 *Dzodzi* ECLI:EU:C:1990:360, Case C-281/98 *Angonese* ECLI:EU:C:2000:296; Case C-144/04 *Mangold* ECLI:EU:C:2005:709; C-555/07 *Kücükdeveci* ECLI:EU:C:2010:21.

the state' (De Búrca and Weiler 2011; see also Arnull et al. 2011), then constitutionalism provides a framework for understanding the roles of law in creating,
sustaining, and legitimating the EU. More recent scholarship, including some of
that mentioned above, reaches beyond 'simple' constitutionalism, towards
pluralist accounts. In the framework of such constitutional pluralism, the
relations between EU and domestic or international law are no longer understood in terms of those between entirely autonomous legal systems, but as
interacting in a pluralist legal order, or 'legal space' (MacCormick 1999; Walker
2002, 2008; Walker et al. 2011; Itzcovich 2012). To the extent that an understanding of the post-Maastricht EU based on a new intergovernmentalism
represents a retreat from traditional constitutional frameworks, it is pertinent
to consider what legal scholarship could offer in its place. Public or private
international law, or comparative law, might offer more appropriate frameworks for understanding the roles of law in determining relations between
actors within (legally) autonomous constitutional orders (states), and hence
understanding what this EU's legal system *is*. The roles of private actors in the
integration process are significantly different too, in terms both of the sources
of their legal entitlements and the roles of litigation in disrupting political
decisions based on consensus of certain constellations of actors.

Furthermore, for much of the post-Maastricht period, the legal construction
of the EU was based on a legally differentiated 'pillar' structure until this was
(largely) abolished at Lisbon. There may be a need, therefore, to distinguish
our analysis into pre- and post-Lisbon phases, given the significant legal
changes that were introduced in 2009.

The mention of 'legal spaces' and 'pluralistic legal order' may seem the
antithesis to a traditional view of EU law as based on a command-and-control
regulatory model with legal characteristics limited to treaties, regulations and
directives, and decisions of the Court of Justice as well as national courts. But,
as we contend in this chapter, law and legal study in the post-Maastricht
period is largely consistent with a new intergovernmentalist perception of
the EU—albeit modified in the ways that we indicate in the introduction.

In order to explain this position, we need to explore some of the principal
changes to the law of the EU—and to our ways of seeing the law and its roles.
We can identify at least four interconnected features of the EU of the 1990s–
2010s to suggest that there is a more limited role for 'law' as traditionally
conceived in the EU legal system, that is to say the dual factors of the extensive
use of the Community method and judicial law-making by an 'activist' Court
of Justice. If true, these would render increasingly redundant those explanations of the integration process that give a central role to law. They would, at
least at face value, support the turn to new intergovernmentalism.

These features are as follows: first, the likely present and future ability of the
EU institutions to maintain the level of legislative output of earlier years.

Second, the 'end' of the development of (constitutional) legal principles by the Court of Justice. Third, a challenge to the EU's 'single legal order' via the emergence of a 'multi-speed' Europe through patterns of differentiated integration. And fourth, the inability of future 'hard' law to adequately explain the workings of EU integration when the rules are not enforced, or where 'hard' law is eschewed in favour of 'softer' political solutions.

3.2 A Relative Decline in Legislative Outputs

In an enlarged EU of 28 member states, the ability of the EU institutions to adopt new legislation or embark on comprehensive legislative programmes is increasingly constrained (Piris 2012). The larger number of EU member states is not a barrier to passing legislation *per se* when one recalls that the 'empty chair' crisis of the mid-1960s occurred when the EU had only six member states. However, the increased economic and political diversity among the member states and need to ensure that legislation passes with as few opposing votes as possible suggests that legislation will be slower to emerge and more contested. The European Parliament, as co-legislator in most areas, has traditionally favoured greater integration but it is more politically fractured than in the past with a more significant Euro-sceptic component. Taken together, if new legislation can no longer be the energy behind European integration, analyses that give a central explanatory place to EU-level legislation will become increasingly irrelevant. Of course, there could be an increase in legislative output if a new Treaty arrangement increased the competences of the EU institutions to act, but this is unlikely to become a reality.

It is true that legislation has not always emerged from the institutions with the same regularity during the European integration process, and pieces of legislation differ greatly in size, significance, and scope. A strictly numerical comparison over time is therefore unlikely to reveal much at all. Regulation 1907/2006 on the Registration, Evaluation, Authorisation and Restriction of Chemical Substances runs to 280 pages in the Official Journal (Scott 2009). What is perhaps more telling is that many of the current policy programmes of the European Commission either rely less on the enactment of legislation, or where this has been the case, the reaction from a majority of member states has often been muted. One might note, for example, the lack of enthusiasm for the Commission's proposed legislative programme in its Single Market Act,[4] as

---

[4] Communication from the Commission to the European Parliament, the Council, the Economic and Social Committee and the Committee of the Regions, 2011. 'Single Market Act: Twelve levers to boost growth and strengthen confidence—Working together to create new growth'. COM (2011) 206 final.

compared to the Single Market project of the 1980s. A further example is the 2009 Stockholm programme on justice, freedom, and security.[5] This signalled an ambitious programme, but when the means to put it in place are compared to its predecessors agreed at Tampere in 1999[6] and the Hague in 2004[7] there are revealed to be far fewer calls for legislation on specific areas, even though there are undoubtedly areas which *could* be legislated on.

The argument here of the increased irrelevance of law to the post-Maastricht EU is that legislation is what matters. For sure, the EU's dense legislative landscape marks it out from other international institutional arrangements. But legislation is not all that makes up that density. Regulatory activity (be that self-regulation; processes of (new) governance; 'steering' through the availability of resourcing; and so on) also plays a significant role here. We also need to take account of the view that the Community method, while generally seen as 'good' by lawyers because of its enforceability, also suffers from a legitimacy problem. Legal accounts that are restricted to analysis of enforceable legal texts are unable to explain even partly some of the most dynamic areas of European integration. The resulting lack of engagement in legal scholarship would be a lack of legal input into some areas where lawyers find a natural 'home' (justice and home affairs being a prime example) but where actual legislation is limited. However, that said, an account of integration processes in such areas that ignores the legal dimension is equally impoverished.

Our central claim here is that one cannot understand regulation or governance without being able to understand law. Although there are competing definitions or descriptions of what governance entails, our view is that governance is both 'law-light' and 'law-like'. A system of governance works because of the 'shadow' or 'backstop' of the law (Sabel and Simon 2003). The system works within a legal framework—law mandates governance activities such as, in the context of the Open Method of Coordination, gathering of data in a particular form; reporting of that data; and comparison (Armstrong 2010). To take a concrete example, cooperation between the judiciaries and other (quasi-) judicial bodies across the EU is on the rise (Rijken 2010; Mégle 2014): this is very much *about* 'hard law' without necessarily being done *through* 'hard law'. Without an understanding of the workings of judicial processes, procedures and principles, it is impossible to account either for what is occurring or what limitations or safeguards need consideration in

---

[5] European Council 2009. 'The Stockholm Programme: An open and secure Europe serving and protecting citizens'. OJ C 115, 1–38.

[6] European Council 1999. 'Presidency Conclusions: Towards a Union of Freedom, Security and Justice'. Available at: <http://www.europarl.europa.eu/summits/tam_en.htm>.

[7] European Council 2005. 'The Hague Programme: strengthening freedom, security and justice in the European Union'. OJ C 53, 03/03/2005, 1–14.

such an important dimension of European integration. This explains our claim that developments in policy-making which do not seem to primarily rely on the Community method do not necessarily represent a 'retreat' from law. An example here is the Commission's 2011 paper on a 'better functioning Single Market for services',[8] which does not rely on new legislation per se, but rather on building on the existing legislation through the use of mutual evaluation processes. This—as the Commission states in its paper—is partly about smoothing out inconsistencies in implementation but also the possibilities for where 'hard' law in the future may be desirable. In this respect, deliberation and consensus could be seen as ends in themselves, even though this is largely irrelevant when discussing 'hard' legislation as a concrete outcome.

3.3 The Lack of Emergence of New Legal Principles

The second feature of the post-Maastricht EU, which resonates with new intergovernmentalism, is the idea that the time for ground-breaking legally driven integration, where new legal principles were developed by the Court of Justice and taken up by the EU legislature, is now over (see also chapter 10 in this volume, on the Court of Justice). As the EU expands into new areas of activity, existing legal principles can be 'written across' from existing areas, so long as they are politically acceptable, or even if they are not, if the Court is involved. We should not expect to see energy for the integration process coming from novel legal principles, especially not from the Court of Justice. If this is so, analyses that put the Court's approach to the development of legal principles at the heart of integration become increasingly unconvincing.

In the EU context, the driving force behind both developing these principles (given the 'traité cadre' nature of the EEC Treaty and its successors) and deciding the contexts in which they apply, is the Court of Justice. According to the standard accounts of Court of Justice-driven integration, the development (or discovery, depending upon your view) of novel legal principles and their application in litigation, often involving national courts and private litigants, is key. These legal principles include both 'constitutional' principles, such as supremacy and direct effect of EU law, implied competence, and 'general principles' of EU law (Weiler 1991), and core principles of EU substantive law, especially on free movement of goods (mutual recognition, market access), but also on competition law, sex equality law, and even

---

[8] Communication from the Commission to the European Parliament, the Council, the Economic and Social Committee and the Committee of the Regions, 2011. 'Towards a better functioning Single Market for services—building on the results of the mutual evaluation process of the Services Directive'. COM (2011) 20 final.

criminal law (Hoskyns 1996; Armstrong and Bulmer 1998; Monti 2007; Baker and Harding 2009; Peers 2011). It is, of course, unfair to characterize the literature associated with a view of Court of Justice-driven integration as representing the position that the Court acts alone in this respect. Rather, the Court is understood in these accounts as acting in collaboration with other actors, especially the Commission (Hunt 2007; Hunt and Shaw 2009; Stone Sweet 2010; Conway 2012), but also, crucially, private litigants, especially legal persons (Cichowski 2007; Kelemen 2011). But, in essence, according to such accounts of the integration process that cast the Court of Justice in a 'heroic' (Hunt 2007) role, at times of stagnation in political drivers towards further integration, we should expect the Court of Justice to 'come to the rescue', and keep the integration process moving 'forward'. In the post-Lisbon settlement, however, it is claimed that the Court has neither the gravitas nor authority (at least compared to national constitutional courts (Chalmers 2012)) nor appropriate judicial architecture (Nic Shuibhne 2009) to develop the imaginative and 'activist' jurisprudence of its supposed heyday.

Our point here is not whether the Court of Justice can be characterized as 'activist' or not (Rasmussen 1986; Arnull 1999; De Búrca and Weiler 2001; Grimmel 2010; Solanke 2011; Arnull 2012; Davies 2012; Dawson 2012; Dawson et al. 2013). In any event there is a significant level of discussion about what 'activism' means when applied to courts (Neill 1995; Green 2009), whether one views judicial 'activism' as a positive or negative trait (Davies 2012), and may in any event now be a rather arid question (Conway 2012). We also do not (need to) refute here the claim that processes of litigation are a crucial mode of governance in the EU (Kelemen 2011; Kelemen and Schmidt 2012). The point we are making is a narrower one, concerning a change in the practice of the Court of Justice, as compared to the 'foundational' (Weiler 1991) period of its jurisprudence. Whereas at that stage, the novelty of the Court's jurisprudence lay in the creation (or discovery) of legal principles that were surprising to, if not most, then many of those whose understandings of the EU were influenced by the prism of international law (de Witte 2011a, points out that even direct effect and supremacy of EU law can be explained through such a prism), our argument is that, at this stage of the Court's 'self-constitutionalization', its *own* self-understanding precludes *that type of* novelty. As the Court of Justice behaves increasingly like a constitutional court, so by definition must it regard itself as bound by the weight, if not exactly of precedent in the common law sense, at least of its previous jurisprudence.

This observation implies a change in the nature of the 'activism' of the Court. Rather than creating novel legal principles, the dominant mode of such activism, probably since the mid-1990s, and certainly in the post-Lisbon Treaty on European Union (TEU), we would argue, is that the Court of Justice 'reads across' already existing legal principles into novel areas. So, for instance, in *Pupino*,[9] the principle of direct effect was 'written across' from 'ordinary' EU law to what was the law of the 'third pillar'; in other cases,[10] direct effect was applied to fundamental rights as 'general principles' of EU law. The case law on goods provided the concept of market access which was subsequently 'written across' to the law on services and establishment (Barnard 2001; Barnard and Scott 2002; Spaventa 2007). The principle of direct effect and the concept of market access were used to challenge collective agreements in the context of a post-2004, enlarged EU,[11] which brought into focus the different levels of economic development of (some) newer and older member states and pitted the EU goals of the promotion of 'harmonious, balanced and sustainable development of economic activities' against 'a high level of employment and of social protection'.[12] Broad concepts of 'restriction', and 'undertaking' were written across from regulation of services or anti-competitive behaviour in the private sector to activities seen as part of national welfare systems, such as health care, pensions, and education.[13] The concept of (social) citizenship as a 'fundamental status' was written across into cases concerning 'third country' nationals.[14] These might seem to be technical points to a non-lawyer, but they are more than this, because of the extension of significant legal principles from one area to another with (especially in the case of *Pupino*) important consequences in terms of what EU law is.

Therefore, our claim here is not that the Court of Justice has not developed *any* novel principles in the last couple of decades (for instance, the concept of 'social solidarity' might be considered to be such a principle; Ross and Borgmann-Prebil 2010), and indeed the revised Treaty appears to be alive to such a possibility (e.g. the jurisdiction of the Court in the field of the CFSP is explicitly ruled out in Article 24(1) TEU (Cardwell 2013)) but rather that this type of activism is very much the exception in the post-Lisbon period.

To summarize, our argument in this section is two-fold. While activism in the sense of Court of Justice-led developments of *true novelty* in legal principles may still form part of the integration process, it is very much the exception.

---

[9] Case C-105/03 *Criminal Proceedings against Maria Pupino* ECLI:EU:C:2005:386.

[10] Case C-144/04 *Mangold v Helm* ECLI:EU:C:2005:709; Case C-555/07 *Kücükdeveci v Swedex GmbH* ECLI:EU:C:2010:21.

[11] Case 438/05 *International Transport Workers' Federation and Finnish Seamen's Union v Viking Line ABP and OÜ Viking Line Eesti* ECLI:EU:C:2007:772.

[12] Case 438/05 *International Transport Workers' Federation and Finnish Seamen's Union v Viking Line ABP and OÜ Viking Line Eesti* ECLI:EU:C:2007:772, para. 78.

[13] Case C-158/96 *Kohll* ECLI:EU:C:1998:171; Case C-372/04 *Watts* ECLI:EU:C:2006:325; Case C-67/96 *Albany* ECLI:EU:C:1999:430; Cases C-180–4/98 *Pavlov* ECLI:EU:C:2000:428; Case T-289/03 *BUPA Ireland* ECLI:EU:T:2008:29; Case C-437/09 *AG2R Prévoyance* ECLI:EU:C:2011:112; Case C-73/08 *Bressol* ECLI:EU:C:2010:181.

[14] For example, Case C-184/99 *Grzelczyk* ECLI:EU:C:2001:458; Case C-34/09 *Gerardo Ruiz Zambrano v Office national de l'emploi* ECLI:EU:C:2011:124; Case C-200/02 *Zhu and Chen* ECLI:EU:C:2004:639).

Because the Court's sense of itself as a constitutional court has changed since the 1970s, the idea that a heroic Court of Justice will once again ride to the rescue of stalling integration processes is unrealistic. This is especially the case for the 'core' areas of integration, which, as Granger has argued (see chapter 10 of this volume), the Court has begun to identify as synonymous with the Community method. The more prevalent form of Court of Justice activism is that of 'write across' of existing legal principles from one context to another. Whichever is at play, understanding integration processes in the post-Lisbon TEU will require an understanding of how law shapes that process of 'write across'. Legal scholarship of a 'doctrinal' nature is classically used to determine the reach or scope of particular legal principles, particularly as unfolding through a body of court decisions, and to discuss in which circumstances such principles are applicable, and which are distinguishable. Comparative legal scholarship proceeds by arguing for the application of legal principles in different contexts, in particular in different jurisdictions.

3.4 The Decline of a Single 'Legal Order'

Third, the idea that the contemporary EU is essentially a 'multi-speed' Europe, or better, a Europe of 'variable geometry', with multiple and complex opt-outs for too many areas to be perceived as exceptions means that notions of the EU as a unitary 'legal order' are increasingly problematic. This is consistent with new intergovernmentalist claims concerning consensus formation, as well as those based on regulation through *de novo* institutions, as entrusting regulatory activities to an under-resourced and geographically remote agency is significantly less politically problematic than entrusting them to the Commission. Legal analysis based on the idea of the EU as a single legal system cannot explain integration processes with variable integration, though neither can the EU's variable legal order be treated on an entirely 'intergovernmental' basis (and hence closer to 'classic' international law). In particular, admission criteria for new member states set conditions which bind them, even if the same obligations do not extend to current member states (e.g. to work towards eventual euro membership for 2004 and 2007 accession states).

Thus, the idea that law is increasingly irrelevant to European integration is bolstered by contemporary moves away from the idea of the EU as embodying a legal order in the singular. Certainly, for the Court of Justice, and also for legal scholars, the EU's landmark declaration of a 'new legal order' in *Van Gend en Loos*[15] as early as 1963 provided the springboard for an entire body of

---

[15] Case 26/62 *Van Gend en Loos v Nederlandse Administratie der Belastingen* ECLI:EU:C:1963:1.

scholarship that understands the EU as having a unitary legal system. In practice, this approach interprets its law as if it were the law of a state. This is particularly strong when we consider scholarship on various areas of EU substantive law, where the assumption that the EU's law can be understood in essentially the same way as national law on the same topic is seldom made explicit (e.g. in competition law or employment law). The approach is, however, also found in EU legal scholarship dealing with the EU's institutions and conceptualizing the EU as having relationships with not only its member states, but also its people(s) (see, e.g. van Gerven 2005), which can be characterized as falling within a 'comparative constitutional law' approach.

Yet, beginning at least with the Maastricht Treaty, if not earlier, and certainly in the post-Lisbon EU, there is increasing 'legalization' of the components of the EU's activities which do not include all the member states. Contemporary examples of departures from the idea of a unitary EU legal order include opt-outs from stage three of Economic and Monetary Union and membership of the euro, the Schengen area of no internal borders, the 'area of freedom security and justice', permanent structured cooperation in defence, the applicability of the Charter of Fundamental Rights and so on. The extent of these examples of variable geometry have gone beyond the stage where they could realistically be counted as exceptions to the general rule, and this has led some lawyers to call for formalization of a 'two-speed' Europe (Piris 2012). One need only look to the sheer number of protocols (37) and declarations (65) attached to the Treaty of Lisbon as proof of the extent to which member states are prepared to publicly make individual interpretations of what the Treaty does—and does not—entail. Nevertheless, all these examples of variable speed all rely on legal tools of integration, even if not all of the 28 member states are bound by the relevant legal instruments.

There is also a change in the metaphoric language used to conceptualize the phenomenon: the term 'legal order', or even 'legal system', is increasingly replaced by terms indicating geographic or physical spaces for circulation and interaction, such as legal 'space' or 'architecture' (Krisch 2008; Piris 2012). This implies 'a new kind of law than can no more be conceived of as being a legal order, as it is pluralist (rather than exclusive), contradictory (rather than consistent), unfinished (rather than complete)' (Itzcovich 2012: 374). Indeed, as already noted, since at least the early 1990s, EU legal scholarship on institutional, if not substantive, EU law, increasingly uses the language of constitutional pluralism (MacCormick 1999; Walker 2002; Maduro 2010; De Búrca and Weiler 2011; Walker et al. 2011).

As for the roles of law in a pluralist legal order, where different systems are in non-hierarchical relationships with one another, the role of *reasoning* takes on increased significance (Itzcovich 2012). In the absence of authority, in the sense of a *de jure* claim based on hierarchy, dialogic relations between systems take place through the accounting of legal reasoning, particularly in the context of judicial activity. Over time, the shared notion of what counts as 'good' and 'less good' legal reasoning (based on internal coherence of the law, the construction of fact patterns as similar to or distinguishable from previous cases etc.) becomes a sort of proxy for authority. Thus, one of the roles of law is to provide a practical solution to the political problem of pursuing integration without going down the road to federal statehood, which relies on the shared European respect for the rule of law and the consequent respect of administrative and executive authorities for the judiciary.

In this context, where scholarship assesses the relative merits of legal reasoning from different 'levels' in a pluralist legal order, it also contributes to that dialogue. Given that it is inherent in legal scholars to scrutinize the quality of legal reasoning, using the classical approaches of 'doctrinal law', alongside comparative legal method, we would argue that it is important for that type of legal scholarship to continue to be heard. We find such scholars grappling with the relationships between the European Convention on Human Rights (ECHR) and the Court of Justice (e.g. Krisch 2008); and the relationships between the Court of Justice and national constitutional courts, particularly with respect to human rights (see, e.g. Sabel and Gerstenberg 2010).

3.5 European Integration is Driven by Politics, not Law

The new intergovernmentalist account of the EU suggests that, in the areas where integration really matters, deliberation and consensus are paramount in explaining the relationships between the governments of the 28 member states, or between EU institutions and national governments. In such an account, the legal position does not explain these relationships. The obvious example is the euro area crisis, where there is no new EU treaty settlement to solve the problem, and where legal rules appear to be easily flouted in view of political necessities or expediencies (depending upon one's view). The role of law here appears to be almost a parody of law—a form of 'hyper-legalism' where law is used simply to be seen to be 'doing something', without any real intention of creating legal effects. A related example is where hard law (such as treaty reform) is used for 'purely political ends to send messages to nervous markets' (Armstrong 2012). The implication is that analysis from other disciplines, in particular political science, but also economics or sociology, is needed to understand the integration process; legal scholarship has little to contribute to explaining the dynamics of deliberation and consensus.

Are there dimensions of European integration where law has no role to play, or where lawyers cannot contribute to the debate? Typically, this question points to issues that have arisen beyond the formal competences of the EU, or the legislative powers of the institutions or even where the Court of Justice has extended the powers of the EU. Our argument here is a simple no—all dimensions of the European integration process involve law (or at the very least, law-like qualities) and an understanding of the politics only is insufficient in itself. This is particularly the case where institutionalization occurs, as Armstrong explains, without necessarily incorporating traditional forms of law: 'the more we treat institutionalization as a product of legalism, the less obvious it might seem to adopt an institutionalist approach to the study of phenomena in which traditional institutional forms of law are displaced or decentred' (Armstrong 2010: 14).

Although this refers to a specific approach to understanding European integration—namely institutionalism—it is nevertheless indicative of the need to understand the law (or law-like) processes and instruments. EU foreign policy serves as a good example. Foreign policy was, historically, the best example of the intergovernmental dimension of European integration, having begun informally (as 'European Political Cooperation') in the 1970s with no formalized framework for cooperation. Some limited treaty recognition came with the Single European Act and, against the backdrop of the fall of the Berlin Wall and a period of renewed Europe-wide enthusiasm for the integration project, became the Common Foreign and Security Policy (CFSP) in the TEU. Legal scholars initially pondered as to whether the instruments of CFSP could be termed as 'law' (Denza 2002; Eeckhout 2004) but since the *Kadi* cases,[16] it can no longer be thought of as an area that is 'immune' from either legal processes or legal analysis. The measure challenged in *Kadi* was a CFSP one after all and brought to the fore the extent to which legal challenges can be made within the EU which involve consideration of the global legal order. Even if the Treaty of Lisbon appears to isolate (or 'ring fence') CFSP from other parts of the Treaty, this does not discount the need for legal analysis, rather, it increases it since the general principles of coherence and so on still apply (Cardwell 2013). The constitutionalization of CFSP in Lisbon is characterized by Thym as 'legal intergovermentalism' (Thym 2011) which aptly bridges any perceived gap between the new intergovernmentalism and legal study in an area often thought to be removed from legal analysis (see also chapter 5 in this volume, on the security and defence aspects of the EU's external relations).

Going back further still, landmark cases such as *AETR/ERTA*[17] dispel the notion that the EU's competence can be defined as 'legal' or 'political' only.

---

[16] Cases C–402/05 P and C–415/05 P *Kadi and Al Barakaat International Foundation* v *Council and Commission* ECLI:EU:C:2008:461; Case C-584-10 P *European Commission and Others* v *Yassin Abdullah Kadi* ECLI:EU:C:2013:518.

[17] Case 22/70 *Commission of the European Communities* v *Council of the European Communities—(European Road Transport Agreement)* ECLI:EU:C:1971:32.

Just as the Court of Justice in *AETR/ERTA* took away the notion that the 'external' is beyond the competence of the EU, owing to the lack of a specific treaty provision giving external competences, but that these are 'implied' by the granting of internal competences, so contemporary legal scholarship can help enrich other areas where law appears secondary—if at all—to the politics.

Our central argument here is that we can only have a partial understanding of the politics (or anything else) if we do not understand the legal context. Even where it appears that there is a limited role for lawyers to play, such as in CFSP, the possibility that a policy area will take on 'legal' features cannot be excluded. With this in mind, legal and political science scholars should (and indeed need to) talk to each other about the methodological tools required to understand the institutional and policy dynamics characterized by new intergovernmentalism.

Conclusion

Our contribution is the conclusion that, despite the changing nature of the EU as we know it, law can still help to account for emerging trends in European integration. To the extent that the new intergovernmentalism incorporates such a position, we agree with its claims. But to the extent that it implies a lack of distinction between the 'political' and the 'legal', we would disagree. Neither would we agree that law as traditionally conceived in the EU context (i.e. the Community method) has been fully replaced by alternative methods of integration, with the consequent decentring of legislatures and courts as important institutional actors in integration processes. There is nothing to suggest that—in general—the Community method will cease to be used as the best way of ensuring the 'unity' of the legal system via the enforceable legal norms that have become familiar over the course of Europe's integration process. In our view, lawyers tend to limit themselves to legally inspired analyses of European integration to the Community method alone. We argue that in seeking to understand trends in European integration legal analysis should aim to do much more than this.

The pursuit of deliberation as an end in itself, rather than as a means to an end (hypothesis 1, set out in chapter 1 of this volume), might be read in a way which suggests a distinction between law and politics. Under the Community method, the purpose of deliberation is clear: deliberation within an institutional framework leads to the eventual adoption of binding and individually enforceable laws. In a way, Community method litigation could also be seen as a form of deliberation—and again its purpose is to resolve a specific dispute between two parties. But even where there has been a retreat from the Community method (e.g. some areas of social policy), or where it has never applied (e.g. Common Foreign and Security Policy), deliberation can often lead to 'law-like' arrangements, with legal norms providing at least procedural legitimacy.

This point also speaks to hypothesis 5 that 'high' and 'low' politics have become blurred. From a legal point of view, the distinction itself is difficult to maintain. To that extent, legal accounts of European integration have always been consistent with the claims of new intergovernmentalism. But even if we take 'high politics' to mean sovereignty-conscious areas of EU activity (such as foreign policy, criminal justice, global migration, health, or social affairs) and 'low politics' to mean areas of technocratic regulation (such as product standards), cooperation between national authorities 'under the radar' takes on 'law-like' qualities. As we have shown in section 3.3, the Court of Justice has set out numerous decisions on the 'constitutional' nature of the EU's legal system (which we can equate with 'high politics') but which have very often emerged through cases which would not have been flagged as constitutional or otherwise significant in terms of either the legal principle at stake, or the financial or other interests involved. But that is not to say that the Court—or indeed the other institutions—necessarily seek further integration at any cost, and the sovereign interests of member states have been underlined by the Court in a number of recent decisions across several areas of EU activity, particularly in litigation concerning the fallout from the euro area crisis (Craig 2013).

In terms of the position of private actors in the integration process, as litigants, private actors may continue to support the integration process by disrupting nationally protectionist or otherwise disintegrationist policies, in areas where 'hard law' remains the dominant mode of integration. But in areas where regulation through *de novo* institutions, or pursuit of consensus, is the dominant mode, private actors may appear redundant to integration. Private actors rarely have standing or any formal place within the work of EU agencies, and they are (by definition) not granted any legally enforceable rights through consensus-based political settlements. However, legal methods based on public international law, or comparative law, reveal that private actors can nevertheless effectively pursue change under such circumstances. For instance, in international human rights law, the discourses of law enjoy power outside litigation processes, through the 'legal cachet' of human rights talk, and processes of 'name and shame', or where the political effects of litigation are not to force change *de jure*, but where 'lost causes' (legally speaking) are nonetheless litigated, in order to raise awareness of injustice and thereby to force political change. Litigation as a *political* act is a subject that cannot be studied through political science methods alone, because the constraining discourses of the law (for instance, modes of legal reasoning) are understandable by definition only through legal methods.

Our other central point here is that there is no single role for law in European integration. If this was true before the Lisbon settlement in 2009, it is even truer today. Different contexts imply different roles for law in the process of European integration. Depending upon the context, the 'driving force' behind integration may be understood as enabled by law empowering, for instance, opportunistic individuals; or EU institutions; or networks; or governments of member states. Or law may be understood as constraining, rather than empowering, certain individuals, institutions, or groups. In each of these cases, the law is understood as playing a different role in the integration process. So our position is consistent with hypothesis 2 of the new intergovernmentalism to the effect that supranational (and national) institutions are not 'hard-wired' for integration. The Court of Justice (and national courts) do not always adopt an 'integrationist' interpretation or approach. Sometimes, EU law is used as a tool to manage different interests in complex settlements of entitlements, such as the position of migrant labour from a less developed Eastern Europe offering services within Western Europe. We should therefore be suspicious of grand narratives that seek to explain *all* European integration through either a central (Kelemen 2011) or a peripheral role for law. The relationships between law and integration are fundamentally context specific. In terms of legal scholarship, it may well be time to begin to articulate a 'turn' from constitutionalism in EU legal studies, perhaps even in its pluralist forms. The kinds of differentiated rather than grand narratives of the roles of law in European integration which we call for in this chapter imply that a range of legal methodologies will be necessary. In addition to pluralist constitutionalism, we suggest a greater role for comparative legal methods, and those drawing on public and private international law, at this post-Lisbon phase of the EU.

The idea that the EU's regulatory agencies are deficient because of comparatively less regulatory power[18] might be another area where we would depart from the new intergovernmentalism, depending on the extent to which regulatory power is understood as embodied in legal authority (as opposed to, for instance, the power of policy isomorphism through comparative data exchange). The emphasis on technocratic decision-making does not necessarily reduce the actual or potential political salience of those decisions (Curtin 2014). Equally, the turn to 'new public management' during the 1980s and 1990s in some member states, and elsewhere, did not involve a retreat from law, but rather a refocusing of the roles of law in determining the balance of interests between the state and others. This can also be said to apply to the various roles played by agencies, which do not have a formal input into the

---

[18] Hypothesis 3: Where delegation occurs, governments and traditional supranational actors support the creation and empowerment of *de novo* institutions.

Community method of law-making but which are responsible for the realization of EU law 'on the ground' (Hofmann and Morini 2012).

This observation speaks also to the idea that the post-Maastricht EU is characterized by a heavy reliance on 'de-politicized' technocratic policy-making.[19] But rather than involving a retreat from law, such technocratic policy-making has been constrained and challenged by legal principles and even by litigation,[20] especially where fundamental rights or the democratic process are concerned.[21]

Overall, and in the final analysis, the roles of law in the post-Maastricht EU can be understood, to a significant extent, through the hypotheses of the new intergovernmentalism. But new intergovernmentalism does not mean a redundancy of law, or legal analysis: it means a differentiated approach. Law's roles in the integration process are too historically significant to be written out of explanatory accounts of the integration process. They are also of enduring contemporaneous significance.

---

[19] Hypothesis 4: Problems in domestic preference formation have become stand-alone inputs into the European integration process.

[20] Case T-135/86 *Union Européenne de l'Artisanat et des Petites et Moyennes Entreprises (UEAPME)* v *Council* ECLI:EU:T:1998:128; Case C-127/07 *Société Arcelor Atlantique et Lorraine and Others* v *Premier ministre, Ministre de l'Écologie et du Développement durable and Ministre de l'Économie, des Finances et de l'Industrie* ECLI:EU:C:2008:728; Case C-506/08 P *Sweden* v *MyTravel and Commission* ECLI:EU:C:2011:496.

[21] Case 280/11 *Council of the European Union* v *Access Info Europe* ECLI:EU:C:2011:496.

4

Institutionalist Dynamics behind the New Intergovernmentalism

The Continuous Process of EU Treaty Reform

Thomas Christiansen

In 2008, Andrew Moravcsik declared that 'the EU has reached a plateau [and that] we are starting to glimpse a "European Constitutional Settlement"—a stable endpoint of European integration in the medium term' (Moravcsik 2008: 158–9). The argument was based on a liberal intergovernmentalist analysis of the driving forces behind the integration process and was written against the background of the failure to formally adopt a European Constitution in the mid-2000s. And while there has indeed been a noticeable sense of 'reform fatigue' among both elites and citizens in the EU, the timing of Moravcsik advancing his vision of a 'boring' Union constituting a 'mature political system' that was 'lack[ing] in salience' (Moravcsik 2008: 181–2) was unfortunate: what followed after the 2008 global financial meltdown has been a roller-coaster of euro area crisis-management, massive sovereign debt bail-outs, several new intergovernmental treaties, ECB activism, challenges in European and national constitutional courts, mass mobilization in the streets, and the formation of new political movements in response to the direction of EU policy-making. The politics of the European Union (EU) have probably never been as salient and as unstable as they have been since the entering into force of the Lisbon Treaty and the outbreak of the euro crisis (see chapter 1).

Decision-making under the cloud of the euro area crisis has advanced European integration into new areas—monitoring of fiscal stability, oversight of national budgets, banking supervision, collectivization of sovereign debt—that were previously considered highly sensitive. The crisis has introduced new dynamics in the integration process, with significant transfers of new competences to the EU level, yet this process has firmly avoided anything like a return to the Community Method. Instead, as chapter 1 demonstrates, the integration paradox has held sway: there has been further integration, yet not with much of a delegation of powers to the traditional supranational institutions. The European Parliament (EP) and, to a lesser extent, the European Commission have been on the sidelines, while crisis-management and decision-making was centralized in the intergovernmental fora of Eurogroup and European Council.

This 'new intergovernmentalist' logic of advancing European integration is not new, even if it has been exacerbated and intensified in recent years. It is, indeed, the continuation of a trend that dates back to the agreement on the Maastricht Treaty. Much of the 1990s and 2000s witnessed a process of fairly constant reform that has continued, in a somewhat different guise, in the 2010s. This chapter charts this process in order to shed some light on the question of how decisions about treaty reform have been made. The chapter proceeds by setting out a particular conception of treaty reform which emphasizes its procedural nature, and then addresses, from this vantage point, a number of the hypotheses advanced in chapter 1. In particular, the chapter demonstrates how an analysis of treaty reform provides evidence in support of two of these hypotheses, namely hypothesis 5 on the blurring of the differences between high and low politics and hypothesis 6 on the EU as being in a state of disequilibrium.

4.1 An Institutionalist Perspective of EU Treaty Reform

Against mainstream assumptions of treaty reform as major events or 'grand bargains' that are best explained in terms of hard bargaining among state leaders, an institutionalist perspective emphasizes four key aspects: first, that treaty reform ought to be understood as a continuous process rather than a series of discrete events; second; that it involves both supranational and intergovernmental actors; third, that actors operate within a particular structural environment providing both opportunities and constraints; and, fourth, that treaty reform occurs through both formal and informal mechanisms.

Understanding treaty reform as a process is key to this perspective—even though it might seem obvious, it sets up an approach to the study of treaty reform that is fundamentally different from the event history perspective that is inherent in both liberal intergovernmentalism and supranationalist accounts of European integration (Sandholtz and Stone Sweet 1997; Moravcsik 1998). Focusing on process implies a recognition that analytically relevant developments occur both before and after the bargaining event, specifically that there is an agenda-setting phase prior to the decision-making within the Intergovernmental Conference (IGC), and that there is an implementation stage after the signatures from the heads of state or government that also has the potential to influence matters. While not denying that there is an element of hard bargaining at play in intergovernmental negotiations, opening the scope of analysis to include both agenda-setting and implementation brings the role of other actors into view.

Supranational institutions such as the Commission, the EP or the Court of Justice of the EU may not have a voice, even less a vote, in the context of an IGC. Their agenda-setting power, however, is clearly evident in instances such as the Delors Committee setting out the blueprint for EMU, the Spinelli Group's Draft Treaty on European Union prior to the Single European Act, or the Court of Justice's case law establishing constitutional principles that were subsequently codified through formal treaty changes. Implementation also matters, not least because, in the process of ratification, the meaning of treaty provisions is being (re)interpreted, if not changed—as happened to the plans to reduce the size of the College of Commissioners which were scuppered after the Irish 'No' on the Lisbon Treaty. On occasion, treaty articles can be seen as 'incomplete contracts' whose actual meaning only becomes evident with the bargains over the detailed legislation that needs to be passed in order to give effect to them (Farrell and Heritier 2003). This is another way in which supranational institutions (as well as other actors) have opportunities to influence the outcome of treaty change *after* the formal decisions have already taken place. The protracted inter-institutional battles about the introduction of delegated acts after the Lisbon Treaty is one such case in point (Christiansen and Dobbels 2012), and the more recent disputes between the European Council and the EP, and among state leaders, about the procedure to appoint—or elect—the president of the Commission is another (*Financial Times*, 27 June 2014).[1]

Beyond recognizing the analytical significance of the agenda-setting and implementation phases in themselves, viewing these as a joined-up process emphasizes the continuity of treaty reform. This includes the recognition that the outcome (e.g. a formal commitment to launch a future IGC)—or indeed the 'leftovers'—of one treaty reform already sets the agenda for the next round. In addition, it is important to consider not only the actors involved—their interests, resources, and strategies—but also the institutional, legal, and ideational structures in which they are embedded. This brings to the fore elements such as discourses (Diez 1999)—e.g. the 'need' for Europe to respond to the pressures of globalization (Rosamond 1999)—and time (Ekengren 2002;

---

[1] *Financial Times*, 'Jean-Claude Juncker nominated for European Commission president', 27 June 2014.

Goetz and Meyer-Sahling 2009) as having a structuring effect on negotiations, limiting the freedom of manoeuvre that actors enjoy. The institutional context of the IGC is a more apparent element of structure, and while rules such as the unanimity requirement for an agreement on treaty change privilege the liberal intergovernmentalist view of this environment, IGCs are not exclusively governed by this rule. The simple fact that the IGC can be convened by the simple majority of the European Council is already significant—as Margaret Thatcher discovered when the IGC on Economic and Monetary Union was launched against her (imaginary) veto.

Finally, there are some important departures from the formal requirements for full-blown treaty change (i.e. those that do indeed require the convening of a European Convention and a subsequent IGC, the signatures of all of the EU's heads of state or government on a new treaty, and the ratification within each member state). For a start, there is, since the Lisbon Treaty, the possibility of using a 'simplified treaty revision procedure' for changes that do not increase the competences of the Union (Article 48 TEU). This provision, as well as other so-called *passarelle* clauses in the treaty, provides opportunities for the member states to agree on 'technical' changes to the treaty that can be adopted by the European Council and thereby do not require a convention or formal ratification domestically. This kind of a 'light touch' mechanism for treaty change has been used on a few occasions, for example on the adjustments of the number of seats of the EP (adopted on 23 June 2010). The fact that it was also used for a treaty amendment to facilitate the agreement on the ESM (adopted on 25 March 2011) demonstrates that even minor changes to the treaty—the ESM revision only required the addition of two short sentences to the Treaty—can have significant impact on European governance, and can become the source of some debate among national governments (de Witte 2011b).

The post-Lisbon distinction between 'ordinary' and 'simplified' revision procedures provides decision-makers with greater flexibility in the means of responding to pressures for change. This is certainly an advantage in the context of a Union having to address the tensions arising from frequent changes in its environment and the presence of inherent tensions within its institutional structure. However, this Lisbon Treaty reform does not go as far as earlier proposals to distinguish between fundamental and non-fundamental parts of the Treaty, with the possibility for the latter to be amended by qualified majority (de Witte 2011b: 2). Nevertheless, there has been a long-standing trend in the EU to modify the meaning of the Treaty in a number of less formal ways, and to maintain through such, more 'informal' mechanisms a capacity for adjustment of the rules or the institutional framework even if formal treaty change is not seen to be possible.

Such 'informal' treaty reform includes a plethora of mechanisms, be it ground-breaking decisions by the European Council, the creation of new institutions outside the treaty or, as mentioned above, key judgments by the Court of Justice as well as new norms and procedures established in the daily practice of EU decision-making. Much of what is being considered today as an essential part of the EU's constitutional order did initially see the light of day through such informal treaty changes: the aspiration towards a common European foreign policy, the principle of supremacy of EU law, the creation of the European Council, or the setting up of trilogues in the legislative procedures are just some of these high-profile examples (Christiansen and Reh 2009).

As these examples indicate, this perspective opens up the scope for recognizing the analytically relevant involvement of supranational actors in the treaty reform process: the Commission and the EP having the capacity to influence the agenda of future treaty change through White Papers, draft treaties, or consultative reports; the Court of Justice setting new legal principles in its case law and thereby contributing to the establishment of a European constitutional order; the EP and/or Commission establishing through their practice new *modi operandi* in inter-institutional relations (e.g. trilogues in the legislative procedure; hearings for prospective Commissioners; the introduction of the *Spitzenkandidaten* idea for the 2014 EP election). However, there is no automatism implied here—emphasizing the role of supranational actors in informally revising (the meaning of) the treaties is a statement about *potential* and not one of absolute facts. It remains a question for empirical research to establish their actual influence in a given circumstance rather than assuming this as being a generalized pattern. Not all opportunities provided by the structure or the contingencies of specific circumstances are being made use of—the reluctance by the ECB to go beyond the strict limits of its treaty mandate during the sovereign debt crisis is a case in point (see chapter 13).

In the same vein, a focus on agenda-setting, implementation and the more informal aspects of treaty reform does not diminish the role of intergovernmental actors, as most powerfully demonstrated by the expansive role played by the European Council (see chapter 8), in particular during the post-Lisbon era of euro area crisis-management when it was in this forum that the new architecture for euro area financial stability was negotiated. In addition, as already mentioned, the European Council's role in formal treaty reform has also been expanded through the simplified revision procedure. In other words, the institutionalist approach, while critical of some of the main assumptions of liberal intergovernmentalism, does tie in with key tenets of new intergovernmentalism.

In sum, an institutionalist perspective on treaty reform casts a wider net, being sensitive to both actors and structures, formal and informal elements, intergovernmental as well as supranational drivers in the process. In doing so, it permits a more comprehensive analysis of treaty reform and promises to provide a better explanation of the dynamics behind the 'integration paradox'. In the following sections, this approach is used to examine two of the hypotheses raised in the introduction to this volume and thus constitute a core part of the new intergovernmentalist argument.

4.2 European Integration from Maastricht to Lisbon: Beyond 'High Politics' and 'Low Politics'

Treaty reform is an ideal testing ground for the traditional intergovernmentalist distinction between 'high' and 'low' politics. Indeed, part of the foundation of liberal intergovernmentalism has been the idea that, while in the 'everyday politics' of the EU the supranational institutions may be able to demonstrate independent influence over decision-making (Wincott 1995), it is during IGCs that member state governments take the key decisions that matter. As a consequence, treaty reform has come to be seen as being 'high politics' by definition, not so much because of the nature or salience of the issues under discussion, but because the decision mode—unanimity and domestic ratification—signifies that member states are in control. Delegation of powers to supranational institutions is agreed by member states through changes to the treaty, and these will therefore only occur if they are, in fact, in their national interests.

The post-Maastricht era is, however, rich in evidence that this distinction between treaty negotiation as 'high politics' and everyday decision-making as 'low politics' is too simplistic, and that hypothesis 5 about the blurring of the lines between these supposedly 'high' and 'low' politics is supported by an examination of developments in the post-Maastricht era.

To start with, there are a number of conceptual problems with the distinction between high and low politics. First, in view of its dependence on the salience of a given issue, it does not lend itself easily to generalization across all member states: something that is highly salient in one country may be less so in another, and as a result it is difficult to draw a dividing line for the whole of the EU. Second, the degree of salience of a particular policy area is subject to change over time—an issue that is of low salience at a certain point in time may become highly salient a few years later, under different circumstances or in the face of crisis. Third, there are an increasing number of regulatory challenges that are either new or increasingly transnational in nature, and as such do not fit into a pre-existing classification between high and low. Food safety, for example, was not very salient at a time when production was predominantly domestic, but in the context of global trade in foodstuffs has become a highly sensitive issue, both within the EU and in its external relations. The regulation of genetically modified organisms used in agricultural products has also become a highly divisive issue, and one that was non-existent during the earlier stage of European integration.

These points indicate that a basic distinction between high and low politics is extremely difficult, and may be impossible. At the very least, it is analytically flawed as a device for distinguishing areas where member states will seek to maintain control, and those where they are willing to give it up. This does not mean that, at any given point in time, there are no issues that are highly salient for a number of member states. What this requires, however, is not the reliance on a static distinction between high and low, but rather the recognition of processes of politicization and de-politicization which help to determine whether an issue will be regarded as salient or not, and whether member states are willing to devote diplomatic capital on the defence of their interest in this field. The real question then becomes what issues are being (de)politicized, and how, rather than an artificial distinction between high and low.

The experience of the Convention on the Future for Europe, the resulting Constitutional treaty and the subsequent Lisbon Treaty illustrates a prime example of such processes of (de)politicization at work. This episode in an attempt to formally constitutionalize the EU, lasting the better part of a decade, had been preceded by two formal treaty revisions—Amsterdam and Nice—which had not delivered on the expectations and the anticipated demands of the upcoming Eastern enlargement of the Union. Partly as a response to the perceived disappointments of these previous IGCs and the continuing need to achieve significant step-change in the nature of EU decision-making to facilitate the 'big bang' enlargement, a number of actors decided to politicize the next round. The Laeken process was a very purposeful attempt to politicize the reform of the Union, involving as it did the engagement with citizens, NGOs, and organized interests via online platforms, the parliamentarization of the treaty reform negotiations through the convention method, the discursive construction of a 'constitution' for the EU, the attraction of significant media attention resulting from these plans, and the requirement of popular referendums in many of the member states.

The idea of politicizing treaty reform in such a manner appealed to a number of different actors in the EU. It was of course in line with the long-standing desire of the EP to become more directly and proactively involved in treaty change, and the idea of a convention, composed largely of national parliamentarians and Members of the European Parliament (MEPs), promised the vision of a parliament-like open debate about the ways in which the EU needed to be reformed. It also tied in with the then Commission President Prodi's view of the Commission as more of a political body, a European 'government' which contrasted somewhat from the non-partisan attitudes of his predecessors and successor in the post. Clearly, both the Commission and the EP could expect a greater involvement in the decision-making process from the convention method, rather than being reduced to largely informal agenda-setting powers as discussed previously.

But there was also, and arguably more importantly, substantial support from among the state leaders, many of whom followed the then German foreign minister Fischer in the discourse about a possible *finalité politique* of the Union. The idea of a European Constitution became a powerful discourse in the early 2000s, with contributions from many leading politicians, opinion-leaders, and scholars. Crucially, it appealed to either side in the wider debate about further integration: for supporters it provided an opportunity for the major reform that neither the Amsterdam nor the Nice Treaty had achieved. For Euro-sceptics, the idea of a *finalité* promised a definite end to the elusive search for an ever closer union.

A more politicized approach to treaty reform ensured that something which had so far been considered to constitute a highly technocratic process which lacked transparency became the stuff of newspaper headlines and evening news. There was, indeed, an element of popular debate about treaty reform, even if this public awareness developed more after the signatures of the state leaders under the new treaty than beforehand. In any case, the convention method had involved a much greater number of decision-makers in the drafting of the new treaty, and created a new level of pan-European debate about the key issues of reform that had not been possible previously. This degree of politicization had two effects: on the one hand, it became possible to cut through many of the difficult issues that had blocked broader agreement at Nice, and led to a far-reaching plan for future reform in the shape of the Constitutional Treaty. On the other hand, it was precisely this level of politicization that proved to be the undoing of the ambitious reform plans when the people of the Netherlands and France voted against the ratification of the Treaty, condemning the attempt at a formal constitutionalization of the EU to failure.

Had history stopped there—as indeed Moravcsik's plateau analogy seemed to anticipate—then it might be plausible to claim that this was an example of the integration process reaching into the domain of high politics only to burn its wings and come crashing down. However, as we now know, the reform process did continue after a period of cooling down, of 'dialogue' with the citizens, and—crucially—of de-politicization. The road to the Lisbon Treaty was as obscure as the European Convention was high profile. The new treaty was negotiated on the basis of the Constitutional Treaty and contained, according to some estimates, 99 per cent of its text. Much of the negotiation took place in the context of bilateral discussions among government officials during the German and Portuguese presidencies, resulting in an extremely detailed mandate document that pre-empted much of what would be negoti-ated in the formal IGC. The IGC itself, when it eventually started, consisted essentially of a group of legal experts debating mainly technical points in the wording of treaty articles, with the key political decisions having already been taken. The group was chaired not by the Presidency, but by a senior official from the Council Secretariat. And once the treaty was agreed and signed, it was—just as with the Nice Treaty—only put to a popular vote in Ireland (where it again failed at the first attempt). In other words, much of the negotiation of treaty changes—which only a few years earlier had been con-sidered as 'constitutional' and in need of public debate and acceptance—were now handled behind closed doors, and the bulk of the detailed work was left to legal experts and diplomats rather than political leaders. Treaty reform, having failed in its incarnation as formal European constitutionalization, continued in an extremely de-politicized manner.

These 'ups' and 'downs' of formal constitutionalization illustrate powerfully the effects of politicization on the process of treaty reform. A highly politi-cized treaty proved impossible to pass in the face of significant popular mobil-ization against further integration, whereas effectively the same reforms could be passed a few years later through a de-politicized and less transparent procedure. This experience of treaty reform demonstrates how its effects are better understood in terms of degrees of politicization and de-politicization, rather than the distinction between 'high' and 'low' politics which is less useful.

Looking back at the post-Maastricht period, it may appear as something of a puzzle that there has been frequent—indeed almost permanent—treaty reform during this period even though there has been little popular pressure for more integration. The treaty was substantially revised on three occasions—Amsterdam, Nice, and Lisbon—with further adaptation occurring between these formal rounds of treaty change through less formal mechanisms. New calls for further treaty change were heard almost as soon the Lisbon Treaty itself had come into force. It is a powerful expression of the 'integration paradox' that treaty reform continued unabated at a time when popular opinion was hardening against deeper integration.

Part of the answer to this puzzle lies in the interconnectedness of the various rounds of treaty change. As was argued earlier, these are best seen not as separate events, but as being linked in various ways: both Amsterdam and Nice were dealing with 'leftovers' from the previous round, and Lisbon was about the realization of the aims contained in the Constitutional Treaty, using a different language and method. The attempt to politicize treaty reform—the public project to create a Constitution for Europe—failed, but this did not stop the continuous push for further reform, a process that continued after Lisbon (see section 4.3).

Pressure for reform is closely linked to the search for greater legitimacy. Each round of reform sought to enhance the EU's democratic credentials by enhancing the powers of the EP, involving national parliaments more directly in the decision-making process or creating new opportunities for participatory democracy through the European Citizens' Initiative. Yet, due to the widespread scepticism within public opinion, each round of treaty reform also required its own legitimation, which has often been difficult to attain. Four defeats for proposed treaty revision in popular referendums during this period are testimony to this challenge. However, the difficulties to legitimate major treaty change and the ensuing reform fatigue did not stop further pressure for constitutional change, specifically in the context of the euro area crisis. The following section looks in more detail at these contemporary challenges and provides evidence for hypothesis 6 on the persistence of disequilibrium in the EU.

4.3 Persistent Disequilibrium and Continuous Reform: Governing the Post-Lisbon, Post-Crisis EU

Another key argument of new intergovernmentalism as presented in the introduction to this volume is the elusiveness of an equilibrium state in the post-Maastricht EU. The presence of disequilibrium is closely connected to the continuity of treaty reform, as EU leaders constantly seek to adjust the Union's institutional architecture and decision-making procedures in the changing environment in which they operate. The challenges here are manifold and originate from a combination of endogenous and exogenous factors. With regard to the latter, the greatest challenge has been the changing structure of international politics after the end of the Cold War, leading to the accession of the countries from Central and Eastern Europe. The changing landscape of Europe after 1989 impacted on the plans for the Maastricht Treaty, caused the setting up of a second IGC on political union and led to the adoption of the pillar structure in order to accommodate the more supranational plans for EMU, as well as the intergovernmental nature of other policy areas.

However, these decisions concerning new institutional arrangements in the Maastricht Treaty are also a good example of how past decisions are endogenous factors in pushing for subsequent reforms. A construction like the pillar structure created its own dynamics due to the close connections between policies governed by different procedures, such as internal security and freedom of movement or foreign policy and external economic relations. The resulting tensions could be managed for a number of years but would eventually require new reforms in order to address the problems arising from such arrangements.

The EU is host to numerous such in-built tensions, indeed the very motto of the Union—'unity in diversity'—points the way to many arrangements which are set up in a contradictory manner and prevent it from achieving equilibrium. The tension between supranational and intergovernmental arrangements not only puts different EU institutions at loggerheads with one another, but is also present within each institution (Christiansen 1997). For example, the leadership of supranational institutions such as the European Commission or the European Court of Justice is composed of nationals of the member states whose views, despite the formal requirement of independence, strongly reflect the interests of 'their' country (Hooghe 2005; Thompson 2008), potentially turning the College into something akin to a 'COREPER III' (Bertoncini and Vitorino 2014: 6). At the same time, the Council, even though it is seen as the essence of intergovernmentalism in the EU, also exhibits elements of supranationalism through the fact that it is an institution with a common purpose, a dedicated civil service, and the potential to influence decision-making (Wessels 1991; Christiansen and Vanhoonacker 2008).

A good example of such tensions within the EU's institutional structure, generating conflict while at the same time preparing the ground for further development of the constitutional basis, was the debate surrounding the election of the Commission president in 2014. A vague wording about the need to '[take] into account the results of the European Parliament elections' (Article 17.7 TEU) when electing the Commission president led to disagreements between the European Council and the EP, and the subsequent power struggle demonstrated again that treaty revision is often not the end of an argument, but rather the basis for further disagreements about the nature of inter-institutional relations. In the end, the majority of the member states in the European Council followed the argumentation of the majority of the EP, that the leading candidate of the largest party group ought to become Commission president, but only after strong arguments had been exchanged between the supporters and opponents of the EP's perspective, and after the first-ever formal vote on the Commission president nomination in the European Council. In other words, it took a serious and public inter-institutional 'battle' to establish the meaning of the above-mentioned treaty provision.[2]

In new intergovernmentalist terms, however, contextual factors behind disequilibrium are considered more relevant, and here also there is much evidence of matters being out of sync. Perhaps the most far-reaching example of such a disequilibrium between what is expected from the Union and what it actually performs has come about in the context of the euro area crisis. In fact, several tensions in the EU have become visible in the context of this crisis:

---

[2] *Financial Times*, 'Cameron's flawed tactics on Europe', 12 June 2014.

- inherent tensions in the Maastricht Treaty construction for EMU, in which monetary policy-making became an exclusive competence of the Union, while fiscal policy remained firmly in the hands of the member states

- the liberalization of financial markets, facilitating significant market integration in this area, without the setting-up of adequate regulatory frameworks at the EU level

- the prevalence of public debates about ways of responding to the crisis, and actual decision-making to address the crisis in the European Council and the Eurogroup taking place behind closed doors

- the highly politicized role played by the EU, both as an actor and as a forum for debate, in contrast with the technocratic manner in which decisions were taken and implemented

- the contestation of EU-level decisions occurring predominantly at the national level, within the member states and among domestic actors.

Each of these tensions caused problems for European governance in a time of crisis, and, together with other factors, contributed to demands for further reforms. In fact, The EU has had to react to what has been widely seen as an existential crisis of the single currency, if not of the Union itself. With the Lisbon Treaty having been agreed long before the crisis broke in 2008, its coming into force in December 2009 did not provide an adequate response to the new challenges facing the euro area. Instead, the onset of the crisis triggered new demands for reform, and the initial inability of EU leaders to come up with quick solutions to address burning problems expanded what was an economic and financial crisis into an institutional crisis.

Adapting the institutional framework to address a range of new problems took time and was eventually successful in averting the perceived disaster of several member states leaving the euro area, putting the entire arrangement at risk. The survival of the single currency and the integrity of the euro area have been assured for the foreseeable future, when both appeared doubtful to many in the early 2010s. A range of agreements addressing financial assistance for countries suffering excessive sovereign debt, improved fiscal supervision of all euro area members, banking supervision and related financial market regulations provide a much stronger foundation for the euro area (see chapter 8). These agreements help to achieve the dual aims that are generally seen as essential to a long-term solution of the crisis, namely, to convince financial markets that the debts of all euro area members will be serviced and ensuring that member state finances are restructured so as to limit the chances of excessive debt in the future.

This particular reform of the EU relied on a plethora of legal instruments: legislative acts on the basis of existing treaty provisions (the European

Semester, the six-pack, the two-pack), two new international treaties outside the EU treaties (the Fiscal Compact, the ESM), a corporation set up under private law (the European Financial Stability Facility), and operational decisions by the ECB (Outright Monetary Transactions) which were partly seen as a far-reaching new interpretation of the existing treaty mandate of the bank. The combined effect of these reforms has gone beyond pure crisis-management, creating a new environment for economic governance in the EU. The newly found capacity of the EU to bail out euro area members facing unserviceable debt, to wind down failing banks and to oversee in detail the fiscal policy of member states amounts to a significant deepening of integration, strengthening the powers of the central institutions vis-à-vis the national level. While there has been no resort to the sort of large-scale formal treaty change that brought us the Lisbon Treaty, the combined effect of these 'little steps' is, nevertheless, a significant change in the constitutional basis for economic governance in the euro area.

From a new intergovernmentalist perspective this deepening has strengthened, in particular, the intergovernmental institutions, above all the European Council and the Eurogroup (Puetter 2012). However, the European Commission and the ECB have also increased their competences as a result (see chapter 9 and chapter 13, respectively). Newly created agencies in the area of financial services supervision add further to the supranational element of economic governance, and the involvement of the IMF in the design and implementation of the conditionality attached to the sovereign debt bail-outs further increases the complexity of the mix. In the face of growing popular criticism of the EU, part of the 'solution' to the dilemma faced by national governments has been their capacity to de-politicize decision-making. In the words of Schimmelfennig (2014: 335), 'governments have been able to shield their crisis policy and deepening of euro area integration, first by excluding Eurosceptic parties from government, second by designing new treaties and the treaty-making procedure so that the threat of referendums and ratification failure was minimized, and third by further empowering supranational organizations or agreeing to the informal expansion of their mandate'.

Arguably, these reforms in the area of economic governance have established more of a balance between three sets of actors: national governments, EU institutions, and financial market operators benefiting from the liberations of capital movements in the EU. Member state governments, having benefited from lower interest rates since the introduction of the euro and increased their borrowing significantly as a result, are now under increased scrutiny from the EU concerning their fiscal discipline, whereas banks and other financial institutions are facing greater regulation and supervision from ECB and the new institutions of the Single Supervisory Mechanism (SSM). Therefore it can be argued that the strengthening of the EU has returned a semblance of equilibrium to this triangular relationship. However, even if euro area crisis-management post-2010 had appeared to address this particular disequilibrium (and it is not certain at the time of writing that it has), it has created new imbalances of a different kind, namely with respect to the democratic legitimacy of the Union. The problem with democratic legitimacy has both an institutional and a popular dimension.

Institutionally, the increase in tasks and competences in EU economic governance has centred almost entirely on the executive institutions and intergovernmental fora. Representative institutions, be it the EP or national parliaments, have not seen a concomitant rise in their powers. The situation of the EP here is particularly precarious: while it has been involved in the passage of secondary legislation to beef up the Stability and Growth Pact—the so-called 'six-pack' and 'two-pack'—it has been largely excluded from those instruments that were adopted outside the EU's treaty structure. This includes both the negotiations and implementations of the bail-outs as well as the provisions of the Fiscal Compact. The deeper problem here is not so much the alleged desire by executives to monopolize power at the expense of the legislature, but the fact that the EP cannot conceivably be seen as the parliamentary body of the euro area, or indeed of arrangements outside the formal treaty architecture. There is no increase in legitimacy if such reforms mean that MEPs elected by citizens of non-euro area countries end up being involved in taking decisions that would not apply to their constituents.

Therefore, even if agreement could be found on giving the EP a greater role in scrutinizing economic governance, it is by definition impossible to see this as the sole answer to any heightened democratic deficit arising from these new arrangements. A number of solutions have been discussed to address this situation: the exclusion of non-euro area MEPs from any decision affecting only the euro area; the creation of new sub-committees of the EP, composed only of members from the euro area or from the contracting states party to any additional agreements; or a greater involvement of MPs from national parliaments of the euro area countries in a new body set up at the European level.

While each of these proposals might have their merits, they also all carry significant problems with them. Most notably, the problem with any such reform is that it would most likely require a revision of the treaty, and one that would need to go through the Ordinary Revision Procedure which, in turn, involves a European Convention and ratification in all member states. Apart from the difficulties that that would involve in terms of getting unanimous agreement, especially in the face of British demands for renegotiation of their position in the Union, it is unlikely to find favour anywhere in a general climate of popular disenchantment with the European project.

As a result, there is little prospect of significant institutional reform in order to address these democratic legitimacy concerns. Ad hoc solutions, such as the creation of the Article 13 Committee in the Fiscal Compact bringing together European and national parliamentarians to debate matters, jointly suffer from both practical and structural weaknesses (Cooper 2014) and have not yet established themselves as credible alternatives to established institutions. It is difficult to see how such joint bodies without genuine decision-making powers can make a positive contribution to democratic legitimacy. In any case, they have to confront the growing antagonism between the EP and national parliaments as to who ought to be the real champion of democratic legitimacy in economic governance.

The second dimension of a Union in disequilibrium is the coincidence of the deepening of integration in economic governance, and more generally the greater relevance of the EU that has become apparent as a result of the crisis, with a marked increase in Euro-scepticism and outright hostility to the European project in many member states. While the rise of Euro-scepticism in the context of the euro area crisis had been tracked for some time, the results of the 2014 elections to the EP made this crisis of confidence obvious and official: a record number of Euro-sceptic and right-wing populist parties gained seats in the EP, leading to the establishment of three sceptical party groups on the right of the EU mainstream (European Conservatives and Reform Group, the Europe of Freedom and Democracy, and the European Alliance for Freedom). This includes electoral success not only of fringe groups or parties in member states such as Denmark or the UK that are well-known for the Euro-sceptic attitudes, but also in countries regarded as the core of the EU. In Germany, the anti-euro Alternative für Deutschland won more than 7 per cent of the popular vote and has sent seven MEPs to Brussels. At the same time, left-wing parties also gained in strength, especially in the Mediterranean member states, after campaigning on an anti-austerity ticket.

The 2014 election result, even though it delivered a majority for pro-European parties around the grand coalition of Christian Democrats, Socialists, and Liberals, was widely seen as a wake-up call that delivered a message from citizens to EU elites that the future ought not to be 'business as usual'.[3] Instead, record votes for stern critics of the EU such as Nigel Farage in the UK, Marie Le Pen in France, Beppe Grillo in Italy, or Alexis Tsipras in Greece, were seen to imply that there would need to be fundamental changes to the way the EU operates. This development coincided with, and indeed further reinforced, the policy of UK Prime Minister Cameron to demand a renegotiation of the British position in Europe, implying a repatriation of (not clearly

---

[3] *European Voice*, 28 May 2014.

specified) powers from Brussels back to the UK. One plank of the Euro-sceptic approach in the UK and other member states has been to demand new powers for national parliaments to be able to block EU legislation—known under the football metaphor of a 'red card'—and even to call back powers previously delegated to the EU (Groen and Christiansen 2015).

However, this rise in popular disenchantment with Europe is clearly at odds both with the deepening of economic governance described above, and also with the perspectives for further integration in the second half of the 2010s. Indeed, as Schimmelfennig has pointed out, the policy of de-politicizing the deepening of further integration that may have been possible during the crisis, may not be possible after it has passed (Schimmelfennig 2014: 336). Nevertheless, this 'dissensus' about the European integration process remains at odds with developments in Brussels: the choices in favour of Jean-Claude Juncker as Commission president and, for a second term, Martin Schulz as EP president indicate that the new leadership of the EU institutions will be of deeply pro-European conviction, unwilling to undo key bargains of the past that have underpinned the EU. If anything, judging by their statements made during the various televised debates during the election campaign, the Juncker-Schulz 'tandem' can be expected to favour a further deepening of the integration process, completing the process of establishing a stronger institutional architecture in economic and financial governance as well as in other areas.

The developments of the first half of the 2010s then point to an ever-widening gap between, on the one hand, elite aspirations and institutional dynamics in the EU, and, on the other hand, popular attitudes to the integration process. The perception is therefore that of a Union moving apparently inevitably towards 'ever closer union' even in the face of a considerable popular revolt. While there are widespread demands for 'less Europe', the EU appears to be locked into a path towards further deepening. In the absence of opportunities for significant treaty reform, the existing institutional structure will continue to deliver pro-integrationist policies.

The Lisbon Treaty was meant to conclude a period of ten years of semi-permanent treaty revision. Proponents of liberal intergovernmentalism regarded this as a moment in which the EU had reached a developmental plateau on which to consolidate. However, as we have seen, in the five years since the coming into force of the Lisbon Treaty, the EU has been confronted by new and substantial disequilibria which, in turn, provide new pressures for institutional adaptation, if not constitutional reform. However, at a time when formal treaty reform itself has become unpopular and difficult to promote, disequilibrium is set to remain a persistent part of the EU's political life. The final section of this chapter provides an outlook towards the dilemmas arising from this state of affairs for the EU.

Conclusion

The previous sections have traced the EU's treaty reform in the face of deep, underlying tensions: on the one hand, the functional pressures to address limitations in the institutional design by further delegating power to the European level; on the other hand, the increasing difficulty to achieve root and branch reform through formal constitutional change due to popular disenchantment with, and populist mobilization against, further integration. The result has been the growing de-politicization of reform, the agreement on technocratic solutions, a greater reliance on ad hoc decision-making in inter-governmental institutions, or the adoption of new intergovernmental arrangements outside the formal treaty structure.

These short-term measures were justified in terms of the urgency required to address market pressures during the euro area crisis, likened by Juncker to 'repairing a burning plane while trying to keep it flying' (Juncker 2014: 2). Whatever their merit in the short term, they remain at odds not only with the long-term requirement to combat the crisis and prevent its reappearance, but also of regaining the badly damaged legitimacy of the Union. Short-term needs, for instance, may have justified the opposition by EU leaders to the idea of Greece deciding on the acceptance of bail-out terms through a referendum—in the context of rapidly rising interest rates on Greek bonds, such a solution may have made sovereign debt quickly unserviceable. In the long run, however, there remains a fundamental dilemma: a highly politicized problem—the euro area crisis—which has witnessed unprecedented popular resistance against austerity policies and record votes for Euro-sceptic political parties, has been addressed essentially through a series of technocratic policy measures and new institutional arrangements that lack transparency. In such a context it is crucial to enhance the democratic legitimacy of economic governance, be it through more powers for the EP (Deubner 2013) or active scrutiny activities by national parliaments (Auel and Hoeing 2015).

The pressure on the EU remains, therefore, to follow up on short-term, technocratic and intergovernmental responses to the crisis with a democratic solution to these problems. In other words, to address not only the legitimacy deficits that have become visible in the course of the crisis response, but also to legitimate the further deepening of integration that the initial reaction to the euro area crisis has brought with it. The answer would point to a return to formal constitutionalization, that is, a comprehensive and large-scale round of treaty reform that would bring extra-treaty arrangements such as the Fiscal Compact and the ESM into the core treaty framework and that would subject decision-making in the euro area to greater democratic scrutiny.

However, such a new round of 'constitutional' treaty reform, involving the convening of a new European Convention and resulting in new referendums in some of the member states, is difficult to imagine in the context of heightened Euro-scepticism within the member states and treaty reform fatigue among the leaders. It is also at odds with the demands from some quarters, in particular the UK, to renegotiate the terms of EU membership and to redraw the balance of powers between national and European institutions. Finally, the search for straightforward democratic reforms, giving the EP a greater say about decision-making in economic governance, is complicated by the institutional fragmentation of the EU in this area. The fact is that institutional solutions are needed only for a subset of member states, and that giving new powers to the common EU institutions serving—and being paid for by— all 28 member states creates new legitimacy problems in itself.

The outlook for the immediate future of treaty reform, then, is one of a continuation of muddling through: novel arrangements being agreed by state leaders if solutions cannot be found within the existing framework, and the selective use of the simplified revision procedure if the wording of the treaty actually requires changing. Central to this remains the role of the European Council: it is here that key decisions are being made, not only concerning operational matters, but also strategically and institutionally. Here the European Council enjoys even greater flexibility than in the past: state leaders can initiate formal treaty change, as they did with the change to Article 136, if the wording of the treaty actually needs to change and no new transfer of competences is involved, or negotiate new intergovernmental arrangements if these are not compatible with formal treaty change.

It remains to be seen to what extent the pressures from the EP and a rising chorus of dissent within the member states to put these arrangements on more legitimate footing can be resisted. What is clear is that the dilemmas between efficient problem-solving and formal treaty change, between short-term reaction and long-term solution, between technocratic governance and democratic legitimacy are persisting and are, if anything, likely to grow in the coming years. New intergovernmentalism, with its focus on the central role of the European Council and other intergovernmental fora of decision-making, on the impossibility of disentangling 'high' and 'low politics' and on the persistence of disequilibrium in the EU, is well-equipped to shed further light on these dynamics as they unfold.

Part II
Selected EU Policy Domains Since 1992

5

The New Intergovernmentalism and Experiential Learning in the Common Security and Defence Policy

Michael E. Smith

The year 2003 marks a pivotal moment in the development of European Union (EU) foreign policy ambitions.[1] After years of debate regarding the EU's desire to become a more prominent global actor, a new institutional framework—the Common Security and Defence Policy (CSDP)—was devised to help achieve this goal.[2] Unlike the 1993 Treaty of Maastricht, which mentioned the possibility of greater EU security/defence cooperation but largely failed to make this goal a reality during the 1990s, the CSDP has launched thirty foreign security assistance missions of various types since 2003, spanning a range of geographical areas and functional problems. These missions have involved civilian security forces and, in several cases, the projection of military forces under an EU chain of command. This record clearly demonstrates that the EU has permanently adapted itself to help meet the growing demand for various forms of international security assistance since the end of the Cold War.

This adaptation raises several questions regarding the nature of European cooperation in such a difficult, and even controversial, issue area: conflict resolution, crisis management, and peace-building. Although the EU has developed a highly institutionalized system—the Common Foreign and Security Policy (CFSP)—for cooperating in foreign/security policy, this

[1] I would like to thank the editors for their comments, as well as acknowledge the generous financial support of the European Research Council (Grant No. 203613) for this research. I am also grateful for the information provided, on a confidential basis, by numerous EU and EU member state officials in personal interviews with the author between 2007 and 2014.
[2] Prior to the Lisbon Treaty, the CSDP was referred to as the European Security and Defence Policy; for the sake of consistency I use the term CSDP throughout this chapter.

mechanism did not provide a clear framework for conducting foreign security assistance operations.[3] Yet how did the EU reform itself in order to implement the CSDP, and in such a fairly short time period? In addition, the CSDP, like the CFSP in general, was devised as an intergovernmental domain of EU policy-making: major decisions are taken by consensus in the Council of Ministers, the European Commission plays a limited role, and related supranational actors like the EP and the Court of Justice of the EU are kept outside normal day-to-day policymaking. How does the CSDP function as an EU policy domain when the supranational 'drivers' of European integration are not allowed to play their usual roles? Finally, CSDP operations quickly expanded in terms of their type and scope, and in ways that cannot be explained by traditional realist approaches to security cooperation: balancing against power or balancing against external threats.[4] Why did CSDP operations expand after 2003, and in ways that were not foreseen by the original architects of the mechanism (i.e. a much greater focus on civilian operations rather than military ones)?

This chapter attempts to address these questions by developing a more general theoretical argument regarding the relationship between experiential learning and various methods of European integration. Specifically, I use the expansion of the CSDP to make three general points about the changing nature of intergovernmental cooperation in EU foreign/security policy—or what might be termed the new intergovernmentalism.

First, I argue that the institutionalization of this issue area over the past several decades created a common frame of reference among EU member states regarding the practice and purpose of European foreign policy. This process can be considered a very general form of EU security policy integration, as various principles and norms are generated as a by-product of taking joint action, although EU member states clearly reserve their rights (as in any intergovernmental system) to pursue independent policies in the absence of a common position. Second, the functional task expansion of the EU (i.e. to cover so many areas of domestic and foreign policy), coupled with the inherent uncertainties involved in security policy,[5] mean that a strict or traditional view of intergovernmentalism does not apply to this policy domain.[6] Instead,

---

[3] The Maastricht Treaty mentioned the possibility of drawing upon the military resources of the Western European Union to manage foreign security problems, but EU member states failed to take advantage of this opportunity throughout the 1990s because of a lack of political will.

[4] For examples of these views, see Pape (2005), Paul (2005), and Posen (2006).

[5] I exclude defence policy from this chapter, as the CSDP does not as of yet involve territorial defence or specify a clear security guarantee among EU member states, as in the manner of NATO's Article V.

[6] That is, EU member states form their own policy preferences in relative isolation from each other, and policy decisions are taken through the use of bargains among the most powerful EU member states.

EU security policy cooperation has expanded primarily through the use of pragmatic and informal working methods involving actors at several levels of analysis: supranational, intergovernmental, and transgovernmental. The driving force behind this integration has been a largely endogenous process of norm development promoted by those involved in the day-to-day making of EU foreign/security policy. Third, the major changes required of the EU to launch the CSDP have involved a high degree of experiential learning, as security policy cooperation cannot be 'regulated' in terms of formal EU treaty articles or directives. As EU member states clearly do not wish to invent each CSDP operation from scratch, on a case-by-case basis, some degree of experiential learning was bound to occur within this domain, particularly as the CSDP expanded into new functional or geographic areas. This flexible, pragmatic, and informal approach to the CSDP follows a long tradition of intergovernmental integration in EU foreign/security policy, as with European Political Cooperation (EPC) in the 1970s–1980s and its successor, the CFSP.

Thus, where the CFSP was already highly institutionalized[7] and touched upon various foreign *security-related* problems, it did not involve complex *security-providing* missions, and it did not involve its own military/policing component. Conversely, under the rubric of the CSDP the EU found itself organizing a range of complex security and state-building operations involving police forces, rule of law tasks, border monitoring, peace monitoring, and, in some cases, the projection of air, land, and naval forces into conflict zones. As the CFSP framework was not specifically equipped to deal with this degree of rapid task expansion, officials involved in the CSDP had to devise a completely new set of institutional rules and bodies to cope with these challenges. These mechanisms include intergovernmental and transgovernmental integration, mimetic learning, and institutional learning by doing (or experiential learning). Taken together, these dynamics can be viewed as a form of new intergovernmentalism in the CSDP issue area.

5.1 The New Intergovernmentalism and the CSDP

What is the new intergovernmentalism, and why did the EU—specifically its member states—resort to this method rather than relying on the 'old intergovernmentalism' (i.e. existing methods, based on the CFSP) or delegate more authority to supranational EU institutions? Before examining these questions

---

[7] However, the CFSP was not 'supranationalized' in the sense of complete delegation to the Commission or the regular use of majority voting to make policy decisions, as compared to traditional economic-centred aspects of European integration. For more on this point, see Smith (1998) and Smith (2003).

in detail, we should first note that the EU's decision to create the CSDP was contingent on several factors that can be viewed as foundational assumptions for the analysis that follows. The most important factor is that while all EU member states agreed on the *general* need for a CSDP capability by the late 1990s, they could not specify in detail the circumstances under which specific CSDP operations would be launched. Indeed, the first CSDP operations were launched before a European Security Strategy (ESS) was even agreed,[8] so that policy improvisation became a core trait of the CSDP right from the start. In addition, and like the CFSP in general, there was clear consensus that the CSDP—and particularly its military/defence aspects—would remain an inter-governmental mechanism with limited policy input by, or delegation to, supranational EU actors (particularly the Commission). EU member states would retain not only the right to decide each CSDP mission on the basis of consensus, but also the authority to provide resources for individual CSDP missions through national contributions on a case-by-case basis. Thus, the resource base of the CSDP, like the ideational foundations or justification of the mechanism, was highly unstable relative to the 'normal' funding of common policies through the Commission-dominated budget process.[9]

In other words, EU member states found enough consensus to create the CSDP mechanism and embed it within the EU's body of treaty law, yet still felt they would need to be able to debate every decision to act jointly, and then finance that action, on an almost ad hoc basis. With (now) up to 28 EU member states involved in every CSDP operation, and a potential range of conflicting preferences as to when and how to act, this approach is a recipe for hesitation and inaction, especially if EU member states are unwilling to delegate more authority to the Commission or another authoritative actor, such as the High Representative of the Union for Foreign Affairs and Security Policy (HR). These problems became apparent when the EU began to launch its own independent CSDP operations in mid-2003, rather than simply take over existing UN or NATO operations or make use of NATO assets under the Berlin Plus arrangement.[10] Independent CSDP military operations are the most problematic, given their high costs and risks, as the EU first realized

---

[8] The first CSDP operation, the EU Police Mission in Bosnia-Hercegovina, was launched on 1 January 2003. Two military operations (Concordia and Artemis) followed that same year before the ESS (Solana 2003) was first published on 20 June and then agreed by the Council of Ministers on 12 December 2003.

[9] Specifically, the EU budget cannot be used to fund military/defence operations, so EU member states must supply such forces, as well as police forces for certain CSDP missions. Some common costs for CSDP actions can be financed by the EU budget.

[10] The first CSDP operation, the EU Police Mission in Bosnia, was a take-over of a UN police mission. The first CSDP military operation (Concordia) was a take-over of a NATO operation and made use of NATO assets under Berlin Plus. The Berlin Plus arrangement allows for 'assured access' to NATO planning capabilities, a 'presumption of availability' to the EU of NATO assets, and NATO European command support for EU-led operations.

with Operation Artemis. This operation was a critical learning experience for CSDP policy-makers, and a major step on the path towards the new intergovernmentalism.

Specifically, EU member states had to devise a number of new institutional arrangements to cope with the expanding CSDP workload. As more delegation to the Commission was out of the question, most of these new arrangements were located in the Council of Ministers, which represents the interests of EU member states (i.e. it is an intergovernmental body). EU member states quickly realized that CSDP operations could be devised along military or civilian lines, so new institutions and procedures had to be created to serve both types of operations. Basic military structures for the CSDP had already been agreed under the terms of the Nice Treaty—mainly in the form of an EU Military Committee (EUMC) and an EU Military Staff (EUMS)—yet mechanisms for conducting civilian CSDP operations had to be created from scratch. They also had to be kept separate from the military structures for legal as well as political reasons, although both sets of structures (civilian and military) were part of the General Secretariat of the Council of Ministers.[11] However, given the extensive functional overlap between civilian and military aspects of the CSDP, as well as the legal budgetary role of supranational actors such as the Commission, the EU had to devise stable ways of involving these actors as well, in both the planning and operational phases of CSDP actions. Thus, and in addition to the EUMC and the EUMS, the EU created a set of supporting institutions for civilian CSDP operations, and (later) created an entirely new bureaucracy—the EEAS—to consolidate many of these mechanisms in a single institution, even to the extent of transferring some Commission staff into it.[12] This represents a remarkable example of how the new intergovernmentalism can impact upon the interests of long-standing supranational mechanisms or actors, even ones as powerful as the Commission.[13]

In addition to general problems regarding unstable preferences for taking CSDP decisions and then financing those decisions (and/or committing police or military forces), the EU also had to consider how to justify these operations in terms of common principles or values. As nearly all CSDP operations have not involved or even dealt with a direct threat to European security interests,

---

[11] They were physically separated as well: the civilian structures were located in the Council's Justus Lipsius building, and the military structures were located in a rented office building nearby, on Avenue de Cortenbergh.

[12] As the EEAS did not start functioning until after 2011, well after the main CSDP learning period under consideration here, I do not deal with it extensively in this chapter.

[13] In fact, the Commission was forced to attempt to defend its long-standing institutional interests in certain areas of external relations (mainly in areas of development policy and humanitarian aid) when the EEAS was being set up. It also had to create its own new bureaucratic mechanism, the Service for Foreign Policy Instruments, to manage certain budgetary tasks that involved EEAS responsibilities. For details, see Smith (2013).

the EU has been compelled to think about the 'value added' aspect of the CSDP in other ways. This problem largely involves a debate about the EU's unique contribution to international security or crisis management, and in ways that (apparently) cannot be achieved by other international organizations (such as the UN or NATO) or by coalitions of European states. As critics of EU foreign policy have argued for years (Wallace and Allen 1977), the process of taking CFSP/CSDP decisions is almost, if not more, important, than the actual substance or consequences of those decisions. In other words, deliberation about the EU's role as a security actor becomes an end in itself, in addition to a means to an end; such discussions are as much about how the EU positions itself as a global actor as they are about how the EU should try to improve its conduct of individual CSDP operations. Yet this is not necessarily a deficiency of CFSP/CSDP; instead, it reflects the fact that EU foreign/security policy actions will lack credibility if EU member states do not agree completely on the need to act. In fact, various mechanisms for consultation and deliberation have been built into the CFSP system for years, mainly for the purpose of what could be called, 'negative integration'; that is, using consultation for internal confidence-building and to avoid disputes over foreign policy issues (Smith 2003). Since the launch of CSDP operations, however, this consultative process has been increasingly oriented towards 'positive integration' as well, in terms of framing of what is now known as the 'comprehensive approach' to crisis management and conflict resolution. In addition, these efforts were increasingly made in the context of experiential learning from specific CSDP actions; they were not merely conceptual or speculative. These differences between the 'old' intergovernmentalism and the 'new' intergovernmentalism in the CSDP domain can be summarized in terms of four general hypotheses (see table 5.1).

Thus, the general argument motivating this chapter is this: the greater the difficulties—political, legal, and financial—in using or reforming existing formal (i.e., treaty-based) methods to deal with major crises or new policy problems, the greater the resort to new intergovernmental methods and various ad hoc arrangements, such as experiential learning. EU foreign/security policy cooperation has always been based on pragmatism rather than legal formalism. However, the implementation of the CSDP in particular pushed the EU well beyond its 'normal' limits of foreign/security policy cooperation, particularly in situations involving the deployment of military or police forces—a completely new area of EU policy authority. In the rest of this chapter, I examine how the EU had to adapt—through the development of the new intergovernmentalism in general and experiential learning in particular—in the critical period between 2003 and 2008, before the various disruptions noted above set in.

Table 5.1 'Old' versus 'New' Intergovernmentalism in the CSDP

Hypothesis	'Old' intergovernmentalism (pre-2003)	'New' intergovernmentalism (post-2003)
Problems in domestic preference formation have become stand-alone inputs into the European integration process.	Preferences mainly involve calculations about economic aspects of foreign policy, usually in stable countries.	Preferences often involve difficult and risky calculations about committing military/ police forces into foreign conflict zones.
Where delegation occurs, governments and traditional supranational actors support the creation and empowerment of *de novo* institutions.	A clear reluctance to create new institutions under the EPC/ CFSP system (i.e., the CFSP Secretariat and the Early Warning Unit).	Extensive changes and involving new bureaucratic actors in the Council of Ministers to cope with CSDP workload (i.e., EUMC, EUMS, CPCC,[14] CMPD,[15] EEAS, among others).
Deliberation and consensus have become the guiding norms of day-to-day decision making at all levels.	Primarily 'negative' integration: confidence-building and preventing conflicting positions on foreign policy from undermining economic integration.	Move towards 'positive' integration: creation of common principles, doctrines, and 'best practices' to justify/legitimate CSDP actions and improve their effectiveness (i.e., the 'comprehensive approach').
Supranational institutions are not hard-wired to seek ever closer union.	Commission acts primarily in an 'offensive' manner (i.e., tries to assert its authority in a new policy domain like the CFSP/ CSDP).	Offensive and defensive (i.e., Commission asserts itself but also attempts to protect its core responsibilities in external relations against bureaucratic competitors).

5.2 Experiential learning in the CSDP

As I suggested when discussing the critical role of deliberation in the CSDP, the fact is that the new intergovernmentalism had to be improvised gradually once the EU began undertaking its own security assistance operations; it was not planned or even negotiated. In fact, EU member states probably did not even realize that they were devising a new approach to intergovernmental foreign/security policy coordination. These changes—new CSDP competencies and new CSDP operations—have provoked a great deal of interest in academic and policy circles, yet there is little consensus on an explanation of why and how the EU is developing this capacity. One major school of thought involves exogenous factors, such as external threats. Yet no CSDP operation, other than the EU's counter-piracy naval operation (Atalanta, or the EU Naval Force [EUNAVFOR]) was inspired by a direct security threat to the EU (Germond and Smith 2009).

---

[14] Civilian Planning and Conduct Capability (CPCC).
[15] Crisis Management Planning Directorate (CMPD).

Instead, I argue that the development of the CSDP—in light of the institutional limitations imposed by formal treaty rules—have compelled EU policy elites to pursue other avenues to improve the EU's standing as a global political actor/security provider. Rather than delegating more authority to a powerful bureaucracy or adopting the use of majoritarian voting rules in the Council of Ministers, EU policy elites have attempted to use social mechanisms, which can be framed in terms of institutional learning processes. These processes are largely endogenous to the EU, and do not involve exogenous factors such as power balancing, responses to major security threats to the EU, or crisis-induced decision-making. Instead, they involve the generation and consolidation of ideas regarding what role the EU can play in international security affairs, based on its resources and experiences, as well as the demonstration effects (both negative and positive) of competing global actors such as the UN, NATO, and the United States in particular. The single most important factor behind these institutional learning processes is the steady accumulation of new CSDP operational experiences since 2003, coupled with intensive and deliberate reflection by CSDP professionals on the EU's performance in these operations. Prior to 2003, much of this thinking was hypothetical or speculative in nature, as the EU had never undertaken its own peacekeeping/conflict resolution operations; since then, however, it has been increasingly based on actual operational experiences that have grown increasingly ambitious in their goals, wide in their geographic scope, and complex in terms of their logistical requirements.

Yet does this change reflect mere adaptation to circumstances or actual learning on the part of the EU (Levitt and March 1988; Haas 1990)? Where adaptation does not involve changes in institutional values or purposes, learning can be conceptualized as a process of deliberate reform, consisting of: 1) regularly benchmarking the existing EU rules/values/purposes in a policy domain; 2) actively generating policy-relevant lessons as a result of new missions; 3) deliberately transforming those lessons into cumulative knowledge through feedback/monitoring/evaluation processes; and 4) institutionalizing and disseminating that knowledge for application to future operations. This new knowledge may represent a fundamental change in how the EU sees its role in the world, as well as involving the creation of new foreign/security policy doctrines, or even a new strategic culture for the CSDP (Cornish and Edwards 2001; Solana 2003; Meyer 2005; Smith 2011).

Experiential learning obviously requires new experiences in order to start the learning process, and there has been no shortage of such experiences over the past decade. In my use of the concept, institutional learning is deliberate, proactive, transparent, collective/social, policy relevant, and progressive. My approach also differs from ideational approaches to foreign policy and international relations (Goldstein and Keohane 1993; Yee 1996), which often do not explain why one policy-relevant idea gets chosen over other, equally plausible, ideas. Based on my previous work (Smith 2003), I have also found that one must also explain how new ideas or lessons are institutionalized, hence my specific focus on social-institutional-organizational, rather than merely personal or cognitive, learning. Some of the major examples of new CSDP experiences are discussed in the rest of this section; these experiences provide much of the 'raw material' for institutional discussions within the EU regarding how to draw lessons from actual problems on the ground.

The first-ever CSDP mission involved an EU police mission (EUPM) in Bosnia-Hercegovina (BiH) intended to succeed the UN International Police Task Force in 2003. Among other stabilization and policing tasks, the EUPM-BiH has helped transform the BiH Police Agency into one with enhanced powers and has helped foster major new state agencies (Osland 2004). This mission was very soon followed by the EU's first-ever military operation: Concordia. In this case, the EU deployed a military force to help oversee the implementation of the EU/NATO co-sponsored ceasefire between the government and rebel forces in the Former Yugoslav Republic of Macedonia (FYROM). Concordia was also the first test of the Berlin Plus arrangement for resource sharing between NATO and the EU. The EU also launched a police mission to FYROM, Operation Proxima, at the request of its government in 2003. Proxima's objectives were to monitor, mentor, and reform the police; promote sound policing standards; fight organized crime; help create a border police; and support the overall political environment in that country. As the EU viewed this mission as a success, it ended operations in December 2005 (although limited police affairs cooperation continued into 2006).

As a reflection of its success with the EUPM and Concordia, in December 2004 the EU increased its commitment to state-building in BiH with Althea, a peace mission involving nearly 7,000 troops from twenty-four EU and ten non-EU member states acting under a UN mandate. This was the EU's third, and largest, military operation to date. As with Concordia, Althea was another test of the Berlin Plus arrangement with NATO, and for the first time, the EU in BiH was able to draw on all instruments of foreign and security policy to achieve desired outcomes.

From June to September 2003, the EU led another military operation, Artemis, in the unstable Ituri region of the Democratic Republic of Congo (DRC) at the request of the UN. Here EU troops helped displaced persons return to their homes, helped reopen markets, protected refugee camps, secured the airport, and ensured the safety of civilians, UN employees, and humanitarian aid workers. Since the operation included troops from several non-EU states, the EU again demonstrated its ability to lead foreign troops in a military operation as it had done in Macedonia. Equally important, for the first time, the EU also demonstrated its willingness and ability to initiate, plan, and execute a military operation completely autonomously of NATO. Artemis was also an important test-case for the EU in terms of its great distance from the European theatre and in terms of setting a precedent for future EU military operations organized independently of NATO. A follow-on CSDP mission, EUFOR RD-Congo, was deployed in 2006 using EU rapid reaction forces to provide security during the DRC presidential and legislative elections. As with Artemis, this was an action carried out independent of NATO and thus independent of the Berlin Plus arrangement.

In addition to CSDP police missions in Afghanistan, Iraq, and the Palestinian territories several other smaller-scale CSDP operations have provided additional experiences for the EU to draw upon. These include rule-of-law missions (to establish independent judiciaries), monitoring missions (to oversee a ceasefire or border crossing), and technical aid missions (to establish effective police and military forces). These missions, which have taken place in Georgia, Indonesia, Moldova, Sudan, and Ukraine (among others), demonstrate increasing confidence on the part of the EU, and on the part of those seeking assistance, in the EU's ability to provide a range of security services. More importantly, the EU also attempted its first-ever CSDP naval operation, Atalanta, to combat piracy and facilitate the delivery of humanitarian aid in the coastal regions of the Horn of Africa. Atalanta (or EU NAVFOR) has a mandate to deter and repress acts of piracy and robbery at sea, including within Somali territorial waters. These goals indicate that the operation goes well beyond the traditional Petersberg-type CSDP tasks (i.e. humanitarian/ rescue missions and peace operations) that originally helped to justify an independent EU military capability in the 1990s, as Atalanta is authorized to use violence on the high seas and within Somalia's territorial waters in order to protect the EU's and its member states' own interests (maritime trade), in addition to protecting the Somali population through the delivery of humanitarian aid (Germond and Smith 2009).

5.3 Learning Processes and Lessons

Given the wide range of CSDP 'firsts' since 2003, it would indeed be surprising if the EU did not engage in some degree of learning based on these experiences. However, this commitment to learning can vary widely, from 'accidental' lesson-drawing on an ad hoc basis to far more deliberate and formalized processes for improving performance. Based on the EU's functioning since the first CSDP mission in 2003, we can state quite conclusively that EU foreign policy elites in general, and CSDP personnel in particular, are developing a far more formalized approach to learning, although the degree of such formality still varies across EU organizations. By using 2003 as a baseline starting point, we can also demonstrate the creation of new procedures and institutional roles involving learning processes devoted to the improvement of CSDP functionality.

For the purposes of this chapter, I define 'institutional learning' as changes in an institution's functions, resource base, and skill set as a result of new information, observation, or experience. More specifically, such learning can be measured in terms of institutional changes across three major dimensions: responsibilities, rules, and resources. *Responsibilities* refers to the EU's own conception of its place in the world and the specific types of foreign/security policy missions that might reflect or advance its role. *Rules* refers to the institutional rules and organizational structures that govern a particular policy domain, in this case the CSDP. Finally, *resources* refers to both material and non-material assets that the EU makes available to the CSDP as a policy tool. Material resources might include financing, personnel, and equipment provided by the EU or its member states; non-material resources might include the provision of best practices, progress reports, data sets, and other sources of knowledge relevant to the functioning of the CSDP.

Given the expansion and close involvement of the EUMS in several major CSDP operations since 2003, it is appropriate to begin our discussion with this body. The EUMS in fact has developed one of the most sophisticated lessons-learned systems within all EU institutions involved in the CSDP. This system involves regular lessons-learned meetings among the key principals involved in every CSDP operation, as well as new organizational roles and responsibilities to oversee the lessons-learned processes. Further, these individuals are not politicians or bureaucrats but tend to be well-trained professional experts with extensive experience in legal, policing, or military affairs. This experience also tends to involve some degree of familiarity in dealing with multilateral international cooperation (for example, past service in the UN system or NATO), and these individuals are keen to improve their skill sets to make the CSDP function better. The EU's mission to support African Union (AU) peacekeeping in Darfur (the African Union Mission in Sudan [AMIS] mission), for example, led to a workshop in Brussels devoted to lessons learned; it involved EU staff from the civilian and military parts of the system. This effort has been repeated with all other CSDP missions over the past few years, meaning that a post-mission lessons-learned debriefing process has been institutionalized within the EUMS and related offices in the Commission and Council General Secretariat. The EU's experience with the Artemis mission in the DRC also led it to create a 'Battlegroup concept', which provides a system of ready-response European multinational forces in various permutations.[16]

---

[16] A battlegroup is a form of rapid-response capacity building, each one consisting of around 1,500 troops reinforced with combat support elements, including relevant air and naval capabilities, which can be launched on the ground within ten days of an EU decision to act.

Many of the specific lessons or best practices drawn from these efforts are then incorporated into an increasingly sophisticated EUMS database, the Lessons Management Application (LMA). The LMA has become a real knowledge base for information produced during specific CSDP operations to be applied to future tasks. It has generated well over 1,000 specific lessons for the EUMS, and is regularly updated with new data. In light of this information, the EUMS has improved its planning procedures to anticipate, rather than merely wait for, the kinds of CSDP missions that might be required in the short to medium term; this process also involves the generation of 'watch lists' for potential hotspots around the globe that might require an EU response. The watch lists are generated by a body created after 2006, the Single Integrated Analytical Capability, which then transforms the lists into 'dossiers' for potential CSDP operations. This information is then coordinated with analysis generated by the EU's Situation Centre, another post-2003 innovation. With these mechanisms, all of which are dominated by intelligence professionals, the EUMS does not initiate or suggest CSDP operations, but offers advice on what the EUMS could contribute to handling a certain problem. This need to engage in planning much earlier in the process was a direct result of the Artemis operation in the DRC, which involved a very short timeline, relative to most other CSDP missions (i.e. instigated in days/weeks rather than months).

The General Secretariat of the Council of Ministers, particularly various offices within Directorate General E (DG-E) for External and Political/Military Affairs, as well as the personal office of the HR, also developed its own lessons-learned procedures. These, however, were not as institutionalized and centralized as those found in the EUMS, even though the EUMS is organizationally part of the Council of Ministers. As DG-E directed civilian CSDP missions (until the creation of the EEAS, which effectively absorbed DG-E), it had to adopt feedback mechanisms and standard operating procedures to avoid creating each new mission from scratch. Its approach to such missions is now far more systematic as opposed to the more ad hoc approach during 2003–5, and it is using a database of lessons similar to that adopted by the EUMS. The Council of Ministers also coordinates its learning efforts with those of other EU actors; these procedures are reviewed on a six-month basis in light of lessons-learned reports and post-mission reports delivered by relevant participants in each CSDP mission. Finally, the creation of two new bodies in the Council of Ministers—the Civilian Planning and Conduct Capability (CPCC) mechanism and (later) the Crisis Management and Planning Directorate (CMPD)[17]—were a direct result of the EU's growing experience in planning

---

[17] Now absorbed into the EEAS.

and executing various civilian CSDP operations, a capacity that grew on an almost 'accidental' basis since 2003 and required new structures to oversee it.

In addition to institutionalized lessons-learned procedures and organizational reforms, both the Council of Ministers and the EUMS have conducted various exercises to improve their performance; these involve both military and civilian/policing tasks.[18] Crisis management exercises involving planning capacities in Brussels have been instigated, partly to determine how much support individual EU member states could provide to a given problem. Policing exercises involve a 'rapid deployment of police elements' planning concept, followed by a training exercise to prepare the police officials who volunteer for CSDP operations. These efforts have produced better coordination with the military during such operations, especially in light of the EU's considerable experience in the Balkans. These exercises also give individual EU member states experience in leading a mission; as various CSDP missions have been led by a range of EU member states, any efforts to develop such experience could improve the EU's response capacity in the longer term. Moreover, the leadership candidates include not just the 'usual suspects' (i.e. the larger EU member states) but have included smaller states such as Lithuania (in the Georgia rule of law mission) and Finland/Sweden (in the Aceh monitoring mission). The involvement of 'officially' neutral EU member states in military CSDP operations (as with Swedish special forces operating in Artemis in the DRC) is similarly useful for providing foreign military experience to non-NATO EU member states.

The specific lessons generated by these new procedures and institutions are far too numerous to list in the scope of a single chapter, and many are actually classified. We can, however, report that they cover a wide range of operational tasks at all levels of analysis during a specific CSDP mission. For example, as with all CSDP operations, the EU has gained experience in negotiating Status of Forces Agreements and Host Nation Support Arrangements with the authorities where the CSDP operates, both of which can be delicate political issues for fragile host nations. More parochial lessons have involved the provision of medical care, evacuation procedures, and food supplies for mission staff, plus other logistical issues; this effort is partly due to the EU experiencing difficulties when relying on other organizations (such as the AU) for the overall chain of command in certain operations.

At the more organizational level, various CSDP missions have given the EU valuable experience in managing a security operation through the coordination of its European Community and CFSP/CSDP policy tools and the establishment of best policing and rule of law standards for future missions.

---

[18] Such as the Common Effort (2002) and MILEX (2005) exercises, among others.

As some of these operations have involved non-EU member states, the EU has become more adept at convincing third states to participate in its CSDP operations. One important side effect of these learning and leadership efforts involves the EU's constant, even vigilant, desire to distinguish itself from other major players in international security, particularly the United States. In fact, the demonstration effects of America's experiences in Afghanistan and Iraq have played an important role in how the EU thinks about, and plans, its own CSDP operations. As more than one EU official put it, Europeans do not want to repeat the mistakes of others in developing this capability.

5.4 Towards the 'Comprehensive Approach'

The discussion above clearly indicates that formal learning procedures are in place, and that many institutional 'lessons' are being generated. But is this activity actually improving the functionality of the CSDP? And if so, do these lessons then improve perceptions of the EU's effectiveness and legitimacy with each new mission? Finally, is it possible to speak now of a 'European approach' to conflict resolution and crisis management that largely involves the new intergovernmentalism?

The evidence that the EU has been attempting to apply various lessons can be seen in terms of changes in responsibilities, rules, and resources. Regarding responsibilities, for example, the EU has taken a strong interest in stopping organized crime and corruption as a result of its CSDP experience. It has also attempted to improve the coordination of its civil and military responsibilities during such operations, hence the explicit combination of military and police forces within certain CSDP missions. Many aspects of CSDP missions also involve teaching European standards to soldiers, police, and legal officials, which requires some degree of self-reflection about what those standards are. Regarding institutional rules, and in addition to the learning processes noted above, the EU learned from early CSDP missions (particularly Concordia and Artemis) that it needed to streamline its CSDP funding procedures where common-pool resources (that is, those not funded by the Community budget) had to be devised; this realization led directly to the institutionalization of the 'Athena' funding mechanism.[19] It was first applied in Operation Althea in

[19] As the EU budget cannot be used to fund military operations, the Athena facility (Council decision 2004/197/CFSP) provides for a common pool of financial and other resources supplied by EU member states. It speeds up the disbursement of funds and, critically, allows for contracts to be signed with sub-contractors and other suppliers of mission resources.

BiH, and was later followed by an additional mechanism, the Instrument for Stability (IFS).[20]

Finally, regarding resources, the EU has improved its ideational inputs to the development of the CSDP, as through the EU Institute for Security Studies, an EU think-tank of independent policy experts which provides analysis and recommendations regarding the EU's new security capabilities.[21] In addition to reports and working papers, the institute produces a regular 'CSDP Newsletter' and other publicly available publications, which are circulated among CSDP policy experts and which often document specific lessons drawn from CSDP missions. The creation of the European Defence Agency (EDA) was similarly intended to improve the EU's military resource base for CSDP missions by reducing duplicated efforts and facilitating joint research and procurement projects. The EU Satellite Centre and related cooperation in intelligence sharing further add to the EU's resources for CSDP operations. In what is another first for the EU, the creation of a 'CSDP College' helps to not only institutionalize the lessons learned regarding the EU's security capabilities, it also aids in the teaching of those lessons to both EU and non-EU nationals. In this sense the EU is already attempting to export its security-related knowledge to non-EU states in the form of a CSDP curriculum.

These changes can also be considered within the context of what the EU is now striving towards: not just a more active and effective CSDP, but rather something known as the 'comprehensive approach'. This involves a stress on preventative action using a full range of EU policy tools directed towards a single target/problem. These tools would include military, policing, law, human rights, and economic development resources. One example of such an approach is the EU's mission in Eastern Chad/Central African Republic (RCA) (EUFOR Tchad/RCA), the most multinational and largest independent EU military operation to date, involving around 3,700 troops. As many as 23 EU member states were represented in the operational headquarters, while 16 EU member states were represented at the mission level in the theatre, and three non-EU member states participated. EUFOR Tchad worked not only to protect civilians and UN personnel but also to deliver humanitarian aid, build up the African Union as a regional security provider, support the return of refugees, and foster long-term political and economic development.

The comprehensive approach is therefore not just about improving functionality; it also has much to do with the EU's conception of itself as a

---

[20] Unlike the Athena mechanism, which involves intergovernmental contributions, the IFS is a new Community budget line that helps to speed up the disbursement of funds controlled by the Commission in situations involving crisis management, conflict resolution, and peace-building.
[21] Formerly the Western European Union (WEU) Institute for Security Studies; the EU assumed control of this Paris-based agency in January 2002.

responsible global actor. As more than one EU official put it, the EU is the 'acceptable face of Europe' in a manner unlike NATO (which is seen as too American and too aggressive), and the comprehensive (or 'European approach') to conflict resolution/crisis management problems is becoming the EU's 'trademark' in international politics. EU insiders who have also worked for NATO (particularly those in the EUMS) also note a distinct difference between the two organizations: the EU simply engages in far more reflection and feedback about its global role as compared to NATO. The EU is also more developed in its support of policing/rule of law missions, which may be more important than military force for securing many troubled states. To develop this capacity, the EU has created its own new civilian crisis management capability.[22]

In this manner, the EU is able to provide a distinct 'rule of law covenant' to govern its missions in third countries, so that the entire process is subject to formal legal rules and some degree of democratic accountability. Police forces, in other words, are far more answerable to the legal jurisdictions in which they operate, whereas military forces can often invent or impose their own rules of engagement for a specific host country. Thus, and although military missions often receive the most attention by outside observers, the EU's comprehensive approach is likely to involve more policing and judicial resources rather than hard military power, and various weak or failing states have been looking to the EU for assistance in these areas. Police forces are also very useful for crowd control and undermining organized crime groups, which often proliferate in weak or conflict-prone states.

Although various EU officials throughout the bureaucracy speak of the comprehensive approach, it does not (as of yet) involve a single model or 'one size fits all' approach. There is still a considerable degree of flexibility when individual CSDP missions go from the planning to the execution stages. Still, as the EU gains experience with working out the complex details of these operations, such as negotiating Status of Forces Agreements with host countries, it increasingly attempts to institutionalize and formalize these tasks to make them more consistent and streamlined. These efforts even extend to requiring ever more legal oversight of such arrangements, involving legal advice from both the Council of Ministers and the European Commission. Legal officials in both bodies confirm that the drafting of CSDP documents has become easier and more consistent compared to the situation just a few years ago; for example, the drafting of the Aceh agreement was much more streamlined compared to the earlier CSDP missions in BiH. The Council legal service

---

[22] As decided by the Feira European Council in June 2000; also see the Council of Ministers, 'Civilian Capabilities Improvement Conference 2006', ministerial declaration (Brussels: 13 November 2006).

has similarly undertaken the use of 'preparatory measures' to quicken the planning/financing process; these measures can be implemented even before a final CSDP mission has been agreed.

Conclusion

Changing the CSDP from rhetoric into reality, while still maintaining its largely intergovernmental nature, was a major challenge for the EU and its member states. Yet the EU clearly met this challenge, and the CSDP is now a fully functional EU foreign/security policy instrument. Moreover, the EU has gained many new experiences in the CSDP, has made active efforts to draw lessons from its experiences, has catalogued various lessons, and has attempted to apply some of these lessons to ongoing CSDP missions. If we use 2003 as a baseline year for comparison against CSDP performance in recent years, there is no doubt that a high degree of institutional learning has been occurring within European foreign policy in general and the CSDP in particular. Thus, as measured against past performance during the 1980s and 1990s, the EU has come a *very* long way in terms of its foreign policy perform-ance and its learning processes in this domain. In fact, it could be argued that in the last ten years there has been more dynamism and institutional innov-ation in this domain than in any other EU policy area. Various EU insiders across the system also consistently report their support for keeping the EU in the business of international security/crisis management; they also clearly believe that the EU can bring a unique capability to this domain beyond the efforts of the UN, NATO, and other international organizations.

However, there is also no doubt that the CSDP mechanism faced new challenges after 2008. The methods of new intergovernmentalism discussed in this chapter were not enough to overcome the institutional lethargy over foreign/security policy that emerged between the 2008 financial/euro crisis and the bureaucratic problems generated by implementing the Lisbon Treaty after 2010. The EU is also faced with a complex security environment: the changing roles of the United States and the UN, the rise of China, the erratic influence of Russia, and the continued unrest in North Africa and the Middle East. In short, while there are still numerous opportunities for CSDP actions, particularly in the EU's 'near abroad', the supply of those actions has dwindled thanks to the inherent limitations of intergovernmentalism as a mechanism to harmonize the foreign policy positions of the 28 EU member states. If EU member states refuse to delegate more political leadership over the CSDP to a stable bureaucratic actor or other authority (such as the HR), then they can only blame themselves when a clear consensus cannot be reached on whether to utilize the CSDP mechanism.

This reluctance can be seen in a range of crises after 2008, where the EU failed to act decisively through the CSDP (or its other foreign/security policy tools): the Arab spring, Mali, Syria, and Ukraine are the most prominent recent examples. The EU therefore seems to still be in some disarray about how to develop the CSDP to cope with such challenges; the December 2013 European Council on security and defence did little to address this problem.[23] If the EU cannot create a central source of political will for deploying the CSDP on a consistent basis, then it will remain in a state of just 'muddling through' various security problems until, or unless, a stable coalition of EU member states emerges to build a broader European consensus on whether to act during a particular crisis. Thus, while the new intergovernmentalism clearly helped to get the CSDP off the ground as a viable EU policy domain, it remains to be seen whether this approach to European foreign/security policy integration will survive as a robust and reliable means of turning the EU into a credible global political actor. The signs so far, however, are not very promising.

---

[23] See Andrew Rettman, 'France, Germany and UK show discord on EU defence', *EU Observer*, 16 January 2014. However, the Council of Ministers did mention maritime security as a new priority area; see the European Council conclusions of 19/20 December 2013 (Brussels), and Smith (2014). The ESS was also set to be revised at the time of writing this chapter.

6

Integrating in Justice and Home Affairs

A Case of New Intergovernmentalism Par Excellence?

Sarah Wolff

In the post-Maastricht era, researchers have been struggling to identify trends in European integration. The 'paradox of Lisbon' is one that has seen negotiations on the 2005 Constitution starting out as a reinforcement of supranationalism and ending in a seemingly strengthening of intergovernmentalism (Schout and Wolff 2011). Beyond the 'either–or' debate, more research on this paradox of European integration, including a reconceptualization of supranationalism and intergovernmentalism is needed. I have argued elsewhere that both visions are part of the same 'concept' that explores political and administrative interdependences at the level of policies.[1] This interdependence can be more or less asymmetrical depending on the policy areas under study or time. What matters in this approach is the study of 'coordination' across the different levels (Schout and Wolff 2011). Building upon this work, this chapter engages with the new intergovernmentalism thesis in the field of Justice and Home Affairs (JHA).

JHA is a prolific area of activities in the post-Maastricht context towards which EU decision-making has shifted both internally and externally. It therefore constitutes excellent testing ground for the assumptions outlined in chapter 1 of this volume. Internally, this area, which started out as an intergovernmental domain, known as the third pillar, has gradually been structured around

---

[1] Rather than conceiving those two approaches as opposites on the European integration scale that you can rank, it is about unpacking the interdependencies across the different layers and understanding that the two are 'interconnected and mutually reinforced' (Schout and Wolff 2011: 30).

common strategic guidelines adopted every five years since Tampere in 1999. The Stockholm Programme, which lays down the multi-annual programme in JHA for 2009–14, lists more legislative proposals than the 1992 Programme that implemented the Single European Act in its time. Also, in 2010 the EU adopted its first EU Internal Security Strategy. Competence-wise every treaty since Maastricht has expended the communautarization of JHA, with the 2008 Return Directive being the first text co-decided between the Council of Ministers and the European Parliament (EP). After Lisbon, the abolition of the pillars and the continuing extension of co-decision have led observers to point to a victory for the Community method and to the end of intergovernmentalism inherent to the third pillar dealing with police and judicial cooperation. External competences have also expanded: migration, terrorism, and intelligence cooperation are among the top priorities of EU external relations and JHA has entered rapidly into the field of EU diplomacy. Visa liberalization, EU Readmission Agreements, Mobility Partnership, Passenger Name Records, Terrorist Financing Tracking Programme are some of the manifold JHA policy instruments used in EU external relations with third countries.

The Lisbon Treaty has nonetheless led researchers to some additional confusion in characterizing JHA integration. Owing to the expansion of the co-decision and qualified majority voting to many old third pillar issues, it is quite natural that academics take the assumption of a gradual communautarization of JHA issues (Ripoll Servent and Trauner 2014). The EP appears, indeed, as the big winner of the Lisbon Treaty and co-decides in most JHA areas, while the European Commission has now two specific Directorate-Generals in charge of 'Justice' and 'Home Affairs'. EU agencies such as Europol, Frontex, or the European Asylum Support Office (EASO) are beloved policy instruments of national and supranational policy-makers. In the field of asylum, the Community method is expanding and has helped member states to improve their asylum standards instead of leading to a race to the bottom (El-Enany and Thielemann 2011). Even in sensitive fields like counter-terrorism, supranational activism is at play (Kaunert 2010). Those developments also challenge the concept of intensive transgovernmentalism (Lavenex and Wallace 2005). JHA is not merely the product of intensive cooperation among 'governmental actors below the level of heads of states and governments, such as ministerial officials, law enforcement agencies, and other bureaucratic actors' (Lavenex and Wallace 2005). While JHA police officers and magistrates continue to cooperate across borders and to use the transnational EU level for new 'policy venues' to bypass domestic constraints (Guiraudon 2001), supranational actors have become active players of JHA governance. The 2014 *In 't Veld* case won by MEP Sophie In 't Veld on transparency of the SWIFT-TFTP agreement in front of the European Court of Justice is another instance that supranational dynamics are at play.[2] At the same time, EU member states are wary of delegating competences to supranational bodies and agencies and remain in control in the design of agencies such as Frontex (Wolff and Schout 2013). EU migration policies are also a prime example of re-nationalization (Angenendt and Parkes 2009).

JHA is therefore a pertinent policy area to debate methods of integration beyond conventional wisdom. This chapter questions what drives JHA integration in the post-Maastricht era and why. Claiming that the intergovernmental-supranational dichotomy is ill equipped, it engages with the concept of new intergovernmmentalism. Does JHA qualify as an instance of new intergovernmmentalism? Building upon prior work on the trends of agencification, politicization, and operationalization (Wolff and Mounier 2012), the analysis that follows shows that some of the new intergovernmmentalism's core hypotheses present some novel explanations for JHA developments, along with traditional explanations. First, the Community method in JHA is under many constraints and has been weakened (hypothesis 2: Supranational institutions are not hard-wired to seek ever closer union). This is instantiated by an analysis of JHA legal competences enshrined in the treaties as well as by the strengthened role of the European Council as agenda-shaper. Second, there is strong evidence that deliberation and consensus between the EP and the Council of Ministers has become an end in itself as exemplified by the informal early agreements' practice of the Civil Liberties, Justice and Home Affairs (LIBE) Committee (hypothesis 1: Deliberation and consensus have become the guiding norms of day-to-day decision making at all levels). Third, JHA is being de-politicized in the EU discourse and by the use of agencies as favourite policy instruments. This agencification and operationalization trend tends to play a part in the blurring between high and low politics, which fuels the state of disequilibrium (hypothesis 4: Problems in domestic preference formation have become stand-alone inputs into the European integration process; and hypothesis 5: The differences between high and low politics have become blurred).

6.1 A Restrained Community Method

In spite of evident communautarization, the analysis of legal competences reveals to some extent an undermining of the Community method. In addition, turf wars over agenda shaping and in particular regarding JHA multi-annual programming confirm the thesis according to which the European

---

[2] Case C-350/12 P *Council* v *In 't Veld*, 3 July 2014, not yet published.

Council has become the political centre of new intergovernmentalism (see also chapter 8 in this volume). JHA integration therefore follows a tortuous path which can restrain the Community method, even in spite of major advances with the Lisbon Treaty: 'rather than seeking any form of "integration" of their systems and policies, member states have therefore opted for gradually increasing interaction and synergy between their national systems, while wherever possible limiting legislation and common structures which may interfere with national control over JHA instruments' (Monar 2011: 119).

In theory, recent developments in JHA point to a very functionally integrated area. The creation of Schengen and the removal of internal borders were linked to the completion of the internal market. In turn, compensatory measures were created to fight borderless crime. Cross-border law enforcement cooperation, databases such as the Schengen Information System, the Visa Information System, and the multiplication of JHA agencies can be seen as functional derivatives of the single market. JHA integration is an area of intense integration, with about 172 measures listed in the Stockholm Programme. This is comparable to the ambitions of the 1992 Programme on the single market. The EP has gained extensive co-decision powers on short-stay visas and residence permits (Article 77 TFEU),[3] legal immigration (Article 79 TFEU), judicial cooperation in criminal matters (Articles 82, 83, 84 TFEU), the rules governing Europol (Article 88 TFEU), and Eurojust (Article 85 TFEU) as well as civil protection (Article 196 TFEU). Non-operational police cooperation is also subjected to the ordinary legislative procedure.[4]

Yet, this communautarization is limited by many exceptions to the rule. This weakens the argument that JHA integration is governed by the Community method. Unanimity in the Council of Ministers is the rule for short-stay and visas, passports, identity cards, residence permits, or any other such document (Article 77 TFEU). Only then is the EP consulted. Unanimity remains for family law (Article 81 TFEU), the establishment for a European Public Prosecutor's Office (Article 86 TFEU), and operational police cooperation (Article 87 TFEU). In addition, the right of initiative is shared by the Commission with one quarter of EU member states in the ex-third pillar, namely draft legislation in the field of judicial cooperation in criminal

---

[3] The European Council and the European Parliament are able to decide together in the field of the common policy on visas and other short-stay residence permits; the checks to which persons crossing external borders are subject; the conditions under which nationals of third countries shall have the freedom to travel within the Union for a short period; any measure necessary for the gradual establishment of an integrated management system for external borders; the absence of any controls on persons, whatever their nationality, when crossing internal borders.

[4] This refers to the collection, storage, processing, analysis, and exchange of relevant information; the support for the training of staff, and cooperation on the exchange of staff, on equipment and on research into crime detection and common investigative techniques in relation to the detection of serious forms of organized crime (Article 87 TFEU).

matters, police and administrative cooperation (Article 76 TFEU). Similarly, if the jurisdiction of the ECJ is expanding on the ex-third pillar, there is a transitional period of five years. In 2014, the ECJ gained the ability to review the entire range of JHA policies with the restriction that it will not be 'review (ing) the validity or proportionality of operations carried out by the police or other law-enforcement services of a member state or the exercise of the responsibilities incumbent upon member states with regard to the mainten-ance of law and order and the safeguarding of internal security' (Article 276 TFEU).

The inclusion of an emergency brake in the Lisbon Treaty illustrates this intergovernmental bias to JHA integration. Article 82 TFEU stipulates that where a member state considers that a draft directive would 'affect fundamen-tal aspects of its criminal justice system', it can request the European Council to suspend the ordinary legislative procedure. This emergency brake or 'right of appeal' (de Zwann 2011) is another legacy of the intergovernmental method whereby the member states usually decide by unanimity, the EP being merely informed or consulted. Most importantly, the Commission does not have an exclusive right of initiative. It shares this right with one quarter of the member states on the ex-third pillar issue (Article 76 TFEU).

JHA is also characterized by fragmentation and several speeds, since there are opt-outs/opt-ins that remain for Ireland, the UK, and Denmark.[5] The year 2014 was a crucial year for the UK government, as it decided to opt out of all the 133 police and criminal justice measures (formerly referred to as the 'third pillar') that were set to come under the jurisdiction of the European Court of Justice (according to Article 10, Protocol 36 TFEU). However, the UK also decided to opt back in to thirty-five of these measures, including the European Arrest Warrant, meaning that the impact of this decision on the UK's influence over the future of police and judicial integration in Europe is as yet unclear.

Behind the politics of opt-outs, often dictated by domestic politics, deliber-ation and consensus have enabled the UK and Denmark to remain important

---

[5] The UK and Ireland can opt out of or opt in to any JHA legislative proposal. Protocol 19 of the Lisbon Treaty provides that the Council would then decide by unanimity of the rest of its members to allow the UK and Ireland to opt in. Protocol 20 of the Treaty stipulates that both countries, which are not part of the Schengen area, can continue to control people entering their territories. Regarding the jurisdiction of the ECJ, the UK and Ireland will be subject to its jurisdiction in the field of asylum, civil law, future policing, and criminal law in the event that they would opt in. However, they are not subject to its jurisdiction when it comes to the existing JHA acquis in the field of policing and criminal law during five years following the entry into force of the Lisbon Treaty (until 1 December 2014). Denmark has an opt-out on border control, immigration, asylum, and civil law. However, it used to take part fully in police and criminal law cooperation. The Lisbon Treaty offers the possibility to opt in to JHA policies after having held a public referendum. This would then enable Denmark to opt in on a case-by-case basis for new legislation. The UK, the Czech Republic, and Poland are also not subject to the Charter of Fundamental Rights of the EU as stipulated by Protocol 30 of the Lisbon Treaty.

players of JHA (Adler-Nissen 2008). This goes against the conventional wisdom that opt-out marginalizes member states and equates a loss of influence and it confirms hypothesis 1. This is illustrated by the role of the UK role in Frontex. While the UK was not allowed to formally take part in the adoption of the 2007/2004 Regulation establishing the Frontex Agency because the country does not implement the Schengen acquis,[6] the UK participates as an observer in Frontex operations. Quite surprisingly, the UK also takes part financially in Frontex since it contributed in 2010 with '€570,000 to the cost of joint operations and other activities in which the UK participates' (House of Commons 2010). In addition, key JHA positions are also held by UK officials in EU institutions such as Rob Wainwright as the director of Europol or Jonathan Faull who remained Director-General of DG JLS for seven years.[7] The UK has also been at the forefront of several JHA initiatives such as the Harmony project in police cooperation which led to the establishment of the policy cycle in police cooperation. Next to legal competences, member states often remain the gatekeepers of JHA and the European Council is increasingly playing a key role in the phase of agenda shaping. Article 68 TFEU codifies the role of the European Council, stating that it 'shall define the strategic guidelines for legislative and operational planning within the area of freedom, security and justice'. Since 1999 and the first multi-annual JHA programme adopted in Tampere, the European Council has constantly renewed and extended its agenda-shaping powers through The Hague and Stockholm Programmes. In those documents, like in the field of economic governance or CFSP, it has gotten used to instructing the Commission.

The Stockholm Programme, adopted in 2009, in the midst of a transition towards the Lisbon Treaty, also epitomized issues of ownership. The Future Group on Freedom, Security and Justice, created in order to provide input on the future of the Area of Freedom, Security and Justice (AFSJ), was composed of the Italian, German, Portuguese, Slovenian, Swedish, and French ministries of Interior (plus the French Immigration minister) as well as the then Commissioner for Justice, Freedom, and Security Jacques Barrot, and Franco Frattini, his predecessor. The EP was excluded from the consultation as well as smaller member states. Being a European Council document, the Stockholm Programme reiterates the heads of state or government's monopoly over the JHA agenda (see European Council 2010). This led to a conflict with the Commission, which was seen as going too far in its 2010 Action Plan implementing the Stockholm Programme. JHA Ministers criticized the Commission for cherry-picking the actions to be implemented. The UK government, for

---

[6] Case *UK v Council* (C-77/05) [2007] ECR I-11459.
[7] Jonathan Faull was Director-General of DG Justice, Liberty and Security between 2003 and 2010 before moving to the Directorate General for Internal Market and Services.

instance, was concerned to see the Commission overstepping the European Council regarding the establishment of a European public prosecutor (House of Lords 2011: 9). What has been labelled as the 'Stockholm Affair' re-emerged when the Commission refused in 2012 to provide a mid-term evaluation of the Stockholm Programme (Carrera and Guild 2012). This time, both the Council of Ministers and the EP had requested the Commission to provide such an evaluation in order to prepare the post-Stockholm guidelines.

This eagerness to deliberate at the highest political level on JHA issues is visible in the practice of 'European Pacts' whereby the European Council agrees on guidelines to the EU and its member states on specific areas of JHA. Several 'European Pacts' were adopted in recent years: the European Pact on Immigration (Council of the European Union 2008), the European Pact on International Drug Trafficking (Council of the European Union 2010), and the European Pact on synthetic drugs (Council of the European Union 2011). Those pacts usually help the positioning of the rotating presidency around operational and pragmatic goals. They do not have any legal basis and therefore remain gentlemen's agreements. This emphatically confirms the trend towards 'high-level intergovernmental policy coordination' (Puetter 2011). Pushed by the 2008 French presidency, the European Pact on Immigration has been viewed as undermining 'the possibilities for the EU to fully accomplish a "common" and harmonised immigration and asylum policy that is coherent, global and integrated' (Carrera and Guild 2008: 5). Reaffirming member states' interests and strengthening the principle of subsidiarity, it brings little added value to a common immigration policy (Carrera and Guild 2008). In the field of EU external migration policy, the European Council has also played an instrumental role in the adoption of the 2005 Global Approach to Migration.

The European Council has moved to the centre of JHA agenda-shaping and uses its deliberative and consensual qualities among national officials over JHA governance as a whole, confirming hypothesis 1. Deliberation also takes place among transgovernmental actors gathered in *de novo* bodies such as the Standing Committee on Operation Cooperation on Internal Security (COSI) or the Justice and Home Affairs-External Relations (JAIEX) Council working groups whose coordination abilities have been strengthened with Lisbon. The COSI, in particular, has a strong operational focus. It is in charge of coordinating, supporting, and implementing the Internal Security Strategy adopted by the Council of Ministers on 25/26 February 2010 and endorsed by the European Council on 25/26 March 2010. This *de novo* institution enables the Council of Ministers to remain as the gatekeeper of JHA through operational cooperation, and to sideline supranational institutions by its priority-setting function (Rijpma 2014: 75).

JHA governance both in its legal competences and in its agenda-shaping phase is thus marked by high-level deliberation. The Commission finds itself, at times, in a position of 'outsider' in the agenda-shaping phase and is relegated to the role of implementing the European Council's tasks. This weakening of the traditional Community method is further substantiated by the practice of early informal trialogues.

6.2 Deliberation in JHA Decision-Making: The Case of Informal Early Agreements

The practice of informal early agreements by the Council of Ministers and the EP verifies hypothesis 1 and hypothesis 2 of chapter 1 of this volume. It confirms that deliberation and consensus between the two co-legislators, sometimes at the highest levels, have become ends in themselves (hypothesis 1) and that even the EP is not necessarily hard-wired to seek ever closer union in the field of JHA (hypothesis 2). MEPs, like policy-makers in the Council of Ministers, are rational actors, eager to appear as credible and effective legislators vis-à-vis their respective constituencies and other EU institutional actors. To this end, the common practice of early agreements weakens the Community method as we know it by sidelining the Commission. The latter is indeed more hesitant in 'the exercise of its right to withdraw its proposals and then deprives it of what used to be a major weapon' (Bertoncini and Kreilinger 2012: 10).

Even though this practice is detrimental to enhanced transparency and legitimacy and is a subversion of the traditional co-decision process (Costa, Dehousse, and Trakalova 2011; Reh et al. 2011), the EP, and in particular the LIBE Committee, are eager to use it. This is most surprising given that the EP is often keen to appear as the civil liberties and personal data freedom defender. However, being a 'competence-maximizer' and an 'efficient legislator' can take precedence over the normative commitment to civil liberties or the Community method. Historically, the LIBE Committee favoured until the Lisbon Treaty the consultation procedure over the co-decision, even though the latter had been available since 2004. This preference for consultation was motivated by the ambition to play the good cop in front of the Council of Ministers and to appear as an institution defending citizens' civil liberties, in particular in the case of data protection (Ripoll Servent 2012: 66). In the practice of co-decision, the EP also needs to secure its own institutional position vis-à-vis the Council of Ministers in the period post-Lisbon (Monar 2013: 136).

A survey of co-decision initiatives between 2004 and 2009 reveals that the LIBE Committee was one of the committees most affected by the extension of the co-decision to migration, asylum, visa, and border issues following the Amsterdam Treaty. During the 6th legislature, it had to deal with 38 co-decision procedures, compared to eight in the 5th legislature (Kratsa-Tsagaropoulou et al. 2009: 7). The LIBE Committee is one of the committees where the practice of 'early agreements' has been the most important, with 84.2 per cent of the 38 co-decision procedures being adopted at 'first reading'. Some 15.8 per cent of the procedures reached the second reading, and none went to a conciliation committee. An informal early agreement is 'a legislative compromise [that] must be reached prior to the EP's first reading. This compromise is negotiated informally by a restricted and secluded group of representatives from the EP, the Council of Ministers, and the Commission. Next, the procedure is 'fast-tracked', as legislation is adopted after one rather than three possible readings' (Reh et al. 2011: 2). Rapporteurs and shadow rapporteurs start early negotiations with the Council of Ministers through informal contacts that are called 'trialogues'. Who exactly is involved and which compromises and package deals are made remains quite secretive. Traditionally, in prior legislatures, 'early-stage conclusion of legislative procedure is reserved for technical texts devoid of controversy or political agendas, or for emergencies' (Costa 2011: 15).

The development of such a practice in the LIBE committee should trigger questions as to why is this practice more important than in other committees, and who benefits from it. Costa, Dehousse, and Trakalova (2011) found that the Council of Ministers' influence is greater through early agreements and that the presidency is keen on having early agreements that lead to concrete deliverables within the short period of time of a 6-months presidency. Reh et al. (2011) have shown that the likelihood of informal early agreements is greater when the number of stakeholders is higher, and therefore it explains why after the 2004 enlargement that practice expanded. They explain that 'fast-track legislation offers an opportunity to regain efficiency by reducing the number of interlocutors in the informal arena and by capitalizing on the simple majority rule in Parliament' (Reh et al. 2011: 21). Other variables that were relevant over the period of the study (1999–2009) were 'EU enlargement, legislative workload, complexity, and the time fast-track legislation has been in use. Evidence also points to the relevance of political and national proximity of key negotiators and to a strong "committee effect"'. However, contrary to other studies they 'find no link between the choice to "go informal" and policy type, issue saliency, or the Council presidency's priorities' (Reh et al. 2011: 21).

The common practice of informal trialogues in JHA fuels the state of disequilibrium whereby the JHA policy-making is uncoupled from national policy-making. De-politicized language and policy instruments are also core features of JHA politics, thereby accentuating the blurring of high and low politics (hypothesis 5).

6.3 De-politicized JHA Language and Policy Instruments: the Blurring between High and Low Politics

Another feature of new intergovernmentalism is the blurring of the frontier between high and low politics (hypothesis 5). In spite of being a highly sensitive policy area, which calls upon national core sovereign prerogatives, JHA integration post-Maastricht has been marked by high-level deliberation, which favours pragmatic and operational cooperation. This is evident in the language on JHA policy instruments found in non-legislative documents and also by an 'agencification trend'.

A content analysis of JHA governance documents reveals that national and Commission policy-makers have had an increased preference for solutions that favour networks, are operational in nature or focus on the implementation of JHA acquis. I analyse a small sample of JHA multi-annual programming documents: Tampere (1999), The Hague (2004), and Stockholm (2009), which set the objectives on a five-year period to achieve an Area of Freedom, Security and Justice. To cover also police cooperation and migration the sample includes the Global Approach to Migration adopted in 2005 and revised through a Communication of the Commission in 2011 (Commission 2011c). The European Pact on Immigration adopted by the Council of Ministers in 2008 is also included. Finally, the EU internal security strategy drafted by the Council of Ministers in 2009 and the Communication of the Commission on 'The EU Internal Security Strategy in Action: Five steps towards a more secure Europe' are also included (Commission 2010c).

The ambition is to identify the priority given to either new modes of soft governance such as 'networks', to intensive transgovernmentalism under the form of 'operationalization' or to coordination through 'interoperability'. A word frequency analysis has been run to identify the importance taken by the terms 'network', 'operational', and 'interoperability' (see Figure 6.1 below). The choice for this discourse analysis is motivated by existing research which shows that executive politics of JHA have been strengthened by operational cooperation (Rijpma 2014: 62). Police cooperation for instance relies a lot on informal operational cooperation networks and practices (Den Boer et al. 2008; Bures 2012). Formal operational institutions have been created with the Lisbon Treaty through the creation of the COSI and with the adoption of the EU Internal Security Strategy (Rijpma 2014: 63). In spite of an important communautarization process, member states remain the gatekeepers of JHA operational activities, which are the exception to the rule in the treaties. A discourse analysis of the term 'operation' reveals an executive bias to JHA. A search has also been made of the use of the word 'network', since most of JHA networks and networked governance are symptomatic of informal practices which de-politicize salient issues and strengthen transgovernmental practitioners reporting to

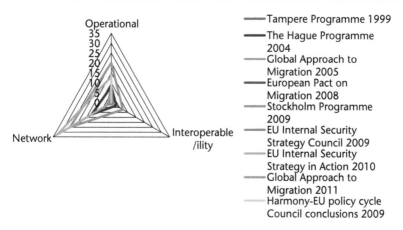

Figure 6.1. Content Analysis of Key JHA Documents: Which Policy Instruments?

the Council of Ministers. Therefore, instead of looking for common EU solutions that would favour supranational solutions, such as a unique European Passenger Name Record system or a European Border Guard Corps, priority is given to operational solutions which are considered to belong to 'low politics' and rely on networked governance. Interoperability can have two meanings. The first is a de-politicized meaning, which involves the 'interoperability' of JHA databases and therefore 'serves as a means to preclude public debate on the interoperability of databases that process essentially personal data, with social and political ramifications' (Balzacq 2008: 93). The second meaning refers to the operational coordination between the different levels of JHA governance and the aim of making national, European and international levels more interoperable. This is another way to refer to 'coordination' at the operational level. Figure 6.1 reveals the importance given, at this stage of the police cycle, and across policy areas (e.g. migration and police cooperation), to networked governance. Figure 6.1 also shows that, over the years, priority is given to operational solutions, and this even more so with regard to the Stockholm Programme and the EU Internal Security Strategy.

The de-politicization trend is not only visible in policy documents but is translated into policy instruments and, in particular, is evident in the phenomenon of agencification. The decentralized nature of EU governance is characterized by new instruments such as networked governance or the Open Method of Coordination (Kassim and Le Gales 2010). This leads to new forms of policy learning (Schout 2009), and specific choices of policy instruments (Lascoumes and Le Galès 2007), for instance in the field of EU external migration policy (Trauner and Wolff 2014). Public policy instruments can be motivated by rational decisions to deliver credible outputs, in the sense of Majone's 'Regulatory Europe' argument (Majone 1996). The choice of instruments can also reveal a 'form of knowledge about social control and ways of exercising it' and is therefore not neutral (Lascoumes and Le Galès 2007:1). Policy instruments 'produce specific effects, independently of the objective pursued (the aims ascribed to them), which structure public policy according to their own logic' (Lascoumes and Le Galès 2007:1).

The role of JHA agencies has been covered extensively in the literature (Wolff 2008; Busuioc and Groenleer 2011; Kaunert et al. 2013; Wolff and Schout 2013). Since the historical third pillar Europol and Eurojust, JHA agencies have multiplied: the European Police College (CEPOL), the EU Joint Situation Centre (Sitcen), the European Anti-Fraud Office (OLAF), Frontex, the European Asylum Support Office (EASO) and a new European Agency for the operational management of large-scale IT systems in the area of freedom, security, and justice. The nature of those agencies is quite diverse. Research has investigated their origins and applied the principal-agent framework to understand why member states were ever willing to coordinate their police or border control cooperation. Some have also questioned the choice of this peculiar policy instrument (Wolff and Schout 2013), in particular, from a legitimacy perspective. If one adopts a Majonian interpretation, agencies should be of added value from an output legitimacy perspective. But many question whether accountability mechanisms are properly in place when it comes to input legitimacy. Frontex, in particular, has attracted attention from NGOs. Given the supposedly independent nature of agencies, many observers have criticized the way they have—as with Frontex—been instrumental in pursuing the pet projects of EU member states. This politicization is also highly visible in the choice of agencies as increasingly preferred modes of governance for JHA.

The choice of policy instruments is never neutral. While the creation of agencies was certainly favoured by member states to avoid supranational solutions proposed by the Commission (see, in the case of Frontex, Wolff 2008), it is today the preferred mode of governance of the EP. The latter has indeed gained scrutiny on those of instruments as it co-legislates on their creation and budget. Consequently, it contributes to the EP's quest for more institutional strength.

JHA agencies also provide operational coordination of the member states law enforcement agencies. This is the case for Europol, Eurojust, and Frontex for instance. The EASO was created in 2010[8] to develop 'practical cooperation among EU states on asylum', provide training, support for translation, and assist in relocation. Its mandate specifies, nonetheless, that the EASO should also show solidarity and support for 'EU states under particular pressure' and

---

[8] Regulation (EU) No. 439/2010 of the European Parliament and of the Council of 19 May 2010 establishing a European Asylum Support Office.

implement the Common European Asylum System. This will involve 'collect [ing] and exchanging information on best practices, drawing up an annual report on the asylum situation in the EU and adopting technical documents, such as guidelines and operating manuals, on the implementation of the Union's asylum instruments'. This confirms some supranational elements although in a weaker form as the newly found arrangements rely on networks, guidelines, manuals, and non-binding instruments.

Agencies are also assisting law enforcement actors pragmatically, while avoiding some constraints imposed by institutionalization and politicization. This operational dimension is visible through the 'operational' work of the above-mentioned agencies and reported in public documents. Both Europol and Frontex have been mandated to do risk analysis. In the field of Terrorism Europol publishes the EU Terrorism Situation and Trend Report and the annual Organised Crime Threat Assessment. Frontex publishes an Annual Risk Analysis every year related to border control, illegal border crossing and cross-border crime. This relies on quarterly reports. Operational outputs are also put forward in the annual reports of both agencies where 'success stories' are highlighted in the Frontex annual report and Europol's operational activities.

Agencies struggle, nonetheless, between politicization and de-politicization, therefore confirming hypothesis 5. In their original design, they were conceived as expert bodies that coordinate the work of the member states. Their creation, mandate, and operations have in fact been highly politicized. Management boards of JHA agencies have ended up being mini-Council formations, which poses a dilemma regarding de-politicization (Wolff and Schout 2013). Some socialization and evidence of a professional ethos are, nonetheless, emerging from this operationalization. Research has shown that knowledge-based network governance matters in JHA. The emergence of a European 'homeland security' culture is due to the presence of transnational actors who encourage integration 'by virtue of their technical expertise and shared norms as they attempt to persuade member states of their policy goals' (Cross 2007: 94). In her use of the concept of epistemic communities, Cross points to a new instance of the operationalization trend in JHA. The development of large IT databases or the use of surveillance technologies necessarily requires expertise, to be found in the networks that fall under the umbrella of JHA agencies. Agencies are also becoming important sources of information for MEPs who need to become experts on very complex technical issues.

This reliance on knowledge-based networks can also be found in the field of migration policy. Commission officials, and also national policy-makers, value knowledge and expertise. In a politically sensitive policy area, it is indeed a way to legitimize policy-making. This leads to the development of 'policy narratives', that rely on expert knowledge and which are 'deployed to legitimise particular actors or preferences rather than to enhance the cognitive plausibility of the narrative' (Boswell et al. 2011: 1). This confirms the fact that the choice of policy instruments, and in particular of agencies as instruments that favour the output legitimacy side of policy-making by remaining independent and fostering expertise, is not neutral. By removing issues from the political debate, agencies and policy networks help legitimize policy making and 'neutralize' the policy debate.

This can, however, be double-sided, as it tends to fuel the state of disequilibrium. Operational cooperation might yield tangible and rapid results such as the diminution of illegal migrants detected by Frontex on the Greek-Turkish borders. Those objectives respond to new public management goals and can be easily quantified. However, this operational cooperation is conducted by decentralized bodies that require intensive network coordination and peer-learning. As we have seen, these bodies are themselves increasingly directed by high-level institutions that deliberate informally, all of which lends credit to anti-immigrant domestic political discourse, which is very critical of this de-politicization of JHA policies.

6.4 JHA Politics and the State of Disequilibrium: the role of the European Parliament

The blurring of high and low politics, which is marked by the involvement of high-level bodies such as the European Council in the day-to-day management of JHA, nourishes the state of disequilibrium of the EU. In this sense hypotheses 4 and 5 are correlated in the case of JHA. National politicians are prompt to blame Frontex and the EU more generally for the dramatic situation of migrants dying at sea on the shores of Lampedusa rather than recognizing their own deficiencies (Wolff 2013). This section explores the role of the EP vis-à-vis this state of disequilibrium. Dynamics of politicization counterbalance the professionalization of MEPs taking place through informal early agreement.

Since the Lisbon Treaty, JHA has been subjected to a high level of politicization and left/right polarization. Politicization widens the circle of actors involved in the deliberations and, by the same token, its contestation (Wolff and Mounier 2012: 317). Unlike CFSP, the EP has been a key player in JHA international negotiations through its right of assent on the Passenger Name Records (PNR), Society for Worldwide Interbank Financial Telecommunication (SWIFT), and the Anti-Counterfeiting Trade Agreement (ACTA) dossiers. This has given rise to highly prominent public debates that led the European Council and the Commission to reconsider their agreements with third countries.

Also, over the years, evidence shows that the LIBE Committee has become more polarized. A report analysing MEPs' votes after Lisbon notes 'increased competition between groups on the centre-left and groups on the centre-right . . . in some policy areas, such as civil liberties, the environment, development and gender equality' (VoteWatch 2011: 15). This is calculated by 'the per cent of times EPP [European People's Party] and S&D [Progressive Alliance of Socialists and Democrats] voted against each other out of the total number of votes cast in each policy area'. For the LIBE Committee it amounts to 50 per cent, which is comparable to the development with 60 per cent. This is much more than, for instance, what happened in a Committee like Budgetary Control with 19 per cent (VoteWatch 2011: 15). Analysing the voting patterns between July 2009 and the December 2010 plenary, they found that a coalition of the centre-left parties, the European United Left–Nordic Green Left (GUE/NGL), the Greens/European Free Alliance (Greens/EFA), the S&D, and the Alliance of Liberals and Democrats for Europe (ALDE) has been particularly successful. It challenges the traditional 'grand coalition' of the S&D, ALDE, and EPP that has only obtained 40 per cent of the total votes cast during this period (VoteWatch 2011: 7).

Thus when the EP legislates on JHA matters, it is acting increasingly as a traditional representative assembly, on salient issues of concerns for citizens. This trend could prove to play against anti-immigrants and the Euro-sceptic movement, and thus to address the deficiencies of the state of disequilibrium highlighted by new intergovernmentalism.

This is, nonetheless, a long-term effort and the short-termism of politicians and eagerness of the EP to gain institutional strength might undermine it. Indeed, if EU member states have been delegating increasing competences to the EP, inter-institutional battles still arise where 'member governments calculate the likely consequences of delegation to the EP, and refrain from delegating powers in areas where they perceive that the EP would move political outcomes away from their collective preferences' (Pollack 2003: 260). Similarly, the EP is much more united when it comes to defending its own institutional interest vis-à-vis the Council of Ministers than when it legislates and is organized around partisan lines.

A case in point occurred in the summer of 2012 when the EP decided to block five major JHA dossiers after the Council of Ministers tried to by-pass the co-decision right of the EP. Following the Arab Spring, member states resorting to anti-immigrant discourses took several initiatives that undermined the freedom of movement in Europe. The most prominent example was the temporary closure of the Vintimille border with Italy by the French government, which prompted the 2011 Franco-Italian pact calling upon the Commission to revise the Schengen Convention and in particular the reintroduction of border controls by member states (normally undertaken only under exceptional circumstances). Other examples include the reintro-duction of internal border controls on the Danish–German border and on the border between the Netherlands and Belgium. Consequently, the Council of Ministers under the Danish presidency proposed to allow more freedom for member states to reintroduce internal border controls. It did so, however, by changing the legal basis of the evaluation mechanism of the Schengen con-vention (Council of the European Union, 2013) from co-decision to only informing the EP as specified in article 70 TFEU.[9] In retaliation, the EP blocked negotiations over some major JHA dossiers in the summer of 2012: the Schen-gen governance legislation, the European Investigation Order, the Internal Security aspects of the 2013 Budget, and a proposal on combating attacks against information systems in judicial cooperation. Beyond playing the good cop in front of a nationally oriented Council, this 'Schengen Affair' was also the opportunity for confronting the Council, building internal institutional unity, and reasserting the EP's prerogatives. This is even more the case where issues regarding evaluation and monitoring or agenda-setting are at stake. Those functions were already at stake before Lisbon (Pollack 2003) and con-tinue to lend some credit to the new intergovernmentalism claims on the paradoxes of Lisbon.

Conclusions

While at first sight, JHA integration in the post-Maastricht era seems to be a difficult case for new intergovernmentalism, this chapter has shown that this trend coexists with other traditional patterns of EU integration. High-level deliberation and de-politicization constitute the core trends of JHA post-Maastricht integration. The Council of Ministers and the European Council remain central to agenda-shaping through practices such as the 'European Pacts' or the extensive use of informal early agreements. The relevant dis-courses and the use of JHA agencies as favourite policy instruments contribute to an operationalization trend that blurs the distinction between high and low politics.

Given the peculiar nature of JHA, which touches upon core sovereign issues as well as citizens' mobility and civil rights, the state of disequilibrium has a

---

[9] Article 70 TFEU specifies: 'Without prejudice to Articles 258, 259 and 260, the Council may, on a proposal from the Commission, adopt measures laying down the arrangements whereby Member States, in collaboration with the Commission, conduct objective and impartial evaluation of the implementation of the Union policies referred to in this Title by Member States' authorities, in particular in order to facilitate full application of the principle of mutual recognition. The European Parliament and national Parliaments shall be informed of the content and results of the evaluation.'

particular resonance in the light of the rise of Euro-sceptic and anti-immigrant movements. High-level deliberation is increasingly confronted with an intense politicization whereby citizens and NGOs are contesting JHA integration. In parallel, the EP and the LIBE Committee seem to be moving towards a more salient left/right cleavage, especially since the entry into force of the Lisbon Treaty.

The state of disequilibrium fuelled by the willingness of policy-makers to provide concrete deliverables, in the sense of Majone's 'Regulatory Europe' argument, poses issues of legitimacy. First, by focusing too much on the output legitimacy, there is a risk of losing any connection with citizens. The number of detections of illegal migrants has not led to social legitimacy and appropriateness for the various stakeholders including civil society. Moreover, the output legitimacy dimension in JHA is subject to competition between EU institutions and governments, with a risk of participating in the rise of the extreme-right and anti-immigrant movements. Politicization of JHA could be a way to overcome this entrapment and further research would need to investigate the interaction between the politicization and operationalization trends of JHA. This would also help the thinking about the sustainability of the new intergovernmentalism trend in the long run.

7

The New Intergovernmentalism in Financial Regulation and European Banking Union

David Howarth and Lucia Quaglia

In the post-Maastricht period, financial market integration gained momentum in the European Union (EU).[1] From the late 1990s, the completion of the single financial market became a priority for the EU and its member states. To this end, no fewer than 42 EU legislative measures were adopted between 2002 and 2007. The global financial crisis that began in late 2007 prompted a revision of financial services regulation in the EU. From 2010 onwards, the banking crisis was followed by the sovereign debt crisis in the euro area, which, among other consequences, increased the fragmentation of the single financial market. The EU's main response was the proposal for Banking Union.

This chapter asks whether the new type of intergovernmentalism outlined in chapter 1 of this volume has emerged in financial services regulation and Banking Union. It is argued that in the post-Maastricht period, financial market policy was an area of intense activism in the EU, as demonstrated by the strides towards the completion of the single financial market (1999–2008) and the attempts to re-regulate it after the global financial crisis (post 2008). Both the pre-crisis regulatory push on financial market integration and the post-crisis reinforcement of regulation were influenced by the different preferences of the member states, which were mainly rooted in domestic political economy—that is, the configuration of their national financial sector. In this context, the reluctance to delegate regulatory and supervisory power to supranational institutions—which led to the creation of the so-called Lamfalussy committees of national supervisors and their subsequent transformation into authorities ('EU bodies') after the crisis—was in line with the new

[1] Lucia Quaglia wishes to acknowledge the financial support from the European Research Council (Grant 204398 FINGOVEU) and the British Academy (SG 120191).

intergovernmentalism. It confirmed hypothesis 3: when delegation occurs, it involves the creation of *de novo* bodies. Moreover, neither pre-crisis nor post-crisis supranational institutions sought an ever closer union in finance, as postulated by hypothesis 2: supranational institutions are not hard-wired to seek ever closer union.

In the debate on European Banking Union the traditional intergovernmental debate on fiscal transfer in the EU—which juxtaposed Germany with other member states, such as France and Italy, in the negotiations of the Maastricht Treaty—resurfaced. However, unlike in the making of Economic and Monetary Union (EMU), the European Commission was not the 'engine' of Banking Union, confirming hypothesis 2. In Banking Union, the new bodies to which supervision and resolution have been delegated retain an intergovernmental imprint, especially in the case of resolution (hypothesis 3). Finally, it is important to note that European Banking Union was designed to complete the 'incomplete' EMU agreed at Maastricht and address the 'inconsistent quartet' that ensued from the state of disequilibrium in the euro area. However the European Banking Union 'light' eventually agreed under German insistence casts doubts on the sustainability of the single currency.

7.1 Post-Maastricht Financial Regulation in the EU

Prior to the mid-1990s, financial services legislation in the EU had been a particularly contested policy area among member states. Indeed, Story and Walter (1997) explained delayed and limited financial market integration as the result of a 'battle of the systems'. Progress on several pieces of EU financial legislation—such as directives on capital adequacy, investment services, Undertakings for Collective Investment in Transferable Securities (UCITS) and accounting—had been slow and painstaking. In some cases (notably on accounting standards), progress had been blocked entirely and by the mid-1990s, the single market in financial services remained highly fragmented.

In the run-up to the launch of the single currency in 1999 and during EMU's first decade, the pace of financial market integration quickened and financial services legislation underwent significant changes in the EU. From the early 2000s onwards, progress in pushing forward the single financial market was achieved through a set of legislative measures outlined in the Financial Services Action Plan (FSAP) (Commission 1999). The plan was proposed by the Commission and endorsed by the member states. Previously, financial services legislation in the EU had been mostly based on minimum harmonization, mutual recognition, and national supervision. It had mainly dealt with banking. By contrast, the legislative measures that ensued from the FSAP mostly aimed at maximum harmonization and focused primarily on securities markets and insurance (Ferran 2004).

The adoption of 42 pieces of financial legislation between 2001 and 2007 was facilitated by the so-called Lamfalussy reform (Mügge 2006; Quaglia 2007). In July 2000, the Economic and Financial Affairs (Ecofin) Council appointed a Committee of Wise Men, chaired by Alexander Lamfalussy. The mandate given to the Lamfalussy Committee was to put forward proposals for the reform of financial regulation and supervision in the EU. It was clearly stated that prudential supervision should not be discussed by the Committee because this was a sensitive issue for the member states, which were keen to retain it at the national level. In the preparation of the report, the Wise Men considered the proposal to create a single European regulator for the financial sector, but quickly concluded that creating such an agency would require years of intergovernmental negotiations, and that such an agency, if it were created, would be hampered by the continuing diversity of national regulations in the area (Committee of Wise Men 2000: 26). The Lamfalussy report was subsequently endorsed by the Ecofin Council.

The Lamfalussy reform architecture was articulated across multiple institutional levels. At level one, the European Parliament (EP) and the Council of Ministers co-decided framework legislation (mainly directives) proposed by the Commission. At level two, the implementing measures (generally directives, less frequently regulations) of the framework legislation were adopted by the Commission through the comitology process, which involved the so-called level two committees of member state representatives. At level three, the committees of national regulators (the level three committees) advised the Commission on the adoption of level one and level two measures and adopted level three measures, such as non-legally binding standards and guidelines (Coen and Thatcher 2008; Quaglia 2008). This delegation of power to *de novo* bodies fits well with the account provided by the new intergovernmentalism (hypothesis 3). There was never any discussion of delegating supervisory functions to the Commission, which neither had supervisory expertise, nor the capabilities to develop it.

Some authors (Posner 2005; Jabko 2006) have pointed out the pace-setting role of the Commission in the completion of the single financial market, with the support of an increasingly powerful transnational financial industry (Van Apeldoorn 2002; Bieling 2003; Mügge 2010). Other authors (Quaglia 2010a, b) have argued that two main coalitions of member states competed in the regulatory process: the market-making coalition, led by the UK, and the market-shaping coalition, led by France and Germany. Overall, the former coalition was more influential than the latter and most of the pre-crisis financial services legislation in the EU was indeed market-making, designed to promote financial services liberalization and increase the competitiveness of the EU financial industry or at least, as Mügge (2010) argues, the most transnational part of it. However, these coalitions were far from homogenous: each member state had its own distinctive preferences, rooted in the distinctive features of the national financial system and its link to the real economy.

In the post-1999 period, especially after the FSAP, financial services regulation in the EU was much more consensual than in the past (Posner and Veron 2010), as demonstrated by the fact that no fewer than 42 new legislative measures were adopted in less than six years and comitology was introduced in the regulatory process. This is not to say that post-1999 financial services regulation was harmonious and conflict free. Indeed, the negotiation of certain pieces of financial services legislation was controversial, as in the case of the Markets for Financial Instruments directive. However, even in these instances, agreement was reached relatively quickly, because of the shared overall objective to complete the single financial market.

In the aftermath of the global financial crisis, a host of new financial regulation was adopted by the EU,[2] suggesting that the regulatory process remained broadly consensual. New EU legislation was issued on rating agencies, alternative investment fund managers, over the counter derivatives as well as capital requirements and liquidity rules for banks. The traditional Community process was followed and, as in the pre-crisis period, the main line of division tended to fall between the market-shaping coalition on one side and the market-making coalition and affected industry on the other. Although, with some notable exceptions, the new or amended rules were generally resisted by the UK, Ireland, Luxembourg, the Nordic countries, and the financial industries directly affected by the new provisions. The main argument used by the coalition eager to tone down the EU's regulatory response was that the proposed rules were overly prescriptive, intrusive and potentially protectionist.[3] The UK stressed the need to retain 'open, global markets' (Darling 2009).

The new or revised rules, as well as the reshaped institutional framework post crisis (discussed below) were actively sponsored, or at least strongly supported, by France, Germany, Italy, Spain, and other members of the market-shaping coalition, as illustrated by national government responses to the Commission's consultation, newspaper accounts and interviews with policymakers. The new EU measures were seen as necessary to safeguard financial stability and protect investors. Some of these rules, such as those concerning

---

[2] Several special issues and edited volumes dedicated to financial regulation were published in the aftermath of the crisis. See for example, *Review of International Political Economy* (2012) 19, 4; *New Political Economy* (2010) 15, 1; *Journal of Common Market Studies* (2009) 47, 5; Helleiner, Pagliari, and Zimmerman (2010); Mayntz (2012); Hardie and Howarth (2013); Moschella and Tsingou (2013).

[3] See: *Financial Times*, 7 July 2009, 14 July 2009, 16 June 2009, 4 June 2009.

hedge fund managers, credit rating agencies, over the counter derivatives, also embodied the deeply ingrained Continental dislike of 'casino capitalism' (Strange 1997), which was seen as serving the fortunes of the City of London.[4] The market-shaping coalition was less preoccupied than the UK government with regard to potential international regulatory arbitrage (Quaglia 2010a, 2010b; Zimmerman 2010).

A somewhat special case was the international Basel III Accord on capital and liquidity requirements for banks (BCBS 2010a, 2010b). As in the case of Basel I and II, after the accord was agreed internationally, it was to be incorporated into EU legislation. To this end, in July 2011, the Commission adopted a legislative package designed to replace the Capital Requirements Directive (CRD) III with a directive that governs the access to deposit-taking activities (Commission 2011a) and a regulation that establishes prudential requirements for credit institutions (Commission 2011b)—this package is often referred to as the CRD IV. Following its approval, the proposed directive would have to be transposed in the member states in a way suitable to their own national environment.[5] On Basel III and the CRD IV, the 'traditional' positions of the competing coalitions were inverted. In a nutshell, the UK authorities called for 'tougher' rules that required a more restrictive definition of what counts as capital, higher capital requirements, and liquidity rules. France and Germany advocated a broader definition of what counts as capital, a moderate increase of capital requirements, and non-compulsory liquidity rules (Howarth and Quaglia 2013a).

The global financial crisis revealed the weaknesses of existing macro-prudential oversight in the EU and the inadequacy of nationally based supervisory models in overseeing integrated financial markets with cross-border operators. In 2009, a group of high-level practitioners and financial experts, chaired by the former governor of the Banque de France, Jacques de Larosière, produced an eponymous report on the issue (de Larosière Group 2009). The report outlined the blueprint for the post-global financial crisis reform of the institutional framework for financial supervision in the EU. The report was endorsed by the member states and most of its recommendations were implemented.

The European Systemic Risk Board (ESRB) was established to monitor macro-prudential risks in the EU. The so-called level three Lamfalussy committees were transformed into independent EU bodies with legal personality, an increased budget and enhanced powers.[6] The newly created bodies, namely

---

[4] *Financial Times*, 30 April 2009.
[5] The CRD IV package was adopted by the Council and the EP in June 2013.
[6] It can also be noted that the legal basis of the authorities (114 TFEU) makes it easier for member states to assign them additional powers (through qualified majority voting in the Council, rather than unanimity).

the European Banking Authority (EBA), the European Insurance and Occupational Pension Authority (EIOPA) and the European Securities Markets Authority (ESMA), were charged with the tasks of coordinating the application of supervisory standards and promoting stronger cooperation between national supervisors.[7] The decision-making board of each of the authorities consists of officials coming from appropriate national supervisory authorities who serve as independent experts working to uphold collective EU interests—and not officially as national representatives. Other supranational institutions (the Commission and the ECB notably) and representatives of the other authorities only have observer status on the boards. While the Commission retains the power to intervene in the operation of the authorities in exceptional circumstances, the authorities enjoy considerable autonomy.

In the negotiations on these institutional reforms, there were concerns about giving the new authorities powers over national regulators and the possibility of supervising individual financial cross-border institutions—with the UK, Ireland, and Luxembourg the most reluctant (Buckley and Howarth 2010). The British government was particularly reluctant to grant decision-making powers to EU-level bodies, on the grounds that public funds to tackle banking crises came from national budgets. Prime Minister Gordon Brown secured a guarantee that the new supervisory system would not include powers to force national governments to bail out banks. That said, a number of other member states, including France and Germany, favoured the limited reform approach and were hesitant about transferring substantial power to the EU level (Buckley and Howarth 2010).

As postulated in chapter 1, the institutional design of the new authorities (the former Lamfalussy committees) reflected 'a clear reluctance on the part of member states to delegate politically sensitive functions to the Commission and a preference for innovative institutional arrangements in which national representatives dominate' (hypothesis 3). As in the case of the Lamfalussy reform, the possibility of delegating some of these functions to the Commission was never contemplated because the Commission was seen as lacking the necessary expertise and manpower. Moreover, national governments were eager to safeguard the competences of national supervisors in this field, at least until the proposal for European Banking Union was put forward. Finally, in neither the pre- nor the post-financial crisis period did supranational institutions, including the Commission, officially propose or push actively for an 'ever closer union' in the area of financial supervision (hypothesis 2).

---

[7] The Commission also proposed a directive amending the existing directives in the banking, securities and insurance sectors and a Council decision entrusting the ECB with specific tasks in the functioning of the ESRB.

7.2 The New Intergovernmentalism in the Push for Banking Union

The June 2012 European Council and Euro area summit agreed to deepen EMU creating 'Banking Union' (Euro Area Summit 2012).[8] The aim of proponents was to stabilize the national banking systems exposed directly to the sovereign debt crisis by breaking the dangerous link between the high and rising sovereign debt in the euro area peripheral member states and domestic banks, which had come to hold an increasing amount of this debt. At the same time, European Banking Union was an attempt to address the increasing fragmentation of financial markets in the EU, which was a consequence of the crisis (see Howarth and Quaglia 2013b for an overview).

The incomplete EMU agreed at Maastricht created a state of disequilibrium in the EU, to be precise in the euro area—as proposed in hypothesis 6 on the EU being in a state of disequilibrium. At the international level, Dirk Schoenmaker pointed out the 'financial trilemma' (2013; see also Schoenmaker and Wagner 2011) based on the interplay of financial stability, cross-border banking, and national financial policies, arguing that any two of the three objectives can be combined but not all three: one has to give. In EMU, there was a fourth element to be added to this trilemma, which became, what we label, an 'inconsistent quartet' (Howarth and Quaglia 2014). The single currency undermined national financial policies, because the function of lender of last resort could no longer be performed at the national level. Moreover, national resolution powers were constrained by euro area fiscal rules.

Consequently, the safeguard of financial stability was outside the control of the national authorities and could only be achieved at the euro area level. For these reasons, euro area member state governments agreed (in some cases with great reluctance) to move to Banking Union. European Banking Union is to replace the third element of Schoenmaker's trilemma, namely national financial policies which include regulation, supervision, and resolution. The European Council proposal of June 2012 had four elements: an EU deposit guarantee scheme; a Single Supervisory Mechanism (SSM) for banks; a Single Resolution Mechanism (SRM) and a common fiscal backstop for struggling banks—the latter two bolstered by an EU legislative framework for bank recovery and resolution. The fifth element of European Banking Union was the so-called single rule book (notably, financial regulation and competition policy rules) which was to apply to all EU member states.

The Deposit Guarantee Scheme (DGS) Directive and the Bank Recovery and Resolution (BRR) Directive were legislative proposals put forward by the

---

[8] On Banking Union, see Schoenmaker (2012, 2013), Schoenmaker and Wagner (2011), Veron and Wolff (2012), and Wyplosz (2012).

Commission prior to the proposal for Banking Union.[9] A DGS directive, dating back to 1994, set the minimum level of deposit protection schemes in the EU at €20,000 per depositor. The directive was based on minimum harmonization, hence national deposit guarantee schemes continued to differ in several important respects, such as the definition of eligible deposits, the level of cover, the types of funding mechanism, and the calculation of member contributions.

In July 2010, the Commission (2010b: 5) put forward a legislative proposal to amend the DGS directive with a view to promoting the 'harmonization and simplification of protected deposits, a faster pay-out, and an improved financing of schemes'. The proposal aimed to establish a network of guarantee schemes as a first step towards a 'pan-European deposit guarantee scheme' to cover all European Union-based banks (Commission 2010b: 5). Such a pan-European scheme, however, presupposed full harmonization of national schemes and could only enter into force after a minimum fund of 1.5 per cent of eligible bank deposits had been reached in each of the member states.

One of the most contentious provisions in the proposed directive was the establishment of a mandatory mutual borrowing facility, whereby if a national deposit guarantee scheme is depleted, it can borrow from another national fund. Several member states tried to remove this provision while discussing the proposed directive in the Council of Ministers.[10] The mutual borrowing facility could have been the first step towards a pan-EU deposit guarantee scheme, which was even more controversial. Indeed, in the preparation of the directive, the Commission considered setting up a single pan-European scheme. However, it soon realized that there were complicated legal issues that needed to be examined (Commission 2010b) and, therefore, the idea of a pan-European scheme was shelved by the Commission for the time being. In this case, the Commission did not pursue an ever closer union, in line with one of the hypotheses of the new intergovernmentalism (hypothesis 2). Ultimately, though, the problem was political—it would have meant fiscal transfers (of taxpayers' money) among the member states. The creation of a pan-European scheme would have implied pooling national sovereignty to an extent unacceptable to most of the member states in 2010.

Member states were principally divided on the pan-European scheme between those that feared that they would be net contributors to the scheme, notably Germany, and those facing dangerous instability in their banking systems, notably Spain and Ireland, and which were more likely to resort to

---

[9] The principal logic behind the establishment of national guarantee schemes—which reimburse part of the amount of deposits to clients of banks that have failed—is to prevent a 'bank run', that is panic withdrawals of customer deposits from a bank because of a fear of collapse.

[10] Interviews, Brussels, July 2012.

the scheme. Moreover, Germany had a high level of depositor protection and a rather complex system of public and private deposit guarantee schemes. The creation of an EU-wide scheme brought to the forefront the old debate, dating back to the Maastricht Treaty, of 'fiscal union' or 'transfer union', whereby some states were set to be net beneficiaries of the transfers and others net contributors.

After prolonged consultations, the Commission put forward a formal legislative proposal for a directive on bank recovery and resolution[11] in June 2012 (Commission 2012d). The proposed directive had the same scope of application as the CRD IV (hence, credit institutions and certain investment firms). It distinguished between powers of 'prevention', 'early intervention', and 'resolution'. The harmonized resolution tools and powers outlined in the directive were designed to ensure that national authorities in all member states had a common toolkit and roadmap to manage the failure of banks. Among the tools considered, there was a bail-in tool, whereby banks would be recapitalized with shareholders' stakes wiped out or diluted, and creditors would have their claims reduced or converted into shares. Resolution colleges were to be established under the leadership of the group resolution authority and with the participation of the EBA, which was to act as binding mediator if necessary (Commission 2012d and 2012e).

The legislation envisaged the creation of resolution funding, which would raise contributions from banks proportionate to their liabilities and risk profiles and would not be used to bail out banks. There was a link between this piece of legislation and the amendment to the DGS directive, proposed by the Commission in 2010, which was to provide funding for the protection of retail depositors. Member states would be allowed to merge these two funds, provided that the scheme had enough funding to repay depositors in case of failure (Commission 2012d and 2012e).

The Commission noted that ideally, a single pan-European fund should be established with a pan-European resolution authority to manage its disbursal, but the absence of a single European banking supervisor and insolvency regime would make this unworkable.[12] Hence, the Commission backed down from proposing a single fund. In both this case and that of the DGS Directive, the Commission did not act as an engine of integration (hypothesis 2). In both cases, the obstacles to these far-reaching changes were ultimately political, the main line of division running between potential net contributors and net beneficiaries of these schemes.

[11] 'Bank resolution' is the organization of an orderly failure, which maintains the continuity of banking service. It is an alternative or complementary mechanism to deposit guarantee schemes in the event of bank failure.
[12] See: <http://europa.eu/rapid/pressReleasesAction.do?reference=MEMO/12/416&format=HTML&aged=0&language=EN&guiLanguage=en>.

Unlike the other aforementioned components of Banking Union, the SSM applies only to the euro area member states and to the non-euro area member states that decide to join Banking Union. In the SSM, responsibility for banking supervision is assigned to the ECB and national competent authorities working collectively in one system. During the negotiations on the SSM, there were two main areas of disagreement among member states: first, the scope of ECB supervision, in particular whether the ECB should directly supervise all euro-area-based banks (plus the banks based in opt-in countries) or only the main (cross-border) banks—and the definition of the threshold between 'significant' and 'less significant' banks; and, second, the relationship between the SSM and non-euro area member states, in particular those that chose not to opt in.

The Germans opposed a broad scope for ECB supervision. In particular, they resisted the ECB's supervision of the country's public Landesbanks and savings banks (Sparkassen). These banks were seen as having a 'public' function in Germany with strong ties to local and regional governments and traditionally reliant on the Länder for financial backing (Hardie and Howarth 2013). The French government expressed concern over the unequal treatment of member states, given that its banking system was dominated by five very large institutions that would all end up being directly supervised by the ECB.[13] Yet, while the extent of the delegation of supervisory power to the ECB was a controversial issue for the member states, different positions were not an insurmountable obstacle to a final agreement.

Over the years prior to the launch of the European Banking Union debate, some senior ECB officials (for example, Tommaso Padoa-Schioppa) expressed support for the ECB to assume control over supervisory functions (Howarth and Loedel 2005; see also chapter 13 in this volume). However, this was never previously an official ECB policy. Nonetheless, the ECB endorsed the Commission's initial September 2012 proposal on the SSM of allocating all supervisory competences to the ECB, regardless of the size of banks. President Mario Draghi made clear that being an effective supervisor included oversight of all 6,000 banks to ensure a level playing field.[14] But in several speeches he also reiterated that day-to-day tasks would remain with national supervisors (see for example, ECB 2012).

In the end, the agreement reached at the December 2012 European Council foresaw that the ECB would be 'responsible for the overall effective functioning of the SSM' and would have 'direct oversight of the euro area banks' (European Council 2012: 2). This supervision however would be 'differentiated' and the ECB would carry it out in 'close cooperation with national

---

[13] See *Financial Times*, 14 November 2012.   [14] See *Financial Times*, 8 November 2012.

supervisory authorities'. Direct ECB supervision was to cover those banks with assets exceeding €30 billion or those with assets representing at least 20 per cent of their home country's annual GDP. The agreement permits the ECB to step in, if necessary, and supervise any of the 6,000 banks in the euro area to bring about the eventual restructuring or closure of banks faced with insurmountable difficulties. In this instance, supervisory functions were delegated to a supranational institution, the ECB, which partly contradicts the third hypothesis of the new intergovernmentalism. It is, however, noteworthy that the Supervisory Board of the SSM (in operation from January 2014) consists principally of representatives from national competent authorities (currently 19 out of 24 Board members). This national presence is similar to that in the Governing Council of the ECB—where 18 of the 24 members are governors of national central banks. There is a permanent cap of 18 Governing Council members from the member states, with the introduction of a rotation system in January 2015 when the number of euro area member states exceeded 18 for the first time. The Supervisory Board has, as of April 2015, 19 representatives from National Competent Authorities (NCAs), a number that will rise as the number of participating member states expands. However, in both the Supervisory Board and the Governing Council, national officials serve officially (if not necessarily in practice) in an *ad personam* capacity as independent experts and are not to take instruction from governments or other bodies in the pursuit of their objectives.

The ECB Governing Council retains formal decision-making power, while the Supervisory Board—which is not a legal entity—possesses drafting power and executes tasks on behalf of the ECB. The maintenance of a 'Chinese wall' between the ECB's prudential and monetary policy-making was a significant legal concern, given the ECB's monetary policy mandate—to be driven primarily by the goal of price stability—and a major preoccupation for several member states, notably Germany, which feared the dilution of the central bank's monetary policy focus in its pursuit of other objectives. The assumption of the institutional compromise involving the Governing Council and the Supervisory Board is that the intervention of the former will be limited and the policy-making autonomy of the latter respected.

As for the relationship with non-euro area members, some euro-outsiders were interested in participating in the SSM and therefore opposed the regulation proposed by the Commission in September 2012, which placed the ECB at the centre of the mechanism and equated SSM membership with euro area membership. The European Council eventually decided that non-euro area member states could opt into the SSM through the establishment of a 'close cooperation agreement' and that 'opt in' countries could sit on the new ECB supervisory board with equal voting powers but not on the decision-making

Governing Council.[15] Initially, the majority of non-euro area member states either signalled clearly their intention to enter European Banking Union or adopted a 'wait and see' policy.

The British government had no intention of joining the SSM. Hence, its main priority in the establishment of European Banking Union was to avoid a potential euro area block within the single financial market. Crucially, the British feared the adoption of subsequent financial legislation that would be detrimental to the British financial sector. They also feared that the operation of the EBA would be heavily influenced by euro area member states. Hence, the British demanded an EBA voting reform, whereby any decision by the Authority should be approved by a minimum number of member states outside the European Banking Union and thus, effectively, by a 'double majority' of member states inside and outside the Banking Union. The outcome of the EU negotiations was a compromise involving the creation of a double-majority system until the number of non-Banking Union member states dwindled to fewer than four. The reform thus creates the strong probability of an over-representation of non-Banking Union member states in EBA policy-making. The reform also demonstrates the intergovernmental character of the EBA, despite legal provisions ensuring the independence of national supervisory authorities sitting on the authority's board.

The proposal and creation of the SRM in 2013–14 goes beyond the timeframe of the analysis in this volume. However, its creation was one of the five elements of European Banking Union outlined in the June 2012 agreement. The outcome can be examined briefly here because it was a messy compromise that nonetheless embedded core features of the new intergovernmentalism. In July 2013, the Commission proposed the establishment of a SRM (Commission 2013), designed to complement the SSM. The Commission's draft regulation envisaged the establishment of a Single Resolution Board, consisting of representatives from the ECB, the Commission, and the national resolution authorities of the member states where the bank has its headquarters as well as branches and/or subsidiaries. A Single Bank Resolution Fund was to be set up under the control of the Board to provide financial support during the restructuring process.[16] Banks would be required to contribute to the Fund.

The draft regulation gave the ultimate decision-making power to the Commission, which would decide whether and when to place a bank into resolution and would set out a framework for the use of resolution tools and the Fund. This would have increased the power of the Commission on bank resolution at the expense of the member states, seemingly contradicting the

---

[15] See *EUobserver*, 29 November 2012.
[16] See: <http://europa.eu/rapid/press-release_IP-13-674_en.htm>.

hypothesis of the new intergovernmentalism that supranational institutions are not hard-wired for the pursuit of ever closer union (hypothesis 2). Yet, the Commission called for a kind of quasi delegation with responsibility for the Single Resolution Board shared between the ECB, the Commission, and national representatives. As such, the Commission proposed the creation of a new body to which to delegate competences, confirming the third hypothesis of the new intergovernmentalism.

Why did the Commission not bid for more power in this field? During the consultation stage in the Commission's preparation of the proposal, it became clear that some member states, first and foremost Germany, would not have accepted the delegation of resolution power to the Commission. Even the hybrid solution eventually put forward by the Commission was not acceptable to Germany, which challenged this proposal on legal grounds, arguing that the Commission had overstepped its authority and that a treaty change was required for such a far-reaching reform.[17]

Beyond the legal argument, there was a financial and ultimately political argument, as with other elements of European Banking Union involving financial assistance. German policy-makers feared that their country would be the main contributor to the Single Resolution Fund and that the Commission would take decisions that might have fiscal implications for the member states. Should the Fund not have enough financial resources to intervene, national governments (and ultimately taxpayers) would have to step in.

In the run-up to the decisive Ecofin meeting in December 2013, Dutch policy-makers floated the idea of splitting the SRM proposal into two parts, to be discussed in parallel negotiations: one part concerned the scope and decision-making mechanism of the SRM, the other part concerned the Single Resolution Fund.[18] With reference to the Fund, a compromise solution proposed by Dutch policy-makers was a system whereby the resolution fund of the bank's home state would be used before other member states' funds were utilized. On 18 December 2013, an agreement was eventually reached in the Council of Ministers on the draft regulation on the SRM.[19] In addition, a decision adopted by euro area member states committed them to negotiate an intergovernmental agreement on the functioning of the Single Resolution Fund by March 2014. With reference to the decision-making process on resolution, the main change advocated by Germany had been that the Single Resolution Board was to be given the power to decide to place a bank into resolution and to decide upon the application of resolution tools and the use of the Single Resolution Fund.

---

[17] See *Wall Street Journal*, 10 July 2013.   [18] See *Bloomberg*, 10 December 2013.
[19] See: <http://www.consilium.europa.eu/uedocs/cms_data/docs/pressdata/en/ecofin/140190.pdf>.

The agreed SRM was to cover all banks in the participating member states. The Single Resolution Board would be responsible for the planning and resolution phases of cross-border banks and those directly supervised by the ECB, while national resolution authorities would be responsible for all other banks, as advocated by Germany. However, the Board would always be responsible if the resolution of a bank required access to the Single Resolution Fund, which in the case of Germany was unlikely. National resolution authorities would be responsible for executing bank resolution plans under the control of the Single Resolution Board.[20] Should a national authority not comply with a decision by the Board, the latter could address executive orders directly to the troubled bank. To guarantee member state budgetary sovereignty—a non-negotiable demand of the German government—the SRM could not require member states to provide extraordinary public support to any entity under resolution.[21]

The version of the regulation agreed in December 2013 created a Single Resolution Fund that would be financed by bank levies raised at the national level. However, the German government refused to include in the regulation the most sensitive elements of the SRM package, notably specific provisions on the transfer and pooling of member state funded compartments into a single mutualized fund. The Germans sought to eliminate EP's involvement on these matters and minimize the Commission's role.[22] The German government insisted upon subsequent intergovernmental agreement among participating member states to permit the transfer of national funds towards the Single Resolution Fund and the activation of the mutualization of the national compartments. The German government also insisted on a delay of ten years, during which the mutualization between national compartments would progressively increase.[23] Therefore, while during the first year the cost of resolving banks (after bail-in) would mainly come from the compartments of the member states where the banks are located, this share would gradually decrease as the contribution from other countries' compartments increased. The intergovernmental agreement also endorsed the use of the bail-in rules set by the BRR Directive in the SRM.

During the negotiations, the ECB president Mario Draghi at his hearing before the EP pointed out that: 'We should not create a Single Resolution Mechanism that is single in name only . . . I urge you and the Council to swiftly set up a robust Single Resolution Mechanism, for which three elements are essential in practice: a single system, a single authority, and a single

---

[20] See: <http://www.consilium.europa.eu/uedocs/cms_data/docs/pressdata/en/ecofin/140190.pdf>.
[21] Statement from the Commission after the agreement in the Council <http://europa.eu/rapid/press-release_MEMO-13-1186_en.htm?locale=en>.
[22] *European Voice*, 12 December 2013.
[23] See: <http://www.consilium.europa.eu/uedocs/cms_data/docs/pressdata/en/ecofin/140190.pdf>.

fund.'[24] The ECB also urged finance ministers to adopt an emergency proced- ure that would ensure resolution decisions could be taken within 24 hours. Like the ECB, Michel Barnier, the EU commissioner responsible for financial services, remained concerned about the ability of the SRM to take difficult decisions to close a bank quickly or secretly enough, arguing that, 'What we are building is a single system and not a multi-storey intergovernmental network.'[25] The EP unsuccessfully attempted to bring the elements of the December 2013 intergovernmental side-agreement into the regulation, win- ning only limited concessions on 20 March 2014 in the compromise with the Council of Ministers that decreased the period during which the national compartments would merge to eight years, increased the proportion of the Fund shared at an earlier stage, and marginally increased the role performed by the Commission in the Single Resolution Board—allowing the Council to reject resolution proposals only under certain conditions.[26] Although the Commission is to have a limited role in the SRM, member state governments retain their vetoes on mutualization and an important say on the use of resolution funds. The creation of the Board reflects the preference of member states to delegate powers to new bodies in which member states retain a presence (hypothesis 3 of new intergovernmentalism).

As for the common fiscal backstop, a link was established between European Banking Union and the European Stability Mechanism (ESM) in the event that temporary financial support was needed. The ESM is a new EU body— with no direct relationship to the Commission—established in September 2012 to replace the temporary European Financial Stability Facility (EFSF) (Gocaj and Meunier 2013). The members of its decision-making body are representatives of the member states. The mechanism has a lending capacity of €500 billion. Member states contributing to the ESM could apply for a bailout from the mechanism if they were in financial difficulty or if their financial sector needed to be recapitalized in order to restore financial stabil- ity. However, the ESM bailouts were to be based on strong conditionality and member states were required to sign a 'Memorandum of Understanding' which would highlight the reforms needed to be undertaken or fiscal consoli- dation implemented in order to restore financial stability. The Commission and several member states proposed that the ESM be used to support failing banks directly (Howarth and Quaglia 2013b), a proposal initially resisted by the German government. The December 2012 European Council agreed that the SSM would allow the ESM to recapitalize banks in difficulties directly, subject to majority voting in both the ECB and the EBA.

---

[24] See *Bloomberg News*, 16 December 2013: <http://www.bloomberg.com/news/2013-12-16/ draghi-says-european-bank-resolution-plan-may-be-too-cumbersome.html>.
[25] See *Daily Telegraph*, 18 December 2013.   [26] See *Financial Times*, 20 March 2014.

Effectively, the Franco-German debate on European Banking Union paralleled long-standing debates on euro area governance and solutions to the euro area's sovereign debt crisis. The French sought support mechanisms; the Germans reinforced fiscal policy commitments (sustainable member state budgets). French support for European Banking Union stemmed from their limited success in convincing the Germans to agree to other measures to tackle the crisis and notably massive support mechanisms—what British Prime Minister David Cameron called the 'Big Bazooka'—able to purchase debt directly from euro area member state governments and engage in bank recapitalization.[27] European Banking Union was seen as a way to establish a kind of fiscal backstop to the euro area—via a lender of last resort style support for banks rather than governments per se. The underlying German and Northern European concern with the fiscal backstop, as with the resolution mechanism, was to be forced into a situation of having to contribute more funds to the ESM in order to bail out banks in other member states (Howarth and Quaglia 2013b).

Conclusions

From the mid-1990s to the mid-2000s, the EU made significant strides towards the construction of a single market in financial services. Following the international financial (banking) crisis, the EU engaged in a major overhaul of its financial services legislation. The massive bailout of banks in a range of EU member states during the crisis highlighted that there was a 'fiscal tag' attached to financial legislation—to be precise, to getting it wrong. The fiscal tag of unfit for purpose financial legislation was not clear prior to the crisis and was generally not present, at least not to the same extent, in other areas of the single market. Hence, post-crisis financial legislation acquired greater political salience than in the past—a crucial difference in comparison to other policy areas of the single market.

As a response to the sovereign debt crisis, EU policy-makers put forward proposals for Banking Union. This crisis was partly caused by the state of disequilibrium created by the incomplete EMU outlined in the Maastricht Treaty. The initial proposals for European Banking Union had far-reaching fiscal and, ultimately, political implications, which went to the heart of national sovereignty—a crucial difference in comparison with other policy areas of the single market. On the one hand, the Banking Union 'light' that was eventually agreed—largely because of German government reluctance—appeared to cast some doubt on the ability of the euro area to deal with the

---

[27] See *Financial Times*, 10 October 2011.

sovereign debt crisis and future banking crises. On the other hand, even in its much-watered down form—compared to the Commission's initial proposal—and despite concerns for moral hazard, the German government agreed for German tax payers and for German banks to contribute (eventually and under a host of conditions) to the recapitalization and resolution of banks based in other euro area member states.

Finally, it is worth reflecting on an interesting feature of the new intergovernmentalism in economic governance, namely the increasing use of intergovernmental agreements—such as the Treaty on Stability, Coordination and Governance (Fiscal Compact), the Treaty Establishing the European Stability Mechanism, and the side-agreement on the operation of the Single Resolution Fund. The logic behind these agreements varied but they all reflect a preference for flexibility not afforded by standard treaty change and the Community method. Most of the member states resorted to an intergovernmental treaty on the Fiscal Compact in December 2011 because they refused to give in to British government threats to veto EU treaty change unless it was given concessions on unrelated demands.[28]

In the case of the Treaty Establishing the European Stability Mechanism, member states preferred to avoid EU treaty change which would have required politically difficult referendums in a range of member states. In the case of the SRM, the member states reached an intergovernmental agreement in order to meet German government demands to maintain national veto power over the mutualization of national resolution funds. The German government was also concerned that enshrining some features of the Commission's proposed SRM into EU law would make German tax payers potentially liable for the debts of banks in other member states, and risk rejection by the German constitutional court.[29] These intergovernmental arrangements curtail the powers of the EP and Court of Justice of the EU in new areas of economic governance, and weaken the Commission's control.

---

[28] See *European Voice*, 12 December 2013.   [29] See *European Voice*, 12 December 2013.

Part III
EU Institutions in the Post-Maastricht Period

Part III

8

The European Council

The Centre of New Intergovernmentalism

Uwe Puetter

This chapter analyses the changing role of the European Council in the post-Maastricht era. It is argued that the European Council represents the political centre of the new intergovernmentalism. The top-level forum, which is composed of the heads of state and government of the member states, the President of the European Commission, the High Representative and, as a guest, the President of the European Parliament (EP), is the main engine of Europe's new intergovernmentalism. Since the early 1990s the European Council has worked both towards the enormous expansion of the European Union's (EU) policy acquis and, at the same time, has prevented the further expansion of Community method decision-making into these new areas of EU activity. Most importantly, the European Council has established itself as a pivotal institutional actor in the context of post-Maastricht integration. This central role of the European Council is a legacy of the Maastricht Treaty. The Treaty assigned the European Council the lead political role in developing economic governance, the Common Foreign and Security Policy (CFSP) and the field of justice and home affairs (JHA). Subsequently, the Amsterdam Treaty authorized the European Council to oversee the new domain of employment policy coordination. The Lisbon Treaty for the first time also formally acknowledged the enhanced role of the European Council in EU decision-making at a more general level by adding it to the list of the EU's main institutions to which it formally did not belong before. Moreover, the Lisbon Treaty enhanced the status of the European Council by creating the office of a full-time president.

It is notable that there is no reference to a formal role of the European Council in classic domains of Community method decision-making—neither at the time of the Single European Act nor in later treaties. Instead, the Maastricht Treaty and all subsequent treaties contain reference to a formal role for the European Council in all new major areas of EU activity which have since been created. The centrality of the European Council in post-Maastricht EU governance is not only the result of treaty changes but also a consequence of numerous acts of self-empowerment by the European Council itself. New policy initiatives were linked to novel oversight functions of the top-level decision-making forum—the Lisbon agenda being a prominent example.

These developments are quite remarkable as they constitute a substantial reconfiguration of the original so-called institutional triangle of Community method decision-making. This is not to say that the European Council itself is a post-Maastricht institution but that it acquired a role in EU decision-making which it originally did not have and which is characteristic for the period of integration to which this book refers to as the new intergovernmentalism. There is no doubt that the European Council's role in forging consensus around the general path of European integration and major political and institutional initiatives mattered already during the heydays of Community method expansion as Simon Bulmer and Wolfgang Wessels emphasized in the late 1980s (Bulmer and Wessels 1987). Yet, the European Council has evolved into an institution which is much more than a forum for building consensus about the medium- and long-term path of EU integration. In the post-Maastricht era it has become a pivotal decision-making institution which directly intervenes in governing the new areas of EU activity on a regular basis. Most importantly, the European Council embodies a particular style of decision-making that involves ongoing efforts at the highest political level to agree on common policy objectives and coordinated policy action among member state governments and, wherever it commands relevant resources, the Commission. This decision-making style gives a pivotal role to member state governments and, in particular, to their top representatives as the members of the European Council. Many of the policy issues which are at the heart of the new areas of EU activity have immediate consequences for domestic politics and concern areas which are particularly sensitive to sovereignty concerns, such as fiscal, diplomatic, and military issues. It is a characteristic feature of the post-Maastricht period that collective EU action in these domains has become possible but only under the condition of prior high-level political agreement among member state governments (see also Smith, chapter 5). As ultimate decision-making powers have not, or only to a very limited extent, been delegated to the supranational level in these domains, the European Council has become a pivotal source of political authority in post-Maastricht integration. It monopolizes policy initiative, oversees policy implementation and often acts as its own referee as the Court of Justice of the EU widely lacks sanctioning powers that can reverse European Council decisions within the contexts of the new areas of EU activity. The European Council also regularly instructs other EU institutions, notably the Commission and the Council of Ministers, to pursue particular policy objectives and implement decisions by the heads.

This chapter starts out by substantiating further the claim that the European Council represents the centre of the new intergovernmentalism, making reference to the expanding scope and changed focus of European Council activity in the post-Maastricht period. Subsequently, the chapter engages more closely with each of the six hypotheses presented in chapter 1 of this book, and provides related examples of European Council activity. The most important point in this regard is the institutionalization of deliberation and consensus-seeking as core elements of intergovernmental decision-making within the European Council (hypothesis 1). The rise of the new intergovern-mentalism implies profound changes in the way the forum operates. By referring to the analytical framework of deliberative intergovernmentalism, which was developed to study the proliferation of policy deliberation in high-level intergovernmental decision-making forums, examples of the internal reorganization, agenda-setting practices and intervention by the full-time European Council President are discussed so as to demonstrate how much the work of the European Council is geared towards consensus generation among member state governments. By referring to the contemporary practice of inter-institutional relations between the European Council and the Com-mission this chapter speaks to the argument that supranational institutions are not hard-wired to seek ever closer union on the basis of Community method integration (hypothesis 2). Instead, the Commission, notably under the leadership of its president, acts as a key partner of the European Council when it comes to the daily management of the new areas of EU activity. Equally, it is shown that the European Council promotes the proliferation of *de novo* bodies in EU decision-making (hypothesis 3). The forum repeatedly played a lead role in establishing *de novo* bodies, several of them were even created outside Community procedures. The European Financial Stability Facility (EFSF) and the European Stability Mechanism (ESM) are prominent examples in this regard. Looking at contemporary European Council activity also helps to detect that difficulties in preference formation become stand-alone inputs to European integration (hypothesis 4). The focus on constitut-ing the European Council as a forum for secretive top-level policy deliberation further reinforces the central role of the most senior national and EU-level executives and may therefore substantially reduce the relative influence of rival domestic actors. At the same time, the European Council has repeatedly diagnosed a legitimacy crisis which is facing EU policy-makers. In a further step this chapter interprets the fact that the European Council assumes a pivotal role in overseeing the day-to-day management of the new areas of

EU activity as evidence for the blurring of the difference between high and low politics in the post-Maastricht era (hypothesis 5). This chapter concludes on a more general note by highlighting that the centrality of the European Council in EU decision-making shows that the EU is in a state of disequilibrium (hypothesis 6). Key issues in EU policy-making prove to be politically so contested that they may even threaten the survival of individual member state governments, if not the integrity of the Union as a whole. Ad-hoc European Council intervention especially at times of economic and foreign policy crisis reveals this.

8.1 The Centre of New Intergovernmentalism

An important indicator for the new role of the European Council in EU decision-making is the increased frequency of European Council meetings.[1] At the time when the Maastricht Treaty was signed European Council meetings were scheduled to take place three times a year. Each meeting was an important event in the calendar of the rotating EU presidency and was carefully planned long in advance (see on the pre-Maastricht role of the European Council Bulmer and Wessels (1987)). From 1996 onwards the baseline figure of European Council meetings per year was four—two meetings during each presidency. Starting from the late 1990s the number of European Council meetings per year has repeatedly jumped up to five, six, and seven. The European Council was convened seven times in 2008—the year when the global economic and financial crisis started to hit the EU—and during the following two years. Not only were there various ad-hoc meetings, there were also meetings which were especially convened for the euro area members of the European Council—a format which later became referred to as the Euro Summit. In 2011 the total number of regular European Council meetings, ad-hoc meetings and euro area meetings reached eleven. In 2012 eight, and in 2013 seven meetings took place. French President François Hollande even advocated regular monthly meetings of the euro area heads of state and government in order to better adapt to the constant demand for short-term decision-making.[2]

---

[1] Unless noted otherwise data on European Council agenda composition as well as interview data relating to European Council activity and internal organization were first presented in Puetter (2014). The author would like to acknowledge research assistance by Adina Maricut in the context of the composition of the European Council agenda dataset. Research interviews were carried out on the basis of anonymity by the author and his research assistants in Brussels and member state capitals during the period of April 2009 and March 2013.

[2] François Hollande, interview with *Le Monde*, 17 October 2012.

Though formally the baseline number of regular European Council meetings has been kept to four per year, the European Council has frequently been convened for extraordinary meetings to address economic and foreign policy crisis situations or which have been dedicated to the discussion of topics of particular importance to the Union. This practice marked a change in the European Council standard working method which previously was tailored towards dealing with long-term decision-making and important personnel decisions throughout the EU decision-making cycle. From 1992 until 2013 there were 29 so-called extraordinary or special meetings convened with an advance notice of less than three months.[3] More than half of these extraordinary or special meetings were even announced less than one month in advance.

Yet, it is not only the significant increase in overall European Council activity in the post-Maastricht period which signals a new role of the European Council in EU decision-making. A closer look at the composition of the European Council agenda reveals that the increase in European Council activity is indeed closely linked to the development of the new areas of EU activity.[4] These policy domains clearly dominate the European Council agenda. It is the proliferation of new policy coordination processes in the new areas of EU activity which has triggered the overall increase in the frequency of European Council meetings from the second half of the 1990s onwards. More than 65 per cent of the overall number of European Council agenda items in the post-Maastricht period can be attributed to the new areas of EU activity. The relevance of these policy portfolios becomes even more apparent if the time dimension of European Council meetings is taken into account. Interview data suggests that already economic governance issues alone normally account for 50–65 per cent of the actual time spent on European Council meetings.[5]

Economic governance did not come to the European Council's attention only in the context of the economic crisis, which started to leave its imprint

---

[3] As official EU terminology is inconsistent in the way the terms 'extraordinary' and 'special' meeting are used European Council agenda data was coded by referring to regular meetings as those meetings which were announced more than three months in advance (normally before the beginning of a new semester) and extraordinary meetings which were announced less than three months in advance.

[4] European Council agenda data was analysed on the basis of European Council conclusions, Agence Europe reporting, other media sources and own interviews. Agenda items were coded and grouped according to so-called activity areas. These areas included 'economic governance', 'CFSP and CSDP', 'employment and social policy coordination', 'justice and home affairs', 'environment' and 'energy policy', as well as major institutional (Treaty reform and enlargement), personnel decisions, and budget and finally intervention in processes of legislative decision-making. The analysis covers all formal and informal European Council meetings as well as the so-called Euro Summit meetings and logs the quantitative occurrence of agenda items. For a detailed presentation of the findings see Puetter (2014: 68–110).

[5] Anonymous interview, 4 July 2011.

on European Council activity from the autumn of 2008 onwards. In fact, ever since the mid-1990s the European Council has devoted substantial attention to the economic governance portfolio. Notably it dealt with the negotiation, implementation, and adaptation of the Stability and Growth Pact (see Hodson 2011a). The European Council has regularly reviewed the work of the euro area finance ministers working in the Eurogroup and monitored the activities of the Economic and Financial Affairs Council (Ecofin). Foreign policy features as the other major agenda item, though considerably less time is spent on it than on economic governance issues. Especially since the outbreak of the economic and financial crisis in Europe in 2008, the heads are said to have spent less than 20 per cent of their average time on external affairs issues, though this is expected to change again.[6] In any case, there is a long list of special meetings of the European Council on foreign policy crisis situations and there have been almost no meetings since the mid-1990s during which both economic governance and foreign affairs issues were not debated at the occasion of European Council meetings. The importance of the foreign policy portfolio for the European Council was further highlighted by the Lisbon Treaty which made the High Representative a member of the European Council. Other major agenda items include social and employment policy coordination which prominently featured on the agenda during the second half of the 1990s and the first years of the new millennium. JHA is another new policy domain which occupies the European Council on a regular basis though this policy field sees less ad-hoc intervention by the heads. The focus is on providing guidance to the Commission and the Council of Ministers on developing JHA policy initiatives. The 1999 Tampere European Council may serve as an example in this regard as it marked the beginning of this particular practice of European Council intervention. Over time, most aspects of the JHA domain were brought under Community method governance, yet the lead role of the European Council in this new EU policy area was preserved and stipulated again by the Lisbon Treaty (see Wolff, chapter 6).

It is noteworthy that the crucial importance of the new areas of EU activity is not diminished by the attention the European Council devoted to the various EU enlargements which took place since the entering into force of the Maastricht Treaty, including the historic 2004 enlargement. Other important tasks of the European Council such as major personnel decisions and the periodic renegotiation of the EU budget account for only a small portion of the overall number of EU agenda items and typically occur only at longer intervals according to the multi-annual cycle of EU decision-making. The European Council also spends very little time interfering with EU legislative

---

[6] Anonymous interview, 8 July 2011.

decision-making in traditional areas of Community method integration—something which may appear to be counter-intuitive from the point of view of the 'old'—pre-Maastricht—intergovernmentalism (see chapters 1 and 15). An exception to this rule are legislative issues which are closely intertwined with the new areas of EU activity. The area of financial market regulation and supervision is a case in point. This policy field is closely tied to the economic governance portfolio but involves decision-making under the single market competences of the EU (see Howarth and Quaglia, chapter 7).

8.2 Institutional Change and Deliberative Intergovernmentalism

As outlined in chapter 1 the focus of post-Maastricht EU decision-making has shifted towards the new areas of EU activity. The integration paradox implies that the pursuit of more integration cannot (or only to a very limited extent) take place within the context of the classic Community method. Simultaneously, there is no lack of ambition to address contemporary policy challenges through collective policy responses. In this context intergovernmental policy coordination and the coordinated use of national and existing EU-level resources becomes a key issue in EU decision-making. Moreover, the inevitable problems and inefficiencies which are typically associated with this decision-making mode become an issue of collective concern in their own right. As delegation to an autonomous supranational political authority is not an option for solving collective action problems, the alteration and improvement of intergovernmental decision-making procedures becomes a key objective in processes of institutional engineering. This explains why the post-Maastricht integration paradox is invariably linked to the proliferation of policy deliberation as a behavioural norm which has become particularly salient in those areas of EU decision-making that involve intergovernmental policy coordination outside the framework of the classic Community method (hypothesis 1). Moreover, the disposition towards a particular practice of intergovernmental decision-making is not only detectable as an attitude of individual officials or political representatives but has become deeply embedded into the post-Maastricht institutional infrastructure for collective decision-making. Intergovernmental decision-making bodies such as the European Council, the Eurogroup, the Political and Security Committee, or the Economic and Financial Committee are geared towards facilitating consensus-seeking through their working methods and decision-making routines. The process of institutional change which involves the (re-)orientation of intergovernmental decision-making in this regard is at the core of the analytical framework of deliberative intergovernmentalism (Puetter 2012, 2014)

171

which was developed to study the work of key forums for collective decision-making within the new areas of EU activity. Deliberative intergovernmentalism holds that post-Maastricht intergovernmentalism is characterized by a particular quest for intergovernmental policy consensus. Deliberative intergovernmentalism thus conceptualizes an important dimension of the new intergovernmentalism as a broader integration dynamic.

It is anticipated that problems in collective decision-making translate into increased levels of policy deliberation rather than into an abandoning of collective decision-making processes. Moreover, the expectation is that with the expanding EU policy agenda this institutional dynamic is amplified and can be traced empirically with regard to changes in the operation of key EU decision-making institutions. Working methods are reviewed and altered. The shift of attention from legislative decision-making towards policy coordination implies that decision-making routines in the Council of Ministers—which is the key forum for the representation of member states in the EU legislative process—undergo a process of significant change. The proliferation of new senior expert committees, which are primarily or solely charged with supporting policy coordination within the Council of Ministers rather than legislative decision-making, is another key indicator for this process of institutional change (Juncos and Reynolds 2007; Grosche and Puetter 2008; Cross 2011).

The European Council is central to this process of institutional change. Processes of policy deliberation are not restricted to the sphere of technocratic circles of policy experts but proliferate up to the highest level of EU decision-making. Without the active political support of the heads many coordination portfolios are not viable. It is often only the heads of state and government who command the necessary political authority at home to forge common EU decisions. Even senior cabinet ministers may lack such authority. The existence of coalition governments in many EU member states further exacerbates this problem. All this implies that consensus formation within the European Council becomes a determining factor with regard to a wide range of policy decisions. Thus, the heads have not only been the key political force in suppressing the further expansion of the Community method; with the creation of the new areas of EU activity they also produced new demand for consensus formation around a wide range of policy issues within the European Council.

Indeed, there is clear evidence of a profound process of institutional change with regard to European Council decision-making. This notably concerns the European Council working method. Though the European Council, based on its original conception, has always been perceived as a forum for informal high-level debate (Bulmer and Wessels 1987; De Schoutheete 2002; Hayes-Renshaw and Wallace 2006) important modifications have been made to the

European Council's working method. First of all, the fact that the European Council is convened much more frequently than in the past implies that there is greater flexibility in agenda setting. It is a common practice now that the forum is reconvened without much waiting time to discuss an issue that could not be resolved. European Council meetings are focused on face-to-face debate among the heads. For a long time the European Council had operated as a forum composed of the heads of state and government and the foreign ministers of the EU member states—a formula that reflected the original mandate of the European Council to focus on the long-term development of the EU and institutional issues. The shift towards exclusive discussions among the heads became clear at the June 2002 Seville European Council, which issued a statement that European Council meetings were to be split into restricted discussions among the heads with a second part under the participation of the foreign ministers (European Council 2002). The Lisbon Treaty eventually abandoned reference to the foreign ministers altogether.

Moreover, the European Council maintains a high level of secrecy. It is not only the foreign ministers who are banned from attending the debates among the heads; advisers also are not allowed in the meeting room; neither can they listen in to the discussion via headphones. This is standard practice with regard to many Council meetings. There is only one part of a regular European Council session during which one senior diplomat from each member state is allowed to follow the debate in a different room. Substantial policy debates and negotiations where a frank exchange of views is required are now, by preference, scheduled to take place during the infamously long 'dinners' of the heads. This part of each European Council meeting takes place in complete isolation on the so-called 80th floor of the Justus Lipsius building in Brussels. Even the interpreters are banned from these meetings and work via headphones from a different room. Moreover, night-time hours are considered to be particularly conducive to debate as the heads are less distracted by urgent communications from their capitals which may reach them during the day.[7]

Since the late 1990s onwards, the European Council agenda has gradually been freed from broad discussions about future policy initiatives and has become more and more focused on debating concrete proposals for decision-making.[8] At the same time, it has been the practice to devote entire European Council meetings (or at least most of the meeting time) to a single policy issue or a set of connected policy portfolios, in order to focus political attention on a particular policy issue and reach agreement on a wider range of coordination

---

[7] Anonymous interview, 4 March 2013.
[8] The issue was also raised by a report on European Council and Council reform adopted by the Helsinki European Council in December 1999. Cf. European Council (1999), Annex III.

objectives. The special 1997 Luxembourg European Council on the employment situation in the EU marked the beginning of this particular practice. The spring meetings of the European Council which since the launch of the so-called Lisbon agenda have been dedicated to socio-economic governance issues constitute another example.

This process of institutional engineering was extended further with the introduction of the office of an elected full-time President of the European Council by the Lisbon Treaty. As the first office holder the former Belgian prime minister Herman Van Rompuy put particular emphasis on enhancing the consensus generation capacity of the European Council through further developing the internal organization of the forum and its working methods. Again, Van Rompuy's initiatives documented the focus of European Council decision-making on the new areas of EU activity as he declared it a priority of European Council activity to unite member state governments on issues related to economic governance and foreign affairs (Van Rompuy 2010). Contrary to expectations that the European Council President would mainly act as a spokesperson of the EU to external audiences Van Rompuy concentrated his activities towards consensus-building by acting as a facilitator for discussions among the heads, by engaging in bilateral diplomacy, and by using his agenda-setting powers to focus attention on important policy issues. For example, he scheduled regular orientation debates which were led without pressure to take a final decision to address issues of strategic importance for EU policy coordination and to explore member state positions.

8.3 The European Council and the European Commission

The European Council President also spends considerable time on maintaining inter-institutional relations with other EU bodies—notably the Commission, the EP, the European Central Bank (ECB) and Council formations which are active within the new areas of EU activity. It is worth considering especially the relationship with the Commission here (hypothesis 2). The Lisbon Treaty remains ambiguous about the precise division of labour between the new European Council President and the President of the Commission. Both represent different institutions but they have overlapping responsibilities both in relation to the external representation of the EU and with regard to their responsibility to coordinate member state activities. This set-up has led analysts to predict inter-institutional rivalries and conflicts between the two presidents (Wessels and Traguth 2010). Yet, this is not what happened, at least during the time of the Barroso and Van Rompuy tandem. The working relationship between the two presidents was described as functioning well and close coordination between the cabinets of the two presidents was established to allow the coordination of external representation obligations.[9] The practice of weekly meetings between the two presidents was introduced.

This confirms that the Commission took a pragmatic stance towards the expanding powers of the European Council which are clearly felt within the supranational institution.[10] Two particular aspects can be highlighted here, which further explain why the Commission did not engage in open inter-institutional conflict with the European Council about its expanding powers and preference for intergovernmental policy coordination and agreement. First, the President of the Commission is a crucial member of the European Council. Not only does the Commission President owe his or her appointment to the European Council, as a member of the high-level forum he or she is also personally bound by the decisions of the European Council. As the European Council essentially governs through reaching informal face-to-face agreement and through releasing jointly adopted conclusions, the moral costs for deviating from these decisions are particularly high for the Commission President who is directly involved in almost all policy issues debated at European Council meetings. The fact that the Barroso Commission is considered to have acted as 'a far more Presidential Commission', as John Peterson puts it (chapter 9) speaks to this point too. Barroso not only made personal commitments according to the consensus reached within the European Council but also implemented them internally.

The second aspect which is worth considering here is that the relationship between the Commission and the European Council is relatively clearly defined within the treaties as regards the new areas of EU activity—which account for, by far, the largest chunk of European Council activity. Though it is true that the Lisbon Treaty did little to specify the precise division of labour between the Commission and the European Council in agenda-setting and external representation at a more general level, it is not the case that there is no constitutional basis for Commission and European Council cooperation in specific policy sectors. An example of the close integration of the Commission with European Council affairs is seen in the annual Spring meetings of the European Council which are devoted to socio-economic governance issues and in relation to which the Commission prepares specific input. Moreover, as the High Representative who is also a Vice-President of the Commission has become the chair of the Foreign Affairs Council and participates in European Council meetings the institutional ties between the two bodies have been strengthened further. Thus, it would be wrong to primarily understand the role of the Commission as a political counterweight to the European Council.

[9] Anonymous interviews, 4 and 8 July 2011.
[10] Anonymous interviews, 3 June 2010 and 17 November 2011.

8.4 The Creation of *de Novo* Bodies

The European Council can be said to have been a pivotal political force behind the proliferation of *de novo* bodies in the post-Maastricht period. How contested further delegation was is evident in the fact that it was the European Council itself rather than the Council of Ministers that finalized decisions even on the location of many of the various regulatory and executive agencies of the EU. The vast majority of EU agencies are located in the member states rather than in Brussels. A memorable episode in this regard is the Brussels European Council meeting of 13 December 2003 during which the heads were able to conclude a year-long debate about the location of nine new EU agencies (European Council 2003).[11] Holding the rotating EU presidency the then Italian Prime Minister Silvio Berlusconi could proudly announce that the European Food Safety Authority would reside in Parma—a location which he saw as being best suited because of the famous ham being produced there.[12] This appeal to local tradition was less welcomed, though, by the Finish government, which had pleaded for Helsinki as the agency's home and was left with the European Chemicals Agency instead. The episode showed how serious member state governments were about the decentralization of delegated powers.

The European Council's preference for creating *de novo* bodies rather than empowering supranational actors along traditional lines was again forcefully revealed in the context of EU efforts to deal with the consequences of the global economic and financial crisis which, by 2010, had turned into a sovereign debt crisis threatening the integrity of the euro area. On the invitation of European Council President Herman Van Rompuy the euro area heads and the Commission President met for an emergency informal euro area summit in Brussels on 7 May 2010.[13] The background to this meeting was the spiralling sovereign debt crisis in Greece. Already at an informal European Council meeting in February 2010 the heads had agreed on a statement that the euro area would stand behind Greece and would provide support if needed. This was the strongest hint so far that the European Council considered breaking the so-called no-bailout clause of EMU. At their May 2010 emergency meeting the heads not only decided to help Greece with an unprecedented €100

---

[11] Formally the decision was taken as a decision of the Council of Ministers meeting at the level of heads of state or government. This is the formula applied whenever the European Council transforms itself into a formal decision-making body which can adopt official EU acts.

[12] See EUobserver, 'Agencies allocated after two years of talks', 13 December 2003. Full text available at <http://euobserver.com/institutional/13890>.

[13] At the time, meetings of the euro area members of the European Council were referred to as informal meetings of the 'Heads of State and Government of the Euro Area' or as emergency summits. All meetings were convened by European Council President Herman Van Rompuy. Later the term 'Euro Summit' was introduced.

billion support package, they also created a *de novo* body for the future provision of financial assistance for euro area countries facing severe problems in refinancing their sovereign debt on international financial markets. The new body—the EFSF—was authorized to disburse an initial sum of up to €440 billion in financial emergency aid to struggling euro area countries and was intended to calm financial market scepticism about the solvency of a number of euro area countries. The EFSF was used to disburse a special credit line to Ireland in November of the same year and a year later, in May 2011, the EFSF provided similar financial assistance to Portugal.

The key point was that the EFSF was not set up as a novel assistance fund of the Union, which operates under the supervision of the Commission. Moreover, unlike the EU's structural and cohesion funds the EFSF was not funded through the EU budget.[14] Instead, the May 2010 informal euro area European Council meeting instructed the Commission and Ecofin to present within days a decision on establishing the EFSF as a special fund of the euro area member states. The EFSF has the status of a public limited company. It is a fund with an initial base capital provided by the euro area countries, which borrows most of its resources on international financial markets. As shareholders of the EFSF the euro area member states guarantee this debt collectively. The member states remain in full control of the EFSF governing structure within which the Commission and the ECB only have observer status.

With the decision to create the EFSF the European Council made a significant step to modify the so-called no-bailout clause. It created, for the first time, an institutional framework with the aim to issue euro area debt. Yet, the special construction of the EFSF allowed it to minimize the influence of supranational actors as much as possible and to avoid the formal transfer of ultimate decision-making authority. This also implied that the EFSF framework, because of its institutional design, was to trigger further European Council activity, as each time the fund was activated unanimous agreement among euro area member states had to be achieved rapidly. This may also help to further explain why the European Council became involved in the finalization of all major EFSF bailout decisions after the approval of the initial aid package for Greece.

The ESM—the successor of the EFSF—continues to follow the above outlined institutional design of the EFSF. The general decision to create a permanent and financially slightly more powerful successor of the EFSF was already made at the May 2010 emergency meeting of the heads. Ultimate approval was given by the European Council meeting of 16–17 December

---

[14] This model was only applied in relation to another much smaller fund—the European Financial Stability Mechanism. For an overview of EU crisis management and a discussion of these assistance instruments see Hodson and Puetter (2013).

2010. This time the European Council also agreed on a limited revision of Article 136, TFEU, which now formally allows for the provision of emergency financial aid through a stabilization mechanism within the euro area. Yet, the ESM, as such, is neither mentioned in the Treaty nor is it a Community institution in the conventional understanding. As with the EFSF the ESM is a fund owned by the member states. The mechanism is based on an intergovernmental treaty and ESM intervention is dependent on unanimous agreement among the euro area member states.

The EFSF and ESM episodes also reveal the degree of political authority levelled by collective agreement among the heads within the European Council. Far from rejecting collective policy responses they, however, do not feel bound by traditional patterns of supranational empowerment, nor do they see existing treaty provisions as an insurmountable obstacle to collective action even if the adopted measures are in conflict with EU law.

8.5 Problems in Preference Formation are Revealed in European Council Activity

Judging from what the inevitable press conferences of heads at the end of a day of European Council deliberations reveal, one could assume that the members of the European Council are staunch defenders of clearly defined national interests who—more or less successfully—make their position clear to their counterparts and travel home with the boxes on their to-do-lists accurately ticked. The fact that the heads give separate press conferences, which all address different national audiences, exacerbates this image. Indeed, interviews with senior EU and member state officials who are in charge of the preparation of European Council meetings confirm that the question of what one can report back to the press is of key importance for the heads when they are locked into the European Council meeting room. Yet, press conferences may reveal a slightly incomplete picture of how much time and attention is devoted to which issues during a particular meeting. For example, interview research reveals that during key stages of the economic and financial crisis European Council members were engaged in substantial policy debates which revealed the high degree of uncertainty under which decisions were made (see Puetter 2012). In other words, clear national or, for that matter, individual policy preferences were not at all fully established. As a forum for collective decision-making European Council deliberations also inform particular outcomes which were not necessarily fully anticipated by member state governments. The markedly different tone adopted during the press conferences can be interpreted as evidence of how uncertain the heads are about attitudes towards these decisions within domestic audiences.

As highlighted in other contributions to this volume (see in particular Bickerton, chapter 2 and Smith, chapter 5) policy evolution is often a network-based process in which senior technocrats within member state administrations and at the EU level play a pivotal role. A peculiar example of how closely political decision-making in the European Council is linked to intergovernmental networks of senior policy experts was provided by the so-called Van Rompuy task force. At its meeting in March 2010 the European Council decided on a mandate for its President Herman Van Rompuy to lead a special task force of EU finance ministers to advance proposals for the reform of EMU. The work of the task force was crucial for the later adoption of the so-called six-pack—a reform of the euro area multilateral surveillance mechanism and the Stability and Growth Pact procedures. The task force also paved the way for later agreement on the creation of the ESM. At the meetings of the task force, which met six times between May and October 2010, each EU member state was represented by its finance minister and a so-called Sherpa. The Sherpas were senior civil servants—most of them with a background as Economic and Financial Committee representatives. The Sherpas also met as a separate group between the meetings with the ministers.[15] The Sherpa group had its own president, the Austrian finance ministry official Thomas Wieser, who directly advised the European Council President. Van Rompuy reported to the European Council on the work of the task force on two occasions before the final report was submitted at the European Council meeting on 28–9 October 2010.

For the final stages of the negotiations, which centred on the adoption of the task force proposals, the heads were assisted by their respective Sherpas. It is the only example where senior civil servants were allowed to play such a role during a European Council meeting. The episode shows how much EU crisis management required political leaders to draw on technocratic expertise and to rely on a process of collective policy formation. The episode certainly was not short of interventions in the defence of particular national interests, yet the particular format of the task force and the role of the Sherpas is evidence that EU-level policy deliberation was constitutive for the eventually adopted reform proposals.[16]

Finally, the extent to which problems in domestic preference formation have become stand-alone inputs to European Council activity is also demonstrated by the various (and at times ad hoc) European Council meetings on the problem around the lack of popular support for particular EU policy initiatives

---

[15] See Annex 2, 'Strengthening Economic Governance in the EU', Report of the Task Force to the European Council, Brussels, 21 October 2010.

[16] The president of the Sherpa group, Thomas Wieser, interpreted his own role in the process to be the one of a 'marriage counsellor'. Interview with Deutschlandfunk radio, Hintergrund, 17 October 2012, own translation, <http://www.dradio.de/dlf/sendungen/hintergrundpolitik/1896250/>.

and institutional reforms. Just to name only a few examples here: the Laeken European Council in December 2001 adopted the so-called Laeken declaration, thus paving the way for the European Convention process, which is intended to enhance the legitimacy of EU decision-making. At its meeting in Brussels in June 2005 the European Council found itself confronted with the failed referendums on the Constitutional Treaty in France and the Netherlands and sought to find a way forward though the declaration issued by the heads left little doubt that they were far away from a solution:

> We have noted the outcome of the referendums in France and the Netherlands. We consider that these results do not call into question citizens' attachment to the construction of Europe. Citizens have nevertheless expressed concerns and worries which need to be taken into account.[17]

Two years later the European Council at its June 2007 meeting dropped the ratification process relating to the Constitutional Treaty altogether and called for an Intergovernmental Conference to work out a revised Treaty. Yet, again, the European Council had to come back to the issue of ratification as it met just a week after the Irish 'no' vote on the Lisbon Treaty on 19–20 June 2008.

8.6 High and Low Politics

Senior EU and member state officials attribute the growing involvement of the European Council with issues related to the day-to-day management of the new areas of EU activity to the political ramifications that contemporary moves in EU policy coordination have for domestic politics. They see an increasing interest on part of the heads in exercising close control of EU policy coordination dossiers such as economic governance or major foreign affairs issues as these dossiers are seen to determine electoral success or failure as well as the fate of coalition governments. It is also highlighted that decisions are increasingly perceived as impinging on national sovereignty and therefore cannot be delegated to the Council of Ministers.[18]

What is interesting is that the issue is often less about whether the EU should or should not act on a particular policy issue but rather that the heads want to be in control of the process. For example, in the context of decision-making in response to the sovereign debt crisis the European Council itself finalized all major bailout decisions except the one related to Cyprus in March 2013. Finalization in these instances implied the decision on the

---

[17] Declaration by the Heads of State or Government of the Member States of the European Union on the Ratification of the Treaty Establishing a Constitution for Europe, Document SN 117/05, Brussels, 18 June 2005.

[18] Anonymous interviews, 7 April 2009, 9 December 2009, 3 June 2010, and 4 July 2011.

amount, timing, and key political conditions of the bailout package. Technical implementation then was left again to the finance ministers in the Eurogroup. What is interesting is that 'technical implementation' in the case of the bailout packages involved controversial and equally far-reaching conse-quences for domestic decision-making in those countries that received finan-cial assistance. Yet the European Council found it less difficult to delegate important oversight functions within the context of the so-called Troika process to the Eurogroup, which in turn made its political decisions based on the assessments and recommendations by the actual Troika representatives who were technocrats from the Commission, the ECB, and the International Monetary Fund. The political controversies developing around the Troika process were finally acknowledged by a European Parliament inquiry into the work of the Troika which was launched in 2014 to review the effectiveness and concerns about the transparency of the Troika process.[19]

The key point here is that in the sphere of the new areas of EU activity the role of the European Council cannot be reduced to dealing with issuing overall guidance to the Council of Ministers and the Commission and making long-term institutional decisions. Situations in which the European Council deals with particular policy issues in great detail are not the exception but occur on a regular basis. That it is often difficult to tell in advance what is considered a matter for the heads and what not speaks to the claim made in chapter 1 that the boundary of high and low politics is often blurred. What is clear is that specific policy decisions can prove to be as, or even more, complicated than long-term decisions over institutional reform.

Conclusion

This chapter highlighted the role of the European Council as the political centre of the new intergovernmentalism. The European Council is the key driver of processes which are aimed at securing member state representatives a key role during all phases of EU policy-making, including policy formulation and implementation. At the same time, the creation of new areas of EU activity according to the institutional doctrine of the new intergovernment-alism has significant repercussions for the functioning of the EU's main forums for intergovernmental decision-making. The changes in the operation of the European Council reflect this. The rise of the new areas of EU activity increases the demand for consensus generation at the level of the EU's most senior decision-makers. This leads to an overall increase in European Council

---

[19] See: <http://www.europarl.europa.eu/news/en/top-stories/content/20140110TST32314/html/Troika-inquiry>.

activity and triggers processes of institutional engineering which are aimed at strengthening the consensus generation capacity of the forum. Thus, the case of the European Council confirms the claim that the institutionalization of policy deliberation becomes an end in itself (hypothesis 1). Another key feature of post-Maastricht European Council activity is that the heads regularly deal with detailed policy decisions and no longer focus predominantly on providing political guidance on the medium- and long-term orientation of EU policy. In fact, both dimensions are often closely interlinked (hypothesis 5).

The European Council decisions to set up the EFSF and later the ESM illustrate the push for creating *de novo* bodies rather than delegating policy functions to the Commission (hypothesis 3). The European Council plays a lead role in such processes. The above review of European Council activity also backs the claim that problems in domestic preference formation become stand-alone inputs to the discussions among the heads. In turn, the European Council itself has become a crucial venue for preference formation, in particular when decisions are made under uncertainty. Examples of direct empowerment of intergovernmental networks of senior technocratic experts by the heads further speak to this point. Finally, this chapter highlighted the practice of inter-institutional relations between the European Council and the Commission. The European Council environment and the method of decision-making firmly bind the Commission President into a system of decision-making which empowers the top executives of the EU member states—and, not least, the Commission President. The Commission is not only complicit in this process but its internal organization and political leadership structure are very much compatible with the new role of the European Council as the political centre of the new intergovernmentalism. These findings confirm the expectation that the Commission as a traditional supranational actor is not hard-wired for the pursuit of ever closer union according to the model of the classic Community method.

It is actually the centrality of the European Council as the lead political institution of the new intergovernmentalism which signals that in the post-Maastricht era the EU is in a constant state of disequilibrium. Regular European Council interventions into specific policy decisions and the close oversight exercised by the heads over the Council of Ministers and the Commission reveal how much is at stake domestically and at the EU-level whenever the Union seeks to act collectively. The economic and financial crisis may be seen as an exceptional scenario. One could, however, also argue that it merely revealed what it implies to be in an economic and monetary union. It is unlikely that the EU can stay clear from decision-making on bailouts or larger scale fiscal transfers in the future. At least it is clear that decisions in the sphere of economic governance are not trivial and have far-reaching implications for domestic politics. The tensions that such decisions may create have the potential to unseat national governments and to threaten the functioning of the EU. In the sphere of foreign and security policy-making the EU may have just avoided similar scenarios so far. However, there is already no shortage of examples of European Council emergency activity in the light of foreign policy crisis. Should the EU or a large group of its members ever decide to become an active party in a broader international conflict, the meeting calendar of the European Council is very likely to resemble the one during the economic and financial crisis.

Already in the 1980s Bulmer and Wessels (1987) argued that consensus formation within the European Council at regular intervals was a precondition for the advancement of European integration. Later, Bulmer referred to the European Council and the Council of Ministers as 'shapers of a European confederation' (Bulmer 1996). The systemic role of the European Council in EU governance obviously pre-dates the Maastricht Treaty. The forum was indeed crucial in paving the way for the establishment of the Maastricht institutional framework. What has changed since then is the degree to which the European Council intervenes in specific policy decisions, how much its activities have been intensified, and how much the scope of these activities has been widened. These changes have been triggered by the rise of the new areas of EU activity as policy fields, which have been largely developed outside the classic Community method.

Whether the European Council always succeeds in managing political tensions around collective EU decision-making is a very different question. What is clear, however, is that European Council intervention is constantly required. A key problem is that the concentration of power in the hands of the heads and the European Council method of decision-making inevitably triggers questions about the democratic control. It is part of the paradoxical character of post-Maastricht integration that the growing attention which heads of state and government devote to European Council proceedings and which Deirdre Curtin (2014) has referred to as the problem of 'executive dominance in European democracy' is a reaction to the repercussions that EU policy-making has for domestic politics. The EU's responses to the economic and financial crisis showed this quite clearly. The concentration on resolving some of the most difficult policy decisions in contemporary EU governance within the context of confidential face-to-face discussions runs counter to calls for increasing the transparency of EU decision-making.[20] The problem of transparency translates into a bigger problem of democratic

---

[20] For example, the European Council safely escaped reforms to increase the transparency of Council decision-making by making public the minutes of formal Council meetings and televising debates about legislative decisions. That these transparency rules are habitually diluted by the practice of holding important Council discussions outside the context of the formal part of Council sessions is another matter for discussion.

control, given the consequences European Council decisions have for Europe's citizens. For example, the European Council's decisions in the field of economic governance may have redistributive implications. They directly and indirectly impact on member states' ability to operate, for example, social security systems. Mark Dawson and Floris de Witte (2013: 842) highlight this dimension of European Council decision-making and warn that the institutional constellation in EU politics that is emerging after the euro crisis with the European Council at its centre may further weaken 'the EU's ability to be politically responsive'.

9

The Commission and the New Intergovernmentalism

Calm within the Storm?

John Peterson

By most accounts, the twenty plus years since the ratification of the Maastricht Treaty in 1993 have been an unhappy epoch in the life of the European Commission. Maastricht seemed to augur a very different scenario. After all, it extended majority voting as well as the policy remit of the European Community, while creating a 'political union' featuring new cooperation on foreign and internal security policy. These new areas seemed ripe eventually to become subject to the Community method of decision-making, in which the Commission enjoys a powerful position through its monopoly on the right of legislative initiative (see Dehousse 1994: 14). An important reason to expect such 'communitarisation' was Maastricht's creation of a new single institutional framework: the same institutions—including the Commission—would preside over all EU policies. Given its successful advocacy of both a single market and currency—the latter enshrined as a core EU objective by Maastricht—the Commission's future appeared bright.

In fact, numerous analyses in the immediate post-Maastricht period took a different view. The first (and, for thirty years, only) Secretary-General of the Commission saw his former institution's position 'eroded' by the elevation of the European Parliament (EP) in Maastricht's new co-decision procedure (Noël 1994: 22). Dehousse's (1994: 8) close reading of the Treaty, particularly its single institutional framework, led him to lament that 'one cannot avoid the impression of institutional weakness'. A leading historian of European integration judged that 'the Commission was lucky not to have had its formal powers seriously curtailed' by Maastricht (Dinan 2008: 252), given numerous proposals by member states to do just that during the Treaty negotiations. Dinan (2004: 258) regarded the Commission as being in a state of 'political decline' by the time it was agreed. Perhaps, then, the Commission's subsequent two lost decades should come as no surprise.

This chapter's focus is on evidence that challenges the view that the Commission is in decline, which is not (necessarily) a claim of the new intergovernmentalism, but still widely shared in the research literature. We argue, first, that the Commission has adjusted—in ways that are sometimes, even often, impressive—to the new political reality of European integration. Second, we present evidence that chimes with the new intergovernmentalist argument that the EU's institutions—including the Commission—are not hard-wired for the pursuit of ever closer union. Third, the Commission has taken a pragmatic view of the creation of new European agencies that, in most cases, have yielded closer European policy cooperation than previously existed, and (mostly) in areas where the Commission's own powers were previously weak. More generally, this chapter argues that the Commission's institutional position in the EU is strong, even if it has never regained its pre-Maastricht role as an 'engine of integration'. Simply put: institutional weakness is not synonymous with modest ambition.

This chapter builds on earlier analysis that began by noting that the EU has entered a 'post-vision' era.[1] The same work asked whether the shift to a College of European Commissioners with the same composition as all versions of the EU Council—one per member state—was 'reflective of a more intergovernmental Commission' (Peterson 2008: 775). Yet, foreshadowing the theme of the present collection, it challenged scholars to consider whether the EU's 'new' intergovernmentalism was of a different quality and character than earlier versions. To shed light on this and other questions, the present analysis draws on the largest-ever attitudinal survey of Commission officials (see Kassim et al. 2013).[2] Its results broadly confirm that the Commission is a bureau-shaping administration—which seeks to 'shape' its work to focus on high status tasks linked to its core goals (see Dunleavy 1991)—rather than a power or budget-maximizing bureaucracy.

Three main themes are developed to help explain why both the Commission and EU more generally have internalized relatively modest ambitions in a post-vision era. First, Maastricht was a strikingly inward-looking treaty that

[1] This characterization was offered by one of the Commission's most senior officials (quoted in Peterson 2008: 762).
[2] The data presented in this chapter were first presented in Kassim et al. (2013), which was supported by the EU CONSENT network and the UK's Economic and Social Research Council's grant RES-062-23-118. Thanks are due to participants who commented on this chapter at a workshop in Budapest on 28–9 November 2013 and those at the 7th Pan-European Conference on EU Politics at The Hague, 5 June 2014, especially Petya Alexandrov.

contained virtually no provisions to prepare for today's radically enlarged and enormously diverse EU. The new intergovernmentalism is largely a product of how collective action in today's EU is, by an order of magnitude, far more complex than was the case in the immediate post-Maastricht era. Second, the Union of yesteryear yielded far 'straighter' delegation of powers to the Commission. Today's EU delegates to *de novo* institutions, such as European agencies or regulatory networks, far more often. But such delegation has overwhelmingly taken place where the Commission's prerogatives and powers were previously either limited or unthreatened. The Commission is thus almost always a willing partner in delegation that, in appearance, smacks of a new intergovernmentalism. Third, any suggestion that the Commission has become a more intergovernmental body must be fundamentally qualified by the emergence of a far more presidential Commission under José Manuel Barroso. Part and parcel of a more centralized Commission is that it is highly task-focused, far more professionally managed, and broadly content with the status quo, even if that status quo deserves to be labelled the 'new intergovernmentalism'.

Section 9.1 takes a historical view of the evolution of the Commission's role in the twenty years since Maastricht was agreed. Section 9.2 asks what is really new about the new intergovernmentalism from the perspective of the Commission. In section 9.3, attitudinal data is mined from the largest ever large-n study of Commission officials to gauge how accepting the administration is of the EU's new status quo. The durability of a new and unparalleled mode of operation of the Commission under Barroso is the focus of section 9.4. The conclusion summarizes evidence about the extent to which the Commission as a case validates or challenges the new intergovernmentalism as a paradigm.

9.1 The Life of the Commission: 1993–2013

The first years of the post-Maastricht era saw Jacques Delors come to the end of his long, ten-year mandate as Commission President. Delors surely ranks as one of the—probably *the*—most successful Commission president(s) in history. His visions of a single market and currency were both realized in large part because he was viewed as a political equal at the top table of the European Council by legendary figures such as Kohl, Mitterrand, and even Thatcher.

It often goes unappreciated that the latter half of the Delors era was a far less successful or dynamic period in the life of the Commission. His second and third colleges (1989–93 and 1993–5) were considerably less cohesive than his first (1985–9), not least due to growing dissatisfaction with his imperious style of leadership (Nugent 2001: 47). Delors clearly got ahead of member states with proposals for Maastricht that were overambitious and mostly ignored.

The Treaty's two intergovernmental 'pillars' for internal security and foreign policy were indicative of suspicions in many national capitals about the Commission's (then) recent record of maximalism in its interpretation of the reach of its own powers. Maastricht's strong commitment to subsidiarity reflected the same concerns. It also was used to justify widespread infringements of EU rules or judgments of the Commission, particularly during the eighteen months between the Treaty's signing and ratification caused principally by Denmark's rejection of Maastricht in its 1992 referendum (Peterson 1999: 52). Delors himself bore a share of the blame for the Danish 'no', because of his personal association with monetary union—a project viewed negatively in Denmark—but also because of ill-chosen utterances prior to the Danish vote about how the influence of small states would decline in the EU of the future (Nugent 2001: 46–7).

These remarks revealed Delors' own aversion to further enlargement of the EU, which—to be fair—was widely shared in west European capitals at the time. The perception that widening would imperil deepening came to dominate debates about Europe's future (see Nugent 1992). These debates were given a shot of urgency by the geopolitical earthquake to the EU's east that began in 1989. In an illustration of how two political worlds coexisted for a time on one continent, the European Council concluded the summit at which the Maastricht Treaty was agreed precisely sixteen days before the Soviet Union collapsed. Despite the urgent need to consolidate democracy, human rights, and working economies in the former Soviet bloc, Noël (1994: 25) mused that '[t]he Maastricht negotiators deliberately decided to ignore these problems. Were they really right to endeavour, as in the past, to "let time take its time"?'

In the event, the masters of the EU's treaties had no choice but to shift focus from deepening to widening as applications to join the Union surged. By the time of the 1995 enlargement (Austria, Finland, and Sweden), Poland and Hungary had already applied for membership. Another eight Central and Eastern Europe states followed in 1995–6. Meanwhile, EU leaders opted for a relatively low profile and pro-enlargement successor to Delors in Luxembourg's Prime Minister, Jacques Santer. The choice reflected both the inevitable tasking of the Commission with preparing the next enlargement(s) and the wish to rein in the ambitions of the Commission with a president who promised to 'do less but do it better'.

The lacklustre performance of Santer's Commission—leaving aside enlargement and EMU—and its unhappy end has been analysed elsewhere (see Peterson 1999, 2012: 101–2). Here it is worth pausing on three points. First, Santer appeared exceptionally weak but he was by no means the first Commission president to have his own authority frequently defied by a College that included a plethora of political heavyweights. In Santer's case, they included six former prime ministers, foreign ministers, or finance ministers, plus the former British Labour leader, Neil Kinnock, and the Italian Radical party firebrand, Emma Bonino. Perhaps Santer's difficulties in leading the College explains why he quietly and constructively engaged with EU leaders as the Amsterdam Treaty was negotiated in 1996–7 to give the Commission president—previously only *primus inter pares* (first amongst equals)—new powers to nominate Commissioners 'by common accord' with member states and preside over a College that would work 'under the political guidance of the President'. Enshrined in the Treaty, these powers would be exploited to the maximum by Santer's successor plus one: Barroso.

Second, the mass resignation of Santer's College in 1999 was mostly a product of his own political misjudgements. But it also exposed how badly managed the Commission had become under Delors, who took next to no interest in managing the house. Ironically, one upshot of Santer's humiliation was a programme of reforms piloted by Kinnock after Santer's departure, which transformed the Commission into a far more efficient, professionally managed and modern administration. Augmented by rules laid down by Santer's successor, former Italian Prime Minister Romano Prodi, internal reform extended to new rules that eliminated national 'flags' on senior Commission posts (for instance, the head of Directorate-General (DG) Agriculture would no longer always be French as Directors-General posts would be rotated between individuals). Commissioners were required to appoint to their private offices (*cabinets*) a head or deputy head (*chef*) who did not share their nationality and ensure that their *cabinet* contained officials of at least three different nationalities. The effect was to place new and powerful constraints on the 'old' intergovernmentalism in so far as it penetrated the Commission.[3]

Third, the choice of Santer—as well as his two successors—gives rise to suggestions that the new intergovernmentalism is reflected in the European Council's post-Delors appointments of one of their own as Commission President on three consecutive occasions (see chapter 1). By this view, the intent is to ensure that the Commission does not revert to its supranational excesses. Yet, at best, this hypothesis is unproven. Roy Jenkins was appointed president in 1977 because a critical mass of member states thought that the Commission should be led by a political figure with the stature to be a potential prime minister in their own country (Peterson 2012: 100). His successor, the far from forceful or dynamic Gaston Thorn, had—like Santer—previously been Prime Minister of Luxembourg. Since Jenkins's appointment, the only outlier from the hypothesis has been Delors, whose

---

[3] Famously, one *cabinet* official claimed in an interview in 1994 that 'Intergovernmentalism starts in the *cabinets*. They're mini-Councils within the Commission' (quoted in Peterson 1995: 74).

previous top job was as French Finance Minister. The Commission and EU more generally both became enormously more powerful in the post-Maastricht period than was the case when Jenkins took the job. What is new is simply that the job of Commission President is far more important and authoritative than in bygone eras.

Romano Prodi's tenure as Commission President reinforces the point. He was the first former Prime Minister of a large EU member state to be appointed as President. Yet, he presided over the most high-powered, talented collection of Commissioners ever appointed to any College. Previous expertise was matched to portfolio as never before in the Commission's history in a sign that member governments (as well as Prodi) were serious about wielding the Commission's formidable power.

Prodi proved to be a poor communicator and less than forceful Commission President. He showed poor political judgement in trying to influence debate within the Convention on the Future of Europe in 2002 (Peterson 2012: 103–4). But he mostly 'got out of the way' and let his Commissioners manage their own portfolios in ways that led to considerable policy success. Prodi also helped to shift the debate on eastern enlargement to the point where EU governments agreed to open accession talks with no fewer than twelve applicant states.

With little support for his reappointment, Prodi left Brussels to contest a domestic election (which led to him serving again as Italian prime minister from 2006–8). Not for the first time, the European Council settled on a consensus candidate to succeed Prodi—nobody's first choice, but everybody's second or third—in Portugal's Prime Minister, José Manuel Barroso. A stinging criticism of Barroso's early performance as President accused him of being an 'intergovernmentalist at heart' (Munchau 2005: 17). An evaluation of his first Commission after his reappointment to a second term lamented that 'Barroso is too politically cautious and too eager to trim his sails to the winds blowing from national capitals, especially Berlin, Paris and London' (Taylor 2010: 12). These comments plus Barroso's own assertion that 'the basic legitimacy of our union is the member states' (quoted in Peterson 2006: 93–4) perhaps lends credence to the new intergovernmentalism as a paradigm on how the EU now operates.

Or perhaps not. By the time of Barroso's appointment, an earlier commitment to move to a slimmed-down College with posts rotating between member states had been abandoned in favour of a simpler, one Commissioner per member state formula. The upshot was that Barroso inherited an unprecedentedly large[4] College of 25 members following the 2004 'big bang'

---

[4] Strictly speaking, this statement is false. For a time at the end of his mandate, Prodi presided over a College of 30—with each of the new member states contributing a Commissioner—even before enlargement officially took place in May 2004 (Barroso took over in January 2004).

enlargement. It also, on paper, appeared to extend the trend towards member states appointing big political beasts, as it included no fewer than eleven former prime ministers, foreign ministers, or finance ministers. Yet, all bar one—ex-Italian Foreign Minister Franco Frattini—were from small member states. Frattini was appointed only after Italy's original nominee—Rocco Buttiglione—stood down under pressure from the EP after airing ultra-conservative views on gays and women (see Peterson 2012: 108). In any event, Barroso made full use of the President's post-Amsterdam Treaty powers to lead and mould the College to enforce an unprecedented strengthening of the Commission presidency, arguing that anything less in an expanded College of 25 (and then 27–8) risked 'fragmentation' and 'Balkanization'. In his words, the enlarged Commission needed 'a President that is seen by members of the Commission as a last resort and authority' (quoted in Kassim et al. 2013: 166).

Barroso stamped his authority on his College from the word go. Franco-German pressure on Barroso to give especially powerful portfolios to their own nominees and designate them 'super-Commissioners' was, in their view, a wholly justified reaction to the loss of their previous prerogative to appoint two members to the College. Yet, Barroso saw off the pressure and publicly refuted the argument. Cleverly, he insisted that he needed all members of his College to be 'super-Commissioners' and, in the process, endeared himself to the drastically expanded share of small member states in the post-big bang EU.

Finally, Barroso's first College (as well as his second) contrasted with Prodi's despite the appearance of continuity in terms of the appointment of senior national political figures. The Barroso Commissions were strikingly more technocratic, and even rather grey and faceless compared to Prodi's collection of big political beasts. In large part, this result reflected the appointment of figures drawn from Central and Eastern Europe's first democratic political classes, in which being apolitical was often a virtue (Peterson 2008: 765). And, as we see in the section that follows, there is strong evidence to suggest that Commissioners under Barroso have been overwhelmingly focused on their own portfolios, as opposed to political signals from their own national capitals.

9.2 What is Really New? The View from the Berlaymont

If a paradigm shift has occurred in EU governance, how does it look from the vantage point of the Berlaymont building, the Commission's headquarters that houses the College and Secretariat-General (responsible for managing the administration)? In important respects, the Commission's view of the EU system is a product of changes that have occurred within the administration.

An overarching change is the emergence of a far more presidential and centralized College. A second is a legacy of changes under Santer and Prodi that have made *cabinets* far less like the partisan, national enclaves that Commissioners' private offices were in the past and made them more focused on their Commissioner's dossier. But the view from the Berlaymont also reveals an EU where (third) far more powers and functions have been delegated to *de novo* institutions than in the past, thus adding to the 'polycentricity' of the EU, or its tendency to sprout ever more distinct, autonomous, and divergent centres of power and control (Greve and Jørgensen 2002). Surely, it would seem, the Commission takes a dim view of being sidelined as a consequence of the eschewing of the more direct, 'cleaner' pre-Maastricht pattern of delegation to the administration.

9.2.1 *A More Presidential Commission*

Any examination of leadership in the Commission should start by recalling how the College makes decisions. First, it works on the basis of collective responsibility. Second, the College decides by simple majority votes when it finds it cannot unanimously agree. Even if (say), thirteen of twenty-eight Commissioners[5] are outvoted, they must publicly support the majority position or else resign. Collective responsibility has symbolic as well as operational implications. By giving all Commissioners the right to a vote on all EU matters, and not only those falling within their portfolio, the institution's right to represent the general interest of the Union—and not the narrow interests of the governments who nominated them—is reinforced (see Dimitrakopoulos 2008).

Historically, the Commission President has had few levers of control over the College. To illustrate, he (there has never been a female President) has only one vote in the College, the same as all other Commissioners. Yet, from the Maastricht Treaty onwards, the President gradually has accumulated powers to influence the nomination of Commissioners by member states, allocate portfolios, appoint Vice-Presidents, and even require that a Commissioner resign (see Kassim et al. 2013: 157).

Officials surveyed in a project that produced the largest-ever data set on the views and attitudes of Commission officials were asked to rate the performance of the presidents under whom they had served. Four different criteria were chosen:

---

[5] Interestingly, the accession of Croatia in 2013 gave the College an even number of Commissioners for the first time. It is unclear what would happen if any measure met with a 14–14 vote, but presumably the action under consideration would not go forward.

1. setting a policy agenda
2. delivering on policy priorities
3. managing the administration (or 'house')
4. defending the Commission in the EU system.

Predictably, Delors received astronomically high ratings from the (relatively few) officials remaining in the Commission who worked under him, leaving aside the partial exception of managing the House. Santer's presidency was rated as woeful. Prodi's ratings were better—especially on the two policy questions—but still not very flattering.

Barroso was rated considerably higher than any president since Delors, especially (again) on policy questions. Intriguingly, his performance was rated as 'strong' by fewer officials on his management of the administration than was the case on any other question. And his defence of the Commission in the EU system was rated negatively by a clear plurality of officials. The fine grain of the data yield further interesting nuggets about Barroso. His performance was rated as considerably stronger by officials from member states that joined the EU after 2004 ('EU-12' officials) than by those from states from the 'EU-15' (Kassim et al. 2013: 271). Officials from administrative DGs[6] were considerably more likely to rate his management performance as strong than those serving in other DGs (Kassim et al. 2013: 166).

The same study supplemented its survey findings with more than 200 interviews, including with a stratified sample of middle and senior managers, *cabinet* officials, and Commissioners themselves. Determining whether Barroso had delivered on his promise to run a highly Presidential Commission was one of the key priorities of both the survey and interviews. The conclusion reached is unequivocal: 'Barroso has largely succeeded in his aim of strengthening the Commission Presidency' (Kassim et al. 2013: 166).

Besides leading (two) Colleges with far fewer political heavyweights than were in Prodi's, the main factor that allowed Barroso to impose a far more centralized, Presidential Commission was a transformation in the role of the Secretariat-General. Pre-Barroso, it acted as a mostly honest broker between the interests and agendas of different DGs. Under Barroso, it was turned into 'an instrument of the Commission Presidency' (Kassim et al. 2013: 170), and even a sort of extension of his *cabinet*. To illustrate, a plurality (37 per cent) of survey respondents disagreed that the Secretariat-General remained a 'neutral arbiter between the services [that is, DGs] in policy coordination'. Meanwhile, a clear majority (59 per cent) agreed that: 'The Secretariat General is becoming

---

[6] Kassim et al. (2013) consider administrative DGs to be those for Budget, Administration, Internal Audit, the Anti-Fraud Office, and Secretariat-General.

more political and more influential in the life of the Commission' (Kassim et al. 2013: 170–1).

Clearly, Barroso had to break a few eggs to make his omelette. His relatively low rating on 'managing the house' in the survey is testament, as are numerous less than happy testimonials about his management style from interviewees (see Kassim et al. 2013: 166–77). Whether or not the 'Barroso model' is sustainable beyond the end of his mandate is uncertain (see section 9.4). But there seems little doubt that he made the Commission subject to strong, centralized leadership during his tenure.

9.2.2 Cabinets: It's the Dossier, Stupid

The political space available to Commissioners to act as channels for impulses from national capitals into the work of the Commission appears to have been narrowed significantly by the emergence of a more presidential Commission. Equally, however, it seems to be reflected in a more secular transformation of *cabinets* since the Delors days. If intergovernmentalism once started 'when proposals hit the *cabinets*' (Peterson 1999: 74), there is evidence to suggest they now act far less as national enclaves than they did in the past.

Kassim et al. (2013: 198) are firm in contending that '*cabinets* are centred on the portfolio of the Commissioner rather than supporting his or her non-portfolio responsibilities'. This argument is based primarily on two findings from post-survey interviews. First, a total of 28 *cabinet* interviewees were handed a list of possible roles for their office and asked to indicate how closely they described the work of their *cabinet*. 'Portfolio support' was deemed to describe their office's role very, or quite, closely by nearly all interviewees (see Figure 9.1). All besides one said oversight of the DG for which their Commissioner was responsible was a key role of their *cabinet*. Meanwhile, roles that accorded with an image of *cabinets* as national enclaves—linking to the political party or home state of their Commissioner or safeguarding the interests of their Commissioner's compatriots in the administration—were viewed by most interviewees as not very closely descriptive of their work.

Second, a series of questions in both the survey and interviews sought to test the tenor of relations between *cabinets* and the DGs. *Cabinets* were viewed in bygone days as national enclaves and populated by (relatively young) officials planted by national capitals who reworked the output of the DGs to serve the national interest of their Commissioner's member state. Thus, '[t]he conventional wisdom is that the relationship between the *cabinets* and the services is one of permanent tension' because relations pit 'the state-centric concerns of *cabinet* members against the commitment

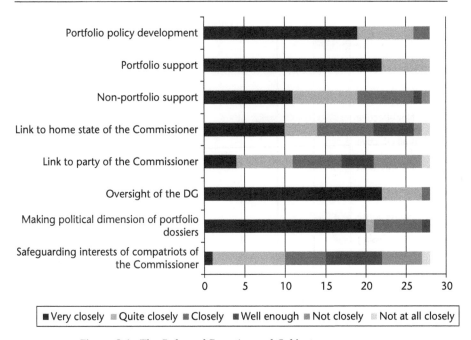

Figure 9.1. The Role and Functions of *Cabinets*

Note: Based on face-to-face interviews with *cabinet* members (n = 28).
Source: Kassim et al. (2013: 199).

to the European ideal of permanent officials in the services' (Kassim et al. 2013: 201).

The survey found that 43 per cent of respondents thought that the *cabinets* respected the expertise of the services, while only 19 per cent disagreed (Kassim et al. 2013: 202). Meanwhile, no fewer than three-quarters of senior and middle manager interviewees judged coordination between their DG and the *cabinet* of the Commissioner responsible to be very effective, quite effective, or satisfactory (Figure 9.2). If the *cabinets* and services fight a sort of perpetual war with one another—in large part because *cabinets* are channels for national political impulses—there is very little evidence to support it in this data.

Two other factors help explain the laser-like focus of Commissioners and their advisors on their dossiers. One is simply how much more difficult it now is to design policy solutions in Brussels that suit the almost infinitely more diverse local circumstances in an EU of twenty-eight. Following the 2004 enlargement, many DGs were reorganized into geographical sub-units with responsibility for specific groups of states or regions.[7] Many EU-12 officials

---

[7] Around 200 new units were created in the Commission in 2005 alone (Peterson 2008: 767).

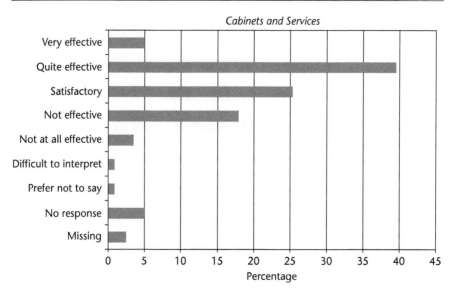

Figure 9.2. DG-Cabinet Relations

Note: Question: How would you judge coordination between your DG and the responsible Commissioner's cabinet? Based on a survey of Commission officials (n = 119).
Source: Kassim et al. (2013: 204).

were deployed in response to the new reality noted by a long-serving and very senior Commission official: 'one of the most striking effects of enlargement is how much more difficult but critical it is to monitor implementation' (quoted in Kassim et al. 2013: 259). The primary function of 52.1 per cent of officials from post-2004 member states surveyed by Kassim et al. (2013: 259) was implementation, compared to 41.5 per cent of EU-15 officials.

Another reason for Commissioners to prioritize their dossier over serving their national capital may be that enlargement had the effect of empowering the services in the relationship between them and the College. The consequence is that Commissioners have to work harder to retain control of their dossier and direct the work of the services over which they preside. One Director in the services (who served in Santer's *cabinet*) argued that:

> Enlargement pushes things down and makes the services more powerful. The Council can't negotiate. The Parliament struggles. So what is actually in the proposal is now more important than before. Even though very few Commission proposals are spontaneous, and dreamt up exclusively by us, more gets pushed down to Commissioners and their *cabinets*. And if either one of those levels are weak, as is sometimes the case in this [Barroso I] Commission, responsibility for the actual content and impact of what we do gets pushed down to the services. (Quoted in Peterson 2008: 768)

9.2.3 *New Delegation = New Intergovernmentalism?*

At the heart of claims that the EU has lapsed into a new intergovernmentalism is the observation that member states have delegated new powers and policy tasks to *de novo* institutions far more often than they have delegated to the Commission post-Maastricht (see chapter 1). The trend towards more agency governance, as well as delegation to alternative bodies such as regulatory networks, is reflected in the research literature's preoccupation with the 'new delegation' (see Rittberger and Wonka 2011; Keleman and Majone 2012; Van Boetzelaer and Princen 2012). It is vividly illustrated in the timeline showing which EU institutions were created and when (Peterson and Shackleton 2012: 9). All European institutions created in the fifty-two years between the Treaties of Paris (creating the Coal and Steel Community) and Maastricht fit on less than a page. Those created post-Maastricht—a grab bag of agencies, institutes, authorities, and centres—stretch on for a page and a half.

We lack hard evidence on attitudes within the Commission towards the rise in agency governance. It is not, for example, a matter on which views were sought by Kassim et al. (2013). However, the Commission has always been keenly mindful of its own institutional dignity. It has often seemed a 'citadel under siege' post-Maastricht, especially since the fall of the Santer Commission (Kassim et al. 2013: 130–50). As such, we might expect it to take a very dim view of the rise of agency governance.

Yet, what evidence we do have suggests otherwise. It is clear that European 'agencification' has been heavily shaped by past patterns of delegation to the Commission. Rittberger and Wonka (2011: 782) conclude that '[t]he Commission, eager to defend its turf, has agreed to the establishment of EU-level agencies only when this strategy promised to enhance the Commission's own objectives'. European regulatory agencies (ERAs) have very few powers to regulate and none have been created with general rule-making power. Most offer the Commission, a generally resource-poor administration, expertise, or personnel, or finance that it lacks, and thus add value where the Commission needs it. For example, the European Food Safety Administration offers scientific advice to the Commission, which itself then takes decisions on foodstuffs. The European Medicines Agency offers a centralized procedure for authorizing medicines but formal decisions are taken via a complicated procedure involving the Commission, a committee of national regulators, and the Council of the EU. Thatcher's (2011: 802)[8] verdict was that:

> Hence the Commission keeps decision-making powers, but gains through ERAs an additional means of rule-making, information and enforcement. Thus in domains

---

[8] See also Kelemen 2002; Kelemen and Majone 2012.

where the Commission had limited discretion and powers, an ERA represented an opportunity for expansion in the Commission's role, not a rival to it.

Clearly, this verdict does not (*could* not) cover all *de novo* institutions. To take one prominent example, the Commission is effectively excluded from any role in the ESM—the permanent crisis resolution system for the euro area—where, presumably, it would wish to have a role.

Yet, more generally, Egeberg and Trondal (2011: 882) find that 'EU-level agencies find themselves much closer to the Commission than to the Council and national ministries'. They go as far as to claim that, because most ERAs have the capacity to act independently of national governments and the Council but are highly reliant on the Commission, they contribute to a 'system transformation' of the European political-administrative order and the creation of a stronger administrative centre. The result is that this administrative centre is 'in practice, *autonomous* from key components of an intergovernmental order' (Egeberg and Trondal 2011: 868; emphasis added).

In short, the view from the Berlaymont is very much a product of changes that have taken place within the house, even within the building. They include the emergence of a far more presidential Commission, which means that eyes have had to look to the thirteenth floor from where Barroso and his advisors—as well as the Secretary-General—have retained a tight hold on the reins of power. The view out of the window from the two top floors that house other members of the College seems very much focused on the DGs that are scattered around Brussels because Commissioners and their *cabinets* concentrate overwhelmingly on their dossiers and associated services. And the Commission's corporate view of the rise of European agency governance seems, perhaps counter-intuitively, an overwhelmingly positive one. System transformation by stealth and the strengthening of an administrative centre autonomous of EU member states suggest that the new intergovernmentalism may not be quite what it seems.

9.3 The New Status Quo: 'OK with Us'

A core assumption (or hypothesis) of the new intergovernmentalism is that the EU's supranational institutions are not 'hard-wired' for the pursuit of ever closer union. Logically, then, they should be broadly content with the new status quo of stasis in the process of European integration. Another proposition is that deliberation and consensus have become ends in themselves in the new European Union. Are these hypotheses confirmed when we test them on the Commission?

To a considerable extent, they are confirmed. We now have abundant evidence that the image of a Commission that is power-hungry is mostly false. Consider Hooghe's (2012) characterization of only about a third of Commission officials as 'supranationalists', based on their support for the notion that the College should become 'the government of the EU' and opposition to the statement that member states—not the Commission or EP—should be the 'central players' in the Union. Nearly the same share (28.9 per cent) of officials may be characterized as 'institutional pragmatists', who support the Community method of decision-making but are not power-maximizers. Surprisingly, around 14 per cent are state-centrists (and, in order of disproportionality, tend to be British, Slovakian, Swedish, Latvian, and Danish; see figure 9.3). More than one-fifth are fence-sitters who defy clear characterization. The claim that Commission officials (particularly managers) 'favour deeper European integration regardless of their national background or their organizational experience' (Ellinas and Suleiman 2011: 923) finds very little support in investigations of the Commission based on far larger data sets (Hooghe 2012; Kassim et al. 2013).

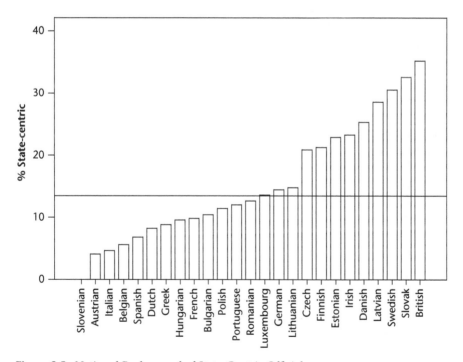

Figure 9.3. National Background of State-Centric Officials

Note: Based on a survey of Commission officials (n = 1,698). The horizontal line represents the mean response.

Source: Kassim et al. (2013: 109).

None of this is to deny that allegiance to European unity is part of the DNA of the Commission. No fewer than 71 per cent of surveyed officials said they were motivated to join the administration by (*inter alia*)[9] their 'commitment to Europe'. Yet, bureau-shaping motivations—especially commitment to a particular policy area or 'quality of the work'—have become more important motivators over time.[10] Enlargement has played a role in this shift: one of the most significant differences between EU-12 and EU-15 officials was that noticeably fewer of the former chose commitment to Europe as a motivator for joining the Commission, while far more cited quality of the work as well as (predictably given the state of many EU-12 national administrations and economies) 'competitive remuneration', 'job stability', and 'career prospects' (Kassim et al. 2013: 251–2).

Moreover, evidence that EU-12 officials are more sanguine about the new intergovernmentalism than their longer-serving colleagues does not stop there. Considerably fewer recent recruits want the College to morph into a 'government of Europe'. Nearly 40 per cent of EU-15 officials strongly disagreed with the notion that the member states should be the central players in the EU, compared to only about a quarter of EU-12 officials. The Commission's recent recruits also show considerably less commitment to the Community method (see Kassim et al. 2013: 252–3). There is even support post-enlargement for Hall's (2007) contentious claim that the Commission has become an outpost of neoliberal fervour. Far more EU-12 (37 per cent) than EU-15 (25 per cent) officials have economics or business degrees. Nearly two-thirds (64 per cent) of recruits from the new member states placed themselves on the liberal side of a 10-point scale gauging their economic philosophy compared to only 43 per cent of EU-15 respondents (see Figure 9.4).

More generally, the Commission does not appear wedded to a federalist agenda. Kassim et al. (2013: 292) maintain that: 'Officials are not overwhelmingly supranational idealists or technocrats. Nor do their beliefs reflect an ingrained institutional credo that there should always be more Europe.' Of course, the Commission is only one of several supranational EU institutions and the degree of satisfaction of the others with the new status quo must also be gauged. But, by way of comparison, the EP's recent, muscular, and integrationist positions on the EU's budget, the rights of migrant workers, anti-human trafficking measures, and female quotas for non-executive company boards suggest that the Parliament is considerably less satisfied than the Commission with the new intergovernmentalism.

---

[9] Survey respondents were asked to choose as many 'motivators' as were relevant to them.
[10] To illustrate, comparing more recent recruits (1–10 years of service) with long-serving (21–45 years) officials, the share choosing commitment to a policy area rose to 25 per cent from 16.5 per cent. Over one-third (36 per cent) of recent recruits cited quality of the work as a motivator, compared with 26.5 per cent of long-serving officials (Kassim et al. 2013: 56).

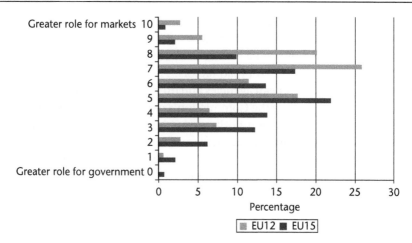

Figure 9.4. Economic Philosophy of Commission Officials

Note: Respondents asked to position their economic philosophy on a ten-point scale ranging from (0) a greater role for government to (5) centrist to (10) greater role for markets. Based on a survey of Commission officials (n = 1,769).
Source: Kassim et al. (2013: 263).

In gauging whether the Commission has accepted the new intergovernmentalist claim that deliberation has been elevated over delegation in EU governance, we must rely on intuition more than hard evidence. Hodson argues (2013) that the Commission's lack of supranational ambition under Barroso was a product of strategic entrepreneurship. That is, the Commission focused on modest or pragmatic proposals that had a chance of success in the new political climate. Barroso's own privileging of the Lisbon agenda and Europe 2020 initiative, neither of which implied much new EU legislation, could be taken as evidence that deliberation trumps delegation.

Yet, the question arises: what is really new here? One of the main findings of Coombes's (1970) classic study was that the Commission had a strong self-interest in its own success, and only rarely pushed the edge of the envelope to propose measures that challenged political limits. Ross's (1995: 234–7) account of the Delors years insisted that the Commission's supranational entrepreneurship depended on three contingencies—geopolitical changes in Europe, a favourable business climate, and (crucially) member state receptivity to European policy solutions—that were unlikely to coincide very often in future. It is revealing—and often forgotten—that Delors' third (abbreviated) term as President was largely focused on the White Paper on Growth, Competitiveness and Employment, which set the tone for the decentralized mode of economic governance that dominated the post-Maastricht period. Very much in line with Ross (1995), Tömmel (2013) finds that only Delors enjoyed the institutional and situational conditions (in addition to possessing the personal qualities) to be a 'transformational' leader, while the Santer and Prodi presidencies were no more than 'transactional'.

If the Commission has been a willing partner in the new intergovernmentalism, it might be due to two broad factors. First, it has had little reason to protest delegation to European agencies and other *de novo* institutions because most operate in areas where the Commission's powers are weak and most offer resources that the Commission both needs and lacks. Second, enlargement has made it somewhere between difficult and impossible to design new, one-size-fits-all policy solutions in Brussels. The enlarged EU now has far more 'varieties of capitalism' and the literature that goes under that name has shown convincingly that common pressures of the kind Europe has faced during the post-2008 global recession can act to sharpen national differences (see chapter 1). Besides, the Commission has its hands full merely monitoring implementation of existing EU legislation in what is now a vast political space. It has had to re-engineer itself internally just to keep up. The new intergovernmentalism may not be the Commission's first choice option as a current state of the Union. But it has always been risk-averse and fearful of failure. Any forward progress on policy cooperation requires deliberation in the new EU, and quite a lot of it. And the Commission is as keenly aware of this fact as anyone.

9.4 The Barroso Commission: a New Normal?

A final set of questions concerns whether the Barroso Commissions—dominated by their President and modest in their ambitions—represent a new normal. In other words, have patterns been set in the work of the Commission over ten years that are durable and will last now that Barroso has passed from the scene? Crystal ball gazing in the social sciences is always risky. However, it is worth considering what kind of Commission is emerging post-Barroso.

Two fundamental features of the twenty-first-century landscape of European integration are worth considering carefully. First, given its buoyant policy agenda, a bloated College that is here to stay, and stark new political limits to European integration, it might be assumed that EU governments would favour choosing Commission presidents who broadly embrace Barroso's style and agenda in future. If a College of twenty-eight or more members is going to do its job and effectively preside over the Commission's formidable policy remit, it needs a strong president who can broker compromises, participate effectively in the European Council, and deliver clear political messages about what the Commission is doing and why. Perhaps—despite all the political noise about the EP's role in choosing (and successfully confirming) its *Spitzenkandidat* (see below)—Barroso's successor, Jean-Claude Juncker, fits the bill.

Second, it is not only 'agencification' that suggests that the Commission is less weakened than it appears by the prioritization of deliberation over delegation. Even in areas where its formal powers range from weak to non-existent, the Commission is almost always essential to achieving successful policy cooperation. Arguably, most policy solutions advance European integration, often by stealth.

After reviewing evidence that points to a much stronger style of leadership under Barroso, Kassim et al. (2013: 179–80) consider reasons to expect that the new normal will outlast Barroso, and reasons why it might not. The latter includes the possibility that his successor(s)—such as Juncker (chosen in 2014)—may approach the presidency differently. They may run, say, a more collegial and integrationist College. The transformation of the Secretariat-General into an extension of the President's own office is not a change that is deeply institutionalized. The new model presidency has been very much a product of Barroso's close personal relationship with the Secretary-General, Catherine Day, who served throughout his two terms, as well as their (liberal) ideological affinity. Barroso had few big political beasts in his College. Their reappearance in future may equate to strong aversion to strong presidential leadership. The Lisbon Treaty's stipulation that the selection of a Commission President had to 'take into account' the results of EP elections led the Parliament's political groups to choose their own lead candidates (referred to by the German term *Spitzenkandidat*) ahead of the 2014 European elections, leading to speculation that Barroso's successor might be an integrationist focused on new *grands projets* in which the Commission's role and power would be maximized. Perhaps Juncker was precisely this kind of Commission President?

Perhaps not. There are few reasons to think that the Commission will not remain, in political terms, a 'citadel under siege' that faces powerful challenges to its authority in a political climate of growing Euro-scepticism. In these circumstances, its officials seem likely to accept and even welcome strong central authority. Barroso's reappointment to a second term suggested that a critical mass of member states were broadly supportive of both his policy programme and personal grip on the Commission, and also admired his skill as a political communicator and performance within the European Council (Kassim et al. 2013: 178). On balance, a similarly critical mass of EU governments seemed likely to want more of the same after Barroso stepped down, insisting on the same of a Juncker presidency.

Finally, it might help us get some purchase on the EU's near-term future to consider some of the fine grain of its current policy landscape. One of its most striking features is that it includes multiple areas of activity where the Commission lacks much (if any) power but is still in the thick of policy-making, or at least deliberation, about policy options. Consider the Digital Economy initiative, which was the closest thing the EU had to a major project (besides ending the euro area crisis) during Barroso's second term. In a sense, the initiative confirmed the new intergovernmentalist contention that high and low politics had become increasingly blurred in the new EU. The drive to complete the digital single market by 2015 was complicated by tension between discussions at the highest political level of the European Council and the deeply technical set of issues targeted by the Commission's action plan. With the clock ticking, and Europe falling behind hi-tech rivals such as the United States and China, the Digital Economy was meant to be the centrepiece of an October 2013 European Council. But France spoke for a number of member states who considered the discussion premature because EU telecommunications ministers had not yet even discussed the Commission's package.[11] Suggestions that EU leaders should focus on stimulating European markets by changing rules on public procurement and new financial support for digital start-ups became moot as the summit became dominated by allegations that the US National Security Agency had extensively monitored communications in Europe, including by tapping the phone of the German Chancellor, Angela Merkel. Thus, it appeared that the gap between high and low politics sometimes still appears, and the former trump the latter. Whatever its eventual fate, it was clear that the Commission's role in surmounting obstacles in the way of the Digital Economy initiative—if they could be surmounted—would be crucial. The initiative as a case seems to validate findings in recent and perceptive works on how the Commission engages in policy-shaping and 'framing' (Rhinard 2010) and achieves Europeanization through policy coordination (Armstrong 2010).

The same could be said about preventing economic migrants from dying en route to Europe, after more than 350 perished off Lampedusa (the Italian island southwest of Malta) in October 2013. Five years previously, EU border control had been delegated to a new European agency (for the Management of Operational Cooperation at the External Borders), Frontex, and not the Commission itself. Yet, work on action to strengthen Frontex and prevent another Lampedusa-style tragedy fell to an anomalous joint task force of the Commission and the Council. More generally, Kostadinova (2013) finds that the Commission's contribution to what she calls the 'configuration' of internal EU borders has been both indirect but also very direct—for example, on internal border controls and rules on the movement of highly skilled non-EU nationals—with the Commission showing considerable leadership in the

---

[11] Besides, the French wanted the initiative to focus on peripheral issues such as protection on the Internet for copyright owners and tax avoidance by hi-tech firms that promised to do nothing to boost European competitiveness (Hirst 2013).

latter cases. Again, policy solutions to many of the problems associated with migration were unimaginable, not least to EU member states, without the full participation of the Commission.

Also illustrative are the Commission's efforts to clarify rules on state aid for energy, especially to make clear what governments could do to promote renewable energy. The EU lacks a common energy policy and is not close to having one that features delegation of powers to the Commission. Rules on state aid for energy seem to validate the new intergovernmentalist hypothesis that what seems highly politicized can be made technocratic simply by shifting the problem to Brussels. Witness claims by large energy firms that high subsidies to renewables threatened the functioning of the energy market to the point where blackouts in the European winter became a real possibility (Keating 2013). In any event, the wider point is that the Commission clearly wields formidable powers to determine how much and how fast Europe moves to a carbon-free future.

It is also worth considering the buoyancy of the policy agenda where the Commission wields clear and strong powers, such as foreign economic policy. As of early 2014, the Commission—despite political noise about spying allegations—was at work on a Transatlantic Trade and Investment Partnership (TTIP) with the United States that promised to unleash a significant amount of cross-investment and economic growth on both sides (see Young and Peterson 2014). One investigation of foreign economic policy uncovers an unusually 'long chain of delegation', from voters to governments to the Council to the Commission to international organizations (Dür and Elsig 2011: 324). It also notes how delegation in the trade realm has continued throughout the post-Maastricht period both by treaty revisions and legal judgments by the European Court of Justice.

And when the Commission is the chosen delegate, it knows how to make the most of what it is given. To illustrate, the Commission became progressively more autonomous of EU member states during the Doha trade negotiations by exploiting the heterogeneity of state preferences (two camps of roughly equal size),[12] a vague mandate, and conflicting signals from its 'principals' (Conceição-Heldt 2011). Meanwhile, Niemann and Huigens (2011) characterize the Commission's expanding role in the Group of Eight as a case of 'agent emancipation' that has moved beyond the original principal-agent design, not least because the Commission—ever the friend of small member states—nurtured an alliance of EU states that desired input despite not being members themselves.

---

[12] Here we find a case that challenges—and certainly does not confirm—the new intergovernmentalist hypothesis that problems in preference formation are now a 'constitutive feature' of European integration (see chapter 1).

Finally, amid claims that Barroso led 'the little engine that couldn't' (Hodson 2013), it must be conceded that he launched major policy initiatives on climate change, the regulation of financial markets, the Europe 2020 programme, successive energy crises, the euro area, and TTIP. Crucially, he managed to do so without 'getting ahead' of key EU member states (Kassim et al. 2013: 178). In a way, the new normal of the Barroso Commission is the old normal. By no means can it be claimed that Barroso's entrepreneurship and enhanced authority within the Commission solved the problem of 'leaderless Europe' (Hayward 2008). The Commission is simply not strong enough to lead the EU, regardless of who its president is. But the Commission remains the straw that stirs the drink when it comes to advances in European policy cooperation.

Conclusion

The new intergovernmentalist paradigm offers a perceptive and testable vision of how the modern EU works, and how it differs from the way it has worked in the past. We have found that it provides perceptive insights into how the role of the Commission has changed. But we have also seen that it has its limits.

Yes, the Commission's ambitions as an engine of European integration were scaled back under Barroso. But this result is a natural response to the exponentially increased diversity of a radically enlarged EU. Arguably, Barroso was politically astute in accepting that policy solutions to shared problems require more deliberation in an EU of 28. His presidency was a generally productive one despite a political climate that allowed very limited space for a Commission that sought to impose its will.

Yes, member states have chosen to delegate powers to European agencies or other alternative bodies, rather than delegating to the Commission. But this pattern of delegation has suited the Commission fine. It has provided it with resources or expertise they did not have before in areas where they play an active policy role.

And yes, a College with a membership that replicates that of the Council might make for a more intergovernmental Commission. There is evidence that 'EU member states still attach a high value to having their nationals represented in the Commission at all levels' (Suvarierol 2011: 181). Occasionally, a policy case arises in which the nationality of the Commissioner(s)—such as for Trade and Agriculture in trade negotiations (Conceição-Heldt 2011)—matters as a determinant of the result. But multiple scholars now concur that Commissioners and their *cabinets* are now mostly 'functionally denationalised' (Egeberg and Heskestad 2010; Kassim et al. 2013: 200–2) and highly dossier-focused. One recent review of the research literature on the

Commission finds it to be an unusually clear case of 'a political organization at the international level in which decision-makers' behaviour significantly transcends an intergovernmental logic' (Egeberg 2012: 946).

So, no, the new intergovernmentalist paradigm cannot be unambiguously endorsed when we consider the Commission as a case. It appears that the Commission mostly gets on with its work and that most of it is focused on closer European policy cooperation. There is no question that this work is more difficult and requires more deliberation than in the past. But the Commission is not going anywhere. Most of what it does leads—in terms of policy cooperation—to a more united Europe. If the EU exists in a state of disequilibrium, maybe the Commission is an oasis of calm within the storm?

10

The Court of Justice's Dilemma—Between 'More Europe' and 'Constitutional Mediation'

Marie-Pierre Granger

Integration without supranationalization—this is the paradox identified by proponents of a new intergovernmentalist account of European integration (see chapter 1).[1] They claim, in particular, that *deliberation and consensus have become the guiding norms of day-to-day decision making at all levels* (hypothesis 1), that *supranational institutions are not hard-wired to seek ever closer union* (hypothesis 2), and that *where delegation occurs, governments and traditional supranational actors support the creation and empowerment of* de novo *institutions* (hypothesis 3).

The Court of Justice of the European Union (EU)[2] is generally heralded as a powerful 'engine' of supranational integration; we should thus expect strong resistance from the Luxembourg judges towards this new intergovernmentalist Europe. Existing scholarly works analysing the role of the Court of Justice in European integration tend, nonetheless, to focus on particular types of cases, which are more likely to emphasize supranational dynamics; when we look at a different set of cases, we obtain a more nuanced picture. This is what I attempt to show in this chapter.

I start with a brief overview of the Court's powers and of its role in European integration, as exposed by the 'supranationalist' perspective, before outlining and addressing a number of empirical blind spots. I then proceed by exploring some of the intergovernmentalist hypotheses,[3] through a selective analysis of

---

[1] I would like to thank the editors and contributors to this volume, and H. de Waele, for their helpful comments on previous drafts. The responsibility for remaining errors is mine.

[2] Located in Luxembourg and also known as the European Court of Justice, its official name is the Court of Justice, and it consists in the highest-tier of the EU judicial body now known as the Court of Justice of the European Union.

[3] The remaining three hypotheses are not systematically addressed in this piece. Studies pertaining to judicial preferences or the impact of judicialization on EU political processes (hypothesis 4) are explored in scholarship addressing the dynamics of EU legal integration (for a

official Court statements on European integration and the role of the Court of Justice, as well as judgments, judicial opinions, and academic commentaries, mostly concerned with the judicial review of EU measures.

First, I scrutinize judicial visions of Europe, to find that the Court of Justice does not systematically project a supranational vision of Europe ('ever closer union'), but a much more complex idea of European integration, infused with social concerns, pluralism, democracy, and constitutionalism. In practice, however, the Court of Justice often fails to live up to these new ideals, suggesting that the 'old' federal and liberal vision dies hard (hypothesis 2). Second, focusing on EU judicial review cases, I reveal that the Court of Justice is generally deferential towards intergovernmental coordination or decision-making processes, and is not so inclined to push for supranational mechanisms at all costs. Rather, the Court of Justice comes out as a supporter of 'more Europe', whatever its takes (intergovernmental, differentiated, bureaucratic, etc.). To preserve its own relevance, it asserts judicial control over a broad range of measures, but exercises its oversight in a flexible manner, which acknowledges some of the specificities of 'new intergovernmentalism', including its informal, deliberative, and consensual features (hypothesis 1). This finding challenges the common association of judicialization with supranationalization. Third, I show that the Court of Justice is generally supportive of the creation and empowerment of *de novo* political or technocratic bodies, even where that entails more (inter)governmental influence, but is protective of its own judicial turf (hypothesis 3). I conclude by suggesting that the Court's overall 'pro-European' stance, the reasons for which can, unfortunately, not be fully explored in this chapter, undermines its ability to act as Europe's constitutional court. The Court's handling of the resulting tensions could bear significantly on the future of European integration, in a manner which could put certain features of 'new intergovernmentalism' to the test.

10.1 The Court and European Integration: The Blind Spots of the Supranational Narrative

The role of the Court of Justice is to ensure that 'in the application and interpretation of the Treaties, the law is observed' (Article 19 TFEU). Political science and legal scholarships which address the nature and dynamics of legal

review, see Conant 2007, Stone Sweet 2010). The blurring of high and low politics (hypothesis 5) has always been a feature of integration through law (i.e. law as a 'mask' and 'shield' for politics, Burley and Mattli 1993). Finally, regarding the state of disequilibrium (hypothesis 6), I refer the reader to Weiler's seminal article (Weiler 1991), which outlined interactions and imbalances between normative (legal) supranationalism and decisional (political) intergovernmentalism.

integration have spilled much ink exposing *how the Court of Justice deployed and expanded its enforcement and interpretative powers to lay the legal foundations of a supranational, federal, and liberal Europe.* They do, however, have some blind spots, which cast some doubt as to the encompassing nature of the supranational narrative.

Seminal contextual legal works described at length the constitutionalization and federalization of EU law by the Court of Justice, its consolidation of enforcement mechanisms against defaulting member states, and the judicial expansion of the EU's substantive scope of action through its far-reaching interpretation of internal market provisions; they stressed the significance of purpose-driven ('teleological') interpretation, the creative use of judicial procedures, inter-judicial dialogues, and political inertia (Stein 1981; Mancini 1989; Weiler 1991; Bengoetxea 1993; Mancini and Keeling 1994a and b; Weatherill 2002, 2004). For long supportive and praising of the Court's heroic pursuit of further integration,[4] legal scholarship has become over the years more critical of its relentless promotion of Europe at all costs (Rasmussen 1986; Weiler 1991; Hartley 1996; De Búrca 1998; Arnull 2007; Hunt and Shaw 2009; Lasser 2009; de Waele 2010; Conway 2012; Horsley 2012, 2013).

Legal accounts inspired neofunctionalists, who embraced legal integration as a spearhead for their theoretical approach. They argued that it was driven by self-interested sub- and supranational (legal) actors, and produced spill-over effects in the political arena that national governments could not resist (Burley and Mattli 1993; Mattli and Slaughter 1995, 1998; Stone Sweet and Sandholtz 1998), an explanation which gave a hard time to 'old' intergovernmentalists (Garrett and Weingast 1991; Moravcsik 1993; Garrett 1995).[5] The supranational dynamics they uncovered were later confirmed by historical and rational choice new institutionalist perspectives, which found in precedent-based reasoning, inter-court relations, and judicial independence a number of key features which insulated the Court of Justice from (inter)governmental influence (Tallberg 2000; Pollack 2003; Stone Sweet 2004; Alter 2010; Kelemen and Schmidt 2012; see also chapter 11).

Existing works on legal integration thus emphasize the supranationalizing effect of legalization and judicialization trends in the EU (Stone Sweet 2010). However, their vision may be partially distorted because of their empirical blind spots. Indeed, their works concentrate on cases related to the development of the EU legal order, and compliance with rules which are at the core of the Community method (e.g. internal market, citizenship, competition,

---

[4] For a review, see Hunt and Shaw (2009).
[5] Moravcsik viewed the Court as an 'anomaly' (Moravcsik 1993, 513–14). Garrett and Weingast (1991) and Garrett (1995) advanced that it was sensitive to political constraints, but their theoretical claims did not stand well the empirical test (Conant 2007; Stone Sweet 2010).

environment, or non-discrimination), generated in the context of interpretative preliminary rulings[6] and enforcement actions.[7] Perhaps a different story would emerge if we shifted the focus to other aspects of the Court's activities, and take stock of post-1992 developments.

Since Maastricht, the EU has not only dramatically diversified its objectives and expanded its substantive scope of action to new and sometimes sensitive policy fields, it has also experimented with alternative modes of governance, such as the Open Method of Coordination, which pose challenges to law and courts (Scott and Trubek 2002; Armstrong 2010, 2013; Dawson 2011). They have also explored different paths towards further integration.

Despite attempts at consolidation and simplification, policy-making at EU level involves increasingly complex and mixed institutional and procedural set-ups. As is well known, at Maastricht, member states created, alongside the 'Community supranational Pillar', two new 'intergovernmental Union pillars', the second Common Foreign and Security Policy (CFSP) pillar and the third Justice and Home Affairs (JHA) pillar, to coordinate their activities more closely and effectively in sensitive policy areas. At first, they excluded the Court of Justice from overseeing activities in these fields, but in later treaty reforms, they extended judicial control over what is now known as the 'Area of Freedom, Security and Justice' (AFSJ).[8] The Lisbon Treaty does away with the pillar structure, but the diversity of *modi operandi* persists, the Economic and Monetary Union being a characteristic mix of intergovernmental coordination and supranational processes. There is, moreover, a growing tendency towards 'differentiated integration', through opt-ins, opt-outs, or 'enhanced cooperation' (Leuffen, Rittberger, and Schimmelfennig 2013), or even actions taken outside of the treaties' framework between all or a group of member states, involving EU institutions in adjusted capacities or the creation of new decision-making bodies (e.g. the Schengen agreement, or the recent Treaty on Stability, Coordination and Governance (TSCG) and the Treaty establishing the European Stability Mechanism). This hybridization and complexity generates procedural controversies and inter-institutional disputes which can end up before the Court of Justice, while the scope and degree of judicial control of these matters is contested. Moreover, the Community method itself has evolved over time with the growing influence of the European Council, an

---

[6] Procedure through which national courts can, or must (in the case of last instance courts) send questions relating to the interpretation or validity of EU law (Article 267 TFEU).

[7] Action whereby the Commission (or, rarely, another member state) may bring a member state to Court where it fails to comply with EU law (Articles 258–260 TFEU).

[8] The Treaty maintains most foreign and security policy measures beyond the reach of the Court (Article 275 TFEU). The Court can only review the legality of restrictive measures adopted against natural and legal persons and check whether measures fall under general Union competence or the special foreign and security policy title. The activities of national police and law enforcement bodies cannot be reviewed (Article 276 TFEU).

increased reliance on informal processes, the growth of comitology commit-tees and agencies, the consolidation of the subsidiarity and proportionality principles, the development of fundamental rights frameworks, and so on. These developments pose new challenges to the Court of Justice, whose implications on integration dynamics have not been fully analysed.

The scale of the transformation, only sketched out above, is well captured by those arguing for a reconceptualization of European integration around 'new intergovernmentalist' lines (see chapter 1). Although there is no shortage of detailed accounts of the case law pertaining to new policy areas, in particu-lar, in relation to the AFSP, there have been few systematic attempts to reassess, empirically, the role of the Court of Justice in relation to the trans-formation of European integration.[9] Scholarship on legal integration not only sidelines many of the post-Maastricht developments, they also overlook an important area of judicial activity, the review of EU measures (annulment actions[10] or preliminary rulings concerning the validity of EU measures), and their consequences on EU policy and political processes.

In the following sections, I try to address these lacunae, and explore three of the new intergovernmentalist claims regarding the nature of integration post-Maastricht: supranational institutions are not hard-wired towards ever closer union (hypothesis 2); political deliberation and consensus are ends in them-selves (hypothesis 1); and decision-making powers are delegated to new bodies (hypothesis 3).

10.2 The Court's Visions of European Integration: Stuck In-Between

Is the Court of Justice really genetically designed (Mancini and Keeling 1994a: 186) to pursue the 'ever closer union'? The objectives and values of the EU as set out in the treaties have evolved and the institutional, political, and social context in which the Court of Justice operates has been transformed; yet, the Court of Justice appears to find it *difficult to move beyond its old vision of Europe, despite a rhetoric infused by social, human rights, democratic, and pluralist concerns.*

The Lisbon Treaty sets out explicitly that all EU institutions 'shall aim to promote [the Union] values, advance its objectives, [and] serve its interests, those of its citizens and those of the member states' (Article 13 TEU). EU commitment to 'ever closer union', which was apparently the driving force behind the Court's constitutional doctrines (Pescatore 1983) is still enshrined in the Treaty, but it is now tempered by democracy, transparency

---

[9] See chapter 3 of this volume.   [10] Article 263 TFEU.

and human rights protection requirements (Articles 1 and 6 TEU). EU objectives also go much beyond the original internal market project (itself subject to
social considerations), to include security, foreign affairs, economic and monetary policy, and so on (Article 3 TEU).

Despite this (con)textual evolution, the Court of Justice nonetheless seems
to hold strong to its old *'certaine idée de l'Europe'* (Pescatore 1983:157), as a
sui generis supranational, federal, and liberal (market-driven) project, tied
together by centrally designed uniformly applicable laws which prevail over
conflicting local norms or policies. Whilst a closer analysis reveals that
the Court of Justice is projecting alternative paradigms for European integration, centred on 'Citizens' Europe', 'Social Europe' or a 'Europe of Rights',
instead of the 'Europe of the Market', it often fails to live up to those new
ideals.

On the CURIA website, the historical contribution of the Court of Justice
is framed as protecting the rights and improving the life of EU citizens.[11]
Recent empirical studies reveal that internal market objectives, prominent
in the foundational years, are losing traction within the Court's ranks,
and other concerns, such as social justice, human rights, democracy, rule of
law, pluralism, accountability, and legitimacy, are gaining ground (Granger
2005; Morano-Foadi and Andreadakis 2011; Petkova and Dumbrovsky 2011;
Malecki 2012).

This normative and cultural evolution resonates in the words of some of the
Court's members, cited here as symptomatic examples of the judicial refram-
ing of the nature and purpose of European (legal) integration. Judge Prechal
insists that there is 'a very important social dimension' in the free movement
case law, since 'we are dealing with human beings and not only with "labour
as a factor of production"' (Prechal 2013). Advocate General Trstenjak asserts
that economic integration should not be 'used indiscriminately' but 'brought
into harmony with the values of other policy areas';[12] she adds that '[t]he
European Union should [not] disregard the social dimension of integration',
since '[t]he promotion of social cohesion in the sense of the idea of "solidarity" is and remains an important aim of European integration'.[13]

Moreover, according to Judge Prechal again (2003), 'EU fundamental rights
will . . . function as factors that integrate the system, keep it together' (see also
Lenaerts 2010). These statements echo the views expressed by Advocate General Jacobs, one of the Court's most influential members in the early 1990s,
who portrayed the (then) Community as 'not just a commercial arrangement'

[11] See: <http://curia.europa.eu/jcms/jcms/Jo2_7024/>.
[12] Case C-324/07 *Coditel* [2008] ECR I-317, para. 81.
[13] Case C-282/10 *Dominguez* [2011] ECR I-559, para. 159.

but 'a common enterprise' of 'all the citizens of Europe', aimed at 'foster[ing] that sense of common identity and shared destiny'.[14]

Furthermore, as put by former Advocate General Maduro, '[t]he traditional concept of European integration flows from the notion of unity of integration', but with 'a greater heterogeneity of structures and interests, the concept of unitary integration can no longer be applied in the same way as [before]'.[15] 'Concurrent claims to sovereignty are the very manifestation of the legal pluralism that makes the European integration process unique'.[16]

Finally, Court members are keen to highlight the Court's due regard for democracy, which in the EU context requires respect for both the peoples and the member states (Mancini and Keeling 1994b; Lenaerts 2013).

These individual declarations do not, however, necessarily translate into collective institutional practices and outputs. The Court of Justice is struggling to move beyond a 'free movement logic' in EU citizenship cases, it has not, until recently, taken human rights so seriously, and it is still attached to a unitary conception of the EU.

The EU citizenship case law is characteristic of the Court's struggle to get beyond the internal market foundations. Before Maastricht, the Court of Justice had developed a so-called 'incipient' form of EU citizenship, based on the Treaty provisions and EU legislation on the free movement of workers and services, which conferred residency rights and equal treatment to 'mobile' and 'economically active' citizens (Plender 1976). At Maastricht, the member states incorporated the concept of EU citizenship and corresponding rights in the Treaty.[17] The Court of Justice consequently upheld EU citizenship as 'destined to be the fundamental status of member states' nationals',[18] and granted far-reaching residency rights to third-country nationals (TCN), family members of 'active' and 'mobile' EU citizens,[19] as well as equal access to certain benefits for 'mobile', although non-economically active, EU citizens, who were sufficiently integrated in the host country.[20] The Court of Justice nonetheless remained within a 'mobility logic', with the consequence that the vast majority of EU citizens, the 'static' ones, derived no benefit from their EU citizenship (Kochenov and Plender 2012).

In a series of controversial rulings, the Court of Justice showed signs of moving away from the mobility logic towards developing a more autonomous EU citizenship status. However, later judgments cast doubts as to the scope of the transformation. In *Zambrano*, which concerned the residency right of TCN

---

[14] Case C-326/92 *Phil Collins* [1993] ECR I-276, para. 11.
[15] Case C-137/05 *UK v Council* (Biometric Passport) [2007] ECR I-420, paras 76–7.
[16] Case C-127/07 *Arcelor* [2008] ECR I-292, para. 15.   [17] Articles 20–5 TFEU.
[18] Case C-184/99 *Grzelczyk* [2001] ECR-I 6193.
[19] E.g. Case C-127/08 *Metock et al.* [2008] ECR I-6241.
[20] Case C-209/03 *Bidar* [2005] ECR I-2119.

parents of 'static' EU citizens (dependent minors), the Court of Justice stated that EU citizenship protected 'all' EU citizens, even non-mobile ones, from the 'deprivation of the genuine enjoyment of the substance of the rights' they derive from EU citizenship.[21] Legal academics interpreted the ruling as signifying that 'the Union has overcome its existence as a functional entity devoted to market integration' (Von Bogdandy et al. 2012: 495) and shifted to a 'right-based' approach to EU citizenship (Kochenov and Plender 2012). However, the Court's narrowing of the scope of application of *Zambrano* in later cases *McCarthy* and *Dereci*[22] challenges this assessment. The Court's members justify the latter restrictive approach based on the respect for the vertical delimitation of competence between the EU and the member states (e.g. Lenaerts 2011: 18). However, it could also reflect the Court's unwillingness to interfere with domestic affairs, which do not impact on cross-border movement, even when the human rights of EU citizens are at stake.

Moreover, the Court's case law on human rights protection questions the reality of a paradigmatic shift towards human rights as an alternative to market integration. The Court of Justice has become stricter in enforcing human rights requirements upon domestic actors, where it supports the authority of EU law; it is more reluctant to submit EU rules and actions to strict human rights scrutiny.

The Court of Justice has developed an impressive judge-made catalogue of rights (Tridimas 2006), now codified in the EU Charter of Fundamental Rights. It checks that member states comply with EU human rights obligations when they implement or act within the scope of EU law, defined broadly,[23] and limit the scope of member states' opt-outs from the Charter.[24] It has even supported the European Commission's use of the enforcement procedure to tackle, although indirectly, systematic disregard for the rule of law or human rights in member states.[25] It declared certain EU general principles binding upon private parties.[26] However, one is entitled to question the Court's genuine interest in human rights protection, where it argues that 'the reason for pursuing [compliance with EU human rights] is to avoid a situation in which the level of protection of fundamental rights varies

---

[21] Case C-34/09 *Zambrano* [2011] ECR I-1177.
[22] Cases C-434/09 *McCarthy* [2011] ECR I-3375 and C-256/11 *Dereci and Others* [2011] ECR I-11315.
[23] Case 260/89 *E.R.T.* [1991] ECR I-2925, C-617/10 *Åkerberg Fransson* [2013] ECR I-280.
[24] Cases C-411/10 *N.S.* and C-493/10 *M.E.* [2011] ECR I-13905.
[25] E.g. C-286/12 *Commission* v *Hungary* (Judges' retirement) [2012] ECR I-687 and C-288/12, *Commission* v *Hungary* (Data Protection Ombudsman) [2014] ECR I-237.
[26] Cases C-144/04 *Mangold* [2005] *ECR* I-9981 and C-555/07 *Kücükdeveci* [2010] ECR I-0036. Note that it did not confer the same effect to the Charter's provisions concerning workers' rights (C-176/12 *Association de Mediation Sociale* [2014] ECR I-2).

according to the national law involved in such a way as to undermine *the unity, primacy and effectiveness* of EU law'.[27]

Furthermore, the Court's human rights' scrutiny of EU-level action has been erratic, to say the least. Admittedly, the Court of Justice has accepted that national measures aimed at protecting human rights could validly 'trump' the Treaty's free movement provisions.[28] Yet, some of the most criticized Court decisions of recent years, the (in)famous '*Laval* quartet', in which social rights (e.g. right to strike, collective bargaining) clashed with the market freedoms, exposed the remaining jurisprudential bias towards market integration.[29] Indeed, analytical priority is granted to free movement, with the consequence that other aims, such as social policy or human rights, must always be 'sufficiently justified' in order to survive, which tilts the balance in favour of economic mobility rights (Barnard 2012).

While the Court of Justice does carry out increasingly rigorous checks over EU individual administrative measures, as well as regulatory schemes (Craig and De Búrca 2011: 378–81; Craig 2012a; Lenaerts 2013),[30] its human rights scrutiny over the activities of the EU legislator or intergovernmental initiatives at EU level is more 'relaxed'. The Lisbon Treaty has now made it easier to challenge EU regulatory measures (i.e. secondary legislation, generally adopted by the Commission); yet, the Court's restrictive *Plaumann* doctrine on the standing of non-privileged applicants (individuals, companies, civil society organization, etc.) continues to protect EU (quasi-)legislative acts from direct challenges by private parties.[31] Where such disputes nonetheless made it to the Court of Justice, brought by member states or EU institutions excluded or outvoted in EU processes, or by tenacious private litigants willing to travel the cumbersome indirect preliminary reference route, the Luxembourg judges normally upheld those EU laws, including those adopted under the intergovernmental pillars, even when their human rights credentials were seriously questioned. The Court of Justice, for example, found that instruments such as the Biotechnology Directive,[32] the Family Reunification Directive,[33] or the European Arrest Warrant (EAW), were perfectly compatible with human rights requirements,[34] observers human rights.[35]

---

[27] Case C-206/13 *Siragusa* [2014] ECR I-126, para. 32. Emphasis added.
[28] Cases C-112/00 *Schmidberger* [2003] ECR I-5659; C-36/02 *Omega* [2004] ECR I-9609.
[29] Cases C-438/05 *Viking* [2007] ECR I-10779–10840; C-341/05 *Laval* [2007] ECR I-11767, C-319/06 *Commission v Luxembourg* [2008] ECR I-4323; C-346/06 *Rüffert* [2008] ECR I-1989.
[30] E.g. Case C-221/09 *AJD Tuna* [2011] ECR I-1655.
[31] Cases 25/62 *Plaumann* [1963] ECR 95 and T-262/10 *Microban* [2011] ECR II-7697.
[32] Case C-377/98 *Netherlands v EP and Council* [2001] ECR I-7079.
[33] Case C-540/03 *EP v Council* [2006] ECR I-5769.
[34] Case C-303/05 *Advocaten voor de Wereld* [2007] ECR I-3633.
[35] E.g. criticism of the negative impact of the EAW on the right to a fair trial by Fair Trial International. See: <http://www.fairtrials.org/justice-in-europe/the-european-arrest-warrant/>.

The Court of Justice has, however, started to apply tighter human rights controls towards EU measures adopted in the context of EU anti-terrorism policy. In the famous *Kadi* saga, the Court of Justice invalidated EU 'Smart Sanctions' Regulations adopted by the EU Council of Ministers to give effect to United Nations Security Council Resolutions for failure to observe human rights requirements.[36] The Court's special vigilance could nonetheless have had more to do with protecting the autonomy of EU law from the UN order, than ensuring respect for individual rights (Ziegler 2009; De Búrca 2010; Conway 2012), although this is refuted by its justices (Kokott and Sobotta 2012).

Still, cases such as *Volker and Schecke*,[37] *Test Achats*,[38] or more recently the *Digital Rights Ireland* (DRI)[39] case suggest that we may be gradually moving into a new stage of human rights protection in the EU. In *Volker and Schecke*, the Court of Justice invalidated Council and Commission regulations requiring the publication of information on the beneficiaries of EU funds. In *Test-Achat*, the Court of Justice annulled an EU Directive which allowed discriminatory practices in the insurance sector. Finally, in DRI, the Court of Justice brought down the controversial Data Retention Directive, which required member states to oblige operators to collect and retain traffic data. Significantly, they also explained that the discretion of the EU legislator is limited when it adopts legislation which imposes 'serious interference' with fundamental rights, and that it would apply 'strict' judicial scrutiny in such cases.

The Court of Justice remains, however, weary of extending human rights supervision over member states 'extra-Treaty' initiatives. In the *Pringle* case concerning the validity of the European Stability Mechanism (ESM), the Court of Justice controversially accepted that where member states acted outside the scope of the Treaty, they must not comply with the Charter.[40] This exclusion, probably also applicable to Memoranda of Understandings adopted by the ESM Governing Council,[41] is remarkable, given their possible impact on due process and social rights in 'beneficiary' member states (Peers 2013: 52).

Finally, case law reveals that, despite talk of respect for pluralism, the Court of Justice remains, after all, strongly attached to the notion of unity. In the recent *Melloni* judgment, the Court of Justice upheld the EAW and enforced its application, even with the result that it would lower human rights standards

---

[36] Joined cases C-402 and 415/05P *Kadi I* [2008]. ECR I-6351; joined cases C-584/10 P, C-593/10 P and C-595/10 P. *Kadi II* [2013] ECR I-518.
[37] Case C-92/09 and C-93/09 *Volker und Markus Schecke* [2010] ECR I-662.
[38] Case C-236/09 *Test-Achats* [2011] *ECR* I-73.
[39] Joined cases C-293/12 and C-594/12 *Digital Rights Ireland and Seitlinger and Others* [2014] ECR I-238.
[40] Case C-370/12 *Pringle* [2012] ECR I-756.
[41] But see Advocate General Opinion, in C-370/12 *Pringle* [2012] ECR-675, para. 176.

at the domestic level. Evidently, concerns related to the supremacy, unity and effectiveness of EU law must take precedence.[42]

The Court of Justice, as it moves away from a supranational vision of Europe and market-driven integration, appears caught between a preference for European solutions, and its professed commitment to a 'Europe of Rights', a more socially oriented 'Citizens' Europe and 'Unity in Diversity'. The Court of Justice is thus not hard-wired for the pursuit of ever closer union (hypothesis 2), but changing cap is proving difficult, probably because of the weight of precedent, and sociological and organizational factors characteristic of the Court's decision-making process (*esprit de corps*, socialization patterns, EU legal training, judicial hierarchy, collegial process, interactions between EU legal, political elites, etc.).

10.3 Intergovernmental Deliberation and Consensus: Luxembourg's Light Shadow on Intergovernmentalism in Brussels

Intergovernmental processes, as alternatives to delegation of law-making powers to supranational institutions, have become deliberative and consensual (see chapter 1). The Court of Justice is more supportive of this trend than is often assumed, as revealed by the way it reviews EU legal outcomes. Whilst the Court of Justice deployed efforts to bring a whole range of EU measure *within the ambit of judicial control*, potentially subjecting them to regular legal and accountability constraints, it has *exercised its control in a manner deferential to political choices*.

We have already noted how the Court of Justice has started to impose stricter human rights standards on the adoption of EU measures, and exercises closer scrutiny, except for intergovernmental agreements adopted outside the Treaty framework. However, formally, the judicial review powers of the Court of Justice go far beyond human rights checks, and extend to controlling the respect of the vertical and horizontal allocation of competences in the EU (including respect for the subsidiarity principle), procedural requirements, and substantive treaty provisions. The Court of Justice has always made it difficult for outsiders to EU political processes to challenge their legal outcomes.[43] Moreover, it tends to rubber-stamp the adoption of EU instruments, as well as unorthodox Treaty reforms.

---

[42] Case C-399/11 *Melloni* [2013] ECR I-107.   [43] See n. 31.

In the past, one of the major exceptions to this judicial deference concerned the so-called 'legal basis' cases.[44] The matter is of utmost importance, since the choice of the Treaty basis determines the relative influence of the EU institutions and national governments in EU political processes. From the adoption of the Single European Act, and even more after Maastricht, such cases multiplied, as institutions and governments disagreed as to whether a Directive or a Regulation should be adopted under consultation or co-decision, or by unanimity or qualified majority in the Council of Ministers. Originally, the Court of Justice very much rallied behind the Commission and European Parliament's (EP) claims for greater involvement and impact (Cullen and Charlesworth 1999; McCown 2003; Jupille 2004; Lenaerts 2011). However, over the last decade, it has apparently been less inclined to automatically support the EP's claim in such disputes (Bradley 2011).[45] One should, however, further analyse these 'inter-institutonal' cases, which concern the determination of the border between the pillars, the use of differentiated integration, the validity of agreements outside of the Treaty, and the choice of policy implementation procedures, for they enable an assessment of the Court's preferences towards modes of integration.

The Court of Justice asserted jurisdiction over the border between the supranational and intergovernmental pillars.[46] However, it exercised its powers without systematically favouring the supranational pillar over the intergovernmental ones (Bradley 2011), and this despite the Treaty suggesting priority for Community legal bases (ex-Article 47 TEU).[47] The Court of Justice nonetheless attempted, at first, to 'supranationalize' the intergovernmental pillar, by claiming interpretation and review powers over measures adopted under the intergovernmental pillar, and 'transplanting' Community rules and principles into these intergovernmental pillars. For example, in *Segi* and *Gestoras*, it accepted challenges brought by individuals against common positions imposing sanctions on individuals adopted under the intergovernmental pillars, even though it did not have formal jurisdiction over them at the time.[48] It also applied rules related to Community annulment actions and preliminary rulings to their functional equivalents under the

---

[44] For another famous exception, see C-376/98 *Germany* v *EP and Council* (Tobacco Advertising) [2000] ECR I-8419.

[45] E.g. cases C-436/03 *EP* v *Council* (European Cooperative Society) [2006] ECR I-3733, C-540/03 *Parliament* v *Council* (Family Reunification) [2006] ECR 1-5769.

[46] Case C-170/96 *Commission* v *Council* (Airport Transit Visa) [1998] ECR I-2763.

[47] The Court considered that the act should have been adopted under the Community pillar basis in some cases (e.g. C-176/03 *Commission* v *Council* (Environmental Crime) [2005] ECR I-7879; C-91/05 *Commission* v *Council* (Small Weapons) [2008] ECR I-3651; C-376/98 *Germany* v *EP and Council* (Data Retention Directive) [2000] ECR I-8419) and under an intergovernmental pillar basis in others (C-440/05 *Commission* v *Council* (Ship Pollution) [2007] ECR I-909; joined cases C-317/04 and C-318/04 *EP* v *Council* (Passenger Name Record) [2006] ECR I-47217).

[48] C-355/04 P *Segi* [2007] ECR I-1657; C-354/04 P *Gestoras* [2007] ECR I-1579.

(post-Amsterdam) Third Pillar.[49] In *Pupino*, the Court of Justice (invoking the aim of 'ever closer union') confirmed the binding nature of Third Pillar Framework Decisions and insisted that member states' authorities were under a duty to interpret national law in line with them (i.e. 'consistent interpretation', or 'indirect effect').[50] In doing so, it undermined the member states' explicit rejection, enshrined in the Treaty, of the direct effect of EU Third Pillar instruments.[51] In *Gestoras*, the Court of Justice nonetheless fell short of extending the Community regime of liability to damages caused by the adoption of CFSP Common Position related to EU anti-terrorist measures, thereby acknowledging the specificities of CFSP matters and procedures.[52] The Court of Justice thus eventually set limits to the 'supranationalization' of intergovernmental matters.

Given its already noted inclination towards a unitary vision of European integration, the Court of Justice has been strangely sympathetic towards enhanced cooperation initiatives. It endorsed AFSP and Schengen opt-outs and opt-ins, with few conditions.[53] Recently, it even allowed member states to use the Treaty Enhanced Cooperation Procedure (ECP) to set up a unitary patent system. The Court of Justice rejected Italy and Spain's challenge to the scheme, confirming that the ECP could be validly resorted to where it had been impossible to reach common arrangements for the whole EU within a reasonable period, and where it contributed to the process of integration.[54]

The Court of Justice treads carefully when checking on initiatives outside the Treaty. It checks intergovernmental agreements' compatibility with EU law, but tends to decline the power to invalidate them, and usually declares them compatible (even when they limit its own jurisdiction).[55] In the now notorious *Pringle* case, the Court of Justice upheld the validity of the intergovernmental treaty which established the ESM, even though it seemed to conflict with the Treaty 'no-bail out' clause, and provided for restricted judicial review mechanisms.[56]

Another contentious field concerns the implementation by the Commission of EU legislation. From the 1980s, the member states introduced a complex and obscure 'comitology' system under which committees composed of national experts oversaw the Commission's adoption of measures adopted for the implementation of EU legislation. This comitology regime was resented by both the Commission (Craig 2012a: 112) and the EP (Bradley 1992).

---

[49] Environmental Crime case, see n. 47.   [50] C-105/03 *Pupino* [2005] ECR I-5285, para. 41.
[51] Ex-Article 34(2)b TEU.   [52] C-354/04 *Gestoras* [2007] ECR I-1579.
[53] It, however, limited cherry-picking possibilities: e.g. case C-77/05 *UK* v *Council* (Border Agency) [2007] ECR I-11459.
[54] Case C-274/11 and C-295/11 *Spain and Italy* v *Council* (Unitary Patent) [2013] ECR I-240.
[55] Joined cases C-181/91 and C-248/91 *EP* v *Council and Commission* (Bangladesh) [1993] ECR I-3685; C-316/91 *Parliament* v *Council* (Lomé) [1994] ECR I-625.
[56] See n. 40.

The Court of Justice nonetheless gave its blessing to it.[57] It asserted control over their legal outputs, held the Commission formally responsible,[58] but for long, exercised little control as to what was to be decided under the comitology system (Scott and Trubek 2002). It also contributed to maintaining its club-like nature, resisting pressure from outsiders seeking participation in these regulatory processes (Mendes 2011).[59] The Lisbon Treaty modified the regime, by distinguishing between 'implementing acts', still subject to a modified version of comitology, and 'delegated acts', no longer subject to it.[60] The Court of Justice recognized the broad discretion enjoyed by the Council of Ministers and EP, acting as EU legislator, in determining which procedure should apply (and thus how much control they wished to exert over the Commission's implementation of EU policies).[61] However, it has now started to set limits to the technocratization and the bypassing of democracy and political deliberations. In one case concerning the power to use force at sea to implement the Schengen Border Code, it considered that measures which interfered significantly with fundamental rights could only be adopted by the EU legislator (and not through technocratic procedures).[62]

As already noted, the Court of Justice displays an ambivalent attitude towards more participatory and open processes in EU law-making. It continues to protect EU (quasi-)legislative, regulatory, and treaty reform processes from challenges brought by outsiders. It is, however, also trying to open up EU deliberation and decision-making processes.[63] In particular, it extended the application of EU access to documents rules to measures adopted under the intergovernmental pillars,[64] and required the Council of Ministers to disclose the identities of member states voting for and against legislative proposals.[65]

There is little agreement as to whether transparency facilitates or undermines deliberative and consensual practices (Curtin 2007), but opening up assemblies of representatives may restrict their ability to deliberate and reach consensus (Stasavage 2007). By turning the spotlight on formal decision-making processes, the Court of Justice may stifle deliberation in formal

---

[57] Cases C-25/70 *Koster* [1970 ECR 1161; C-5/77 *Tedeschi* [1977] ECR 1555; C-259/95 *EP* v *Council* [1995] ECR I-5303; C-378/00 *Commission* v *EP and Council* [2003] ECR I-937; C-156/93 *EP* v *Commission* [1995] ECR I-2019; C-417/93 *EP* v *Council* [1995] ECR I-1185.

[58] Case T- 88/97 *Rothmans* [1999] ECR II-2463.

[59] E.g. case C-49/88 *Al-Jubail Fertilizer* [1991] ECR I-3187.

[60] Article 290–291 TFEU.

[61] Case C-427/12 *Commission* v *EP and Council* (Biocides) [2014] ECR I-170.

[62] Case C-355/10 *EP* v *Council* (Schengen Border Code) [2012] ECR I-516.

[63] E.g. cases C-514, 528 and 532/07 *Sweden* v *ApPI and Commission* [2001] ECR; C-64/05 P *Sweden* v *Commission* [2007] ECR II-11839; C-39/05 P, C-52/05 P *Sweden and Turco/Council* [2008] ECR I-4723; C-506/08 P *MyTravel* [2011] ECR I- 496.

[64] Case C-174/95 *Svenska Journalistforbundet* [1998] ECR II-2289.

[65] Case C-280/11 P *Access info Europe* [2013] ECR I-671.

settings, and encourage informal discussions, which offer more favourable conditions.

Looking beyond judicial review cases, the Court of Justice has not always followed the strict enforcement line, which supranationalists stress, as revealed by decisions delivered in the context of hybrid policy areas, such as the EMU. In 2004, the Court of Justice, despite the Commission's insistence, refused to force the Council of Ministers to ensure compliance with the Stability and Growth Pact by France and Germany.[66] It left it to intergovernmental relations to determine the modalities of states' compliance with fiscal discipline principles, thereby undermining its effective application. One can only speculate how the Court of Justice would fulfil its enforcement mission under the TSCG.

To conclude, the Court of Justice, overall, left a wide margin of discretion to the EU and the member states when acting in (quasi-)legislative and regulatory capacities. It asserted judicial control over a wide range of EU acts, and imposed itself as the ultimate umpire of what, and how much, EU institutions and member states could do in different institutional and policy contexts. However, it exercised a light touch review, shielding them from 'outsiders' challenges, and refraining from substantial interference with political choices, even when those amounted to controversial or 'unorthodox' EU treaty- and law-making. This light shadow of Luxembourg probably facilitated intergovernmental deliberation and consensus (hypothesis 1), but it also contributed to insulating EU processes from societal concern. The Court's recent moves towards greater transparency requirements and stricter human rights control over the EU legislator may impose new constraints on formal intergovernmental deliberations in the Council, and paradoxically, encourage further intergovernmental experimentation with 'irregular' modes of policy-making, in particular as the Court of Justice seems willing to endorse such initiatives *ex post facto* and to subject them to 'specifically catered' legal constraints (including human rights exemptions) and judicial control.

10.4 The Court and New Bodies: Conditional Endorsement and Judicial Turf-Protection

The Court of Justice has been portrayed as a strong ally of the Commission (Stein 1981), and a protector of its legislative and regulatory prerogatives. The developments reviewed above already revealed that the Luxembourg judges did not systematically support enhanced powers for supranational actors.

---

[66] Case C-27/04 *Commission v Council* [2004] ECR I-664.

Moreover, despite some initial resistance towards institutional diversification in the EU, they eventually *backed up the creation and delegation of discretionary powers* to *de novo* bodies, including 'intergovernmental' ones, especially where these result in the further transfer of powers to the EU. They, however, *defend their own judicial turf with strong determination.*

EU legislators created, over the last decades, forty or so EU agencies and other bodies to assist in the implementation of EU policies. Some perform only consultative or informative roles, whilst others could adopt binding non-discretionary individual decisions.[67] The Court of Justice had, early on, placed formal legal obstacles to the creation of fully fledged EU regulatory agencies. Institutions could not delegate discretionary powers, but only 'clearly defined executive powers . . . subject to strict review' (*Meroni*)[68] and bodies other than the EU institutions could not adopt regulatory acts (*Romano*).[69] The Commission long successfully relied on these 'anti-delegation' doctrines to prevent the delegation of discretionary regulatory powers to concurrent EU agencies (Majone 2002; Chamon 2011), but it has now become supportive of the empowerment of EU agencies (see chapter 9).

When the United Kingdom tried to challenge the transfer of regulatory and discretionary decision-making powers to the European Securities and Markets Authority (ESMA) under the Short Selling Regulation, relying on the 'anti-delegation' jurisprudence, the Court of Justice concluded, summarily that such transfer did not contradict the *Meroni/Romano* requirements.[70] Given the scale of discretionary powers granted to the ESMA, the ruling empties the anti-delegation doctrines of their substance, and opens the way to the further delegation of discretionary powers to *de novo* bodies.

The Court of Justice has also been unwilling to closely scrutinize the creation and empowerment of bodies outside of the Treaty framework. In *Pringle*, it rejected an Irish parliamentarian's challenge to the creation of the ESM, a new intergovernmental body under member states' control operating as a permanent bail-out mechanism, outside of the Treaty, but drawing upon EU institutional resources (albeit in modified configurations).[71]

The Court of Justice leaves much discretion to the EU legislator or the member states to decide on the creation and delegation of discretionary and regulatory powers to *de novo* bodies; yet, it does assert formal judicial control over their establishment and empowerment, as well as over the measures they adopt. Despite a lack of formal jurisdiction at the time, the Court of Justice had

---

[67] Although formally, these agencies did not have discretionary decision-making or regulatory powers, *de facto*, many did (Craig 2012a).

[68] Cases 9/56 *Meroni* [1957–58] ECR 133.   [69] Case 98/80 *Romano* [1981] ECR 1241.

[70] Case C-270/12 *United Kingdom* v *Council and EP* (22 January 2014).

[71] See n. 40.

agreed to review measures taken by Third Pillar agencies, such as Eurojust,[72] as well as those adopted by EU bodies, such as the European Central Bank (ECB).[73] Since Lisbon, the Treaty explicitly grants the Court of Justice the power to review legal acts adopted by EU bodies, offices or agencies.[74]

The Court of Justice thus rubber-stamps the setting up and empowerment of *de novo* bodies, even when it involves greater intergovernmental influence, where it results in further transfer of powers to the EU level, and provided that they fall under judicial control. The open question is how much deference it will show towards these new bodies. The forthcoming preliminary reference case forwarded by the German Constitutional Court which questions the legality of the ECB's bond buying programme will be testing on the Court of Justice.[75]

Although the Court of Justice has welcomed newcomers on the EU politico-administrative scene, it has relentlessly laboured to keep judicial competitors at bay. The Court of Justice asked for the creation of a Court of First Instance, now renamed 'General Court', and more recently a Civil Service Tribunal, to assist with its workload, but it exercises hierarchical control over them. The Court of Justice is, however, not keen on the creation of decentralized courts.[76]

Putting forward arguments based on the autonomy of EU law, but which reflect concerns for its own institutional integrity and competence, the Court of Justice has generally blocked international agreements which envisaged the creation or empowerment of concurrent judicial bodies (Lock 2011).[77] For example, the Court of Justice prevented the establishment of a unitary patent system outside the framework of the EU treaties (and including non-member states), which would undermine its interpretative and enforcement powers.[78] The member states had to redesign the scheme, eventually adopted through Enhanced Cooperation, to integrate the new Unified Patent Court within the legal and judicial framework of the Treaty (e.g. preliminary references).[79]

---

[72] Case C-160/03 *Spain v Eurojust* [2005] ECR 1-2077.
[73] Case C-15/00 *Commission v EIB* [2003] ECR I-728.   [74] Article 263(1) TFEU.
[75] Case BVerfG, 2 BvR 1390/12 vom 17.12.2013, <http://www.bverfg.de/entscheidungen/rs20131217_2bvr139012.html>; BVerfG, 2 BvR 2728/13 vom 14.1.2014, Absatz-Nr. (1–105), <http://www.bverfg.de/entscheidungen/rs20140114_2bvr272813en.html>.
[76] See 'The Future of the Judicial System of the European Union' (Proposals and Reflections), May 1999; 'Report by the Working Party on the Future of the European Communities' Court System', May 2000.
[77] *Opinion 1/76 Inland Waterway Vessels* [1977] ECR 741; *Opinion 1/91 EEA I* [1991] ECR I-6079; Case C-459/03 *Commission v Ireland (Mox Plant)* [2006] ECR I-4635.
[78] *Opinion 1/09 Unified Patent Litigation System* [2011] ECR I-1137.
[79] The Court confirmed the compatibility of the agreement with the Treaty enhanced cooperation provision. See n. 54.

Furthermore, the Court of Justice protected its turf from international competitors, such as the World Trade Organization (WTO) dispute settlement bodies and the European Court of Human Rights (ECtHR). It refused to confer direct effect (and thus be bound) by decisions of the WTO dispute settlement bodies.[80] In 1994, it barred the way to the Community's accession to the European Convention on Human Rights (ECHR),[81] allegedly for lack of competence, but more likely because it did not wish to be subjected to the ultimate jurisdiction of the European Court of Human Rights (De Búrca 2013: 53). The Lisbon Treaty now requires the EU to accede to the ECHR.[82] The Court's members have eventually warmed to the idea of Strasbourg having the final say on human rights in Europe (Granger 2005; Morano-Foadi and Andreadakis 2011). Yet the Luxembourg Court is setting tough conditions for accession, to preserve its interpretative and judicial authority and the autonomy of the EU legal order.[83]

The Court of Justice has thus supported the creation and empowerment of *de novo* politico-administrative bodies. However, it has fought hard against the creation or empowerment of new specialized judicial bodies, over which it would not have full hierarchical control, which restricts the validity of hypothesis 3 to political and administrative bodies (to the exclusion of judicial ones).

Conclusion: The post-Maastricht Court—A 'Die-Hard Integrationist' or a 'Constitutional Mediator' for a 'Europe of Rights'?

Looking at the transformation of European integration from Luxembourg partially confirms some of the new intergovernmentalist hypotheses, and confronts previous accounts of legal integration in Europe. The Court of Justice is *no longer projecting an idea of Europe based on market integration and supranational and federal solutions* (hypothesis 2). Judicial opinions are infused with notions of *human rights, social justice, citizenship, democracy, and pluralism as core elements of European integration*; however, for a number of reasons which are not fully explored here, *the Court of Justice is struggling to live up to such ideals*. It still operates largely within a free movement logic, and tends to

---

[80] Cases C-377/02, *Van Parys* [2005] ECR I-1465; C-120/06 P and 121/06 *FIAMM* [2008] ECR I-6513.
[81] Opinion 2/94 [1996] ECR 1–1759.   [82] Article 6(2) TEU.
[83] 'Discussion document of the Court of Justice of the European Union on certain aspects of the accession of the European Union to the ECHR', 21 May 2010; 'Joint communication from Presidents Costa and Skouris', February 2011; Oral Hearing on the *Draft Agreement for the Accession of the EU* to the ECHR, Luxembourg, 4–5 May 2014.

support EU-level political solutions (i.e. 'more Europe'), whatever they are (inter-governmental or supranational, unitary or differentiated, political or bureau-cratic, within or outside of the Treaty, etc.). To remain relevant, the Court of Justice claims jurisdiction over EU politico-administrative processes, which result in binding legal outcomes, but save for measures which have a direct and serious impact on important individual rights, it tends to exercise a light touch control in practice, which imposes limited substantive constraints on such processes. The Court of Justice is, furthermore, refraining from 'su-pranationalizing' intergovernmental processes, and ready to accept their specificities.

The Court of Justice has welcomed new players on the EU political scene, but it does not tolerate any encroachment on its own judicial functions. In that sense, hypothesis 3 is only confirmed in relation to political and administrative *de novo* bodies, but not in relation to the potential transfer of judicial powers to competing judicial bodies.

The Court of Justice has largely helped *keep EU policy-making processes largely free from broader societal interferences*, which most likely contributed to people's alienation from EU elitist processes, and the blurring of high and low politics (hypothesis 5). There are, however, signs that the tide is changing, with the Court of Justice appearing more inclined to take human rights seriously, and to open up political processes, which could affect the deliberative and con-sensual dynamics of intergovernmental processes (hypothesis 1), and the operation of *de novo* bodies (hypothesis 3). However, as the Court of Justice remains evasive in relation to what occurs 'outside' the Treaty, or in informal settings, it may also encourage further actions through intergovernmental agreements which fall outside of EU legal frameworks,[84] or more decision-making 'in the corridors' (hypothesis 1).

As European integration is moving towards an 'unknown destination' (Weiler 1993) on untravelled roads, the Court of Justice is having a harder time driving the process, and is refocusing its efforts on a constitutional, rather than integrative, role. The transition is a delicate one, and in doing so, the Court of Justice must also come to terms with the evolution of judicial roles globally, which require greater and more diverse participation in judicial processes and a more mediating role for judges (Ost 1990; Koopmans 1996). The Court's mutation from the Hercules of integration into its Hermes-like messenger[85] may at times challenge, at other times accentuate, some of the new intergovernmentalist features of post-1992 Europe.

---

[84] Although in such a context, member states would still be subject to national constitutional requirements and those of the ECHR, and the respective courts.

[85] There are signs the Court is increasingly willing to play such a part. In the *DRI* case (see n. 39), the Court, before the hearing, invited the parties to consult with one another, addressed specific questions to them, and called for further external expertise.

11

Legislative and Judicial Politics in the Post-Maastricht Era

The Intergovernmentalist Paradox in the Council of Ministers

Marzena Kloka and Susanne K. Schmidt

This chapter looks at Community method decision-making in the post-Maastricht period. We understand the Community method as a mode of integration, in which the Court of Justice of the European Union (EU) and the European Commission enjoy considerable powers, given their exclusive rights to interpret EU law and propose further action, and in which member states hold a decisive position in the formal legislative process through the Council of Ministers. This method of integration originally applied to the single market and we show that it extended to further policy areas. We discuss the interplay between the Court of Justice, the Commission, and the Council of Ministers in an area of shared competence, namely, health care. On the one hand, health care is very close to the single market law, as medical treatment has been interpreted as a 'service' by the Court of Justice. On the other hand, it is a domain in which member states' responsibility is protected by the Treaty (TFEU Article 168(7)). Thus, our contribution differs from other chapters in this volume, as we deal with a policy matter that had been subjected to integration decisions in the past and, therefore, does not constitute an entirely new area of the EU's activity (see chapters 5 and 6). The temporal scope of our analysis extends to the two decades 1990–2010, the period of interest for the new intergovernmentalism.

Our argument is two-fold. First, we argue that the absence of formal competence transfer does not prevent *de facto* integration from happening.

Our story diverts from the new intergovernmentalism in so far as the latter links the lack of an explicit policy integration in the post-Maastricht period with the unwillingness of member states to delegate further competences. In line with previous literature, we show that the Court of Justice can make integrationist decisions even if member states have previously made choices to maintain national autonomy. As the case law is ongoing and the majority threshold in the Council of Ministers is high, member states cannot be seen as exclusive gatekeepers of integration. Member states might wish to regain control over the policy area in question and to respond to the Court's action with a codification of the case law. The directive discussed here shows that member states take recourse to legislation as a means of restoring legal certainty. In our case, however, responding to the judicial avant-garde came at a high price. Member states had to accept very high level of contention as well as an empowerment of the Commission.

This chapter makes two contributions to the theoretical debate around the concept of the new intergovernmentalism. First, we claim that the traditional Community method remains resilient, at least in the policy areas close to the single market. Second, we show that member states are not only aware of, but are also willing to challenge, supranational activism. This observation confirms that member states have been sceptical about delegating further competences since Maastricht and it can provide an explanation as to why not so much explicit competence transfer happened in other policy areas. Moreover, Council negotiations on cross-border health care illustrate that preference formation became, indeed, much more complex in the recent decades (hypothesis 4: Problems in domestic preference formation have become stand-alone inputs into the European integration process). Member-state governments not only take up the concerns of their key domestic constituencies, but also have to position themselves towards supranational (legal) developments, which they cannot control. Thus, the process of domestic preference formation cannot be seen as isolated from the broader inter-institutional dynamics.

We begin by summarizing the literature on the Court of Justice's strength and presenting accounts of the Court's impact on legislation. Then we broaden the institutional context and show that, strangely, the research on the Council of Ministers (as the central legislative institution) has so far omitted to acknowledge that this intergovernmental institution might be subjected to supranational influences. We engage with the judicial-intergovernmentalist interaction while following two specific questions. First, how do member states react to legal uncertainty caused by case law and what is the impact of case law on member states' preferences for further integration in the relevant policy fields? Second, how does the Council of Ministers as a legislative institution position itself towards judicialization?

We then inform these questions in an exploratory analysis of a legislative case, whose background exemplifies the tension between intergovernmentalist and judicial politics particularly well. The Directive on Patients' Rights in Cross-Border Healthcare is crucial for our analytical concern, because health care has been excluded from the EU's legislative competence and yet, the Court of Justice has pushed integration in this field quite far. Between July 2008 and June 2010, the Council of Ministers negotiated a directive which aimed to clarify Court of Justice case law. The decision-making process was accompanied by intense contestation, as member states differed in their recognition that case law is in fact an alternative to legislation—and that the formulation of secondary law may be an option to steer the development of future case law in a way that corresponds more closely to their political preferences. By tracing how much member-state negotiations were pushed by case law, with the directive being explicitly framed as a 'codification of case law', we point to an 'intergovernmentalist paradox', with the intergovernmental Council of Ministers being much supranationally shaped. We conclude by reflecting how the diagnosis of the new intergovernmentalism relates to the supranational dynamic of Council decisions.

11.1 Conceptualizing the Judicial-Legislative Interplay

In the EU, integration through legislation coexists with integration through case law. We argue that this state of affairs—and in particular the development of the body of case law on the four freedoms in the last decades—fundamentally transforms the legislative activity in the EU. To highlight this particular aspect of the Community method, we contrast the observation that the Court of Justice has advanced integration in areas which would have fallen in the competence of the legislature with the intergovernmentalist concept of member states forwarding domestically shaped preferences, which forms the core of the Council literature.

11.1.1 *The Court vis-à-vis the Legislature*

One of the central characteristics of the Community method is that a strong judiciary is coupled with a relatively weak legislature at the European level. There are different sources of the Court of Justice's power. Through the preliminary reference procedure the Court of Justice can control the conformity of national law with EU law (Alter 1998: 126–8) and member states have no real possibility to object to these interpretations (Weiler 1991: 2421). Member states cannot control the flow of cases to the Court, allowing the Court to develop its case law in an incremental building up of legal interpretations (Stone Sweet 2010: 29). The integrated court system thus strengthens the Court of Justice considerably, starting with the constitutionalization of the Treaty via declaring it directly effective and supreme.

Next to this strong judiciary exists a legislature whose own room for manoeuvre is limited by the procedural requirements of the overall decision-making framework. As the revision of secondary law requires a qualified majority in the Council of Ministers, the support of the Commission and the European Parliament (EP), and the revision of the Treaty even unanimity among member states, the Court of Justice is somewhat shielded from having its case law reined in legislatively. The joint-decision trap applies, making the status quo prevail (Scharpf 2011)—also when it is a status quo that has been changed via the case law (Schmidt 2011b).

Only a few examples of legislative overrule are mentioned in the literature. Among them, prominently, the *Barber* judgment, where the European Council decided on an addition to the Maastricht Treaty to reject a retrospective application of this judgment on equal access to occupational pensions for women working part time (Pierson 1996: 151). Institutionally, the Court of Justice is thus in a very strong position. Already Weiler (1981, 1991) pointed out how the strength of the Court of Justice and the weakness of the Council of Ministers are interdependent. The power of the Court in the EU is a matter of institutional design. This structural element should be stressed also with regard to the new intergovernmentalism, which asks whether the post-Maastricht period represents a distinct era in European integration.

Nevertheless, as rational choice critics contend, the strength particularly of international courts is limited as they depend not only on cases reaching them, but also on member states complying with their judgments. Conant (2002) has argued that 'justice contained' is a problem for the Court of Justice. Given the many ways that member states can defer compliance with judgments, it is certainly wrong to conceptualize the Court of Justice as an external force, pushing for policy changes that find no support domestically. As Davies (2012) and Stone Sweet and Stranz (2012) have shown, domestic courts often include their desired answer in their preliminary request to the Court of Justice, managing to instrumentalize the latter for their preferred legal changes (see also Nyikos 2006). While the Court of Justice can be assumed to follow a pro-integrationist line, its far-reaching case law in general has the support of domestic actors, be they companies, courts, or parties that would not be able to succeed with these policy reforms domestically, which leads them to try to realize their policy aims via European law. It is well established in the literature that Court of Justice case law can act as an alternative to legislation (Weiler 1981, 1991). If case law exists, it must influence Council negotiations fundamentally. Interestingly, this influence of European legislation is often ignored, making it more common than not to regard European decision-making as involving exclusively the Commission, Council of Ministers, and the EP, rather than recognizing that court rulings interpreting European law form a crucial impact in their own right.

What does the literature hold? Schmidt showed very early how the Commission can complement its agenda-setting powers with the opportunity to draw on the Court in order to influence Council negotiations. Based on the example of electricity liberalization in the 1990s, she showed that by lodging parallel infringement procedures against member states' import and export monopolies of electricity, the Commission put pressure on the Council of Ministers to agree on liberalization. The alternative of having the Court of Justice decide would have implied significant legal uncertainty, being inimical to the long-term investment needed for infrastructure services (Schmidt 2000). Other examples include the different liberalization processes in telecommunications, postal services, transport (road, air, rail), the services directive, games of chance, and even sports (Schmidt 2004, 2011a). In all instances, case law of the Court of Justice alters the default condition of decision-making for the actors involved. Those actors favouring the changes brought about by existing and pending case law are strengthened in negotiations.

Next to the single market's four freedoms (goods, services, persons, and capital) and competition law, case law has had a particular impact in the area of non-discrimination, building on the provision of Article 141 on equal pay for men and women, and showing that the impact of case law is not limited to economic policies (Cichowski 2004). Most work, however, focuses on the way that litigants, in this area women's groups, and lower-level courts combine to bring about significant changes to member states' policy regimes: Martinsen, in particular, has shown how the broad interpretation of single-market rules has also captured the welfare state, most notably in the area of health services, and constrains national regulation (Martinsen 2005; Martinsen and Falkner 2011; Martinsen and Vrangbaek 2008).

Wasserfallen has shown how case law has undermined the possibility for member states to keep control over their national systems of social benefits. Most prominently in the *Grzelczyk* case the Court of Justice argued that exchange students could claim social assistance.[1] When negotiating the citizenship-directive,[2] member states had to position themselves towards this case law. While member states were opposed to the case law, it was at the

---

[1] Case C-184/99 *Grzelczyk* [2001] ECR I-6193.

[2] Directive 2004/38/EC of the European Parliament and the Council of 29 April 2004 on the right of citizens of the Union and their family members to move and reside freely within the territory of the member states amending Regulation (EEC) No. 1612/68 and repealing Directives 64/221/EEC, 68/360/EEC, 72/194/EEC, 73/148/EEC, 75/34/EEC, 75/35/EEC, 90/364/EEC, 90/365/EEC and 93/96/EEC, 29 April 2004, 2004/38/EC, OJ L 158/77, 30.04.2004, pp. 77–123.

same time clear that secondary law could not fall behind it, as the Court's interpretation was based on the Treaty (Wasserfallen 2010: 1140). In the end, the position of the Court of Justice was codified in the directive, even though 'Representatives from Luxembourg, the UK, Belgium, Ireland and Denmark still remained critical about this legislative confirmation of the Court's jurisprudence. But throughout the policy-making process, the leverage of reluctant member states continuously declined to the point where this coalition was too weak to prevent the institutionalization of case law' (Wasserfallen 2010: 1141). At the same time, Wasserfallen (2010: 1142) points out that member states took the legislative process as an occasion to signal to the Court of Justice that they did not approve of EU nationals' rights to social assistance, which they had to grant to students. However, this did not stop further case law (Wind 2009).

Importantly, it is only certain rights that can be furthered via the Court of Justice, these being generally of a liberal, individualistic nature, and not of a republican one, emphasizing solidarity (Scharpf 2009). Crucially, the Council of Ministers cannot go back on the extent of existing case law.

11.1.2 *The Council of Ministers vis-à-vis the Case Law*

Section 11.1.1 outlined several examples of how case law, across many policy fields, can significantly influence European legislation. Given that our literature review covered the period from the early 1990s onwards, we may safely say that the strong judiciary is resilient, even in times of the new intergovernmentalism. This empirical observation bears an analytical challenge. How does the growing judicialization in the EU affect intergovernmental decision-making? More specifically, how can the Court's strength be integrated into our understanding of the Council of Ministers?

The Council of Ministers is the core of the EU's decision-making system. The 'standard' intergovernmentalist account of how the EU works makes integration highly dependent on member states' preferences and their configuration (see chapter 1). Member states expose their sovereignty deliberately when they prefer integration over national autonomy. Once they achieve the required majority threshold, the Council of Ministers makes a formal decision and passes a binding law. In this way, member-state governments, who are responsible for their country's citizens, maintain control over EU-level policies, and, thus, the substance of further integration.

The key question is, thus, where do member states' preferences come from and how do they come about? The standard intergovernmentalist literature points to the domestic origin of supranational preferences and the role of cost–benefit calculation in the formulation of national positions. Moravcsik was the first to point explicitly at domestic organized economic interests, which, driven by the will to exploit economic interdependencies to their advantage, push their respective governments to support further integration of markets (Moravcsik 1998). In regulatory, or market-correcting matters, governments tend not only to protect national regulatory systems from reform pressures, but even aim to model European governance according to their domestic regimes (Héritier 1996, 1999; Callaghan and Höpner 2005; Fioretos 2009; Hennessy 2008).

Neither the (domestic) origins nor the (rationalist) nature of member states' preferences have remained unchallenged. As regards the former, there is a debate about the extent to which structural characteristics of member states, such as wealth or regulatory regimes, can be overshadowed by the governments' ideological affiliation, in particular their left–right orientation. There exists large-n empirical evidence for both the former as well as for the latter claim (Aspinwall 2007; Hagemann and Høyland 2008; Thomson 2011).

Researchers working in constructivist traditions claim that preferences do not rely on domestic calculations, carried out separately from Council negotiations, but that they are discovered during the course thereof, and through deliberation (Checkel 2003, 2005; Risse and Kleine 2010). Empirical evidence pertinent to this point is mixed and rather inconclusive (Lewis 2005). Yet, one argument advanced by critics of 'standard' intergovernmentalist approaches deserves particular attention. To make calculated, rational choices in EU-level policy-making, governments ought to have a good understanding about the decision-situation (Wallace 2002: 334–5). This is unlikely given the complexity and the nature of the EU policy-making system, where different stakeholders are involved at various levels, relevant communities are strongly knowledge-based (experts) and policies are de-centrally implemented, which makes their pay-offs in the long run difficult to predict. Although EU-level decision-makers operate under considerable uncertainty (Richardson 2006: 15), this notion has been absent in theoretical accounts of member states' preference formation.

As argued above, case law adds significant legal uncertainty to the policy-making process. Case law is concerned with particular incidents and its impact on whole regulatory systems is subject to legal doctrines and interpretations. Furthermore, it is ongoing, as it develops in dependence of the litigants' activities. Although case law enters the legislative arena, as shown earlier in this chapter, it clearly differs from factors which figure prominently in the preference literature. In contrast to national institutional regimes or organized interests, which put governments in a relatively comfortable position with regard to information and impact assessment, case law can neither be controlled, nor can it be predicted. The current Council literature, however, tells us little about how governments respond to uncertainty stimulated by case law and how judicial strength influences the workings of the Council of Ministers. Taking up these two questions would enhance our understanding of intergovernmental politics and of integration dynamics. Both are of great interest for the new intergovernmentalism, which calls for a more differentiated analysis of the preference formation processes (see chapter 1 of this volume, hypothesis 4).

11.1.3 *Research Design*

We aim to inform the questions about member states' reactions to the case law and the Council's positioning towards judicialization in an exploratory analysis of a legislative case, whose background exemplifies the tension between intergovernmentalist and judicial politics particularly well. The patient mobility directive, negotiated between 2008 and 2010, is a response by the Council of Ministers to case law which has been developing from the late 1990s.[3] Although health care has been excluded from the EU's legislative competence, the Court of Justice has pushed integration in this field quite far, being called by patients who, on the grounds of freedom of services, claimed (public) reimbursement for medical treatment they received in another EU country. The wish of member-state governments to codify Court of Justice case law was explicit and much more pronounced than in other cases referred to earlier in this chapter.

Our case is relevant for the debate on the new intergovernmentalism as it shows two interesting developments. First, the Court of Justice overruled an intergovernmental agreement safeguarding member states' autonomy to organize their health care systems and limiting EU intervention. This shows that supranational institutions are resilient, even in times of new intergovernmentalism. Second, we argue that the negotiations represent an attempt by member states to control judicial advancement, and that the success came at a high price. The decision-making process was accompanied by intense contestation, as member states differed in their recognition that case law is in fact an alternative to legislation—and that the formulation of secondary law may be an option to steer the development of future case law in a way that corresponds more closely to their political preferences. The patient-mobility directive is, thus, an interesting case for scholars of Council politics and preference formation, as it reveals that legal expertise and attitudes towards the case law shape the negotiation behaviour of member states.

---

[3] Directive 2011/24/EU of the European Parliament and of the Council of 9 March 2011 on the application of patients' rights in cross-border health care, OJ L 88, 04.04.2011, pp. 45–65.

11.2 The Directive on Patients' Rights in Cross-Border Healthcare

Originally, an article on patient mobility, based on the freedom of services, was part of the services directive, and was dropped after a resolution of the EP in 2005, arguing for a separate approach to healthcare.[4] Following a round of consultation, the Commission published its proposal for a directive on patient mobility in 2008, leading to its adoption by the Council of Ministers and the EP in March 2011 (de la Rosa 2012: 26). Crucial for the agreement on this directive was the case law of the Court of Justice on patient mobility, which had accumulated since the late 1990s. It raised concerns about legal certainty with the member states, particularly with regard to the reimbursement of costs for cross-border health treatment. The literature commonly sees the directive as 'codifying' the case law (Hancher and Sauter 2010: 117; de la Rosa 2012). In the following, we first detail the case law development that put pressure on having a clear, legislative solution. We then discuss the Council negotiations, with a focus on member states' actions and the dynamics of conflict.

11.2.1 Existing Case law on Patient Mobility

The Treaty sees health as a shared competence between the Union and the member states (Hatzopoulos 2002: 685). The legislation on social security coordination (Regulation 883/2004) limits the transnational provision of medical services to cases of emergency. Patients actively seeking (reimbursed) treatment in another member state are subject to authorization procedures by their home insurance institutions.

It was these authorization procedures which the Court of Justice was asked to comment upon in preliminary references, where patients sought treatment in other member states and attempted judicial redress against limited or failing reimbursement offered by their health insurer. Already in the 1980s a basis for future judgments had been established, when the Court of Justice argued that health care fell under the services freedom (*Luisi and Carbone*)[5] but this did not have much impact (Hatzopoulos 2002: 688). The services freedom of the Treaty covers not only the freedom of service providers to cross borders and to offer their services on a temporary basis in other member states (active services freedom), but also the freedom of consumers, to receive services in other member states (passive services freedom).

---

[4] Directive 2006/123/EC of the European Parliament and of the Council of 12 December 2006 on services in the internal market, OJ L 376, 27.12.2006, pp. 36–68.
[5] Joined cases 286/82 and 26/83 *Luisi and Carbone* [1984] ECR 377.

In 1998, the *Kohll*[6] and *Decker*[7] cases were initiated by Luxembourg citizens. Decker had bought glasses abroad, while Kohll's daughter had had dental treatment. Neither had sought prior authorization and their reimbursement was refused, which led to the court cases. With Luxembourg and eight other member states submitting an opinion, it was transparent to the Court of Justice that member states attributed high importance to the prior authorization procedure. While recognizing 'the powers of the Member States to organize their social security systems' (§17 *Kohll*; §21 *Decker*), the Court of Justice argued that the freedom of services applied, making a prior authorization into a disproportionate burden on patients. Thereby, it directly contradicted the existing regulation which required such authorization. The next relevant case, *Smits/Peerbooms*[8] of July 2001 concerned two Dutch patients who had gone to Germany and Austria respectively to receive treatment that was not listed in the Dutch catalogue of eligible health care costs and therefore not reimbursed. This time hospital care was at issue and ten member states intervened to keep this outside single market rules (Hatzopoulos 2002: 691). The Court of Justice, however, argued that these were services like any other. To require prior authorization was a restriction, which could only be seen as proportionate if related to hospital planning. The Court of Justice, moreover, established that the authorization procedure needed to be transparent, timely, and based on non-discriminatory procedures, and that standard treatment needed to be based on 'international medical science' (Martinsen 2005: 1042).

Vanbraekel[9] is notable as the Court of Justice held—should non-domestic treatment be less expensive—that the patient could claim a right to the surplus as otherwise the use of the freedom of services could be hampered (Rz 45, 53) (Hatzopoulos 2002: 690; Krajewski 2010: 172). In *Müller-Fauré and Van Riet*[10] decided in May 2003, nine member states, together with Norway and Iceland submitted opinions. Again, reimbursement in the Netherlands had been refused for dental treatment and hospital care, owing to lack of prior authorization. In these two cases, the Court of Justice saw an authorization procedure for non-hospital care as not justified, as the jeopardy to the financial balance of the social security system was not proven, while for hospital services the necessary planning could justify authorization. The case is interesting because it explicitly referred to the fact that the transborder reimbursement concerned contracted suppliers not having a contract with the health insurer, which mattered in the negotiations.

[6] Case C-158/96 *Kohll* [1998] ECR I-1931.   [7] Case C-120/95 *Decker* [1998] ECR I-1831.
[8] Case 157/99 *Geraets-Smits* v *Stichting Ziekenfonds; Peerbooms* v *Stichting CZ Groep Zorgverzekeringen* [2001] ECR I-5473.
[9] Case 368/98 *Vanbraekel* [2001] ECR I-5363.
[10] Case 385/99 *Müller-Fauré and Van Riet* [2003] ECR I-4509.

In the case of *Watts*,[11] Ms Watts went to France to get a hip replacement, cutting short the waiting times in the NHS (National Health Service). The case is notable for two aspects. For once, the Court of Justice engaged with the issue of waiting times, providing criteria of what it held to be undue delay. Second, Ms Watts tried to recoup her additional travel and accommodation expenses, which the Court of Justice denied. As the NHS is a pure benefits-in-kind system, the Court's ruling forces member states to come up with transparent cost calculations of their hospital services.

While putting member states' practices to authorize and reimburse foreign treatment under scrutiny, the Court of Justice has advanced integration in an area which the member states aimed to keep under national control. Member states have been observing these developments with concern. Consequently, member states have welcomed efforts to restore the clarification of patients' rights and to define a balance between those and general principles and values in EU health care systems (Commission of the European Communities 2004; Council of the European Union 2006).

11.2.2 *The Council versus the Commission*

After the failed attempt to include health services in the general services directive, the Commission proposed its directive on patient mobility in 2008, as part of the programme on 'the social dimension of the internal market'.[12] It put forward an interpretation of the Court of Justice's case law which left member states only limited options in controlling medical tourism. The proposal differentiates between the member state of affiliation and the host member state where the treatment takes place. The respective rights and duties of both member states are detailed, mostly regarding the right of *ex-ante* authorization of the member state of affiliation, which is limited to cases where the financial viability of the health service is otherwise at risk. The directive complements the authorization procedure (Regulation 883/2004), which fully reimburses patients after authorization. The passive services freedom, as detailed by the case law and the directive, only grants the right to reimbursement up to the cost of medical treatment in his/her member state of affiliation.

Next to codifying the case law, the Commission suggested a series of measures to promote member states' cooperation in health care matters. Innovations such as European Reference Networks, eHealth or comitology procedure may, in the end, prove to be highly significant, as they will pave the way for further supranationalization of health care policy (Sauter 2009:

---

[11] Case C-372/04 *Watts* [2006] ECR I-4325.
[12] The information in the case study is based on Kloka (2013).

121). The support for these measures in the Council of Ministers was rather limited and member states recognized a 'competence creep by the Commission'.[13] Yet, although member states acted in concert to weaken the wording of these provisions, most of these innovations became binding law. The case, thus, follows a 'familiar sequence whereby negative integration [...] breeds the need for positive integration' (Sauter 2009: 121). The Commission is now endowed with new prerogatives and power, helped by comitology.

Thus, in order to restore legal certainty in the field of patients' rights in cross-border health care, the Council of Ministers not only had to endorse the case law, but it also had to accept a significant supranationalization of the health care policy and an empowerment of the Commission. As the editors of this volume suggest, while 'supranational institutions are not hard-wired to seek-ever closer union' (hypothesis 2), they also 'act strategically: when faced with a favourable environment for entrepreneurialism they may well take advantage of it' (see chapter 1).

11.2.3 The Conflict within the Council

While the Commission's advance does not really surprise given the latter's traditional role as a motor of integration (Schmidt 2000), the intergovernmental dynamics which emerged once the proposal reached the Council of Ministers revealed very different perceptions of the case law, different approaches to it and, consequently, opposing preferences on codification among member states.

The member states were divided into two groups: the supporters of codification, mostly Northern member states and the opponents of codification consisting of Southern and Central and Eastern member states. The first group saw case law codification as a necessary evil and employed the tactic of 'taking the bull by the horns', which consisted of limiting the directive to what the Court of Justice actually said and taking precautions so that key national health care arrangements would not be put under pressure. The second group placed less value on legal certainty, as it feared a destabilizing impact of EU-level patient-mobility rules on their mostly state-centred health care systems. This group opted for a more passive bargaining tactic which consisted of questioning the project and, eventually, working against the directive with all available means, including blockage. This strategy failed and the directive received the necessary majority after one of the opposing countries, Spain, assumed the Council presidency and significantly moderated its criticism towards the directive. Yet the high number of outvotes and the fact that

---

[13] Interview, Permanent Representation of the UK to the European Union, 02.12.2010.

'symbolic' concessions contributed to the disarmament of the opposition, make clear that the conflict over codification and case-law implications has not been resolved.

What motivated countries such as the UK, Germany, France, Sweden, or the Netherlands to become so eagerly involved in the codification activity? All these countries, although sceptical about the Court of Justice's advances, had been working for several years on the reconciliation of the contentious case law with their domestic systems (Greer and Rauscher 2011). Restoring legal certainty was important to them and in binding legislation they saw an opportunity to influence the future direction of the Court of Justice's rulings in this area. Moreover, they could shape the directive with specific suggestions to take into account the institutional particularities of their health care systems. Over the last decade, these countries switched from opposition towards binding EU action in the field towards the recognition of a window of opportunity.[14]

Germany, for instance, wanted to exclude long-term care from the directive. In Germany, it is not a medical service, but rather a 'solidary support of the society for families who care for their members' (Ulla Schmidt, Minister of Health, quoted by TAZ, 30.12.2008; see also Schulte 2009). Germany opted for exclusion, although the Court of Justice already interpreted care services as medical services (AOK Bundesverband 2008: 6), and there were cases pending during the negotiations (*Chamier-Glisczinski*).[15] Consequently, the Council presidency was very reluctant, pointing out that the Court of Justice's interpretation would, after all, prevail (Council 10026/09: 6). However, having extensively explained to other member states why its system of long-term care is a 'social' rather than a 'medical' service, Germany mobilized enough allies to have its demand accommodated (Council 12532/09: 12).

In the British case, the two top priorities were the gate-keeping role of general practitioners (GPs) and the competence of regional health systems to determine the scope of covered services, both being characteristic features of the British NHS. In the British state-funded health system the individual GP decides who should get what treatment. There are no entitlements decided by national legislation. As the British minister for health put it: 'We want to ensure that the NHS retains the ability to decide what care it will fund.'[16] In practice, this meant that the directive would take into account the decisive role of GPs and the fact that entitlements may vary across the NHS.

---

[14] In Germany, as late as in 2007, there were still influential critical voices about binding legislation in the health care area (GKV Spitzenverband, 2007), but the topic was nonetheless advanced during the German presidency in the first half of 2007.

[15] Case C-208/07 *von Chamier-Glisczinski* [2009] ECR I-6095.

[16] See: <http://www.ehealthnews.eu/research/1351-uks-consultation-on-patient-mobility-in-the-eu>.

Like Germany, Britain was successful. It started with a suggestion made to the Commission at the proposal formulation stage, to include an article stating that the same conditions apply to both outgoing and staying patients. During the negotiations, this provision was then specified, so that the compromise proposal by the Swedish presidency also included a reference to 'administrative formalities at the local, regional or national level' and to the 'assessment by a health professional or healthcare administrator' (Article 8.5 Council 12532/09).

The core of the German and the British negotiation success was the intensive engagement with the case law and input into the Commission's proposal.[17] With specific wording proposals and a handful of supporters, both countries turned to the presidency requesting that their concerns be accommodated. The latter was eager to accede to those demands, as the interest of both countries to conclude the negotiations made them important partners, given the presidencies' interest in effective Council work. The examples of the UK and Germany show that countries which are able to react strategically to the case law, engage with it, and 'take the bull by the horns' can also be quite successful in the negotiation process, as legal expertise and anticipation help them when approaching the presidency and when mobilizing allies.

In contrast, neither Spain, Portugal, Greece, Italy, Ireland, Poland, nor Slovakia were very impressed by the codification rationale. A Spanish representative, for instance, claimed that since the Court of Justice only deals with single cases there was no reason to transform case law into binding rules.[18] In particular, these states feared the introduction of market mechanisms into an area traditionally overseen by the state and solidarity based institutions.[19] Formally, the EU had no competence to intervene in national health care. Southern, Central, and Eastern European member states were heavily critical of the fact that the proposal was based on the internal market Treaty article, rather than on Article 168 TFEU (public health; former Article 152 TEC). In December 2009, Slovakia and Italy conditioned their readiness to continue negotiating upon this change. Given the support by a 'large number of delegations'[20] the legal services of the Council of Ministers and the Commission accepted the additional legal base for selected articles of the directive.

Why did these states object so strongly? Admittedly, the state plays an important role in their health care systems, as it does in the UK or in the Scandinavian countries. Also, Southern, Central, and Eastern European member states had less experience with the case law; most of the court cases

---

[17] Interview, Permanent Representation of the UK to the European Union, 02.12.2010, Interview, former employee of the Permanent Representation of France to the European Union, 15.12.2010 (phone).
[18] Interview, Permanent Representation of Spain to the European Union, 28.10.2010.
[19] Agence Europe, 2.12.2009.   [20] Press release 9721/2/09 REV 2.

concerned the Netherlands, the UK, or Luxembourg. On the other hand, these cases were very well known, discussed in various forums and all the member states had an opportunity to submit their opinions to the Court of Justice. The new member states had to implement the rulings as part of the acquis. It seems that a bundle of domestic factors, such as judicial culture, policy style, stakeholder involvement, and the public's attitude contributed to the fact that these countries preferred to ignore the supranational development rather than engage with it.

The poor domestic engagement resulted in poor negotiation strategies. The countries constituted a large, but not an effective coalition. They remained very general with their claims and, lacking legal expertise, did not participate in the detailed article-by-article work.[21] The presidencies accused this group of being 'active in blocking, not active in making proposals' and often felt they had to remind the group delegations of the legal status quo. Although they never admitted it openly, it appeared that both Southern, Central, and Eastern European countries preferred an unregulated status quo to an agreement with potentially destabilizing implications.[22]

Later in the process, the countries specified their demands. Most Southern, Central, and Eastern Europeans were reluctant to include non-contracted providers in the directive's regulatory regime. The system of contracting is widespread across the EU, as it enables the public insurers to control both prices and the quantity of services supplied to the population. The case law of the Court of Justice, by contrast, did not allow such differentiation for cross-border transactions. The inclusion of non-contracted providers accordingly resulted in more favourable treatment for providers in other member states compared to domestic ones and was therefore rejected by the Council. Southern, Central, and Eastern European delegations feared that this provision would challenge the organization of their domestic systems, though several countries such as the UK, Germany, or the Netherlands had included the reimbursement of foreign non-contracted providers without any domestic repercussions (Krajewski 2010: 195). 'More than half of the Member States have expressed their preference for the limitation of the scope of the directive to providers contracted to the local public health insurer or otherwise defined public system' (Presidency progress report, Council 10345/09). However, the exclusion of these providers from the directive's scope was denied by the presidencies, pointing to the Council's legal service and the Commission, which saw an open violation of case law.

---

[21] Council of the European Union, Progress report, 16514/08; Interview, former employee of the Permanent Representation of France to the European Union, 15.12.2010 (phone).

[22] Interview, former employee of the Permanent Representation of France to the European Union, 15.12.2010 (phone).

The opposition stood united when the Swedish presidency suggested a vote on the directive in December 2009 and blocked the proposal. The demonstrative hostility of Spain, Portugal, Greece, Poland, Romania, and Slovakia was shared by many others, however, the group gradually lost members. The Swedish presidency exploited the incoherence of the group and used tailored wording proposals to convince previously sceptical countries, such as Italy or Hungary, to join the supporting majority. In this way, a large group of opponents was gradually reduced. The climax of this development was achieved when Spain, once the most outspoken opponent of the dossier, took over the presidency and devoted its attention to one highly specific provision important exclusively in the Spanish context, namely the question of who would pay for foreign pensioners residing in Spain and going back to their home country for treatment.[23] Celebrating the 'saving of 2 billion Euros for pensioners' (El Pais, 09.06.2010), the Spanish government performed a U-turn in its negotiation strategy and left its former combatants Poland, Slovakia, Portugal, and Romania outvoted.[24]

The fate of the Southern, Central, and Eastern European countries suggests that member states which, for whatever reasons, have ignored the case law in the past, are in a much weaker bargaining position when the Council of Ministers approaches codification. Once the negotiation process starts, time becomes short to reflect on specific concerns. Keeping an opposing coalition firm and resisting the presidency's efforts to conclude negotiation successfully is very difficult. In our case, a large opposition failed. With so many countries sceptical about a directive, it remains to be seen whether implementation succeeds.

Conclusion

Our analysis of the patient-mobility directive has highlighted the interplay between supranational actors, the Court of Justice, and the Commission, and the traditionally intergovernmental Council of Ministers. Case law of the Court may shape the legislative activity in the Community method to a surprising degree, when assessed through the analytical lenses of the Council literature. We argued that the motivation to legislate does not come exclusively from the bottom of the domestic systems of the member states, but that there are policy developments which member states do not entirely control, and to which they are willing and able to respond. There is an 'intergovernmentalist paradox'.

---

[23] Presidency compromise proposal 9001/19.   [24] Press Release 10760/10.

Our case exposed a legislating Council of Ministers, whose decision-making process revolved around the question what obligations and restrictions the Court of Justice applied on member states and how their key institutional arrangements could be preserved nevertheless. The focus on codification was convenient for the presidencies as it allowed the Chair to argue that legislation by the Council is 'better than legislation by the Court', thereby motivating the delegations to conclude the negotiations.[25] It is interesting to see that this normative-institutional argument worked so well.

Furthermore, the Council revealed a divide between countries interested in adopting a directive (despite reservations about the specific proposal) and those unwilling to discuss health policy in the language of individual rights at the EU level.[26] This divide resulted from differing (domestic) engagement with the case law (Wind 2010; Sack 2012). Member states valued legal certainty at the EU level differently, as they perceived the potential impact of internal market law on their domestic systems differently. Although it appears perfectly legitimate that member states cultivate individual views and advocate diverse bargaining approaches, our case suggests that the capacity to react to judicial developments may shape the bargaining success of member states. The new intergovernmentalism is right when pointing out that national preference formation as an important, yet still poorly understood, piece in the integration puzzle (hypothesis 4).

Finally, the contestation around the directive was not fully resolved, despite formal agreement. These divisions might lead to implementation problems (Zhelyazkova 2012). Moreover, the symbolic concessions impair legal clarity and might invite future judicial and legislative action (Greer 2013). As legal certainty may not (yet) be achieved, the negotiations may impact on the future health policy of the EU. The 'need' to codify case law allowed the Commission to introduce measures of positive integration, which may prove momentous in the future. Furthermore, the reimbursement of all suppliers of transnational services, whether they are recognized according to national standards or not, may make it necessary to agree on European criteria of adequate treatment, furthering the supranationalization of health policy.

At first glance, our case study might read as a story of the Council's 'victory' over the Court of Justice. Indeed, member states demonstrated assertiveness about their prerogatives in the area of health care and at least some of them were willing and able to react to the advancement of the case law. Still, we would hesitate to proclaim the new intergovernmentalism the ultimate successor of supranationalism. Contrary to the new intergovernmentalist assumptions, we claim that integration in areas of significant member-state

---

[25] Agence Europe, 30.09.2008.   [26] Interview, European Commission, 25.10.2010.

prerogative can happen without explicit transfer of competences. The expansion of the legal doctrines of the single market to areas which interfere with the four freedoms remains an important engine of integration.

We have also shown how intergovernmental action is shaped by the case law as an alternative route to policy integration. Case law not only motivates member states to take action, but may be the source of intergovernmental conflict. Our case revealed that member states have fundamentally diverging approaches towards key policy principles such as legal certainty or national autonomy. Strategic engagement with the case law impacts upon the bargaining success, since, as we have seen, case-law opponents face severe difficulties when working against codification. This diversity not only triggers conflict, but might have negative implications for the legitimacy of the collective decisions and on their implementation by the member states. We agree with the new intergovernmentalism that the nature of preference formation might have changed—also because of the growing body of case law and the different patterns of engagement.

In this chapter we have argued that this supranational embedding of Council negotiations is an important backdrop to the new intergovernmentalism. In order to be aware of comparable developments as in the single market writ large, member states have aimed to keep additional competence transfers under control. But how does the national assertiveness of the new intergovernmentalism combine with the supranational pressure we have described? The EU is fundamentally a multi-level system, where governments have long lost their monopoly of access to the higher level. Thus, we observe that private actor litigants and lower courts drive much of the case law dynamic. And their interest in policy change facilitates accommodation at the national level.

12

The European Parliament

Adversary or Accomplice of the New Intergovernmentalism?

Johannes Pollak and Peter Slominski

It is a widely shared view that the European Parliament (EP) has increased its power enormously during the post-Maastricht period and now enjoys considerable legislative control and budgetary power. This remarkable growth in power and status has made the EP not only the 'winner' of all treaty reforms since Maastricht (Pollack 1999; Hix 2002; Craig 2008; Burns 2013), but also one of the most powerful parliaments in the world (Shackleton 2012). Not only are we witnessing a continuous decline in areas from which the EP is excluded (Winzen, Roederer-Rynning, and Schimmelfennig 2012), with the EP meanwhile operating on par with the Council of Ministers in terms of EU legislation; but also a strengthening of its say in executive areas that are traditionally dominated by intergovernmental actors, notably comitology, the establishment and control of EU agencies, the appointment/dismissal of EU personnel, and treaty reform. For some EU scholars, the gradual upgrading of the EP has finally led to an institutionalization of representative democracy of such an extent that it can already be regarded as a core constitutional principle of the European Union (EU) (Rittberger and Schimmelfennig 2006; Rittberger 2012).

For most scholars, EU member states empower the EP, not because they hope to increase legislative efficiency or benefit from policy gains, but to strive to enhance the overall legitimacy of the EU (König 2008; Rittberger 2012). Since the EP has used its powers in a responsible and constructive manner (Rasmussen 2012), member states' governments feel that a further empowerment is beneficial. Some scholars even argue that the gradual expansion of the powers of the EP can be explained by a 'habitual response' on the part of the member states to address not only the EU's 'democratic deficit' (Goetze and Rittberger 2012) but also the growing distrust in the political system as a whole, including both EU as well as national institutions (Gros and Piedrafita 2014; see also hypothesis 4: 'Problems in domestic preference formation have become standalone inputs into the European integration process'). However, the gradual strengthening of a supranational institution such as the EP does not necessarily mean that supranational decision-making modes have also been strengthened. For proponents of the new intergovernmentalism, the willingness of member states to transfer more and more competences to the EU, without simultaneously strengthening the supranational machinery, constitutes a prevalent 'integration paradox' of the post-Maastricht era (see chapter 1). Even more so, supranational institutions are expected to show little commitment to pursue supranational decision-making but instead are broadly satisfied with decentralized, non-hierarchical approaches to decision-making, dominated by intergovernmental bodies such as the European Council, the Council of Ministers (and its ancillary bodies such as the Committee of Permanent Representatives (COREPER)) or EU agencies (see hypothesis 2: 'Supranational institutions are not hard-wired to seek ever closer union' and hypothesis 3: 'Where delegation occurs, governments and traditional supranational actors support the creation and empowerment of *de novo* institutions'). This chapter's objective is to assess whether the institutional upgrading of the EP can be regarded as an exception to the claims of new intergovernmentalism or whether the EP has accepted the intergovernmental approach and is far more complicit to the new intergovernmentalism than its supranational rhetoric suggests.

We conceive of the EP as a 'competence maximizer' that seeks to enhance its authority in the policy-making process, relative to that of the member states, and to extend its influence to areas in which it has little or no say. We also argue that this strategy is by no means a recent strategy. Since the 1970s, the EP has used its budgetary power as leverage to gain influence in other policy fields. At first sight, our argument seems to run contrary to one of the main tenets of the new intergovernmentalism, but we see that it partly confirms the hypothesis that the EP is not necessarily hard-wired for the support of supranational decision-making (hypothesis 2). Although the EP is often critical of the rise of intergovernmental influence (Sebag 2012; Schulz 2012), it is also pragmatic enough to accept that an increasing number of national competences are transferred to the EU level, leading to a growing influence of the European Council, the Council of Ministers, EU agencies, and other informal bodies and working groups. This is not to say that supranationalism is not the preferred mode of policy-making for the EP. But it seems to be the case that the EP is more concerned with preserving and/or extending its influence by using its growing competences, as well as its legitimacy, as bargaining chips, rather than forcefully advocating a supranational mode of decision-making. This can also be observed with regard to its legislative function. Since the Treaty of Amsterdam, the EP has gradually 'informalized' its co-decision powers thereby strengthening formats such as trilogue meetings in which only a handful of Members of the European Parliament (MEPs) are involved at the expense of open and transparent discussions in the plenary. The willingness to informa-lize and seclude its most important legislative procedure seems to confirm the EP's readiness to act as an accomplice to the new intergovernmentalism once it has secured its influence.

Empirically, we assess how the EP has used its various legislative, budgetary, and control functions[1] in two policy areas that can be regarded as key for the new intergovernmentalism: foreign as well as border and migration policy. Both policies touch upon the core of national sovereignty and are of particular political sensitivity, but have been significantly 'Europeanized' ever since the Maastricht Treaty. While foreign policy has long been regarded as a classic case of intergovernmental policy-making, even this field has witnessed a loss of influence by national capitals. For instance, the creation of a European Exter-nal Action Service (EEAS) has led to a considerable 'Brusselization' of the field, thereby eroding traditional assumptions of intergovernmentalism (Juncos and Pomorska 2011). Other core domains of national prerogative, border and migration policies have moved even further in the direction of suprana-tionalization. However, although a growing acquis has been adopted under co-decision, whose compliance is closely watched by the European Commis-sion and Court of Justice of the European Union, we can also identify counter-trends such as opt-outs, weak harmonization, national cooperation outside the EU framework, as well as a considerable amount of newly created *de novo* institutions that inhibit a fully fledged supranationalization of the field (Lavenex 2010).

This contribution proceeds as follows: The next section provides an over-view of the growing legislative and budgetary control and appointment rights of the EP. This is followed by an assessment of how the two most important powers, co-decision and budgetary rights, have been applied since the 1990s. This is illustrated by a case study on the EP's contribution to the establishment of the EEAS. Finally we deal with an important feature of the new intergov-ernmentalism, the rise of EU agencies, and investigate how the EP manages to shape the institutional design of such bodies. Particular emphasis is given to the EU border agency, Frontex.

---

[1] A brief overview of parliamentary powers in general and those of the EP in particular can be found in Craig and de Búrca (2011: 54–7); Corbett, Jacobs, and Shackleton (2011); Judge and Earnshaw (2009).

12.1 The European Parliament's Influence on EU Politics in the Post-Maastricht Era

Although the power of the EP has increased since the 1990s, the EP does not appear satiated and is still trying to further extend its influence. Given that the EP is still facing numerous formal as well as practical disadvantages vis-à-vis the Council of Ministers, the strategy of maximizing its competences seems perfectly rational. But it must be emphasized that the EP's strategy of maximizing its power does not necessarily mean that it is also pursuing the extension of supranational decision-making with the same verve. In fact, the EP has had a certain reputation for extending its influence, in particular by using its existing *formal* budgetary, legislative, or appointment/dismissal powers as leverage to acquire an *informal* say in other policy areas. This increase in informal power usually occurs where formal law is incomplete and provides some room for specification by informal means, where the EP is in a position to veto crucial policy decisions, and in cases when other actors are convinced that including the EP enhances the effectiveness and efficiency of the decision-making process concerned (Hix 2002; Stacey and Rittberger 2003; Crum 2012). The EP's striving to secure its influence by all means implies that it is also hard-wired for supranational decision-making (see hypothesis 2). Examples where the EP has successfully extended its influence through informal means, notably interinstitutional agreements (IIAs), occurred in the fields of co-decision, comitology, and the EU budget, as well as with regard to the appointment procedure of the Commission (Eiselt and Slominski 2006; Eiselt, Pollak, and Slominski 2007; Kietz and Maurer 2007; Röttinger 2010).

Moreover, the very fact that the EP has been continuously empowered neither implies that the EP has 'enough' formal power nor that it operates on par with the Council of Ministers in practice. While the extension of co-decision has mainly occurred within policy fields that have long been transferred to the EU, new shifts of power to the EU are usually dominated by intergovernmental actors. However, as the case of the creation of the EU's external action service illustrates, the EP meanwhile possesses a 'critical mass' of various powers that can be used as a lever to gain influence even in such policy fields.

The power maximizing strategy employed by the EP follows the logic of consequentialism. But the fact that it is increasingly accepted by the member states also shows that parliamentary involvement in EU affairs is more and more seen as the 'appropriate' standard of EU decision-making (i.e. following the logic of appropriateness). In fact, both logics are ultimately intertwined. The more the EP successfully reinterprets existing treaty provisions which are in turn subsequently codified in treaty reforms, the more the EP polity moves towards a model of parliamentarization (which has been confirmed by the

Lisbon Treaty in Article 10 TEU). Although it is by no means settled that we are witnessing a parliamentarization of the EU, normative arguments are often used by the EP to underline its claims (Rittberger and Schimmelfennig 2006; Rittberger 2012). That member states accept this loss of influence is mainly due to their interest in upholding their reputation as legitimate political actors. In other words: once the principle of parliamentarism emerges as the accepted standard of legitimacy in the political discourse, it is costly to object outright to the EP's claim of power enhancement. Thus, the only politically viable option for member states is to operate within and not beyond the principle of parliamentarism (Rittberger 2012: 30).

Accepting parliamentary involvement as the proper standard of legitimacy helps to explain why member states have difficulties in excluding the EP in the decision-making process and why they usually agree to offer the EP 'some' involvement, even if it is only informally agreed upon. While this might be used by proponents of the new intergovernmentalism to argue that member states are running the show, others might argue that the EP has a proven track record of getting its foot in the door in ways that might later open the door more fully to formal hard law powers (Kietz and Maurer 2007: 24–5). Assessing informal involvement of the EP from a normative perspective is ambiguous. Although informal arrangements are widely seen as not being transparent, rendering public scrutiny and accountability difficult (Puntscher Riekmann 2007), any EP involvement through informal arrangements may be defended on the grounds that at least a certain degree of parliamentary scrutiny is injected into the EU body politic dominated by intergovernmental or *de novo* institutions (Christiansen and Neuhold 2013: 1203). However, by relying on informal rights, the EP is running the risk of legitimizing an executive-dominated institutional arrangement that may turn out to be even more persistent than originally thought.

12.2 Legislative Politics: The Case of the Co-Decision Procedure

The growth of the EP's legislative power appears to be at odds with one crucial argument of the new intergovernmentalism, namely that EU policy-makers are reluctant to empower supranational institutions such as the EP. Contrary to the early days of European integration, the Maastricht Treaty formally introduced legislative co-decision rights for the EP that put it on par with the Council of Ministers. Although this was without doubt a remarkable achievement, back then it only applied to 15 treaty articles. After three additional treaty reforms, co-decision (or the ordinary legislative procedure as it is now called) applies now to 86 policy areas transforming the EP into a 'genuine

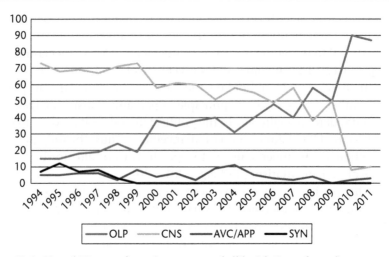

Figure 12.1. Use of EP-procedures (percentage of all legislation adopted)

Note: OLP: ordinary legislative procedure; CNS: consultation procedure; AVC/APP: assent/consent procedure; SYN: cooperation procedure abolished by the Amsterdam Treaty in 1999.

Source: Obholzer, Frantescu, Hagemann, and Hix (2012: 5)

co-legislature' (Corbett, Jacobs, and Shackleton 2011: 248–50). The Lisbon Treaty alone extended co-decision to 40 new policy areas (Ruiter and Neuhold 2012: 103). As a result, EU laws adopted under the co-decision procedure have increased dramatically since the early 1990s (period 1993–9: 153 laws; 2004–9: 454 laws) and it is also by far the most important legislative procedure (figure 12.1).

Although these data indicate a clear trend towards the parliamentarization of the EU polity, we also witness a development of the growing informalization of co-decision (Burns 2013; Burns et al. 2013) that is also more in line with arguments put forward by the new intergovernmentalism. The informalization of co-decision was triggered by the Amsterdam Treaty, as it introduced the possibility of adopting a legal act at the first parliamentary reading (also known as 'fast-track procedure' or 'early agreement'). The consequences of this amendment have been significant: While in the first period after Maastricht (1993–9) nearly 40 per cent of the dossiers to be adopted under co-decision were approved at the third hearing (i.e. conciliation), this figure dropped to around 20 per cent for the period 1999–2004, and subsequently to a meagre 5 per cent in the period 2004–9. The inverse trend can be observed with regard to the early agreement. While in the first period after Amsterdam (1999–2004) 28 per cent of all co-decision dossiers were adopted at the first reading, this figure sharply increased in the following period to a remarkable 72 per cent (figure 12.2). Research suggests that enlargement, legislative

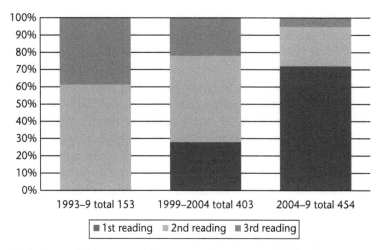

Figure 12.2. Stage of Adoption within the EP (percentage of all legislation adopted in parliamentary session)
Source: European Parliament (2009: 8)

workload, and workload complexities have played a crucial role in pushing the EP to 'go informal' (Reh et al. 2011).

The growing relevance of the fast-track procedure also affected intra-institutional power relations and strengthened 'relais actors' within the EP, such as rapporteurs or other committee members that are involved in inter-institutional bargaining with the Council of Ministers (Farrell and Héritier 2003; Naurin and Rasmussen 2011). As in most modern national parliaments it is no longer the plenary of the EP that is in the driving seat but the responsible EP committee. It is the relevant committee that mandates the EP negotiation team and makes crucial *de facto* decisions regularly endorsed by the plenary of the EP (Obholzer and Reh 2012). Once trilogue negotiations among Commission, Council of Ministers, and EP officials have reached an agreement it will usually be rubber-stamped by the plenary of the EP, rendering any amendment highly unlikely (Rasmussen and Shackleton 2005). Notwithstanding a few public controversies with the Council of Ministers, the huge number of first-reading agreements indicate that the EP has transformed itself from an antagonistic actor, who used to clash with EU member states on a regular basis, to a consensus-seeking decision-making machine that feels the need to behave 'responsibly' (Ripoll Servent 2013; see also hypothesis 1). The shift of legislative policy-making from 'public inclusive' to 'restricted secluded' arenas and the resulting informalization of the political process (Reh et al. 2011), has not only led to an acceleration of the legislative process but also to a significant reduction of the deliberation time within the EP. While the transformation from an arena of publicly debating MEPs into a 'committee parliament'

(Kohler 2014: 612) might have made the supranational decision-making process more efficient, it has had negative effects on the normative role of the EP. MEPs seem to be more concerned with coping with the ever-increasing legislative workload and conceive themselves more as bureaucrats, whose primary responsibility is to get deals done on a technical level rather than debate and communicate policies in the plenary (Fouilleux, De Maillard, and Smith 2005: 617). It is somehow paradoxical that, while transparency in the Council of Ministers increased and co-decision has become the ordinary legislative procedure, a 'culture of secrecy' and a lack of parliamentary debate and communication within the EP has been established that may make its legislative machinery more efficient but at the same time may constitute an 'undemocratic form of parliamentary representation' (Auel 2013: 18).

Furthermore, some scholars have pointed out that the introduction and gradual strengthening of the EP's legislative rights have not fundamentally changed the inter-institutional power balance of the EU (Burns et al. 2013: 943). Although treaty provisions provide the EP with equal power within the ordinary legislative procedure, scholars have pointed out that the Council of Ministers still has more bargaining successes than the EP because it is often closer to the status quo and also enjoys information advantages (Burns et al. 2013: 945; Costello and Thomson 2013). Hence, although the EP has increased its legislative powers significantly, the Council of Ministers still dominates the legislative process (Costello and Thomas 2013: 1036). In addition, the quest to cope with the growing legislative workload and adopt a consensual approach can also affect the EP's policy positions. As the case of migration and asylum policy illustrates, since the EP gained co-decision rights in this field, it has been more concerned with behaving 'responsibly' and finding consensus with the EU member states, thereby giving up large parts of its previous liberal immigration policy and moving towards the more restrictive Council position (Lopatin 2013; Ripoll Servent and Trauner 2014) (see also hypothesis 1). This development has been reinforced by the 'technocratization' of the legislative process that excludes many MEPs from the decision-making process, thus reducing the range of policy options available to the EP (Ripoll Servent 2013: 983).

In sum, empirical evidence on co-decision suggests that the EP is struggling to cope with an increasing and increasingly complex workload and tries to resolve this by 'going informal' and 'behaving responsibly', which has caused the EP to bring its ideological position closer to that of the Council of Ministers in order to keep the legislative ball rolling. The EP still has a clear interest in increasing its say and extending co-decision to as many policy fields as possible. However, the application of the co-decision rights, including its informalization and the limited number of MEPs involved, coincides with central features identified by scholars of the new intergovernmentalism such as the creation and wide use of informal working methods (Puetter 2012: 162). In other words: although the growth of the EP's legislative power serves as an exception to the new intergovernmentalism, the practical use of co-decision reveals features such as informalization and structural disadvantages of the EP that render the achievements of supranational parliamentarization a bit less impressive.

12.3 Budgetary Politics: Maximizing Influence Through the 'Power of the Purse'

Since the budgetary treaties of 1970 and 1975, the EP has played a prominent role in the annual budgetary procedure. By granting the EP the final say over one of the two pillars of budgetary politics, that is the non-compulsory expenditure, the EP was given a 'genuine right of decision making for the first time' (Ehlermann 1975: 325). From the outset, the EP has been prepared to use its strong budgetary power as a lever to increase its influence in other fields of EU policy-making in which the EP has less or—as it was in most cases—no say at all (Eiselt, Pollak, and Slominski 2007: 80; Craig 2008: 129). The inter-institutional struggle culminated in the 1980s and was partly resolved by the budgetary reform in 1988 that embedded the annual budgetary procedure into a multi-annual financial framework. Instead of an annual budgetary conflict, we are now witnessing a substantial conflict among member states and between them and the EP every seven years. With the Lisbon Treaty, the distinction between compulsory and non-compulsory expenditures was finally abolished and the say of the EP over the entire EU budget significantly enhanced. Together with the Council of Ministers, the EP is now responsible for the entire annual EU budget. Besides its increased influence on the annual EU budget, the EP also has a veto with regard to the multi-annual framework, which led to a serious conflict over the multi-annual financial framework in 2012, which was finally resolved in late 2013.

Despite the regular heated negotiations between the EP and the member states, the entire process requires that a consensus be reached and failure is not considered a viable option. True, we witnessed some hiccups in the negotiations at the end of 2012, but although this was widely regarded as a failure by the media, it had no significant impact and was little more than a simple 'game of chicken' in which both players had conflicting interests and preferred the other player to swerve but had, nonetheless, a shared interest in avoiding the crash and securing the finances of future EU activities (Schimmelfennig 2014: 9). For the EP, this search for consensus is of particular importance as it often uses its budgetary power, together with its legislative rights, as bargaining chips to extend its influence to other EU policy fields in which it has little or no say (Kietz and Maurer 2007). Using the example of the creation of the EEAS, we assess the extent to which the EP is able and willing to influence issues in a classic intergovernmental area. We argue that, although it is beyond doubt that these areas remain firmly dominated by intergovernmental policy-making, the EP was nevertheless able to use its existing powers to successfully extend its influence even as far as these intergovernmental areas.

12.3.1 *The Use of Co-Decision and Budgetary Rights in the Creation of the EEAS*

The EU's Common Foreign and Security Policy (CFSP) has traditionally been an intergovernmental affair, rendering parliamentary input modest at best. Apart from securing some information rights in the wake of the creation of the Second Pillar by the Treaty of Maastricht, leading to a regular pattern of meetings and exchanges of views, the EP had virtually no say in this field. This was strikingly obvious with regard to the appointment of the first High Representative in the late 1990s, when the EP failed to exert any influence over the appointment procedure (Crum 2006). Whether the EP has had some influence in substance is a matter of controversy in the literature (Maurer, Kietz, and Völkel 2005; Crum 2006). However, with the entry into force of the Treaty of Lisbon, and the establishment of the EEAS, as well as the modification of the appointment rules of the High Representative, the EP's influence has increased considerably.

From the outset, the EP advocated that the EEAS should be incorporated into the EU institutional architecture, notably within the Commission, instead of being treated as sui generis (European Parliament 2005). The rationale of the EP is evident: only an EEAS firmly rooted within the supranational institutional framework provides the EP with a clear mandate to use its co-decision and budgetary rights and thus plays a powerful role in foreign policy (Duke 2009: 222). This was made clear in a report in which the EP declared 'its intention to fully exercise its budgetary powers in relation to the setting-up of the EEAS' (European Parliament 2009b: 15).

Although the EEAS was adopted by the Council of Ministers alone (2010/427/EU), providing the EP with only a consultative role, the EP was heavily involved in the negotiations leading to the final adoption being treated *as if* it were a co-legislator (Raube 2012: 66). After five quadrologue meetings between the Council of Ministers, the High Representative, the Commission, and the EP between mid-April 2010 and mid-June 2010, the four parties reached a 'political agreement' on the proposal for the Council

Decision in their meeting on 21 June 2010, paving the way for the formal establishment of the EEAS (see IP 10/772; Agence Europe 10164, 22 June 2010). This agreement was approved by the plenary of the EP on 8 July 2010. One of the MEPs involved in the negotiations, Roberto Gualtieri, explicitly stated that the EP had managed to turn the consultation procedure (that is legally required) into a real co-decision procedure (Agence Europe 10165, 23 June 2010). That this achievement might be the first step in 'communitarizing' all foreign affairs issues (Agence Europe 10165, 23 June 2010) could well be an exaggeration, but it shows that the EP is able to use its formal powers as a lever to extend its influence to other areas.

How can the strong involvement of the EP be explained? The creation of a functioning EEAS not only requires the adoption of a Decision by the Council of Ministers but also needs additional amendments concerning the staff regulations of EU officials and the financial regulations. Since the latter two acts fall under co-decision, this puts the EP in a very powerful position. Thus, since the EP made clear that it was willing to treat all issues concerning the setting up of the EEAS 'as a single package' (European Parliament 2010), it became obvious that the EP also has *de facto* co-decision rights on the Council Decision (Christoffersen 2011: 6). In addition, the EP also plays an important role with regard to the appointment of the High Representative. Although she or he is selected, as well as formally appointed, by the European Council, the candidate is subject to a hearing before the EP and a vote of consent by the Parliament (Article 17(7) TEU). Finally, the treaty empowers the EP with the right to dismiss the entire college including the High Representative (Article 17(8) TEU). In terms of institutional design, the EEAS is currently located between the Commission and the Council of Ministers under the supervision of the High Representative. Thus the EP has not succeeded in integrating the EEAS entirely within the Commission. However, the EEAS budget is fully under parliamentary control which allows the EP to continue influencing EU external policy-making by using the 'power of the purse' (e.g. Maurer, Kietz, and Völkel 2005) or other (in-) formal means. While the EP has gained remarkable rights in a classic intergovernmental domain, it remains to be seen whether its institutional power will also translate into substantive influence. The creation of the EEAS seems to confirm hypothesis 2 of the new intergovernmentalism, that the EP might not be hard-wired for the pursuit of supranationalization. Being aware that the 'shadow of renationalization keeps looming' over CFSP, the EP seems to be satisfied with 'any common foreign policy adopted at the EU level' (Crum 2012: 371), as long as it can use its established powers with regard to staff or financial matters to gain some informal influence in the field. Whether this influence is substantial remains to be seen.

12.4 The Rise of EU Agencies: Shaping Design and (Informal) Accountability

Many EU policy fields have witnessed a significant degree of 'agencification' during the post-Maastricht period. More than 30 EU agencies have been established, operating in diverse areas such as pharmaceutical regulation, energy, food safety, the environment, railways, but also border control, fundamental rights, and police and judicial cooperation. The rise of EU agencies is inextricably linked with the incremental extension in both scope and depth of EU competences that required an EU-wide monitoring of rule implementation as well as information gathering, knowledge building and facilitating of cooperation. Since the member states have been reluctant to confer these functions to the Commission, they chose to transfer competences to newly created autonomous EU agencies. Both the Commission and the EP accepted the development of an autonomous EU-wide agency structure as a second-best option, as long as it ensured the Europeanization of more and more policy fields since the Maastricht Treaty (Kelemen and Majone 2012: 226).

There follows a brief discussion of three types of parliamentary control: *ex ante*, ongoing, and *ex post* (see Vos 2014: 31). Initially, the institutional design of EU agencies fell under the exclusive competence of the Council of Ministers. The EP enjoyed consultative powers only. The first attempts by the Commission to suggest a stronger involvement of the EP, by proposing the cooperation procedure, was overruled by the Council of Ministers indicating that it had no interest in enhancing the influence of the EP on the institutional set-up of EU agencies (Kreher 1997: 232). Following the introduction of co-decision and the continuous strengthening of co-decision rights since Maastricht, the EP was concerned about being sidelined in the implementation phase of EU agencies. Hence, it was determined to extend its influence to the design and oversight of EU agencies, basing its claims largely on normative grounds, such as democratic accountability and transparency (Kelemen 2002: 104). As a result, and in line with the gradual extension of the EP's co-decision rights, an increasing number of EU agencies' founding regulations are now adopted or amended under co-decision procedure.

While the EP's say over the design and mandate of EU agencies has increased over the years and may probably continue to do so in the future, the organizational structure of EU agencies is largely dominated by EU member states. This holds true for the two institutional features of every EU agency: the management board and the executive director. While the former is the principal steering body of the agency and thereby responsible, inter alia, for the adoption of the work programme and the budget, the latter is the legal representative of the agency and runs its day-to-day business. The management board consists mainly of national representatives who are expected to ensure the continuous influence of EU member states over the work of the agency and prevent the much-feared phenomenon of 'agency-drift' (Wonka and Rittberger 2011). While management boards are still dominated by EU member states, there are already examples, such as the European Food Safety Authority (EFSA) or the EU Agency for the Cooperation of Energy Regulators (ACER), where the EP has used its co-decision rights to influence the composition of the management board. Having an EP representative present on the management board may also raise the ongoing accountability of the respective agency, and the EP seems to pursue this strategy already, in order to enhance its control of EU agencies (Jacobs 2014). Following principal-agency literature and also existing empirical research on this matter, we may be sceptical as to whether members of the management board (be they EP representatives or not) are able to control the activities of EU agencies (Busuioc 2011). But even if this remains doubtful, we have to acknowledge that the inclusion of EP representatives on the management board of an EU agency can be regarded as a further example of how co-decision also strengthens parliamentary involvement in other stages of the EU policy cycle.

The same holds true with the post of executive director. For instance, the establishment of the EFSA in 2002 was not only the first EU agency to be created under co-decision, but the EP was also conferred with important rights regarding the appointment procedure of the Executive Director. Although the final decision is made by the management board, candidates for the post of Executive Director have to appear before the relevant EP committee and answer questions put forward by MEPs (Article 26 EFSA Regulation 178/2002/EC). Although there is no consistent pattern, the EP has extended its right to influence the appointment procedure with regard to other EU agencies, including the European Fundamental Rights Agency (FRA), the European Medicines Agency (EMA), the European Centre for Disease Prevention and Control, and the European Chemicals Agency.

Another aspect of increasing parliamentary control may result from the 'Joint Statement' on EU agencies, which has recently been adopted by the EP, the Council of Ministers and the Commission and which inter alia foresees the creation of an 'early warning system' in cases where the management board exceeds its mandate, violates EU law or is not in line with EU policy objectives (Joint Statement 2012: 13 para. 59). In such cases, the Commission may request the management board to refrain from adopting the relevant policy and will inform both the EP and the Council of Ministers 'to allow the three institutions to react quickly' (Joint Statement 2012: 13 para. 59). Apart from obtaining some informal control power over management boards, the fact that the EP adopts a tripartite inter-institutional agreement dealing with design principles of EU agencies, mirrors the increasing normalcy of parliamentary involvement in EU affairs (Rittberger 2012).

Ex post control aims to obtain information about past activities of agencies and asks questions that result in a thorough evaluation of their performance. Concrete tools constitute the production of various published reports, the executive director's invitation to parliamentary committees and parliamentary questions that are addressed to the Council of Ministers and/or the Commission that deal with agency-related activities. An important part of *ex post* control is the capacity of the EP to control the budget of EU agencies (Busuioc 2009). In 2010, the EP gave its first negative discharge decision to the European Police College. Other agencies followed, including the EMA, the European Environment Agency, and the EFSA (European Parliament 2012). It has to be pointed out that the EP's budgetary instruments also include the adoption of a resolution in which the EP is able to address problems of financial (mis-)management, insufficient transparency, or potential conflicts of interest. If the EP is of the opinion that such problems are severe, it may even postpone the budgetary discharge as long as these issues have been resolved by the agency concerned (Jacobs 2014). Although the discharge power of the EP entails considerable political pressure ('naming and shaming'), the EP has no right to remove the executive director or dissolve the management board that may be responsible for the budgetary problems. If the EP wants further sanctions, such as the dissolution of the agency, it needs the cooperation of the Council of Ministers and the Commission (Scholten 2010). Thus, the EP's involvement in the institutional set-up of EU agencies and control over their ongoing activities and ex-post control has increased in the recent past. This is not to say that the EP is on equal footing with the Council of Ministers or that the EP has already sufficient control over EU agencies. We merely argue that the increasing involvement of the EP in agency governance can be understood both as a result of existing powers (e.g. co-decision) as well as a reflection of a normative consensus for a greater involvement of the EP in EU affairs.

The role of the EP in shaping the institutional design of the EU border agency Frontex is particularly interesting because, despite its supranationalization, border control is still regarded as being dominated by EU member states (Lavenex, Lehmkuhl, and Wichmann 2009).[2] However, we argue that the EP's legislative and control rights in the field of border control have gradually improved the accountability of Frontex, in spite of the reluctance of the member states.

Frontex was established in 2004 by a Council regulation (2007/2004/EC) that mainly dealt with facilitating the collaborative effort of border control, yet remained silent regarding human rights obligations (Pollak and Slominski

---

[2] The following case study largely draws on Slominski (2013).

2009). Due to widespread criticism put forward by the EP and international organizations, as well as human rights groups, this situation changed and fundamental rights issues have gained increasing political relevance. This is particularly true with regard to the exterritorial application of the so-called non-refoulement principle, which is of relevance because an increasing number of Frontex operations take place outside the EU in international waters or territorial waters of third countries. Although the EU member states refuse to acknowledge the extraterritorial application of this principle, it has become increasingly costly for them to uphold their initial ignorance of fundamental rights in general, and the restrictive interpretation of non-refoulement in particular, without risking an abandonment of crucial normative standards of EU governance (Schimmelfennig 2001). The EP used its various rights, including the hearing of the responsible Commissioner Cecilia Malmström, parliamentary questions, its co-decision rights, as well as its power to take legal action.[3] For instance, the EP used the EP hearing of Malmström as an opportunity to raise the controversial issue of the non-refoulement principle, thereby providing Commissioner Malmström with the occasion to explicitly confirm the exterritorial application of this principle.[4]

Although the EU member states have resisted making a clear statement on this issue up to this day, they have been engaged in a continuous process of explanation, justification and clarification of the fundamental rights obligations and have come forward with new ideas of observing the law and enhancing its accountability (Heijer 2011: 309). One result of this dialogue was the Council Decision 2010/252 that sought to improve many fundamental rights issues with regard to maritime surveillance. While the Commission's proposal included an explicit and unambiguous recognition of the exterritorial application of the non-refoulement principle, the wording of the finally adopted Decision reflected, once again, the Council's internal division and allowed interpretations that suited the particular interest of the actor concerned. While Commissioner Malmström argued that the Decision makes the principle of non-refoulement applicable in Frontex coordinated joint operations, even when they take place in international waters (E-005651/2011; see also P-6871/2010; Malmström 2010: 2), the Council of Ministers, by contrast, answering a similar parliamentary question, avoided such unambiguous language quoting instead the more open wording of the Decision including mere formal references to the non-refoulement principle as such (instead of the

---

[3] See Case C-355/10 *European Parliament* v *Council of the EU*, 5 September 2012, available at <http://curia.europa.eu/juris/document/document.jsf?doclang=EN&text=&pageIndex=0&part=1&mode=DOC&docid=126363&occ=first&dir=&cid=2202160>.

[4] As reported on euobserver.com on 24 February 2012 and 23 June 2011.

contested issue of its exterritorial application) (E-6872/2010). Although this Decision can be regarded as an important step in the right direction of clarification, it 'epitomizes rather than resolves the contested applicability of fundamental rights and EU law to operations undertaken outside EU territory' (Heijer 2011: 317). However, in September 2012 the Court of Justice annulled the Council Decision on procedural grounds (C-355/10). The Court of Justice stated that the clarifications of border control issues in the Council Decision entails political choices that have the power to interfere with the fundamental rights of migrants to such an extent that they must be adopted by the EU legislature including the EP, instead of constituting a mere comitology procedure which includes only a weak involvement of the EP. Apart from that, the Management Board of Frontex adopted two legally non-binding documents (the Frontex Fundamental Rights Strategy and a Code of Conduct), which strengthened its fundamental rights obligations and enhanced its accountability. But it was the EP that made sure that most of these improvements were finally included in the legally binding Frontex recast regulation of 2011.

The Frontex case illustrates that EU member states not only have an interest in tackling irregular migration, but they also conceive of themselves as law abiding and respected members of the international community. The EP (along with others such as the Commission, the UNCHR and human rights groups) exploited this and engaged the member states in a continuous dialogue on fundamental rights that made it increasingly costly for EU member states to uphold their initial ignorance of fundamental rights in general and the restrictive interpretation of non-refoulement in particular. This shows that the EP's consensual behaviour and informal decision-making do not necessarily rule out the notion that significant policy changes can be achieved. Although the extraterritorial application of the non-refoulement principle is still not explicitly recognized by the EU member states, the EP succeeded in including many fundamental rights improvements, including references to the non-refoulement principle in the new Frontex regulation.

It remains open to debate whether these changes advocated by the EP belong to the normative core, the policy core or are only secondary aspects of the policy concerned (Sabatier and Jenkins-Smith 1993; Ripoll Servent and Trauner 2014). Since the wording of the Decision, as well as the draft regulation, avoids unambiguous language and explicitly recognizes the extraterritorial application of the non-refoulement principle, it can be argued that the EP has not been successful in changing the policy core of the contested issue but only in changing secondary policy aspects. However, it cannot be ruled out that the various secondary aspects the EP has achieved in the legislative process add up to big results that come close to a change in the policy core (i.e. a *de facto* recognition of the extraterritorial application of the non-refoulement principle).

Conclusion

Proponents of the new intergovernmentalism argue that the post-Maastricht period is marked by an 'integration paradox'. Although EU member states have been willing to transfer more and more policy areas to the EU level, they have been at pains to avoid supranational decision-making. The rise of the EP, which has been transformed from a mere 'talking shop' to a political power-house (Kohler 2014), seems to be in conflict with this interpretation. While member states have successfully avoided transferring significant competences to the Commission and the Court of Justice, they have indeed conceded substantial powers to the EP throughout the post-Maastricht period. The institutional upgrading of the EP can be explained by the member states' interest in strengthening the overall legitimacy of the policy-making process both at EU and national levels. The controversy revolving around the nomination of Jean-Claude Juncker as Commission President is a case in point here. Although pertinent treaty law on selecting the Commission president is less than clear and can be interpreted both ways, national governments were, in the end, unwilling to challenge the EP's *Spitzenkandidaten* approach. This is even more remarkable as national governments have not only had reservations about the top candidates process in general but also about Juncker in particular (Pop 2014; Traynor 2014). Notwithstanding these concerns, member states realized that it would have been 'inappropriate' to cut off the process and engage in a full-blown confrontation with the EP. Not only would such a move have rekindled well-known complaints about the EU's 'democratic-deficit', including the dominance of executive power at the expense of parliamentary control (e.g. Follesdal and Hix 2006), it would have also been hard for (most) governments to explain why they first contributed to the nomination process by choosing the candidates at the respective party congresses only to abandon the successful candidate after the election. The latter also shows that the unwillingness of member states' governments to take on the EP because of supranational as well as national problems of legitimacy may be sweetened by the fact that they continue to play a pivotal role in the selection of the candidate for the Commission president office (Incerti 2014).

We have shown in this chapter that the EP has been effective in using its existing powers to gain informal powers in areas which were originally not intended to fall under EP scrutiny. Interestingly, the rise of informalism can also be observed in those fields where the EP already enjoys considerable formal powers. For instance, the case of co-decision shows that the EP has significantly informalized its legislative behaviour both within the EP and in relation to the Council of Ministers. The informalization of legislative politics has been interpreted as a consequence of the increasing workload of the EP. But it also shows that the EP has gradually overcome the inter-institutional rivalry that shaped its relationship with the Council of Ministers since the early 1970s. Reducing rivalry with the Council of Ministers and instead working together on more and more legislative dossiers also contributes to 'technocratization or depoliticization of EU decision-making and makes it difficult to observe what decisions are made and how the different actors involved in the game contribute to them' (Raunio 2012: 371). To what extent the EP is able to influence policy content is still a matter of scholarly contestation in the literature. However, proponents of the new intergovernmentalism claim that many powers that have been transferred to the EU are mainly, if not exclusively, shaped by the member states and not by supranational institutions such as the EP. While this seems true, it is far from clear that it has to stay like this. It has been emphasized that there is a pattern that when policy areas are first included in the EU decision machinery, the policy mode is intergovernmental but may later be (gradually) supranationalized (Beach 2012: 49). This process of 'uneven Europeanization' has been explained by the fact that the Europeanization of the economy or law has happened faster than the Europeanization of political actors, political culture, and thereby democratic structures (Jachtenfuchs 1997). It is an empirical question whether newly integrated policy fields (e.g. fiscal policy and fields related to the Open Method of Coordination) will also follow this trajectory or whether they will remain within the intergovernmental policy-making mode.

13

De Novo Bodies and the New Intergovernmentalism

The Case of the European Central Bank

Dermot Hodson

A key claim of the new intergovernmentalism is that supranational institutions are not hard-wired for the pursuit of ever closer union (hypothesis 2).[1] Two broad explanations for this phenomenon are considered in the introductory chapter to this volume. The first sees these institutions as being reluctant to champion a further centralization of decision-making in the EU because of a lack of political and popular support for such measures in the post-Maastricht period. The second suggests that preference formation by supranational institutions is more complex than traditional assumptions about bureaucratic self-interest or ideological motivation allow. Other chapters in this volume explore these claims in relation to the Commission (chapter 9), the Court of Justice of the EU (chapter 10) and the European Parliament (EP) (chapter 12). This chapter extends this analysis to *de novo* institutions, the creation and empowerment of which is another distinctive feature of the new intergovernmentalism (hypothesis 3). It focuses on what is arguably the most important *de novo* body to be created in the post-Maastricht era: the European Central Bank (ECB).[2]

[1] Previous versions of this chapter were presented at the Central European University, Budapest in June 2012 and November 2013 and at the University Association for Contemporary European Studies Annual Research Conference in Passau in September 2012. Thanks to Paul James Cardwell and Simon Bulmer, in particular, for helpful comments. The usual disclaimer applies.
[2] The question of why EU member states delegated control over monetary policy to a *de novo* institution is not dealt with here. For Simon Bulmer (see chapter 14) it owes more to the power of economic ideas than new intergovernmental dynamics. This is a debate for another day but it is worth adding here that the ideational turn to central bank independence in the 1980s and 1990s, while important, was compatible with a range of institutional designs. EU member states could

Although much has been written on the Bank's monetary policy preferences (e.g. de Haan, Eijffinger, and Waller 2005; Geraats, Giavazzi, and Wyplosz 2008), comparatively little attention has been paid to the Bank's wider political aims.[3] An important exception to this rule is Heisenberg and Richmond (2002), who conclude that the ECB performed much like a traditional supranational institution during EMU's first two years by pushing for further integration in the fields of tax harmonization, financial supervision, and fiscal coordination, albeit without success.

This chapter explores the ECB's political preferences across a wider range of policies over the period 1998–2013. Focusing on the ECB's approach to, and public pronouncements on, European integration, it finds the Bank to be highly ambivalent about the pursuit of ever closer union. In the spheres of regulation and, to a lesser extent, allocation, the Bank did push for supranational decision-making. In the sphere of stabilization and in relation to wider questions of European integration, the Bank was generally sceptical, however, about seeing either itself or other EU institutions extend their competences. This ambivalence about the European project is explained with reference to interests rather than identity. With regard to the former, selection bias and socialization effects may not be as strong in the ECB as they were once thought to be in supranational institutions, it is argued, but support for the European project seems robust in the upper echelons of the Bank. As regards the latter, the concept of contingent competence maximization is put forward to understand the ECB's willingness to back supranational decision-making only in those cases where such schemes are consistent with the pursuit of price stability and the bureaucratic interests of national central banks. Ever closer union mattered for the ECB in the post-Maastricht period, in other words, but only once other preferences had been satisfied.

The remainder of this chapter is divided into four sections. The first revisits classic debates about why supranational institutions have traditionally been thought to favour ever closer union and considers why the ECB rests uneasily with these assumptions. The second explores the ECB's approach to supranational decision-making in the fields of regulation, stabilization, and allocation and in relation to wider questions of European integration between 1998 and 2013. The third section seeks to explain why the ECB supports further integration in some cases but not others. The final section concludes by

---

have given traditional supranational institutions a more prominent role in euro area monetary policy, for example, by allowing the Commission or the EP to set an inflation target but they chose not to.

[3] That the ECB is a technocratic body does not explain this lack of interest since political scientists are accustomed to thinking about central banks as bureaucratic institutions (see, for example, Franzese 1999).

considering the wider significance of these findings for the themes of this volume.

13.1 Should the ECB Want Ever Closer Union?

Before looking at the ECB's track record on questions of European integration, it is worth recalling the reasons why scholars have traditionally seen supranational institutions as being hard-wired for the pursuit of ever closer union. A recurring claim in the literature is that the officials who make up such bodies are likely to have convergent beliefs about the desirability of the European project (see Pollack 2003: 36). Scholars differ as to the source of this convergence, with some looking to the socialization effects of international institutions (Checkel 2005) and others emphasizing the selection bias that brings individuals with intense preferences for the pursuit of ever closer union to work for EU institutions (Hooghe 2005). These arguments owe a debt to Deutsch et al. (1958: 76), who underlined the importance of 'partial identification in terms of self-images and interests' for successful political integration. This shared 'sense of community', as the authors called it, is not exogenously determined but the result of social learning between the individuals involved in integration (Deutsch et al. 1958: 76). Whether supranational institutions are the outcome of, or a catalyst for, such social learning is a point of ambiguity in Deutsch's work, although he does allow for the possibility that social learning may progress more rapidly among members of a 'unifying institution' (Deutsch 1953) and that this institution could, in turn, help to drive forward the process of integration (Deutsch 1963).

Haas (1958) was undoubtedly influenced by Deutsch but the former's concept of loyalty is often erroneously equated with the latter's sense of community and more generally misunderstood. Loyalty, for Haas (1958: 5), describes a 'condition in which specific groups and individuals show more loyalty to their central political institutions than to any other political authority, in a specific period of time and in a definable geographic space'. A shift in loyalty from the national to supranational level among trade associations, trade unions, and political parties, for instance, is paramount for political integration, Haas argued, but he remained equivocal on the question of whether the members of supranational institutions must be similarly inclined to provide political direction to the integration process. Jean Monnet, he notes, brought federalist fervour to his role as founding President of the European Coal and Steel Community's High Authority but such views were not necessarily shared by the other members of this institution or, indeed, Monnet's successor, René Mayer (Haas 1958: 456–7).

What motivates supranational institutions if not ideological commitment to integration is often left implicit in Haas's work, although he alludes to the possibility of bureaucratic self-interest in some of his writings. A case in point is Haas (1964: 153), which describes the tendency of the Commission to propose policy solutions that 'upgrade its own power at the expense of member governments'. This theme has been developed in greater detail by a succession of scholars, with Peters (1992) and Cram (1994) among the first to conceptualize the EU executive as a competence maximizer. This line of reasoning is taken further by Majone (1994: 65), who sees the Commission as maximizing the scope of its competences because constraints on the size of the Community budget rule out a strategy of budget maximization. Stone Sweet, Sandholtz, and Fligstein (2001: 13) also leave room for bureaucratic politics when they acknowledge that institutionalization in the EU 'is partly a process whereby powerful actors seek to shape the rules of the game in their favour'.

Viewed against this backdrop, and putting to one side for the time being the question of whether the preferences of supranational institutions themselves may have shifted in the post-Maastricht period, there are a number of reasons to presuppose why the Bank might not support the pursuit of ever closer union in all cases. First is the suspicion that selection bias or socialization effects, to the extent that they matter for the ECB, are more likely to produce a convergence in economic beliefs rather than support for further integration. The ECB's preference for recruiting economics PhDs is one reason for this suspicion.[4] Another is the fact that the Bank is headquartered in Frankfurt, thus reducing the scope for social learning with officials from the Commission and other EU institutions. Of potential significance too is the fact that ECB Executive Board members typically have a background in national central banking.[5] Indeed, of the nineteen men and women who served on the ECB Executive Board during the period under review, seven had previously served as governor of their national central bank and all but three—Christian Noyer, Benoît Cœuré, and Jörg Asmussen—had prior experience in central banking.

Whether national central bankers constitute an epistemic community is a matter of debate in the academic literature (see Kapstein 1992) but Verdun (1999) convincingly shows that central bank governors of EU member states did so in the run-up to EMU. The members of this community, she suggests, shared both causal beliefs about, inter alia, the importance of low inflation and stable exchange rates for growth and normative beliefs about the desirability of monetary integration, but she finds no evidence that a common

---

[4] See the ECB Graduate Programme: <http://www.ecb.int/ecb/jobs/apply/html/index.en.html>.
[5] The ECB Executive Board includes the President and Vice President of the Bank, and four other members.

commitment to the European project bound national central bank governors together. To the contrary, European central bankers seem to have been united in their view that the establishment of a political counterweight to the ECB posed a threat to the smooth functioning of EMU (Verdun 1999: 320).

Turning from ideas to interests, pure competence maximization is not the only strategy open to bureaucratic actors with 'protecting an organization's essence' among the available alternatives (Allison and Halperin 1972: 48). That the latter might apply to the ECB is another reason to doubt its commitment to the pursuit of ever closer union. Of central importance here is the narrowness of the Bank's mandate compared to the traditional supranational institutions. Whereas the Commission is instructed to 'promote the general interest of the Union',[6] the ECB is required to 'maintain price stability' and without prejudice to this goal 'support the general economic policies in the Union with a view to contributing to the achievement of the objectives of the Union'.[7] Economists have long feared that this mandate could create a deflationary bias by forcing the Bank to prioritize low inflation over economic aims such as higher growth and employment (see Begg et al. 1999). A corollary of this point is surely that the ECB's support for the objectives of the Union will also take a back seat. Williams (2005) suggests as much when he argues that the ECB's mandate can be understood as a form of institutionalized 'monomania' in which narrow policy aims take precedence and the incentive to seek out new areas of cooperation is reduced. This argument, in turn, recalls Deutsch's (1963) distinction between institutions with diffuse and specific goals, with the latter likely to be limited in their ambition for federal arrangements and less inclined to engender a shared sense of Community.

Relevant here too is the 'remarkable' degree of statutory independence afforded to the ECB compared to the traditional supranational institutions (Pollack 2003: 392). Members of the ECB Executive Board, it should be recalled, serve eight-year non-renewable terms of office and can be removed only by the Court of Justice and only then with the backing of the ECB Governing Council.[8] Such independence could, in principle, be put towards integrationist ends but this need not necessarily be the case. The Treaty, it should be recalled, underlines the ECB's independence not only from national governments but also from 'Union institutions' (Article 130 TFEU) and places

---

[6] Article 17 TEU.   [7] Article 127 TFEU.
[8] Members of the Commission serve five-year renewable terms of office and Judges and Advocates General of the Court of Justice can be reappointed after six years. The ECB Governing Council includes the six members of the ECB Executive Board and the national central bank governors of the member states that share the single currency.

no direct obligations on members of the ECB Governing Council to uphold the Community interest.[9]

A final reason why the ECB might not want ever closer union is that the involvement and interests of national central bank governors are of potential relevance for bureaucratic politics within the Bank. Under the Treaty, the ECB must be consulted on EU or national legislation within the euro area monetary authority's sphere of competence; the Bank also has the right to issue an opinion addressed to the relevant EU body or national authority on such matters. Such opinions are adopted by the ECB Governing Council, meaning that national central bank governors are in the majority when the Bank forms a view on legal changes at the EU or national level. Whether these governors would support plans for further integration in such circumstances is not certain, especially in those cases where national central banks stand to lose competences as a result.

13.2 Does the ECB Want Ever Closer Union?

In his analysis of what supranational institutions want, Pollack (2003: 39) focuses on the preferences of the Commission and Court of Justice for 'the liberalization of the European internal market and the reimposition of social regulation from the European level'. This section focuses not only on the ECB's approach to EU regulation but also on its pursuit of greater centralization in relation to two other classic functions of economic policy: stabilization and allocation (Musgrave 1959). While some scholars equate political union with supranational economic decision-making, others see it as involving a centralization of policy-making beyond the economic sphere (see Hodson 2009). In keeping with the second of these approaches, consideration is given to the ECB's views on wider questions of European integration.

The ECB's views are ascertained from a review of key ECB decisions in relation to EU policy-making during 1998–2013 alongside a detailed examination of what euro area monetary officials said in public about such issues.[10] The focus here is on those in the upper echelons of the ECB—primarily the President and five other members of the Executive Board—but the views of national central bank governors are considered where relevant. The source material here includes more than 500 speeches from the ECB President alone, the transcripts of 190 press conferences, scores of interviews by Executive

---

[9] Clause 3.2 of the Code of Conduct for ECB Governing Council Members imposes an obligation to 'act in the general interests of the euro area'. This contrasts with the Commission's Code of Good Administrative Behaviour, which requires 'The Commission and its staff...to uphold the Community interest'.

[10] The ECB was founded in June 1998.

Board members with the financial press, a host of official ECB publications and correspondence on legal issues, and questions relating to international and European cooperation. A full content analysis of this material is beyond the scope of this chapter, which instead seeks to paint a broad-brush picture of what the ECB's position was on the pursuit of ever closer union during the post-Maastricht period.

13.2.1 *Regulation*

The ECB was a clear and consistent champion of reforming product and labour market regulation during the period 1998–2013. Statements in support of the Lisbon Strategy—a coordinated approach to product and labour market reforms launched by EU leaders in March 2000—and its successor, Europe 2020, are plentiful. In the ECB's annual report for 2000, for example, the Bank welcomed 'the impetus given by the European Council to the economic reform process' in Lisbon earlier that year (ECB 2001: 98). This message was reiterated in July 2005, when the ECB backed the 'ambitions of the renewed Lisbon strategy and . . . the efforts undertaken in that context by governments, parliaments and social partners' (ECB 2005a: 84). In his remarks on the tenth anniversary of the euro, likewise, the ECB President, Jean-Claude Trichet, noted that 'the resolute pursuit of structural reforms in line with the Lisbon process' was among the most important challenges for the future of EMU (Trichet 2008). Trichet was equally effusive about Europe 2020, declaring the ECB's full support for this initiative in a speech at the University of Liège in February 2011 (Trichet 2011a).

Such support was strong but also passive in so far as the ECB sought new competences for neither itself nor the EU when it came to reforming product and labour market regulation. Altogether more assertive was the Bank's approach to financial market regulation, which saw the ECB Governing Council taking several steps to establish an integrated system for cross-border payments and securities in Europe during this period. A key initiative in this respect was the ECB's launch in January 1999 of the Trans-European Automated Real-Time Gross Settlement Express Transfer System (TARGET), which was designed to facilitate transfers in euros between member states sharing the single currency and some other EU members (see ECB 2005b). Under TARGET national Real Time Gross Settlement Systems (RTGs) were integrated via a so-called interlinking module. The launch of TARGET2 in November 2007 introduced a more centralized approach that saw national RTGs replaced by a single shared platform for cross-border payments.

Other ECB-led initiatives in this domain include the establishment in January 1999 of the Correspondent Central Banking Model (CCBM) to allow counterparties seeking credit from their national central bank to use assets issued by all euro area members, as opposed to just the country in question, as collateral. In July 2008, the ECB Governing Council launched plans for CCBM2, a more centralized system of collateral management based on a common technical platform. July 2008 also saw the launch of TARGET Securities 2, with its eventual aim of creating a single platform for the settlement of securities in euros and other currencies in Europe. Another important initiative here was the Single European Payments Area (SEPA), a project launched in January 2004 with the aim of establishing an integrated system of retail payments (cross-border credit transfers, direct debits, and card payments) in the euro area and beyond. The ECB did not lead on SEPA—it fell to representatives of the banking industry to devise new rules for cross-border retail payments and to the Commission to propose a legislative basis for the SEPA in the form of the Payment Services Directive—but the euro area monetary authority was a vocal champion of this initiative from the outset (Quaglia 2009).

The ECB's pursuit of supranational decision-making in relation to TARGET (2), TARGET 2 Securities, CCBM(2) and SEPA was very much in keeping with the Treaty, which instructs the ECB 'to promote the smooth operation of payments systems'.[11] The Bank's pursuit of a more substantial role in relation to financial supervision was bolder by comparison since the Treaty states only that the Bank should 'contribute to the smooth conduct of policies pursued by the competent authorities relating to the prudential supervision of credit institutions and the stability of the financial system'.[12] In spite of this modest language, the ECB wasted little time in raising the prospect for a more centralized approach. A key champion of supranational financial supervision at the ECB was Executive Board member Tommaso Padoa-Schioppa who had argued in February 1999 for a 'true and effective collective euro-area supervisor' (Padoa-Schioppa 1999). ECB President Wim Duisenberg put this point more delicately in a speech delivered in Amsterdam in 2002, when he argued that the ECB should take the lead in 'co-operation between central banks and supervisory authorities'. Duisenberg's successor, Jean-Claude Trichet, stuck to this cautious line until the publication of the de Larosière Report in February 2009. This report, which was commissioned by José Manuel Barroso amid the global financial turmoil of late 2008, called for the ECB to take charge of a new EU watchdog: the European Systemic Risk Board (ESRB). Trichet's response to this idea was positive: the 'ECB and the Eurosystem', he insisted, 'have the technical capacity to assume a stronger role in macro-prudential supervision', adding that an advisory role 'would be a natural extension of the mandate already assigned to us by the Treaty, namely to contribute to financial

---

[11] Article 127(3) TFEU.   [12] Article 127(5) TFEU.

stability' (Trichet 2009). This paved the way for the launch in January 2011 of the ESRB with Jean-Claude Trichet as its first chair.

The ESRB is a purpose-built intergovernmental body without formal decision-making powers (see Hodson 2012). Its governing council includes not only the President and Vice-President of the ECB but also the national central bank governors of the 27 EU member states, the heads of the European Banking Authority (EBA), the European Insurance and Occupational Pensions Authority (EIOPA), and the European Securities and Markets Authority (ESMA), the Chair and the two Vice-Chairs of the Advisory Scientific Committee, and the Chair of the Advisory Technical Committee. Representatives of each national supervisory authority and the Chair of the EU Economic and Financial Committee (EFC) are also invited to attend. This governing council was tasked with safeguarding the financial stability of the EU as a whole, but in the event of systemic risks being identified it was empowered to issue non-binding recommendations to the national authorities concerned.

The ESRB had been open for less than eighteen months by the time that euro area leaders came to the view that a more centralized approach to financial supervision was necessary. This shift came against the backdrop of a sovereign debt crisis that began in Greece in late 2009 before spreading to Ireland and Portugal in 2010. By mid-2012 this crisis had engulfed Spain, which was struggling to rescue its troubled financial sector. As part of a package of measures designed to reassure financial markets, euro area heads of state or government invited the Commission to come forward with a proposal for a single supervisory mechanism for euro area banks involving the ECB (see chapter 7 in this volume). The ECB Governing Council reacted favourably to the resulting proposal, which was presented by the Commission in September 2012. In this opinion, the Bank made clear its preferences for a supranational approach. The single supervisory mechanism, it insisted, should apply to all credit-bearing institutions and be accompanied by a 'conferral of macro-prudential supervisory powers', the latter position going well beyond the soft-law character of the ESRB.[13]

If the ECB thus sought new powers for itself in relation to financial supervision it was not content to leave matters there. In its opinion on the single supervisory mechanism, the Governing Council made clear its views on the need for progress towards European Banking Union. Here the ECB argued that

---

[13] Opinion on a proposal for a Council regulation conferring specific tasks on the ECB concerning policies relating to the prudential supervision of credit institutions and a proposal for a regulation of the European Parliament and of the Council amending Regulation (EU) No. 1093/2010 establishing a European Supervisory Authority (European Banking Authority) (CON/2012/96).

OJ C 30, 1.2.2013, p. 6. These regulations became law in October 2013, paving the way for the ECB to assume its new responsibilities in relation to financial supervision in 2014.

the broad outline of an agreement on a European Resolution Authority should be in place before the single supervisory mechanism was fully operational. Mario Draghi remained insistent on this point in late 2013 at a time when member states seemed to be having second thoughts, telling members of the EP that a 'priority for 2013 from the ECB's perspective is the completion of financial union with the establishment of a single resolution mechanism' (Draghi 2012a).

13.2.2 *Stabilization*

Whereas the ECB sought a greater role for itself and the EU in relation to financial regulation during 1998–2013, it was much more circumspect with regard to stabilization policy. The Bank was at its most sceptical here when it came to plans for a closer coordination of macroeconomic policy in EMU. An early indication of such scepticism was the spat between ECB President Wim Duisenberg and German Finance Minister Oskar Lafontaine. The latter was a vocal proponent of a more active approach to exchange rate stabilization by the euro area, raising the prospect of a 'target zone' between the euro and the US dollar in a meeting with his French counterpart, Dominique Strauss-Kahn, in October 1998 (Norman and Barber 1998). This was followed in January 1999 by a joint statement from Lafontaine, Strauss-Kahn, and Japanese Finance Minister Kiichi Miyazawa on 'the possibility of creating an exchange rate regime among major currencies' (Ministry of Finance Japan 1999). Such calls for greater exchange rate stabilization received short shrift from the ECB, with Duisenberg insisting in a speech in Berlin in October 1998 that the 'exchange rate should be seen as the outcome of all relevant economic policies rather than as an objective to be set independently' (Duisenberg 1998).

The ECB's disquiet about macroeconomic policy coordination during this period was more discernible still in relation to the monetary and fiscal policy mix. Although the Bank accepted euro area finance ministers' invitation to attend the Eurogroup, an informal body created in June 1998 to discuss the 'shared specific challenges' associated with the single currency (see Puetter 2006), the euro area monetary authority remained implacably opposed to a strengthening of this body. In April 2001, for example, Wim Duisenberg rejected calls by Belgian Finance Minister Didier Reynders for closer dialogue between the Eurogroup and the ECB, stating that euro area monetary and fiscal authorities 'cannot and will not co-ordinate our respective policy areas *ex ante*' (Duisenberg 2001). Jean-Claude Trichet's reaction to Eurogroup President Jean-Claude Juncker's calls in 2006 for an enhanced dialogue with the ECB was equally unfavourable, with the ECB President insisting that existing arrangements facilitated 'as much contact as possible' (Trichet 2006a).

Sceptical of grand plans for supranational macroeconomic stabilization, the ECB defended the status quo for much of the post-Maastricht period. This can be seen most clearly in the Bank's consistent calls for both member states and EU institutions to honour their commitments to the stability and growth pact. In October 2002, for example, the ECB Governing Council issued a statement of support that underlined the stability and growth pact's importance not only for 'budgetary discipline' but also for maintaining 'macroeconomic stability' (ECB 2002). This was followed in March 2005 by a statement on 'improving the implementation of the Stability and Growth Pact', which described sound fiscal policies as a prerequisite 'for macroeconomic stability, growth and cohesion in the euro area' (ECB 2005c).

A recurring theme in the ECB's defence of the pact prior to the global financial crisis was that a decentralized fiscal framework in which member states keep their own house in order circumvented the need for a fiscal federation.[14] Speaking in New York City in April 2002, for example, ECB President Wim Duisenberg argued that euro area members 'do not require the assistance of [a] "federal budget"' providing they meet the requirements of the stability and growth pact (Duisenberg 2002). Jean-Claude Trichet returned to this theme in Washington DC in April 2004, arguing that the macroeconomic stability provided by the pact rendered EMU possible 'without a political federation' in general and a 'federal budget' in particular (Trichet 2004a).

Supportive of the stability and growth pact in principle though it may have been, the ECB was not slow to acknowledge instances in which EMU's fiscal rules fell short in practice. The Bank was especially critical of the March 2005 reform of the pact, with the ECB Governing Council warning that changes to the agreement could 'undermine confidence in the fiscal framework of the European Union (EU) and the sustainability of public finances in the euro area Member States' (ECB 2005c). This view was tempered somewhat in the ECB's report on ten years of EMU, with the Bank acknowledging that 'implementation of the reformed Stability and Growth Pact [had] been facilitated by the onset of more favourable economic conditions and particularly buoyant government revenue growth' (ECB 2010: 74). Significantly less temperate was the ECB's line in the light of the euro area sovereign debt crisis, with Jean-Claude Trichet arguing in March 2011 that the crisis had exposed 'flaws in the Stability and Growth Pact that allowed countries' fiscal policies to become a problem—not just for themselves, but for everyone else within the monetary union' (Trichet 2011b).

Once the global financial crisis hit, the ECB found itself drawn into the domain of macroeconomic stabilization in ways that were hard to imagine in

---

[14] The economic logic of the pact, as Artis and Buti (2000) explain, is that member states could avoid excessive deficits during economic slowdowns by meeting the medium-term requirement to keep government borrowing close to balance or in surplus.

advance. The first indication of this fact was the Bank's decision in October 2008 to provide a €5 billion credit line to Hungary, which faced a burgeoning current account deficit at a time of extraordinary turmoil on international financial markets. In early 2010, as concerns over Greece's fiscal situation mounted, the ECB saw its involvement in crisis management deepen still further. In January of that year, officials from the ECB and the Commission travelled to Athens for discussions over Greece's stability programme, an unusual move for the Bank but one that paved the way for its involvement in the troika. This informal grouping, which brings together representatives of the ECB, Commission, and International Monetary Fund (IMF) conducted joint negotiations over the provision of a €110 billion package of loans to Greece in May 2010 and, thereafter, took the lead in assessing compliance with the conditions attached to these loans. What began as an ad-hoc arrangement emerged as a standard operating procedure over the period 2010–13 in financial support programmes for Ireland, Portugal, Spain, and Cyprus, putting the ECB in the vanguard of efforts to manage the euro crisis.

The euro crisis revealed significant shortcomings in the stability and growth pact, which, inter alia, had failed to pick up on significant inaccuracies in the reporting of public finance statistics in Greece. Having long criticized the enforcement of the stability and growth pact, the ECB could, by its own logic, have initiated a debate on the need for a fiscal federation. Instead, it sought in the immediate aftermath of the global financial crisis to make the case for a more stringent enforcement of EMU's decentralized approach to fiscal policy. The ECB's proposals in June 2010 may have been billed as a 'quantum leap in the institutional foundations of EMU' but they sought to centralize neither the institutions nor the instruments of euro area fiscal policy to any significant degree (ECB 2010). Instead, the Bank called for greater automaticity in the enforcement of the stability and growth pact and for the creation of a new fiscal agency with precious few powers other than the ability to apply peer pressure in the event of threats to public finances. ECB President Jean-Claude Trichet, it is true, went further in June 2011 by raising the possibility of one day creating an EU ministry of finance with responsibility for a large federal budget, but such views were valedictory rather than revealing of a shift in ECB thinking on this issue at the time (Trichet 2011c).[15]

If Jean-Claude Trichet thus steered largely clear of debates over a supranational fiscal policy, Mario Draghi pursued a more circuitous route. During the early months of his presidency, which began in November 2011, Draghi

---

[15] Trichet's remarks were delivered four months before he retired as ECB President in his acceptance speech for the Charlemagne Prize. In proposing an EU finance ministry, Trichet took the unusual step of stating that he was speaking '[o]n a personal basis, as a European citizen' (Trichet 2011c: 5).

followed much the same path as his predecessor, stressing the need for a stricter enforcement of EMU's fiscal rules. This can be seen, for example, in the new ECB President's call in advance of the December 2011 European Council for a fiscal compact to reinforce the stability and growth pact (Draghi 2011). Thereafter, a noticeable shift in rhetoric is discernible with Draghi talking openly in September 2012, for example, about the need to construct a 'fiscal union' alongside plans for financial union (Draghi 2012b). The concept of a fiscal union, as employed by Draghi, should not be confused with a fiscal federation, however. In speaking about the former, the ECB President emphasized the need for 'true budgetary oversight at the European level' rather than a centralized budgetary instrument.[16] Here the ECB President departed from Herman Van Rompuy's report on the future of EMU in December 2012, which made the case for 'a well-defined and limited fiscal capacity to improve the absorption of country-specific economic shocks, through an insurance system set up at the central level' (Van Rompuy 2012).[17] Interesting in this regard is the difference between the ECB's 'reading' of the Van Rompuy report and that of the Commission. While the ECB focused on fiscal union as a means of reinforcing EU fiscal rules, the Commission pre-empted Van Rompuy's call for a fiscal capacity by raising the prospect in November 2012 of a *de novo* budgetary instrument backed by own resources and capable of supporting 'important structural reforms in a large economy under distress' (Commission 2012f).

13.2.3 *Allocation*

The EU budget's size means that its impact on stabilization is minimal but it remains the primary instrument through which the Union engages in allocation and redistribution. During 1998–2013, the ECB largely refrained from public comment on the question of how the EU raises revenue and allocates expenditure, even where such issues were of potential salience for the smooth functioning of EMU.[18] In taking stock of the first decade of the euro, for example, the ECB acknowledged the potential problem of high regional unemployment in monetary unions but made no comment on what the remedial role of EU regional policy might be under such circumstances (ECB 2008). This contrasts

---

[16] The nature of this oversight is not clear from Draghi's public interventions, although he did support German Finance Minister Wolfgang Schäuble's call in 2012 for the creation of a 'Super Commissioner' with veto powers over national budgets. The ECB Governing Council did not take a position on this proposal, which seems, in any case, to have been a bargaining chip to be conceded in negotiations over euro area governance reform.

[17] The report was prepared in close cooperation with Draghi and the Presidents of the Commission and Eurogroup but it was presented in the name of Van Rompuy only.

[18] For a rare exception see ECB (1999: 36), which reproduces the European Council's calls for budgetary restraint at the EU and national level.

with the Commission's Report, 'EMU@10', which explored at length the role of regional policy in promoting catch-up growth in the geographic periphery of the euro area and underlined the continued importance of the Cohesion Fund for the smooth functioning of EMU (Commission 2008: 111).

Although the ECB kept its own counsel on the EU's budget, the Bank had little choice but to offer a view on the Community's role in allocation as concerns over Greece's sovereign debt crisis mounted in early 2010. Asked in March of that year about German Finance Minister Wolfgang Schäuble's plan for a European monetary fund to provide emergency liquidity support to member states facing financial difficulties, Jean-Claude Trichet offered a cautious welcome. Such an arrangement, he suggested, could be understood as 'a possible source of financing' to prevent future financial crises from occurring, while insisting that 'such a fund, if created, should be strictly controlled and confined to cases of an extremely serious and specific threat' (Trichet 2010a).

Schäuble's idea provided little consolation for Greece, which faced mounting pressure from financial markets until EU heads of state or government finally agreed in March 2010 on the necessity of a financial rescue package co-financed by EU member states and the IMF. It took two further months of negotiation before this package was in place, by which time the threat of contagion to other euro area members had intensified. EU leaders responded by establishing two new ad hoc instruments of allocation: the European Financial Stabilization Mechanism and the European Financial Stability Facility, a move that the ECB Governing Council had not sought *ex ante* but which it welcomed *ex post* (Trichet 2010b).

Thereafter, EU policy-makers' attention turned to the creation of a permanent crisis resolution mechanism for the euro area, with the European Council putting in place plans in December 2010 to establish a European Stability Mechanism (ESM) by mid-2013. Reluctant to cede control over a powerful new instrument of allocation to the Commission, EU heads of state or government agreed that the ESM would take the form of a public limited company registered in Luxembourg with finance ministers acting as shareholders and the Commission enjoying only observer status on the body's board of management. The ECB, for its part, revealed a clear preference for supranational decision-making here, calling in its formal opinion on the ESM Treaty for this body to become 'a Union mechanism' rather than 'an intergovernmental mechanism' in due course.[19] Brief though this statement was, it went further than the Commission, which promised in May 2010 to put forward ideas for a permanent crisis resolution mechanism 'in the medium

---

[19] ECB Opinion of 17 March 2011 on a draft European Council Decision amending Article 136 of the Treaty on the Functioning of the European Union with regard to a stability mechanism for Member States whose currency is the euro (CON/2011/24).

to long term' but failed to do so before political agreement on the ESM had been reached (Commission 2010a).

13.2.4 *European Integration*

Turning to wider questions of European integration during the period 1998–2013, the ECB remained largely silent on institutional developments that went beyond the immediate sphere of economic policy. An exception to this rule concerns the recurring controversy over the Bank's precise status in EU law. This controversy first came to light in October 1999, with the ECB Governing Council's decision to create its own independent anti-fraud committee rather than open its doors to the EU's new anti-fraud office (OLAF).[20] The latter was launched by the Commission in April 1999 in response to the financial scandal that forced the resignation of the Santer Administration. An inter-institutional agreement between the Commission, Council of Ministers, and EP shortly afterwards transformed OLAF from a Commission body to a Community one and called on 'other institutions, bodies, offices and agencies to accede to this Agreement', an appeal that the ECB Governing Council took note of in its October 1999 decision, but put to one side.[21]

The Commission successfully appealed this decision, the Court of Justice ruling against the Bank in July 2003. In its judgment on this case, the Court rejected several strands of the ECB's defence, including its claim that it was not included under the scope of the inter-institutional agreement on OLAF since the Bank should not be counted as an institution, body, office, or agency of the Community in this context.[22] On this point, the Court concluded: 'It is sufficient to point out in that connection that, regardless of the distinctive features of its status within the Community legal order, the ECB was indeed established by the EC Treaty, as is apparent from the actual wording of Article 8 EC.'[23]

Although it is tempting to dismiss the *OLAF* case as a mere matter of administrative reform, the ECB Governing Council's October 1999 decision can be viewed as a self-conscious strategy of limiting the scope of EU legislation and, by so doing, exerting 'an expansive...claim of autonomy from the Community's framework' (Goebel 2006: 600). A similar strategy is discernible in the ECB's opposition to the redesignation of the Bank as an EU institution in both the European Constitution and its successor, the Lisbon Treaty. The trigger for this controversy was the decision by the Praesidium of the European Convention to list the Bank as an EU institution alongside the EP,

---

[20] ECB Decision 1999/726/EC.   [21] Regulation EC No 1073/1999 Article 1.
[22] ECJ Judgment Case C-11/00 ECR 2003 I-7147: para. 64.
[23] ECJ Judgment Case C-11/00 ECR 2003 I-7147: para. 64.

the European Council, the Council of Ministers, the Commission, the Court of Justice, and the Court of Auditors in the draft of the Constitution published in May 2003.[24] The ECB Governing Council did not issue a formal opinion on the Constitution until after the Convention had finished its work, but ECB President Wim Duisenberg did raise the issue of the ECB's institutional status in a letter to the President of the European Convention Valéry Giscard d'Estaing in May 2003, insisting that 'no changes in substance should occur' when transferring the Bank's statutes from the existing Treaty to the proposed Constitution (Duisenberg 2003).

The European Convention gave some ground on this issue, with its final draft of the Constitutional Treaty, published in July 2003, recognizing the ECB as part of the EU's 'other institutions and bodies' rather than its 'institutional framework' proper. This change did not go far enough for the ECB Governing Council, which argued that the Bank should be part of the EU's 'institutional framework' but distinct from the 'Union's institutions' by virtue of the its 'specific institutional features'.[25] This drafting suggestion was overlooked by the Intergovernmental Conference that followed the European Convention, with the former placing the ECB under the heading of 'other Union institutions and advisory bodies' in the final draft of the Constitution signed by EU leaders in October 2004.

When it came to drafting the Lisbon Treaty, the ECB's institutional status was one of a comparatively small number of issues over which negotiations were reopened after French and Dutch voters rejected the Constitution. The results of this renegotiation went against the ECB, with the final draft of the Lisbon Treaty, which was signed by EU leaders in December 2007, including the ECB in the list of 'full' EU institutions. In so doing, the Treaty's drafters ignored a formal opinion from the ECB Governing Council, which called for the Bank to be designated instead as one of the Union's other institutions and clarified the ECB's status once and for all as a Union institution bound to 'act within the limits of the powers conferred on it in the Treaties, and in conformity with the procedures, conditions and objectives set out in them' (Article 13 TFEU).

The link between EMU and political union is a recurring one in debates about EMU but it is an issue on which those in the upper echelons of the ECB said relatively little between 1998–2013. Speaking about this issue in November 1999, ECB President Wim Duisenberg described the concept of political union as 'indeterminate' and suggested that by some definitions of the term, EMU already rested on sufficiently solid political foundations (Duisenberg

---

[24] Article I-18, Title IV.
[25] Opinion of the ECB of 19 September 2003 at the request of the Council of the European Union on the draft Treaty establishing a Constitution for Europe (CON/2003/20)(2003/C 229/04).

1999b). When asked about the relationship between EMU and political union in an interview with *Yediot Ahronot* in November 2006, Trichet distinguished between his professional view as ECB President that 'Economic and Monetary Union is fully consistent and coherent' and his personal view that political union was desirable (Trichet 2006b). A similarly personal view was heard during Trichet's final few weeks as ECB President during which he called for a 'significantly stronger political union' while recognizing that this was a matter for the longer term (Trichet 2011d).

The appointment of Mario Draghi paved the way for a more significant shift in the ECB's stance on political union. This can be seen, for instance, in the President's speech to the Federation of German Industries in Berlin in September 2012 in which he argued that political union should become a 'fourth pillar' of EMU alongside the monetary, economic, and financial pillars (Draghi 2012b). As in the case of fiscal union, however, Draghi employed the term 'political union' in a way that did not necessarily entail supranational decision-making. In his Berlin speech, Draghi spoke of political union as being 'essential to ensure that where sovereignty in selected policy fields is pooled, democratic participation is deepened in parallel', but he did not say what form such participation should take. What the ECB President had in mind was suggested in an opinion piece in *Die Zeit* a month earlier in which he called for unspecified measures to enhance the legitimacy of the EU Council (*sic*) and EP alongside efforts to 'better anchor European processes at the national level' (Draghi 2012c). This approach to political union, the ECB President was quick to stress in this interview, would not require the creation of a 'United States of Europe' (Draghi 2012b).

In summary, then, this section has argued that the ECB's preferences for ever closer union in the post-Maastricht period have been ambivalent at best. In the domains of regulation and allocation, the Bank did seek greater competences for itself by taking forward plans for a more centralized approach to cross-border payments and securities settlement in Europe, by supporting plans for a permanent EU crisis resolution mechanism, and, above all, by pushing for a greater role for itself in the field of supervision and for the EU in general in relation to European Banking Union. In the domain of stabilization, in contrast, the ECB remained circumspect about the idea of a fiscal federation even when the euro area sovereign debt crisis exposed serious shortcomings in EMU's decentralized approach to economic governance. The Bank was more sceptical still about plans for closer cooperation in the fields of exchange rate policy and with respect to the monetary and fiscal policy mix. The ECB's involvement in wider issues of integration, meanwhile, was rare but the period in question was marked by a recurring controversy over the Bank's status in EU law. The ECB was also circumspect during this period about the need for, and nature of, European political union. The next section switches from evaluation to explanation, asking whether this reticence about the pursuit of further integration can be reduced to the reasons of identity and interest discussed earlier.

13.3 Explaining ECB Ambivalence About Ever Closer Union

Beginning with the question of identity, there is little evidence to suggest that the ECB's ambivalence about supporting more Europe can be explained by patchy support for the idea of integration. Belief in the European project appears to have been strong in the upper echelons of the ECB, at any rate, with members of the Executive Board missing few opportunities to talk about the importance of the single currency for ever closer union during the period 1998–2013.[26] Jean-Claude Trichet, in particular, talked openly about his own sense of Europeanness during his time as ECB President, even giving a speech on the subject of European identity in Maastricht in September 2004. In this intervention, which was well outside the comfort zone of most central bankers, Trichet not only waxed lyrical about the contribution of 'Dante and Boccaccio, Cervantes and Saint John of the Cross, Shakespeare and Sterne, Goethe and Heine' to Europe's cultural canon, he also spoke of the 'profound sense of... European identity' within the ECB and its mission, along with national central banks, to build a shared sense of Europeanness (Trichet 2004b). Wim Duisenberg and Mario Draghi were both more plainspoken about such matters but consistently positive about the European project during the period examined in this chapter. Duisenberg, for example, made no secret of his hope that the single currency would contribute in time to the aim of 'ever closer union' (Duisenberg 1999a). Mario Draghi, meanwhile, argued that the aim of a 'more perfect union' was a more appropriate one in a speech to the John. F. Kennedy School of Government in October 2013. In the question and answer session that followed this speech, the ECB President expressed his view that establishing a European identity was perhaps the most important political priority for the EU over the medium term (Draghi 2013).[27]

Such beliefs do not appear to have been confined to holders of the ECB presidency. Tommaso Padoa-Schioppa and Otmar Issing were among the members of the ECB Executive Board to have argued consistently about the need for, and desirability of, embedding EMU within a wider political union (see Padoa-Schioppa 2000 and Issing 1999). National central bankers were less

---

[26] In the absence of survey data on the preferences of individuals working in the ECB and national central banks, it is difficult to judge from the bottom up whether beliefs within the Eurosystem have or have not coalesced around the idea of ever closer union.

[27] See, for example, Draghi's response to the question at 0:55:21 in: <http://www.youtube.com/watch?v=i0EJqnC0M0Q>.

forthcoming about the desirability of further integration during this period but positive nonetheless. The need to embed EMU within a wider political union was raised repeatedly by the Bundesbank, for example, with President Ernst Welteke praising the 'slow but steady' progress toward this goal (Welteke 2003) and the Bank's Executive Board welcoming the European Constitution in December 2003 'to the extent that it represents a major step on the road to political union' (Bundesbank 2003).

If questions of identity struggle to explain the ECB's ambivalence towards supranational decision-making in the post-Maastricht period, then what about its interests? One possibility here is that the ECB was engaging in a form of strategic entrepreneurship by supporting ever closer union only in those cases where centralized modes of decision-making stood a realistic chance of success. This line of reasoning explains aspects of the Commission's behaviour during this period but it rests uneasily with the ECB. A case in point is Commission President José Manuel Barroso's reluctance to come out decisively for or against proposals for Eurobonds, a financial transactions tax and an EU crisis resolution mechanism during the period 2007–2011, three issues on which the three largest EU member states were divided (see Hodson 2013). In contrast, Jean-Claude Trichet wasted little time in making clear his doubts about the first two of these proposals and in expressing his support for the third.[28] The idea of strategic entrepreneurship also struggles to explain those instances in which the ECB found itself less enthusiastic than member states about plans for ever closer union. This includes the Bank's opposition to Franco-German plans for closer macroeconomic policy coordination and its reticence in the *OLAF* case and over the European Constitution and Lisbon Treaty.

A more convincing explanation of the ECB's reticence regarding ever closer union during the post-Maastricht period is that the Bank was engaged in a process of contingent competence maximization. This contingency hinged, in part, on the extent to which integrationist initiatives were compatible with the ECB's commitment to price stability. In cases where price stability was perceived to be at risk, the euro area monetary authority showed little inclination for supranational decision-making. This is certainly true in relation to plans for a more centralized approach to macroeconomic stabilization, with Wim Duisenberg responding to calls for a target zone between the euro and other currencies by warning that 'an exchange rate objective for monetary policy...might not be consistent with the objective of price stability' (Duisenberg 1998). Jean-Claude Trichet had a similar reaction to Jean-Claude Juncker's calls for an enhanced dialogue with the ECB, implying that anything

---

[28] See *EU Observer* (2010) 'Trichet Puts Dampener on Financial Transaction Tax', 1 October.

more than existing channels of communication would be incompatible with the 'independence of the monetary authority' (Trichet 2006a). Trichet's colleague on the ECB Executive Board, Jürgen Stark, put this point less diplomatically when he suggested in January 2008 that plans for stronger economic governance in the euro area could be understood as a veiled attempt 'to establish political influence on monetary policy in the euro area and thereby to undermine the independence of the ECB' (Stark 2008).

The idea of contingent competence maximization is also consistent with the ECB's response to the centralization of EU anti-fraud policy and its reticence about being designated as an EU institution by the Lisbon Treaty and the Constitution before it. In the *OLAF* case, the ECB argued before the Court that the 'mere threat' of an OLAF investigation 'is capable of bringing pressure to bear on the Members of the Governing Council or the Executive Board of the ECB and of jeopardising their independence when taking decisions'.[29] That the ECB's designation as an EU institution raised similar concerns is suggested, meanwhile, by the Bundesbank's warning in November 2003 that the Constitution 'may open the door to assigning objectives other than price stability' (Bundesbank 2003).

In cases where the ECB's commitment to price stability was not perceived as being at risk from further centralization, the Bank was more positively disposed towards the idea of supranational decision-making. This can be seen clearly in the ECB's desire to play a greater role in relation to financial supervision. In February 1999, for instance, ECB Executive Board member Tommaso Padoa-Schioppa (1999) acknowledged the concerns of some economists over 'the potential conflict between controlling money creation for the purpose of price stability and for the purpose of bank stability' but rejected the view that 'one model [i.e. the delegation of supervisory powers to central banks or independent agencies] is right and the other wrong' in this regard. Padoa-Schioppa's successor on the ECB Executive Board, Lorenzo Bini Smaghi, offered a similar view a decade later when he argued that his own prior concerns that responsibility for financial supervision could undermine central bank credibility warranted reconsideration in the light of the financial crisis (Bini Smaghi 2009). ECB Executive Board member Yves Mersch went further in a speech in February 2013 demanding that the 'refragmentation of euro area financial markets' in the light of the global financial crisis 'hamper[s] the proper transmission of monetary policy...thereby impeding the ability of central banks to safeguard price stability' (Mersch 2013). Considered thus, he suggested, 'restoring financial stability and reintegrating financial markets'

---

[29] ECJ Judgment Case C-11/00 ECR 2003 I-7147: para. 118.

could be seen as paramount for achieving the ECB's price stability mandate (Mersch 2013).

The ECB's desire to protect its price stability mandate is also consistent with the Bank's response to the global financial crisis. One reading of Jean-Claude Trichet's cautious welcome of Wolfgang Schäuble's proposal for a European monetary fund in March 2010 is not that such a mechanism was considered conducive to price stability so much as the fact that the alternatives being considered posed more of an inflationary risk (Trichet 2010a). Of specific concern in this regard was that an IMF financial support package for Greece would impose conditions not only on Greek officials but also on the ECB. The ECB's subsequent decision to join forces with the IMF and the Commission to negotiate the conditions attached to financial support for Greece and others also allowed the Bank to protect its bureaucratic interests up to a point.[30]

If the ECB's preferences for competence maximization were contingent on its commitment to price stability, a concern for bureaucratic politics within the Eurosystem was evident too. Tensions between the ECB and national central banks certainly appear to have played out over the European Constitution, with the Bundesbank Executive Board adopting a significantly more hawkish line than the ECB Governing Council over the Bank's institutional status. Whereas the latter made clear in its formal opinion on the European Constitution that the proposed text 'does not imply, and is not meant to imply, any change to the substance of the current institutional status of either the ECB or the ESCB', the Bundesbank Executive Board's subsequent warning 'against receding to a situation which falls short of the achievements of the monetary constitution established by the Maastricht Treaty' offered an altogether darker reading of this issue (Bundesbank 2003).

Bureaucratic politics within the Eurosystem also appear to have shaped the ECB's approach to financial market integration during 1998–2013. In seeking more centralized modes of decision-making in the field of payments systems and securities settlements, for example, the ECB sought to empower rather than disenfranchise key national central banks; the Bundesbank, the Banque de France, and the Banca d'Italia were invited to build and operate the single shared platform TARGET II as part of the bureaucratic quid pro quo for this arrangement (Quaglia 2009). The ECB pursued a similar strategy in relation to EU financial supervision, accepting the de Larosière Report's proposal to involve national central banks and the ECB in new arrangements for macro-prudential oversight, even though the sheer number of individuals involved in such an approach raised concerns about effectiveness and accountability (Hodson 2012). The single supervisory mechanism is a more centralized

---

[30] Olivier Blanchard called in February 2010 for central banks to raise inflation targets to 4 per cent in a proposal described by Trichet as 'plain wrong' (Trichet 2010c).

arrangement, although national authorities will again play a key role in its operation. Under the legislative package adopted by EU finance ministers and the EP in September 2013, the ECB will be involved in the direct supervision only of those banks with assets of more than €30 billion or in excess of 20 per cent of national GDP with national authorities conducting direct supervision for the rest, albeit under the gaze of the ECB.

Conclusion

Students of European integration have traditionally assumed that supra-national actors are hard-wired for the pursuit of ever closer union but the new intergovernmentalism challenges this view. This chapter argues that such ambivalence may also apply to *de novo* institutions. It has shown that the ECB, which is arguably the most important *de novo* institution created during the post-Maastricht period, had mixed views about the pursuit of competences for itself and/or the EU during 1998–2013. It was in the fields of regulation and allocation that the Bank came closest to conventional assumptions about what supranational institutions want. This was seen, in particular, in the ECB's push for the integration of cross-border payments and securities settle-ments, in its efforts to carve out a greater role in relation to EU financial supervision, and in its eventual endorsement of a permanent EU crisis reso-lution mechanism. In the field of macroeconomic stabilization, in contrast, the ECB was circumspect about calls for a fiscal federation and openly critical of plans for a more centralized approach to exchange rate policy and monet-ary and fiscal coordination. The ECB also showed itself to be uneasy about certain wider questions of European integration by seeking to limit the scope of EU anti-fraud legislation and resisting moves to designate the Bank as a fully fledged institution of the EU under the European Constitution and, later, the Lisbon Treaty.

Two avenues of explanation were considered to explain the ECB's circum-spection about ever closer union. The first focused on the importance of identity. While there is good reason to suppose that the selection bias and socialization effects that scholars traditionally associate with supranational institutions are likely to play out differently in the Bank, this does not appear to explain the Bank's preferences regarding European integration. Those in the upper echelons of the ECB appear to be committed to the European project and they missed few opportunities during 1998–2013 to note the contribution of the single currency to ever closer union. The second line of explanation looked to the importance of interests. Scholars typically treat EU institutions as competence maximizers, but the Bank was shown to be more interested in protecting its organizational essence through the pursuit of price stability above all other goals. In cases where further integration was perceived to be compatible with price stability, the ECB showed itself to be supportive of supranational decision-making, with the Bank's desire to play a more prominent role in relation to financial supervision a case in point. Where the condition did not hold, the ECB showed a preference for the status quo over further integration, dismissing plans for closer macroeconomic coordination as an attempt to apply political pressure over monetary policy and expressing concern that the designation of the Bank as an EU institution could open the door to objectives other than price stability. Bureaucratic tensions within the Eurosystem also played a role here, with the Bundesbank adopting a particularly hawkish position over the European Constitution and plans for further financial market integration proceeding in a way that empowered rather than undermined national central banks.

In thinking about the generalizability of these results, it is tempting to dismiss the ECB as *a sui generis* institution that bears little relation to other *de novo* institutions. That the ECB's strategy of contingent competence maximization is a product of the Bank's institutional idiosyncrasies is true up to a point. The intensity of the Bank's preferences for price stability is partly a function of the Treaty, which puts the pursuit of this goal above all others, and partly of the anti-inflationary norms that bind euro area central bankers together. The point here is not, however, that other *de novo* institutions will have the same priorities as the ECB for the same reasons but that further research is required to understand what makes each of these institutions tick. EU scholars have devoted considerable attention since the 1990s to understanding the process of preference formation by national governments on key EU policy decisions. The challenge now is to do likewise for institutions operating at the EU level rather than relying on simplifying and simplistic assumptions about what such actors want.

Part IV
Critique and Conclusions

14

Understanding the New Intergovernmentalism

Pre- and Post-Maastricht EU Studies

Simon Bulmer

European integration has developed in fits and starts from the foundation of the European Coal and Steel Community in 1952 through to the current post-Lisbon 'hangover', caused by the euro area crisis, the financial crisis and the associated rise of populism and growing Euro-scepticism across the European Union (EU). The time is therefore ripe for a reappraisal of the state of integration, since—with some notable exceptions—the focus of EU studies has shifted since the mid-1990s to the less grandiose issues of, for instance, the governance agenda or the impact of the EU on member states (Europeanization). The editors of this volume are therefore to be congratulated on their aspiration to advance a new approach to understanding integration in the post-Maastricht era. In doing so, they are able to build on the governance literature but with a view to scaling up its insights in order better to identify the 'nature of the beast'.

The purpose of this chapter is to step back and interrogate the new intergovernmentalism, not least as an observer who first studied integration during the 'doldrums era' of the 1970s and early-1980s. I focus on the editors' chapter 1 but refer to other chapters along the way. Does new intergovernmentalism correctly diagnose the character of the EU when building this new approach? Does it meet the aspirations of any theory, namely to provide some ordered understanding of an often chaotic empirical reality? Do its hypotheses ring true? What is the significance of the Maastricht Treaty being taken as the transformation-point in the timescape of integration for the emergence of new intergovernmentalism? Is new intergovernmentalism really so novel?

In addressing these questions I start with new intergovernmentalism's theoretical aspirations.

14.1 New Intergovernmentalism and Theory

Theoretical advances owe their origins to two sets of impulses: advances in wider social-scientific theorizing or to political developments in the subject being studied (Rosamond 2007: 20–5; Wessels 2006: 236–7). New intergovernmentalism, with its emphasis on the pattern of EU politics in the post-Maastricht era, clearly falls into the latter category. Among the developments in the object of study that the editors identify are the growth of the deliberation of national governments within the European Council and the empowerment of *de novo* bodies rather than the European Commission or the Court of Justice of the EU. This method of securing advances has the advantage—see Rosamond (2007: 21)—that 'EU studies has drawn valuable lessons from its object of study through a process of intellectual "catch-up"'. That is not to say, however, that new intergovernmentalism is without reference to wider theorizing. As Ben Rosamond puts it (2007: 21), 'The description of the EU at particular moments in history is an act that cannot occur independently of an a priori conceptual vocabulary that facilitates that description.' Thus the new intergovernmentalism clearly takes its cues from the intergovernmentalist literature, whether in its original form as propounded by Stanley Hoffmann (1966) or in its subsequent elaboration as liberal intergovernmentalism by Andrew Moravcsik (1993, 1998). These observations therefore suggest two initial approaches to examining what new intergovernmentalism brings to the table. First, does it correctly diagnose reality in the EU and, second, how does it build on the existing legacy of intergovernmentalist analysis?

14.1.1 *Diagnosing Developments in the EU*

One of the key risks that any new analytical approach faces is that it re-describes the EU by over-reliance on a particular period of the EU's evolution. An obvious potential trigger for the case at hand is the euro area crisis. The recurrent process of summit meetings (both as the European Council and in a smaller euro-area format) was a characteristic of this period. The need to create innovative mechanisms like the European Stability Mechanism, cited by the editors as an example of the *de novo* bodies to which power has been delegated, is a similar development arising amidst the crisis (see chapter 1). Furthermore, the rising levels of distrust of the EU and of Euro-scepticism have stemmed in some instances from the adverse public reaction to the prescription of austerity measures to tackle the euro area and/or financial crises. And, in Germany by contrast, public opinion was critical of having to bear the perceived costs of the euro area rescues. Whilst these developments are invoked as context to the new intergovernmentalism, so are other examples of new agencies, such as Frontex (established in 2004) in regards to policing the EU's frontiers and the European External Action Service, set up in the aftermath of the implementation of the Lisbon Treaty in December 2009. A further contributory factor lies with the several rejections of new EU treaties via referendums—from the Danish rejection of the Maastricht Treaty in 1992 through to Ireland's initial rejection of the Lisbon Treaty in 2008. The rejection in 2005 of the Constitutional Treaty in two founding member states—the Netherlands and France—arguably demonstrated most forcefully the new challenges from the wider public to the key assumptions of an elite-driven ever closer union.

There are further developments to note that reinforce the new intergovernmentalism's diagnosis of post-Maastricht EU politics. First, the Maastricht Treaty embedded the notion of subsidiarity in the EU, with its emphasis on the Union only taking responsibility for policy areas where it could offer better solutions than the member states. The subsidiarity principle has served as a brake on the traditional pattern of delegation to supranational bodies through legal integration empowering the Commission and the Court of Justice. A further contributory factor to the new intergovernmentalism, but arguably under-played in this volume, is the widening of integration. Having expanded since the Maastricht Treaty from 12 to 28 member states, the pattern of negotiations has been impacted, first and most obviously in terms of the layout of a venue comprising 28 delegations, but also on the wider dynamics of finding agreement in the EU. The traditional reliance on the Franco-German tandem to advance solutions for the EU as a whole has become less feasible due to the sheer diversity of interests. In the case of the euro area crisis, the preeminence of Germany as the decisive member state became evident owing to France's weaker underlying fundamentals (Bulmer 2014). However, the broad point is that enlargement has made the management of intergovernmental relations less stable and especially complex where unanimity prevails, such as is the normal practice in the European Council. These new patterns are consistent with the assumptions of new intergovernmentalism.

Other post-Maastricht developments are worth identifying in support of the new intergovernmentalism. First, the initial supranational policy areas—coal and steel—disappeared from the EU's remit with the expiry of the Treaty of Paris in 2002. Similarly, the Common Agricultural Policy (CAP), the policy from the European Economic Community that entailed the most supranational intervention into markets, had to be reformed in this time-period because its price support system and discriminatory approach to third countries fell foul of emerging rules in international trade negotiations. The CAP is now less supranational in character as a result. A second development was the rise of new methods of governance, notably the Open Method of Coordination (see, for instance, Héritier and Rhodes 2010). Its growing use in the 2000s—especially in connection with the Lisbon Strategy on EU competitiveness—came about precisely because member governments eschewed supranational patterns of governance in favour of benchmarking and peer review mechanisms (Bulmer 2012). It is worth noting here that the changing character of the CAP and the growth of the Open Method of Coordination came about in part because of factors external to the EU: respectively further moves to neoliberalism in international trade, and changes in modes of governance. In other words, the forces promoting new intergovernmentalism are not necessarily endogenous to the EU itself. Third, and confirming this observation, it is worth noting that the growth in agency governance, such as the so-called *de novo* bodies identified with new inter-governmentalism, was part of a wider trend in public administration towards 'new public management' rather than being confined to the EU. Finally, as confirmed by the Lisbon Treaty maintaining its separate intergovernmental treaty base, moves towards greater supranational control over foreign and defence policy have been very limited. These remain areas where member governments are very reluctant to transfer powers to supranational institutions or to pursue integration through law.

All this evidence suggests that the new intergovernmentalism is well grounded in empirical reality. Yet not all of the drivers are EU-specific, never mind 'post-Maastricht' in a strict sense, since the impact of neoliberalism and new techniques of governance practised elsewhere have also placed their imprint on the contemporary character of integration.

Nevertheless, it is now worth interrogating the assumption that the characteristics fit neatly with the EU and consistently with new intergovernmentalism. What, from the position of devil's advocate, would be the counter-arguments? The first would be that, notwithstanding the supportive evidence identified by the editors and above, new intergovernmentalism is a strong trend but it has not supplanted existing more supranational forms of integration. For example, competition policy has retained its very strong supranational characteristics in the post-Maastricht period (see Cini and McGowan 2009), with the Commission enjoying 'exceptional freedom from the Council and the member governments' (Wilks 2010: 152). A wider review of policy and institutional practice edited by Renaud Dehousse (2011a, 2011b) noted the continuing resilience of the supranational Community method despite the challenges posed. Indicative of the way events can shape theoretical debates, the challenges identified in this study were the intergovernmental turn in the mid-1960s (the empty-chair crisis) and the emergence of new governance in the early-2000s. By selecting difficult cases like Justice and Home Affairs or security policy to go alongside 'easier' policy areas where governance takes place through law, the insights and resilience of the Community method are striking, even though Dehousse concludes (2011b: 203–4) by emphasizing the hybrid nature of the EU. The experiential learning identified by Michael E. Smith (chapter 5) in the Common Security and Defence Policy represents a nod towards shared norms, although the reluctance of the member governments to go beyond the boundaries of new intergovernmentalism is a large part of the explanation for the failure to develop a truly common policy. An analogous 'hybrid' reading is possible from Sarah Wolff's analysis of JHA policy (chapter 6). The findings of Marzena Kloka and Susanne Schmidt arguably fall on the other side of this divide by revealing how Court of Justice case law may still advance integration in spite of new intergovernmentalism, as evidenced by patients' rights in cross-border health care.

The new intergovernmentalism is not just at odds with the Community method, for it does not align so well with other forms of governance that make up the state of integration. In the early post-Maastricht period (and arguably a further example of an event-driven phase of research) the multi-level governance (MLG) interpretation of cohesion policy and integration was particularly influential (e.g. Marks et al. 1996; Bache and Flinders 2004). Has this thesis, with its emphasis on the distribution of power across supranational, national, and subnational levels of governance been rejected? Or is it simply the case that the MLG research agenda, as opposed to its practice, is approaching exhaustion and attention has been diverted elsewhere. Indeed, this point could be extended through reference to the policy-making literature in general. Helen Wallace (2010: 90) identified five modes in the EU: the Community method, the EU regulatory mode, the EU distributional mode, policy coordination, and intensive transnationalism. Of these, only two—intensive transgovernmentalism and policy coordination—can be directly identified as consistent with the assumptions of the new intergovernmentalism. The regulatory mode, while entailing the delegation of authority does not stipulate the creation of *de novo* bodies. Indeed, in the all-important single market policy area the Commission and the Court of Justice are the recipients of delegated powers. The other methods of policy-making practice, I suggest, have not disappeared; they have simply slipped down the research agenda.

A further feature of post-Maastricht integration sits slightly uncomfortably with the new intergovernmentalism, namely differentiated integration. Although differentiated integration takes different forms, for instance variable geometry or multi-speed integration (see, for example, Dyson and Sepos 2010), it is not clear how the new intergovernmentalism or indeed other integration theories persuasively deal with this emergent post-Maastricht characteristic. Differentiated integration is evident in membership of the single currency, the passport-free Schengen zone, in other aspects of the Area of Freedom, Security and Justice and the failure in 2012 of the United Kingdom and the Czech Republic to sign the Treaty on Stability Coordination and Governance (or, more popularly, the Fiscal Compact). Differentiated integration is a key feature of the post-Maastricht EU, so it is striking that it receives little specific attention in the new intergovernmentalism (but see Cardwell and Hervey's related argument in chapter 3 on the decline of a single legal order). Is differentiated integration another manifestation of new intergovernmentalism?

Finally, given the new intergovernmentalism's attentiveness to the euro area crisis, it must be recalled that there is some contradictory evidence from this policy area. The original delegation of responsibility to the European Central Bank (ECB) as part of the Maastricht prescription for monetary union entailed a substantial transfer of authority to a supranational body. This is not in my view a *de novo* body comparable to others that are cited, and here I depart somewhat from Dermot Hodson's starting point (chapter 13). To be sure, the ECB is a *de novo* body but central bank independence had become a new orthodoxy well beyond the EU. To see the ECB's creation as evidence of the new intergovernmentalism would seem problematic, since it could equally be considered as a paradigmatic case of the Community method. Moreover in the discussion on the euro area crisis, while noting the deliberative intergovernmentalism practised in the European Council (see Puetter 2012), surely some recognition of the powers that have been delegated to the Commission to supervise fiscal policy as part of the Fiscal Compact needs to be made? This step could also be interpreted as in line with the Community method that the new intergovernmentalism considers to have faded away.

To summarize in respect of the way the new intergovernmentalism has drawn on developments in the field of study, it clearly diagnoses important trends in European integration but at some risk of neglecting other ongoing features of the EU and a few recent innovations. Its focus on the post-Maastricht period may lead to assumptions that the new intergovernmentalism derives from developments emanating from within the EU, when some are part of wider international changes in governance (*de novo* bodies). The new intergovernmentalism is a strong tendency rather than a blanket characterization of EU integration, since there is conflicting evidence of post-Maastricht moves to greater supranationalism. Of course, this criticism could be leveled at other innovations in the integration literature, such as MLG, but it must be noted in the interests of a critical reading of the new intergovernmentalism.

14.1.2 *The New Intergovernmentalism and the Theoretical Inheritance*

The theoretical aspirations of the new intergovernmentalism can be judged in four ways. What are its objectives; what sort of theory is it; how does it build on the theoretical inheritance of intergovernmentalism; and how do the hypotheses stack up?

First, 'the new intergovernmentalism ... [is proposed] ... as a way of thinking through the dynamics of integration after Maastricht' (chapter 1, p. 39). This is a quite modest claim but justifiable and consistent with the research prospectus. A more specified and articulated model of integration, perhaps with predictive capacity, would be needed if the aspiration were to present new intergovernmentalism as a new 'grand theory'. The new intergovernmentalism certainly amounts to a theory in the sense of 'select[ing] out certain factors as the most important or relevant in providing an explanation' (Stoker 1995: 16–17). Although briefly set out, the new intergovernmentalism is internally coherent and hypotheses can be derived. Second, in terms of the theoretical function of the new intergovernmentalism, its objectives are explanatory rather than critical or normative.

How, third, does the new intergovernmentalism build on its theoretical inheritance? Like Stanley Hoffmann and Andrew Moravcsik, the editors share the view that member state governments rather than supranational institutions are the drivers of integration. Hoffmann and Moravcsik have both been mischaracterized at times as to the theoretical tradition within which their versions of intergovernmentalism are situated. Despite emphasizing the role of governments, neither was a neorealist (for discussion, see Rosamond 2007: 24). While Hoffmann did not open up the 'black box' of the state to the extent that Moravcsik subsequently did, in later reflections in an often-neglected article four characteristics relating to nation states and the EU were highlighted by Hoffmann (1982: 26–9):

- the important distinction between state and society;
- that whilst the state has autonomy, its action can be severely constrained by internal social and political forces;
- that the autonomy of each state is different and the product of state structures and those of social and political forces; and
- European states have a constrained margin of manoeuvre.

These dissections of state and society chime with Bickerton's analysis of the re-casting of state–society relations associated with EU member statehood (chapter 2).

Stanley Hoffmann's favoured general-theoretical approach was derived from international relations (1982: 33):

> to look at the EEC as an international regime, as defined by Keohane and Nye: a set of norms of behaviour and of rules and policies covering a broad range of issues, dealing both with procedures and with substance, and facilitating agreements among the members.

This approach is arguably consistent with the editors' view, although they do not make it explicit and would presumably do so in terms reflecting the passage of more than thirty years since this article by Stanley Hoffmann.

Their discussion of Moravcsik's liberal intergovernmentalism (1983, 1988) is brief but it is clear that the editors do not share his rationalist approach to preference formation, regarding it as an 'unnecessarily reductive notion of domestic politics' (chapter 1.3). I share that critique and an interesting side-question is to wonder what Hoffmann made of Moravcsik's liberal intergovernmentalism. The neoliberal institutionalist foundations of Moravcsik's theory see domestic preferences as the product of economic or geo-political interests (Moravcsik 1998: 24–38). However, the result is to screen out political interests arising from Euro-scepticism or everyday politics. The consequence is that preference formation is understood—absent regular clashes of geo-political interest—with a rationalist, neoliberal bias accounting for the outcome of contestation among economic interests. And yet Hoffmann (1982: 26) was critical of such approaches on the basis of a three-fold reductionism. First, social phenomena are reduced 'to mere effects of economic factors' . . . and thus 'discount the autonomy of politics'. Second, they neglect the 'complex and conflictual agglomerations' that make up society, reducing it instead to a teleological model of industrial society. Third, the state is reduced to 'an epiphenomenon, produced by economic and social relations' (Hoffmann 1982: 26). Are these critiques not also applicable to a large degree to Moravcsik's liberal intergovernmentalism? Indeed, similar 'orthodox' assumptions are also shared by much of the integration theory literature, including neofunctionalism, as has been argued by Magnus Ryner (2012: especially 651–5).

14.2 The Hypotheses of the New Intergovernmentalism

The editors' efforts to break free of such reductionism are to be welcomed. They can be interpreted as developing a post-Maastricht interpretation on Hoffmann's intergovernmentalism. Nevertheless, they are exposed to two criticisms. First, they utilize the language of preference formation, which is a discourse that is firmly rooted in a rationalist approach to politics. And, more significantly, they do not spell out a view of how state–society relations are to be understood in the new intergovernmentalism. Indeed, the new intergovernmentalism only flirts with general political theory, so matters of ontology or how this new approach connects with wider social scientific theorizing is limited.

I now turn to the hypotheses (see chapter 1). All six look plausible on the face of it. Hypothesis 1 proposes that deliberation and consensus have become guiding patterns of decision-making at all levels. In many ways this looks like intergovernmentalism in the era of Stanley Hoffman's theorizing. At that time, and following the Luxembourg Compromise of 1966, consensus was literally the only way to reach agreement in the European Communities. The hypothesis is strongly supported by the workings of the European Council: the hub of the new intergovernmentalism (see Uwe Puetter, chapter 8). But beyond this institution the hypothesis is more open to challenge, for there have been successive moves to qualified majority voting (QMV) in successive treaty reforms from the Single European Act (SEA) onwards. The Council of Ministers is important (as per the new intergovernmentalism) but there is a wealth of difference between where it operates deliberatively and consensually to where it uses QMV.

VoteWatch Europe (2012) examined Council voting over the period July 2009–June 2012. The data revealed that during that time 90 per cent of decisions were subject to QMV provision, while unanimity applied in the remaining cases. Where QMV rules applied, 65 per cent of votes were taken unanimously. In the remaining 35 per cent of cases some disagreement or abstention was noted, although a formal vote might not have been called. These quantitative data challenge the hypothesis in that they indicate a significant departure from consensual decision-making, although they give little impression on the political significance of individual votes. This hypothesis therefore needs to be tested with qualitative data to establish whether the practice of QMV is confined to lesser-order items on the EU's political agenda.

A further observation is in order in relation to the argument that vetoes are ineffective, as illustrated by Greek Prime Minister George Papandreou's overruled wish to have a referendum on its euro area bailout. Perhaps one or two examples from the United Kingdom's European diplomacy might be revealing of the alternative situation: that the veto on the Fiscal Compact resulted in a Treaty that does not apply in all states. Prime Minister Cameron appears to be 'off message' in not adhering to deliberative and consensual politics in the European Council on some issues! The Fiscal Compact also highlights an earlier question, namely where differentiated integration fits in with the new intergovernmentalism and its assumptions about consensus and deliberation.

Hypothesis 2 proposes that not all of the supranational institutions are pre-programmed to seek ever closer union. Again, this hypothesis would have held to a large degree in the period between the Luxembourg Compromise and the SEA. In other words, supranational institutions need to be attentive to the political environment. However, there is one exception to this rule, namely the Court of Justice. It was from the mid-1960s that its rulings on supremacy and direct effect were handed down, advancing the EU's supranational character. In fact, the hypothesis invites a nuanced alternative view.

The three supranational institutions referred to in the discussion of this hypothesis —the Commission, Court of Justice, and the European Parliament

(EP)—are subject to quite different dynamics (both in the mid/late-1960s and in the present). The Commission was, and remains, responsive to the wider political climate as expressed by the policies of the member governments and broader public consent for integration. During the 'golden age' of the Commission under Jacques Delors it was his ability to fit in with the aspirations of the member governments for a single market and then push for linked policy developments through 'cultivated spill-over' that gave rise to the assumption that the institution had an agenda of expanding its own powers. By the same token, though, it should be expected that the Commission has to take a much more cautious approach when faced with the headwinds of more difficult economic times. The fact that the member governments tied the hands of the Commission through subsidiarity constraints introduced at Maastricht should also be recalled as an additional constraint.

The Court of Justice is a rather different body embedded in a different environment (see chapters 3 and 10). It is primarily following legal and jurisprudential dynamics rather than political ones (although Marie-Pierre Granger suggests the latter are not ignored). It might be worth recalling the debates of the 1980s and 1990s about the Court of Justice and integration theory. Some analysts insisted that the key rulings that expanded supranational powers and authority were simply based on legal interpretation of the treaties and legal dynamics. Others, by contrast, argued that the Court of Justice was developing in a neo-functionalist manner, finding a willing set of supporters in the national court systems (see Burley and Mattli 1993 for this interpretation and a critique of legalism). That the Court of Justice is now a more cautious supranational player may simply be a reflection of the fact that: key clarificatory decisions have been taken about the legal system; a more stable legal order exists; and its role has shifted to a more routine one. Or as Cardwell and Hervey emphasize, the Court of Justice is involved much less in constitution-building and acting more like a constitutional court (chapter 3). This transformation of the EU's legal order and the fact that it is now more difficult to speak of a single legal order is key to understanding the Court's role in contemporary integration. Its responsiveness to political context deserves further examination to follow on from Granger's analysis in chapter 10.

The EP, which receives little consideration from the editors, is in a different situation again. In this case the parallel with the *status quo ante* is not very illuminating. The EP was a rather marginal institution during the 'doldrums era' from the late-1960s to the SEA. It is in the period since direct elections in 1979 that it has set upon an agenda of increasing its powers. Adrienne Héritier (2007: 69–120) set out how the EP sought after each round of formal institutional reform to further strengthen the new powers accorded in each treaty through informal means. In more recent times it has arguably been the EP that has—to use the phrase—been 'hard-wired to seek ever closer union'. Some support for this view is evident in the analysis of Johannes Pollack and Peter Slominski (see chapter 12).

In light of the outcome of the 2014 elections it will be interesting to see how far this remains so during the 2014–19 parliamentary period, or whether the editors' hypothesis is confirmed. The fact that a significant number of members of the EP are Euro-sceptics or on the extremes of the political spectrum may well moderate its long-standing efforts to increase its powers, thus confirming the new intergovernmentalist hypothesis. Equally, it might be that the Christian Democrat, Liberal Democrat, and Socialist and Democrat groups in the EP continue to work together in the way identified in the past. Despite apparently being on the opposite sides of the political spectrum the Christian Democrats and Socialists voted together in the EP on between 61 and 71 per cent of occasions in roll-call votes between 1979 and 2000 (Hix et al. 2003: 318). Cooperation between the two parties is incentivized by the rules of the Ordinary Legislative Procedure (Hix and Høyland 2011: 144), for these parties need to work together if they are to secure the necessary majority in the readings of legislation and in the struggle with the Council. The circumstances have changed in numerous respects, but that does not prevent the party groups in the middle ground of EP politics working together to outsmart their less well-organized counterparts even to the extent of seeking additional powers. This pattern cannot be ruled out for the period 2014–19, as the EP's work in the current electoral period unfolds. Research on this issue will be important and will offer evidence on the applicability of the second hypothesis.

Hypothesis 3 proposes that, in the event of delegation of powers to the EU level, *de novo* institutions are preferred to the Commission or the Court of Justice. Unsurprisingly, this hypothesis necessitates detailed empirical research. The editors argue that this preference arises from an unwillingness to assign power to traditional supranational bodies. Howarth and Quaglia's analysis of the European Banking Union (chapter 7) provides supporting evidence for the hypothesis. However, as noted earlier, the ECB is arguably a traditional supranational body; it was simply that member governments (notably Germany) wanted it to have independence from politics, like the Bundesbank, and this necessitated a *de novo* body. Another issue merits further analysis. There has indeed been a growth of *de novo* bodies but some of the new ones are playing a coordinating role among national agencies. Why would, for instance, the Commission want to take on the roles of two policing-related agencies—the European Police Office (EUROPOL) or the European Police College (CEPOL)—when it lacks policing expertise? The same might be held for cooperation between border forces in Frontex (the European Agency for the Management of Operational Co-operation at the External Borders), between judicial authorities in Eurojust (the European Union's

Judicial Cooperation Unit) or between various regulators in ACER (the Agency for the Cooperation of Energy Regulators) or BEREC (the Body of European Regulators for Electronic Communications). These *de novo* bodies are embedded in a transgovernmentalist pattern of governance (see Wallace 2010: 100–3 on 'intensive transgovernmentalism') that departs from the classic methods of EU governance. As John Peterson has noted (chapter 9) these bodies have mostly been welcomed by the Commission and correspond to areas where it lacked powers. Increasingly, these administrative functions had been assigned to agencies in the EU member states as well, so it remains open to debate whether the significance of these bodies is as distinctive to the arguments of the new intergovernmentalism as the editors propose. The dynamics behind *de novo* bodies might be attributable to global trends in governance, thus making this hypothesis less attributable to the new intergovernmentalism.

In any event it seems to this observer that there needs to be a prior hypothesis proposing that national governments prefer transgovernmental cooperation or the Open Method of Coordination over delegation to the long-established supranational authorities. This hypothesis would propose a set of governance arrangements; the arrangements for the agencies would then be the next step in relation to policy execution. A rival hypothesis-relating to the spread of the techniques of new public management to the EU—would be important to have in mind for putting this hypothesis to the test.

Hypothesis 4 proposes that 'problems in domestic preference formation have become standalone inputs into the European integration process' (chapter 1.4). It will perhaps come as no surprise that I find this hypothesis persuasive, having argued along these lines in the 1980s (Bulmer 1983). The presence of competing political forces in member-state European policy formation is by no means a new development. Together with Willie Paterson I drew attention in the 1980s to the way in which the sectoral interests representing German farmers managed for many years to trump taxpayers and consumers in the Federal Republic in shaping what the 'German interest' was in EU negotiations (Bulmer and Paterson 1987: 71–7). Where additional clarification is arguably needed is in spelling out whether member state institutions are understood as being simply neutral or epiphenomenal (cf. Hoffmann 1982: 26). The new intergovernmentalism departs from the reductionist critique of Moravcsik, namely that member government policy is a product of domestic economic and geo-political interests. However, it would be helpful to have clearer guidance on how member governments are perceived. Are they mere arbiters of the political and economic inputs into member state preference formation, or are their own institutional characteristics of importance? This is an important issue when coalition governments may have internal conflicts on European policy; when federal or devolved governmental systems open up further internal institutional pluralism; and when other member state institutions and rules, such as those on ratifying EU constitutional reform or stipulations of constitutional courts, can present opportunities to be exploited by the political forces.

Hypothesis 5 on the distinction between high and low politics is also a plausible one. The editors suggest that the boundaries between these categories have become blurred in the post-Maastricht period. Bickerton, Hodson, and Puetter (chapter 1.4) are not the first to criticize Hoffmann for the way he classified low and high politics. Hoffmann himself later revised his views away from fixed categories and even wrote of the 'momentary saliency' of particular issues (1982: 29–30). What seems clear is that member state governments are caught on different policy issues between the rational dictates of managing interdependence and the need to be attentive to domestic constituencies and institutional rules. The tensions that have to be managed occur not only in everyday policy-making but are also at the root of the dilemmas for treaty reform identified by Thomas Christiansen (chapter 4). Precisely *how* they are caught differs from state to state and differs over time.

Finally, in this section I turn to hypothesis 6: that 'the EU is in a state of disequilibrium'. In one sense this sounds correct and many of the contributing authors identify with it. However, hypotheses should be refutable, and this one is quite difficult to refute. In what sense is there a state of disequilibrium: in the balance between actors and institutions; a lack of stability of its provisions over time; the possible collapse of a policy...? It may be the case that academic analysis has been sparing in its identification of crises in the EU, as the editors argue. However, those concerned with the EU's architecture have certainly noted the ongoing cycle of institutional and policy reform since the SEA (e.g. see Falkner 2002). For journalists the EU is about nothing other than crises. I well recall in my first radio interview in 1983 being asked by a local radio journalist if the EU would recover from the particular crisis (an abortive European Council meeting that had broken up acrimoniously in relation to Britain's contributions to the European Community budget) and whether I would still have a subject to study in the future. Within twelve months the Fontainebleau European Council had provided a settlement of this issue. Similar crisis judgements have been made by academics each time a treaty reform has been rejected at referendum, for instance. Disequilibrium and crises are in the eye of the beholder, and that is what makes this hypothesis difficult to (dis)prove as well as making it normatively loaded.

It is certainly true that the euro area crisis and declining public support have brought increased uncertainty to the EU. Perhaps what is also as surprising, however, is the way in which an integration process, launched in the shadow of European wartime conflict as well as of the subsequent Cold War, has proven to be so resilient. The EU has served as an ongoing 'political opportunity structure' that has been able to offer to member governments solutions to the dilemma of managing international interdependence while responding to pressures from domestic politics.

14.3 The Maastricht Treaty and the Novelty of The New Intergovernmentalism

The new intergovernmentalism certainly offers a new focus for debate on the EU. A key issue in identifying its novelty is associated by the editors with developments following on from the Maastricht Treaty. Like the empty-chair crisis and the SEA, the Maastricht Treaty was a critical juncture in the evolution of integration. However, unlike the other two cases, the Maastricht Treaty instantiated a number of conflicting processes: a three-pillar structure in which member governments remained predominant in two of three pillars; Justice and Home Affairs (JHA), and the Common Foreign and Security Policy (CFSP). It embedded the principle of subsidiarity. In treaty terms it was the first to set down differentiated integration (British opt-outs from the Social Chapter and the single currency). Its attention to the engagement of subnational government in policy-making gave rise to the claims for multi-level governance, when combined with the rapid growth of cohesion funding. It reinforced supranational policy processes, including co-decision and strengthened provision for QMV in the original 'pillar' of the EU. It extended the EU's remit to new policy areas, notably monetary union and JHA. The treaty also encountered the first explicit rejection of a treaty reform through the initial Danish rejection. This step can be credited as the first overt challenge to the permissive consensus.

From the perspective of an historical institutionalist concerned with the time, timing and tempo of integration, the Maastricht Treaty is of considerable importance. Historical institutionalists see politics as a movie rather than a series of snapshots. They use concepts such as path dependence, timing, sequence, and the nature of long-term processes (Pierson 2004) or layering (Thelen 2004) to explore the 'movie'. I would argue that the Maastricht Treaty was a highly complex outcome of intergovernmental bargaining. It developed and reinforced divergent patterns of governance and integration. It even shaped the constitutional-legal basis of integration by creating an intergovernmental treaty (the Treaty on European Union) alongside the more supranational ones now consolidated into the Treaty on the Functioning of the European Union. As Gerda Falkner (2002: 6) has noted, 'EU-level institutions in a wider sense, such as the process of institutionalized negotiation, can be interpreted as causes that unfold in the long run only. They also show short-term and long-term outcomes.' My principal concern about, and the fundamental empirical challenge to, the new intergovernmentalism is that it seeks to superimpose one tendency on a very internally differentiated EU reality. This reality could be interpreted as the way in which diverse characteristics of integration have entailed discrete trajectories that have developed their own 'logics' supported by the sunk costs arising from inter-institutional and inter-governmental politics. That is not to suggest that the EU is simply path-dependent, since the transfer of JHA out of an explicitly intergovernmental pillar to a more hybrid part of EU business reveals what can happen if the institutional constraints are detrimental to achieving policy goals.

So, just as the editors argue for a move away from micro analysis to the wider picture of integration, so I would welcome a similar shift from snapshot analysis to exploring the 'movie' of European integration. The new intergovernmentalism chimes with dominant trends that can be traced back to Maastricht but not exclusively so. And the temporality of how those features and trends have unfolded over that period would be an interesting complementary account to the focus of this volume.

Is the new intergovernmentalism really new? Here, from a historical institutionalist perspective, I think some continuities can be traced back to before the Maastricht Treaty. Was 'old' intergovernmentalism a 'retreat from European integration' or 'renationalization' (chapter 1)? I am not so sure. I think it was perceived that way because it was a pause in the integration process and halted the move to QMV in the Council. And cannot some of the deliberative 'informal and secretive' settings of the new intergovernmentalism not be found in bodies such as Trevi that pre-dated Maastricht? There are continuities from earlier times.

Conclusion

This study on the new intergovernmentalism is an important contribution to understanding today's EU and offers much food for thought. In particular, it builds out from the findings of the governance literature in order to provide a 'bigger picture' analysis of the state of integration. The new intergovernmentalism provides the building blocks for further theorizing. It is there 'to stimulate debate rather than settle it'. My conclusion therefore is simple: let that debate commence!

15

Conclusions

The Post-Maastricht Period and Beyond

Christopher J. Bickerton, Dermot Hodson, and Uwe Puetter

Although the precise meaning of European integration is still unsettled, it is frequently associated with the delegation of policy-making powers to the 'engines of integration': the European Commission and the Court of Justice of the European Union (EU). Seen in these terms, the two decades since the signature of the Maastricht Treaty have given rise to an integration paradox as the scope of EU policy-making has increased dramatically but without the delegation of new powers to old supranational institutions along traditional, Community method lines. While existing theories of European integration look at developments in this period and see either the slow road to supranationalism or the end of the line for integration, neither claim is satisfactory. Even if EU member states somehow 'return' to the Commission and Court in the future, we still need to explain their reticence towards these institutions over such a prolonged period. Appeals to stasis rather than change sit uneasily with the EU's new activism in fiscal policy, financial supervision, and foreign affairs, to name but a few areas. Students of EU governance have been quicker to spot the changing dynamics of policy-making, especially in those new areas of EU activity which have been established since Maastricht, but they have shied away from studying the EU as a whole or the economic and political dynamics of European integration.

This book has put forward the new intergovernmentalism as a way to think through the paradox of post-Maastricht integration. In keeping with the intergovernmental tradition, the new intergovernmentalism sees the intensification of European integration since Maastricht as a choice by national governments. Economic interests remain central for EU member states but these institutional choices are also products of shifts in political economy and a crisis in representative politics. The post-Maastricht period is, we argue, characterized by a convergence in the beliefs of political elites about the limits of national economic policy but also the need for decentralized policy coordination and elite-level deliberation. In other words, there appears to be a consensus between national governments in the post-Maastricht period that economic policy should be closely coordinated but in ways that avoid the imposition of centralized policy solutions on what remains a very heterogeneous and uneven European economy. Other core areas of national sovereignty, including foreign, security and defence policy, employment policy and various aspects of justice and home affairs (JHA) have been framed in a similar way. As regards representation, the weakening of interest organizations and political parties has created a cleavage: between policy elites who remain more committed, in principle, to finding collective solutions to shared policy challenges; and a general public that has grown sceptical about the benefits of European integration. The EU's reluctance to delegate new powers to supranational institutions offers a partial concession to public sentiment but it rests uneasily with the intensification of European integration through other means.

Building on these claims about the changing politics of post-Maastricht Europe, chapter 1 of this volume put forward six hypotheses that together help to elucidate, explain, and understand the implications of the integration paradox. Although the contributors to this volume all engaged with these hypotheses, the contributions themselves vary in their focus on macro- and micro-level analysis. This diversity is intentional and reflects an ambition of the new intergovernmentalism to elaborate a conceptual framework that allows scholars to link the analysis of individual institutional contexts to broader developments in post-Maastricht integration and vice versa.

In this final chapter, we first provide a detailed review of the findings of the various contributions of this volume in relation to the six hypotheses set out in chapter 1 (section 15.1). We then turn the issue of the scope and range of the new intergovernmentalism as an analytical framework, considering in turn the matter of how old and new policy areas are related to one another, the application of new intergovernmentalist claims to 'differentiated integration' and the relevance of the ideas in this book for our understanding of global governance dynamics (sections 15.2, 15.3, and 15.4 respectively). We then ask what a 'post' post-Maastricht period might look like, by revisiting our claims about political economy preferences and Europe's crisis of political representation (15.5). In the final section, we conclude.

15.1 The Six Hypotheses Reconsidered

Hypothesis 1: Deliberation and consensus have become the guiding norms of day-to-day decision-making at all levels

A number of chapters in this volume present evidence and analysis that chimes with this hypothesis. For Uwe Puetter (chapter 8), this deliberative intergovernmentalism is exemplified by the changing role of the European Council in the post-Maastricht period. Until the late 1980s, summits of EU heads of state or government were regular affairs that focused on providing long-term guidance to the Commission and Council of Ministers, and deciding on institutional reforms. Since the mid-1990s, Puetter notes, summit agendas have shifted their focus from long-term institutional questions to short-term challenges and the day-to-day governance of the new areas of EU policy-making. The latter now account for the largest share of European Council activity. Heads of state or government also meet more frequently, often on an ad-hoc basis to discuss unfolding international political crises. Processes of institutional engineering which are aimed at enhancing the consensus generating capacity of the European Council signal how deeply the new intergovernmentalism is linked to the institutionalization of policy deliberation.

Michael E. Smith (chapter 5) sees deliberation as playing a key role in the intensification of EU foreign and security policy—one of the major new policy areas of post-Maastricht integration. Decisions in this domain have always been based on consensus since the launch of the European Political Cooperation in 1970 initiated informal and intergovernmental modes of foreign policy cooperation. However, the new intergovernmentalism goes beyond deliberation as a decision rule. For Smith, it includes experiential learning aimed at developing a common frame of reference between EU member states over the operation and objectives of EU policy-making in this domain. Here he gives the example of the lessons management application, which is used by the European Union military staff to review Common Security and Defence Policy (CSDP) operations and generate specific lessons learned.

Paul James Cardwell and Tamara Hervey discuss the role of law in the new intergovernmentalism (chapter 3). Deliberation and consensus-building have become guiding norms in the post-Maastricht period, they accept, citing a growing reluctance on the part of EU policy-makers to propose new single market legislation, a lack of new legal principles emerging from the Court of Justice and the recourse to reforms following the euro crisis, which give the appearance of law without intending there to be the accompanying legal effect. This retreat from the Community method should not be seen as a retreat from EU law as such, Cardwell and Hervey warn, because deliberation and consensus can lead to a form of hyper-legalism in which appeals to legal reasoning, procedural legitimacy, and legal differentiation play prominent roles. The new intergovernmentalism, in other words, may shy away from hard law but it can give rise to law-like arrangements that are driven by the need for legitimation felt by member state governments. Cardwell and Hervey cite the *Kadi* cases as evidence that intergovernmental modes of decision-making in sensitive areas such as the Common Foreign and Security Policy (CFSP) are still subject to legal processes and, therefore, open to legal analysis. David Howarth and Lucia Quaglia (chapter 7) argue that the intensification of EU financial regulation in the post-Maastricht period would not have happened so rapidly without deep deliberation between national and EU regulators. Far from being an end in itself, however, such deliberation served as a catalyst for regulatory activism after the launch of the euro in 1999 and, once again, after the global financial crisis hit in 2007–8.

Several contributions highlight that the commitment to deliberative practices in elite-level policy dialogue is not only detectable as an activity which concerns intergovernmental coordination and cooperation but characterizes inter-institutional relations among the EU's core decision-making bodies. Smith (chapter 5) sees the new intergovernmentalism at play in EU member states' willingness to integrate the Commission into the planning and operational phases of the CSDP but without empowering the EU executive along traditional lines, the creation of the European External Action Service (EEAS) being a case in point. The close integration of the Commission—notably its president—into policy deliberations within the European Council relating to core policy coordination procedures is an aspect highlighted by Puetter (chapter 8).

Johannes Pollack and Peter Slominksi (chapter 12) see some evidence that the European Parliament (EP) pursues a similar approach in relation to the Council of Ministers as far as the exercise of its co-decision powers is concerned. Sarah Wolff's (see chapter 6) analysis of the practice of informal early agreements between the EP and the Council of Ministers within the Civil Liberties, Justice and Home Affairs (LIBE) Committee reinforces this point too. This sort of deliberation, however, has little relationship to a more public sort of deliberation that one might associate with elected chambers and it is possible that trialogue discussion have had an impact upon the deliberative quality of parliamentary committees.

Whereas deliberation and consensus-seeking have become firmly established as the key operative norms for EU decision-making, therefore, this is not to suggest that the EU is a deliberative democracy in the making. These operating norms of elite-level interactions may be embedded within a wider institutional framework that is itself democratic or they may be conduits for outcomes that may be considered violations of basic democratic procedures.[1]

Hypothesis 2: Supranational institutions are not hard-wired to seek ever closer union

There is a fair amount of evidence in this volume to support this claim, although further research is clearly required here to understand what makes supranational institutions tick. John Peterson (chapter 9) challenges claims that the Commission is 'in decline' since Maastricht but accepts that the EU executive has internalized ambitions that are modest compared to earlier periods, as regards the expansion of its own powers. Drawing on the results of Kassim et al. (2013), who have conducted a large-n survey of attitudes within the Commission, he shows that less than one-third of officials are supranationalist in their outlook with most of the rest alternating between 'institutional pragmatism' or a 'state-centric outlook'. How these micro-attitudes map onto the macro-preferences of the Commission is a matter for further research but there is sufficient evidence from this survey to challenge preconceptions of the Commission as a collection of individuals motivated by intensive preferences for deeper integration. As noted above, Puetter (chapter 8) and Smith (chapter 5) see the Commission taking a pragmatic and constructive approach towards its role within the new areas of EU activity and the relevant decision-making bodies such as the European Council and the Council of Ministers.

Marie-Pierre Granger's examination of the Court of Justice in the post-Maastricht period also calls for a reconsideration of what supranational institutions want. The Court, she argues, has not systematically pursued supranational integration since 1992 but instead has been selective and pragmatic in its response to new intergovernmental modes of decision-making. Such ambivalence can be seen, for instance, in *Gestoras*, which saw the Court claim review powers in relation to the European Arrest Warrant while endorsing the essentially intergovernmentalist character of this measure. Deference to member states' political priorities may be at play in such judgments, Granger argues, although she also sees evidence that the Court's priorities remain in flux. Concerns for closer union are by no means absent from Court judgments since 1992, she notes, but concerns for 'Citizens Europe' or a 'Europe of Rights' also shine through. How far the Court is willing to push such constitutional concerns is not yet clear, she concludes, but its preferences are already more

---

[1] For a useful overview of the idea of deliberative democracy, and on the relationship between deliberation and bargaining and between deliberation and institutional settings, see Bohman (1998). Bohman's view is that as the term has evolved and been applied to practical situations, so the ideal of deliberative democracy as a public activity engaging citizens with one another has been replaced with a more constrained, less participatory, and less public understanding of deliberation.

complex than the literature on European integration typically allows. In making this argument, Granger joins a growing number of scholars who have begun to question the pro-integration assumptions of many of those studying the Court of Justice (e.g. Kelemen and Schmidt 2012; Saurugger and Terpan 2014). The debate, however, is only beginning and is far from conclusive (e.g. Scharpf 2012). What is clear is that we have moved on from the era of certainty about 'integration through law' (Cappelletti, Secombe, and Weiler 1986) and the role of the Court in 'judicial integration' (Dehousse 1998) to one where the role of the Court in the dynamics of European integration is considered a worthy and open-ended topic of study.

The EP has frequently sought to portray itself as the defender of the Community method in the post-Maastricht period but Pollack and Slominski (chapter 12) challenge this preconception. The EP is undoubtedly a competence maximizer, they argue, but its approach to competence maximization does not always map on to the pursuit of formal competences for other Community institutions. A case in point, Pollack and Slominski suggest, is the EP's role in the creation of the EEAS. Whereas the EU legislature had initially pushed for this diplomatic corps to be fully integrated into the EU's existing institutional structures, such demands were later dropped when the EP enhanced its powers of financial oversight over the EU's new diplomatic service. The authors observe a similar strategy at play in the EP's willingness to accept an intergovernmental border agency, Frontex, in return for concessions on this body's accountability to the EP and its commitment to human rights.

If the Commission, Court, and EP are not hard-wired for the pursuit of ever closer union, therefore, might this finding be extended to *de novo* institutions? Given the sheer number of *de novo* bodies created in the last two decades, this volume makes no claims to have answered this question. Instead, it offers an in-depth treatment of what is arguably the most powerful *de novo* body created in the post-Maastricht period: the European Central Bank (ECB). Dermot Hodson (chapter 13) argues that the ECB showed a high degree of ambivalence towards the pursuit of ever closer union, especially during the first decade of the euro. Instances in which the Bank resisted integrationist initiatives include the establishment of the EU anti-fraud body OLAF and periodic schemes for closer macroeconomic policy coordination in the euro area. The ECB was also uneasy about the European Constitution and the Lisbon Treaty, which sought to clarify the ECB's institutional status. Conversely, the ECB showed itself willing and able to take on new competences in the area of financial regulation and supervision, making the case for greater EU involvement long before the euro crisis paved the way for European Banking Union. In seeking to explain this ambivalence, Hodson finds little evidence that members of the ECB Executive Board were anything other than favourable towards the idea of European integration. Instead, the ECB's decentralized governance structure, which assigns significant influence to national central bank governors, and its commitment to a rigorous price stability mandate, offer more plausible explanations for ECB attitudes towards European integration. Other *de novo* institutions are unlikely to be quite so single-minded as the Bank but further research is, nonetheless, warranted into what these bodies want.

Hypothesis 3: When delegation occurs, governments and traditional supranational actors support the creation and empowerment of de novo institutions

In their study of financial supervision and Banking Union, Howarth and Quaglia (chapter 7) provide strong evidence for this claim. A first round of institutional reforms in reaction to the financial crisis produced a plethora of *de novo* institutions among them the European Systemic Risk Board, the European Banking Authority, the European Insurance and Occupational Pension Authority, and the European Securities Markets Authority (ESMA). In this context Howarth and Quaglia also point to the fact that governments and the Commission alike advocated the creation of *de novo* bodies. A similar picture emerged in the context of the later negotiations regarding Banking Union, Howarth and Quaglia argue, with the institutional design of the Single Resolution Mechanism and the Single Resolution Fund reflecting similar preference.

Puetter (chapter 8) highlights the European Council's lead role in advocating and establishing *de novo* bodies. For Peterson (chapter 9) the Commission's support for the creation of *de novo* bodies in the post-Maastricht period is consistent with this line of reasoning. He sees that the EU is delegating more competences and more often to *de novo* bodies. A case in point for him is the European Food Safety Agency (EFSA), which is tasked with providing scientific advice to the Commission that the EU executive is not bound to follow. The case of the European Stability Mechanism (ESM) is more complex, however. This *de novo* body directly impinges on the European Commission's policy-making powers but the EU executive tacitly accepted its creation nonetheless.[2]

Granger (chapter 10) sees the Court of Justice as protective of its own turf in relation to *de novo* bodies but not opposed on point of principle to the empowerment of such institutions. Here she cites the Court's defense of the ESMA and Eurojust, under the proviso that they be subject to judicial review from Luxembourg. The EP appears to be similarly self-interested and pragmatic when it comes to *de novo* bodies. It has not always been happy with this

---

[2] In creating the ESM, EU member states agreed to wind down the European Financial Stabilization Mechanism, an ad-hoc crisis resolution mechanism created under Article 122 TFEU and over which the Commission exercised significant powers.

development. As Johannes Pollack and Peter Slominski observe in chapter 12, the EU legislature has sought to exercise a degree of *ex-ante* and *ex-post* oversight by, inter alia, seeking to influence the composition of management boards, appointment procedures for executive directors and financial management for bodies such as the EFSA and the European Police College.

Simon Bulmer (see chapter 14) sees the rise of the new public management as an alternative hypothesis to explain the rise of *de novo* bodies in the post-Maastricht period. Yet, though we do not rule out the influence of new public management on the proliferation of *de novo* bodies—especially in the field of regulatory agencies—we see sufficient evidence for the reluctance of member state governments to empower traditional supranational actors. The evidence presented in this volume speaks to this point. Moreover, the new public management can be seen, in part, as the product of tensions within the traditional social-democratic state (Bresser-Pereira 2004) and, as such, is not unrelated to problems of domestic politics underpinning the post-Maastricht period.

Hypothesis 4: Problems in domestic preference formation have become stand-alone inputs into the European integration process

In seeking to make sense of the integration paradox, the new intergovernmentalism looks to problems of preference formation within EU member states. This volume makes no claim to have offered an in-depth treatment of domestic politics in EU member states over the last twenty years. Instead, what this hypothesis suggests is that as a process European integration has been shaped by problems in preference formation at the national level. Rather than treating national governments as direct and unproblematic conduits of national strategies and of aggregated socio-economic preferences, the problems that governments face with their own domestic populations have come to exert an independent effect on the EU.

Various examples of this exist, such as the national referenda on the Constitutional Treaty. In France, for instance, the Treaty was so closely associated with the political elite and the establishment that much of the dynamism behind the 'no' vote came from anti-elitist sentiment. Far from being simply a national problem, this came to influence directly the institutional development of the EU itself. This contrasts with the French rejection of the European Defence Community (EDC) in 1954, where the dividing line was not between the political elites and the public but rather it was internal to political life itself, with Gaullists and Communists at the time coming together in a shared opposition to the EDC and voting against it in the national assembly (Aron 1957). Were the UK to have its referendum on EU membership in 2017, one can imagine that the result would owe as much to prevailing attitudes towards the political class as a whole as it would on opinions on the EU as such.

For Christopher J. Bickerton (chapter 2), these problems in preference formation are part of a wider process of state transformation, where state–society relations across Europe have been slowly recast since the 1970s. Specifically, Bickerton argues that state–society relations have become more attenuated and have thinned in comparison to earlier epochs: governing elites have converged in their attitudes and opinions, while domestic publics have retreated from collective political activities. The steady uncoupling of states from societies has led governing parties to look to the EU not only as a convenient venue for the management of interdependence but also as a site of legitimation, authority, and identity. Nation-states have become member states, meaning that governments increasingly use their participation in transnational networks of governance as sources of authority at the national level. This has spurred forward an integration of national administrative apparatuses as well, with the result that there are now few parts of national administrations that are not engaged in some degree of cooperation with their European counterparts.

The problem is that whereas national bureaucracies and their political masters have become enmeshed in EU policy-making, national polities remain focused on domestic rather than European issues. This can be seen in the lack of attention given to European issues in elections to national parliaments, in the low turnout for European elections and in the tendency to use referendums on EU treaty revisions to punish incumbents. The recent 2014 European elections are a useful illustration of this point. The elections were marked by a widespread endorsement of anti-establishment parties, leading to the arrival of many Euro-sceptic MEPs to Brussels. However, what these parties had in common was their virulent criticism of their own political classes: this unites the Italian Five Star Movement with France's Front National and the UK Independence Party in Britain. On matters of substance, in contrast, these parties agree on little and the French National Front was unable to create a grouping in the 2014–19 Parliament for this reason. The response of governments in Europe to the election results was unanimously directed at the EU and the need for reform, rather than at the domestic origins and concerns of these anti-establishment 'populist parties'. The alienation of domestic publics from their own political rulers was transformed into a conflict between nation-states and the EU (Bickerton and Invernizzi 2014).

Given the diversity that exists between individual European states, this particular hypothesis needs to be explored within individual national contexts. For instance, the evolution in state–society relations in Eastern Europe has differed considerably from the Western European experience. Has a demobilization of national publics taken place in Eastern Europe and, if so, how has it impacted upon the relationship of Eastern European governments to European integration? In those instances where a government's commitment to the European project seems to be decidedly lukewarm, as in the UK, does an explanation for this lie at the level of state–society relations or elsewhere? Comparative research on preference formation and the respective difficulties that exist in relations between states and societies across EU member states can serve as a first step to exploring this particular hypothesis further.

Hypothesis 5: The differences between high and low politics have become blurred

Students of European integration have struggled to locate the border between high and low politics since long before the Maastricht Treaty was signed. What we have seen in the post-Maastricht period is a further blurring of this line such that few areas can be definitively classified in either category. In the case of low politics, such is the strength of popular opinion concerning the European project, that there are now few areas of EU policy-making that can be counted as uncontroversial. We see this in the area of financial regulation, which was once described as the plumbing of Economic and Monetary Union (EMU) (Norman 2008) but which, in the light of the global financial crises, is inextricably linked to questions of financial solidarity, fiscal integration, and national control (see Howarth and Quaglia chapter 7). Less dramatic but still symptomatic of this heightened sensitivity over seemingly anodyne policy domains are periodic tensions over the governance of the single market. The confluence of legislative and judicial politics over patients' mobility rights, as discussed by Marzena Kloka and Susanne Schmidt (chapter 11) illustrates this point.

If this sudden politicization of areas traditionally thought of as 'low politics' speaks to Hoffmann's concept of momentary salience then the difficulty of designating areas as high politics in the post-Maastricht period is more difficult to reconcile with traditional approaches to intergovernmentalism. Of all policy areas touched upon in this book, defence is perhaps the one area that appears to be off limits to the EU member states, Smith argues (chapter 5). These limits are hardly sacrosanct, however, as evidenced by member states' willingness to subsume the Western European Union, including a close approximation of its mutual defence clause, in the Lisbon Treaty. Part of the explanation for the EU's encroachment into these areas of activity lies in its ability, thus far, to apply comparatively depoliticized modes of decision-making in what have traditionally been thought of as highly politicized domains. This can be seen, for example, in the involvement of military, legal, and policing experts in the activities of the European Military Staff. This blurring of the line between high and low politics is more profound still in the area of JHA. For Wolff (chapter 6), the emphasis on operational solutions and the deployment of expert networks can be seen as a fairly conscious attempt on the part of national governments to keep cooperation in this domain out of the public eye while it is clear that the consequences for domestic authority are far from trivial.

Thomas Christiansen (chapter 4) offers a different perspective on this hypothesis. Students of European integration, he notes, have traditionally distinguished between the high politics of treaty reform at discrete moments and the low politics of everyday decision-making, but this distinction is no longer tenable. For one thing, treaty reform in the post-Maastricht period became a feature of everyday decision-making in the EU, such was the frequency of treaty negotiations from Amsterdam to Lisbon and beyond. Such negotiations swung, Christiansen argues, not from high to low politics but between politicization and de-politicization as EU member states sought to balance their preferences for institutional reform with the Union's problems of legitimacy. If the European Constitution represented the high-watermark of politicization, he suggests, then the low tide was the Lisbon Treaty, which was negotiated by legal experts behind closed doors and ratified where possible without recourse to referendums.

Uwe Puetter (chapter 8) sees the blurring of differences between high and low politics documented by shifts in the European Council's agenda. Day-to-day issues of policy-making including even technocratic matters regularly become subject to European Council discussion whereas, at the same time, the European Council finds it acceptable to delegate decisions with potentially far-reaching consequences to the Council of Ministers and senior expert committees.

Hypothesis 6: The EU is in a state of disequilibrium

A key claim of the new intergovernmentalism is that European integration in the post-Maastricht period is an unstable and contradictory process that is tending towards a state of disequilibrium. With this claim we seek to understand the causes and consequences of the EU's intensifying legitimacy deficit since 1992, as evidenced by the string of 'no' votes against EU treaties, the low turnout for EP elections and the decline in public support for the European project. In so doing, we challenge contemporary theories of European integration, which tend to downplay the significance of such developments. The supranationalist school sees supranational modes of policy-making as subject to a self-reinforcing logic that would appear to be largely immune from public opinion on, and political attitudes towards, European integration (Sandholtz and Stone Sweet 2001). Liberal intergovernmentalism has been much more attentive to these debates but equally dismissive. For Moravcsik (2002, 2006), the EU is more or less accountable to its member states, whose preferences for further European integration appear to have petered out post-Maastricht.

The new intergovernmentalism departs from these traditional approaches by seeing European integration since Maastricht as both a response to, and contributory factor towards, the EU's legitimacy deficit. The result is an unstable system rather than one that is tending towards a state of supranational or intergovernmental equilibrium. As Claus Offe has remarked, the EU is 'entrapped': it is criticized for being overly technocratic and undemocratic and yet the only way in which further integration can proceed is via the new intergovernmentalist route of executive-dominated agreements that are implemented by national administrations and not subject to domestic political contestation (Offe 2013). Though driven by the choices made by national governments, the new intergovernmentalism and its associated disequilibrium is not something that can be easily undone or changed: conflicts between governments and their own domestic publics have become a structuring feature of European integration. Although they are a condition for the EU's existence, they are also a leading source of its fragility.

Several chapters in this volume take up this theme of legitimacy and disequilibrium directly. Smith (chapter 5), for instance, sees EU member states' reluctance to delegate in relation to the common and security policy as resulting, in part, from a sense that each instance of collective decision-making must be debated and designed afresh. Wolff (chapter 6) goes further here by arguing that delegation to agencies in the area of JHA was deliberately designed to avoid supranational solutions. National governments' determination to press ahead with integration in spite of such concerns is testament to their influence, but it also raises profound concerns about the legitimacy of the European project post-Maastricht. Different chapters in this volume approach this point from different perspectives. Bickerton (chapter 2) challenges the idea that European integration is legitimated via national governments that are accountable to the people. EU heads of state or government have shown their willingness to set aside the will of the people on more than one occasion in the post-Maastricht period so that member states can fulfil their obligations to one another. Cardwell and Hervey (chapter 3) ask whether too much is being asked of EU law in such circumstances. The law-like quality of the new intergovernmentalism is contentious they argue, especially when it leads to treaty reform and other legal measures. As a means of showing that member states are taking action, these measures in fact result in the locking in of particular policy commitments. Pollack and Slominski (chapter 12) are sceptical of the ability of the EP to bridge this legitimacy deficit. The emphasis on informal decision-making in inter-institutional negotiations, they argue, can lead to less rather than more time for deliberation within committees and plenary meetings of the EP. This is an argument that scholars of the EP have increasingly turned to. As Charlotte Burns, Anne Rasmussen, and Christine Rey, remark, the routine use of early agreements by the Parliament 'risks undermining the legitimacy gains that the formal rule change was supposed to bring' (Burns et al. 2013: 946). Co-decision, they surmise, 'has not been successful in strengthening support for the EU's political system' (2013: 948). What this implies, and what the new intergovernmentalism claims, is that the

EU's state of disequilibrium is not simply the result of the specific faults of individual institutions but rather is a more enduring and structural feature of contemporary European integration.

15.2 The New Intergovernmentalism and the 'Old' Areas of EU Policy-making

The new intergovernmentalism attaches particular importance to the post-Maastricht practice of expanding the scope of EU policy action through new mechanisms of governance that diverge from the traditional Community method. While documenting this development in detail, we have deliberately refrained from making broader claims about these domains of Community method decision-making, the implication being that these 'old' policy areas have remained more or less as operational as they were before the entering into force of the Maastricht Treaty. Simon Bulmer is quite right to point out in his commentary (chapter 14) that this should be a matter of debate as there are indeed examples in which traditional domains of supranationalism have become more intergovernmental. This raises for us the broader, and crucial, issue of the precise scope and range of the new intergovernmentalist claims. As an analytical approach, is it merely applicable to those new policy areas brought within the scope of EU activity since 1992, or does it also have something to say about those policy areas that have been long-standing components of the EU's action, from competition policy through to agriculture and trade?

Very much aware of this issue and keen to explore the boundaries of the new intergovernmentalism's claims, we assembled contributions which cover traditional domains of Community method decision-making (chapter 11 by Marzena Kloka and Susanne Schmidt), areas in which Community decision-making intersects with the new areas of EU activity (chapter 7 by David Howarth and Lucia Quaglia) and new domains of EU activity which have seen the introduction of Community method decision-making procedures (chapter 6 by Sarah Wolff). Kloka and Schmidt (chapter 11) offer the strongest indication that it is business as usual as regards the 'old' domains of EU integration. What is interesting about their contribution is the degree to which supranational institutions and the inherent logic of conventional legislative and judicial politics prevent the Council of Ministers from rolling back established Community competences. Though there is no lack of such efforts, they do not seem to be very effective. This particular case study would suggest that the new intergovernmentalist dynamics contribute to reproducing the dual constitutional character established by the Maastricht Treaty (i.e. the coexistence of supranationalism and intergovernmental policy coordination).

Our collection of contributions, however, is far too small to turn this finding into a general argument about the resilience of the traditional domains of Community method decision-making.

Our own sense is that, given the scope of the changes implied by the new intergovernmentalism, it would seem very unlikely that the 'old' policy areas are immune from the political economy shifts and the crisis of representation that have come to define European politics since 1992. Further research into pre-Maastricht policy-making is required, however, in order to determine whether they are resilient or not to new intergovernmentalist dynamics.

The potential breadth of the new intergovernmentalism's claims becomes particularly evident when we turn to policy issues that are located at the intersection of Community method competences and the intergovernmental policy coordination agenda. As Howarth and Quaglia (chapter 7) show, this is the case with European Banking Union. On the one hand, it is built on a classic domain of single market governance that deals with the regulation of a single European financial market and is subject to Community method decision-making. On the other hand, the boost in political attention, which makes this field of single market integration stand out as one of the few dynamic areas of seemingly supranational governance in the post-Maastricht era, is largely explained by the broader EMU economic governance agenda and the EU's attempts to manage the consequences of the financial crisis. This also had consequences for how key decisions on European Banking Union were taken. As Howarth and Quaglia show, the European Council directly intervened with the decision-making process by defining specific aspects of the institutional set-up of European Banking Union and charged the Commission and the Council of Ministers with implementing these decisions through new legislation which was marked by a reluctance to empower traditional supranational institutions. The case of European Banking Union rather suggests that traditional domains of supranational policy-making are subject at least to *de facto* modification. Notably, the Commission's role as initiator of policy is in question, and so is the doctrine of a single institutional and legal framework which applies to a given domain of EU policy-making—an aspect which is discussed further by Cardwell and Hervey (chapter 3).

In a similar vein, Wolff's contribution focuses on the question of how domains of supranational authority and intergovernmental policy coordination intersect through JHA. This particular context identifies an opposite trend to the above case of modified single market governance: in JHA, intergovernmental policy coordination has been (at least partially) replaced by a modified version of the Community method. Notably, the 1999 Tampere and the 2004 Hague programmes constituted a boost for new legislation in the field of JHA. Yet, Wolff's findings are not without parallels to the case of European Banking Union. Though the EU has acquired substantial new legislative competences in the field of JHA, policy initiative is heavily controlled by the European Council and the Council of Ministers. Moreover, the reformed governance structure blends elements of conventional legislative politics with the institutionalization of policy coordination routines, which involve member state and Commission representatives at all levels of decision-making. What is not yet clear is how sustainable the dynamism of new legislative activism in the field of JHA is. Cardwell and Hervey (chapter 3) see the 2009 Stockholm programme as documenting a drop in enthusiasm for new legislative initiatives.

What is clear from the findings of this volume is that the new intergovernmentalism does not exclude the possibility of new legislative initiatives altogether. Yet, where new domains of legislative activity are identified or where existing areas of supranational decision-making intersect with policy coordination, significant modifications of the Community method have taken place. Environmental policy, energy security, and climate policy could be added to the examples discussed in this volume. The precise nature of the resilience or openness of 'old' policy areas to new intergovernmentalist dynamics remains an issue for further research but the potential for change within 'old' policy areas is obviously there. As a framework, the new intergovernmentalism also suggests that it is too simplistic to align member states with policy-making in new post-1992 policy areas and to identify supranational actors with older policy areas. As the integration paradox shows, member state governments are keen to pursue closer integration for a number of reasons whilst supranational actors are sensitive to the changing political and social context within which integration has taken place since 1992. The possibility of indeterminacy in the relationship between a body of institutional rules and the behaviour of national and supranational actors is a clear implication of the new intergovernmentalist claims, and one that merits further research.

15.3 'Differentiated Europe'

The new intergovernmentalism could say more about differentiated integration, a point that Simon Bulmer makes (chapter 14). This reticence is not because we deny the existence of differential integration as a key feature of post-Maastricht integration. On the contrary, differentiated integration is an institutional and juridical fact: not all member states participate in all policy activities in the same way. What is less clear is how the phenomenon of differentiated integration relates to the underlying drivers, dynamics, and patterns identified by the new intergovernmentalist framework. Much like the discussion above regarding the relationship between 'old' and 'new' policy areas, at issue here is the correspondence between concrete institutional determinations and the systemic features of post-Maastricht integration. Does the existence of legal or *de facto* differentiation necessarily obviate attempts at generalizing about the nature of post-Maastricht European integration as a whole?

A striking feature of the case studies discussed in this volume is that they provide little evidence of any differentiation leading to a formal reorganization of EU governance or the formation of clearly identifiable groups of EU member states whose preference is strongly towards being at the centre, or at the periphery, of integration. It is difficult to map differences on the subject of EU economic governance, for instance, directly onto the formal map of euro area membership. It is also the case that even when an opt-out has been negotiated, this does not imply that a member state will not be involved in individual policy initiatives. In fact, we have often seen that precisely in those policy areas where member states have negotiated an opt-out, their governments and national officials play an influential role in collective policy-making.

What this volume has concentrated on is the type of integration that flows from the paradoxical attitude of national governments and officials to EU policy-making: committed to closer integration but very wary of transferring in a last way decision-making powers to supranational institutions. Differentiated integration, or at least certain variations on it, implies a distinction between a pro-integrationist group of member states and a more sceptical group of outliers (the so-called Europe à la carte or a 'two speed' Europe). The new intergovernmentalism, in contrast, highlights the tensions and contradictions *internal to member states themselves* and how these work themselves out at the pan-European level and refashion the integration process.

What this volume suggests is that while legal or *de facto* differentiation has established itself as an important characteristic of the present day EU, it coexists with a number of other characteristics—most notably, the integration paradox and the problematic state–society relations and political economy structures it rests upon—that provide a more comprehensive and determinate explanation of the trajectory taken by the EU in the post-Maastricht period.

15.4 The New Intergovernmentalism and Global Governance

The new intergovernmentalism tries to strike a balance between the search for generalizability and the provision of specific, contextualized explanations for the peculiar trajectory taken by European integration in the post-Maastricht period. We agree with Walter Mattli and Alec Stone Sweet that EU studies should situate itself conceptually and empirically within the wider field of political science. However, we do not think that this precludes inquiring into the nature of the EU and engaging with these erstwhile 'methods of integration' debates. As Alex Warleigh-Lack and Ben Rosamond have argued (2010: 1103) both goals are laudable and mutually complementary to one another. One should certainly not consider that there exists a choice to be made between them. The discussion in this volume has focused on the new intergovernmentalism as an analytical framework for understanding post-Maastricht integration in Europe. We make no claim, neither have we presented evidence, that our findings could be immediately applied to other settings of regional integration or global governance. Yet, it is worth highlighting that we think that a number of our findings could have application beyond the context of the EU in three ways, each of which is discussed below.

First, the integration paradox as set out in chapter 1 may also serve as a useful characterization of global governance in the post-Cold War era. Growing cooperation among states across a variety of different policy areas has been a hallmark of this period. However, it has also been remarked that much of this cooperation has occurred outside formal institutional settings. In fact, cooperation in the absence of legal institutional frameworks is a key feature of post-Cold War global governance. Even those policy areas that had been firmly institutionalized at the global level—such as finance—have seen their respective institutions weaken. Miles Kahler and David Lake have observed that global economic governance is characterized by a 'missing supranationalism': instead of seeing a shift from national to global forms of macroeconomic regulation, states have pursued hierarchy and network governance as functional alternatives to further supranational integration (Kahler and Lake 2009). Practitioners and policy-makers have also voiced their frustration at what they consider to be a puzzle of growing collaboration in the absence of global institution building (e.g. Malloch-Brown 2011). Historians of international organization have also noted that the dense cooperative global networks of the twenty-first century coexist alongside a marked decline in appetite for global political integration (Mazower 2012).

Second, there are similarities between the manner and form of cooperation between EU member states post-1992 and instances of regional and international cooperation elsewhere in the world. For instance, there are parallels between the EU's Broad Economic Policy Guidelines (Deroose, Hodson, and Kuhlmann 2008) and the Association of Southeast Asian Nations (ASEAN) Surveillance Mechanism (Manzano 2001), two soft law instruments designed to encourage consensus-building and facilitate peer pressure in relation to national economic policies. Other scholars have observed parallels between the EU's turn to new modes of governance and the dynamics of regional integration in Asia. Hameiri notes that a number of regional regulatory instruments were created in the wake of the Asian economic crisis. These included the Chiang Mai Initiative and the Asian Bond Market Initiative (Hameiri 2013:

331). In his words, 'in both Asia and Europe, despite their differences, similar mechanisms such as meta-governance and functional specialization have been used in the establishment of new modes of regional governance... aimed at managing transnational problems of various kinds' (2013: 331). Turning to a different region, there is also a strong family resemblance between operations under the EU's Common Security and Defence Policy and the African Union's peacekeeping missions (Murithi 2008). The EU also converged in the post-Maastricht period towards the governance arrangements employed in international organizations. In adopting benchmarking and the exchange of best practice as guiding principles of the Lisbon Strategy, for example, the EU mirrored an approach that has long been employed by the Organization for Economic Cooperation and Development (Hodson and Maher 2001). What the new intergovernmentalism approach contributes to comparative regionalism *empirically* is a framework where on the European-side the accent is on informal cooperation and novel forms of institutionalization. This challenges the traditional image of regional integration in Europe, namely as a formal and legalistic process oriented towards the pooling of sovereignty. In turn, this can help us to rethink the conventional wisdom on regional integration elsewhere, such as with the Association of Southeast Asian Nations (ASEAN) and its own departure from its state-dominated and openly non-interventionist mode of regional cooperation.

Third, owing to the nature of the explanations for the new intergovernmentalism provided in this volume, it is possible to see similar or cognate causal mechanisms at work at the global level and in other regional settings. That the EU has come closer to other regional and international organizations over the last twenty years is not entirely surprising since the political economy shift that characterizes the post-Maastricht period is by no means confined to Europe. Although talk of a Washington consensus (Williamson 1990) is too simplistic, the international monetary system did see the emergence in the 1990s of shared beliefs about the importance of price stability, fiscal discipline and well-functioning markets (Roberts 2010). Industrialized states may not have followed euro area members' lead by creating their own monetary union but many tied their hands by giving statutory independence to central banks and embracing fiscal rules. In the case of Asia, it is no coincidence that its turn towards more 'regulatory regionalism' came on the back of the collapse of the 'embedded mercantilist' model of state–society relations that had prevailed in the region until the economic crisis of 1997–8, and had underpinned the 'open regionalism' project of the 1980s and 1990s (Hameiri 2013: 332–3).

As in the EU, this ideational convergence paved the way for deliberation rather than delegation. The launch of the Group of Twenty (G20) in 1999 exemplifies this trend. Inspired by the Asian financial crisis, the G20 brings together representatives of systemically important economies to discuss shared policy challenges. As with the Eurogroup, the G20 finance ministers and central bank governors styled themselves as a deliberative body operating at one remove from more formal bodies such as the International Monetary Fund (IMF). This trend towards informalization can even be seen within the IMF, which saw the creation in 1999 of a new International Monetary and Financial Committee, bringing together a small group of finance ministers and central bank governors to advise the IMF Governing Board.

As with the EU in the post-Maastricht period, international economic governance is characterized by a reluctance to delegate. Meetings of the G20 conclude with the adoption of communiqués that are politically rather than legally binding and limited in their demands for concrete follow-up. Delegation, where it occurs, also involves the empowerment and creation of *de novo* bodies. The launch of the Financial Stability Forum in 1999 stemmed in part from a reluctance on the part of finance ministers to cede additional powers to pre-existing bodies such as the Basel Committee on Banking Supervision. The G20's willingness to invest significant new powers in the IMF at the height of the global financial crisis is an exception to this rule, of course, but it reflects the scale of this crisis and disguises the increasingly modest role and ambitions of the Fund in the run up to 2007.

If the political economy dynamics of the post-Maastricht period also played out on the international stage then the same could be said of the crisis of representation. A key assumption of the new intergovernmentalism is that a divide opened up between elites, interest groups, and the general public that created a space for policy-makers to pursue closer cooperation on the international stage, albeit in ways that rested uneasily with popular concerns over the legitimacy of such arrangements. This trend is by no means germane to the EU. The international system saw its own share of contested cooperation since 1992. This is exemplified by the Group of Seven (G7), which saw a dramatic increase in the scope of its activity over the last two decades. Writing about the G7 in the early 1990s, G. John Ikenberry (1992) called for the group to be transformed into a 'Liberal Concert of Powers' with a permanent secretariat, a quasi-legal basis and a Council of Ministers with a mandate to cover 'the full range of economic, political and security issues'. Ikenberry's vision proved prescient in so far as the G7 extended its activities over the following decades into policy domains such as health, JHA, science and technology, employment, and development. His implicit idea that the Community method might be transplanted to the international arena was wide of the mark, however, since the intensification of the G7 during the following years occurred without the significant formalization of decision-making structures. Nor did Ikenberry foresee the backlash against the G7 from anti-globalization protestors at Genoa in 2001 or the forum's uneasy interaction with national and transnational social movements thereafter.

Just as the 'permissive consensus' in Europe has given way to growing contestation in the post-Maastricht era, so was the permissiveness vis-à-vis global governance overcome by the rise of a more critical global civil society movement in the post-Cold War era that has challenged the legitimacy of inter-state cooperation in areas ranging from trade policy to the environment (Kaldor 2003). The new intergovernmentalism provides a useful analytic approach, we contend, for understanding how such tensions played out in the G7 and the changing governance of regional and international organizations more generally. A key question that arises from this book for IR scholars is thus whether global governance institutions, and regional institutions such as ASEAN or the Mercado Común del Sur (Mercosur), find themselves beset by the same problems of systematic disequilibrium that have come to characterize the EU in the post-Maastricht period.

15.5 On the Possibility of Post-Post-Maastricht Politics

Having summarized the key findings of this book and considered the scope and range of the new intergovernmentalism, we return finally to the political dynamics that underpin the post-Maastricht period. A key question to address is whether the dynamics of European integration, having shifted after Maastricht, could shift again? Although we see no evidence that the post-Maastricht period is coming to an end, it is worth considering what such a change might look like and how conceivable it appears at the time of writing. We do so not because our crystal ball is any less opaque than those of other scholars but in the hope of giving a clearer sense of where the conceptual limits of the new intergovernmentalism lie. For the purpose of this discussion, two questions stand out. The first is whether the post-Maastricht political economy explored in chapter 1 could yet be overturned. The second is whether the problematic system of political representation underpinning post-Maastricht politics is here to stay.

A key assumption of the new intergovernmentalism is that European political economy changed in the post-Maastricht period thanks to a combination of ideational convergence, institutional diversity, and the final unravelling of the post-war consensus. A return to neo-corporatism in the economic sphere would seem to be a remote possibility at this juncture but what about the prospects for ideational and institutional change? Of the two, institutional change that causes a radical rethink of the EU's role in economic governance seems less likely. Whereas the supranationalist school treats supranational policy-making as a self-propelling process, the new intergovernmentalism sees the institutional complementarities underpinning different models of capitalism as providing a hard constraint on the centralization of economic policy-making in the EU. Institutional differences, as we see it, help to explain why EMU paved the way for a decentralized rather than a centralized approach to fiscal policy and structural reform in the two decades following Maastricht.

Models of capitalism are slow to change, if at all, so we see little reason, as things stand, to expect a convergence towards a more homogenous European political economy in the coming years. What is clear from the euro crisis, indeed, is just how uneven the European economy remains. Sharing the same currency has not given rise to the convergence that some economists hoped for (Frankel and Rose 1998) but instead has highlighted significant divergences between some member states, especially in terms of wage and price competitiveness, levels of indebtedness, and current account positions. National economies in Europe have found themselves organized along systematic dividing lines, such as debtor and creditor, or exporter versus importer. Discussions around modernization and problems of backwardness and poor growth have re-emerged alongside cultural stereotypes about the profligate South and the hard-working North. If institutional diversities served to propel forward decentralized policy cooperation between national elites in the 1990s and 2000s, there is little reason to expect this trend to come to an end.

The evolution of European Banking Union could have a significant impact if it sets in motion plans for a fiscal union to underwrite European bank guarantees but, thus far, member states have resisted moves in this direction. A more plausible scenario from a political economy perspective is that pressures for decentralized economic policies would intensify in the event of further fiscal and financial crises. EMU, it is important to remember, came close to unravelling in the period 2010–12 in spite of national governments' high degree of commitment to monetary integration. This crisis may have de-escalated at the time of writing but it is by no means over.

The prospects for continued ideational change in the EU are more difficult to assess because it is impossible to know in advance what economic ideas will take hold with policy-makers (McNamara 1998). One possibility is that EU member states will come to accept what UK Chancellor George Osborne referred to as, the 'remorseless logic' of moving from EMU to political union (Giles and Parker 2011). Plans for a European Banking Union, a possible first step in this direction, are already bearing fruit but, as Quaglia and Howarth (chapter 7) note, they have confirmed member states' reluctance to delegate new powers to the ECB and, to an even greater extent, the Commission. Plans for fiscal union seem less realistic still. That European Council President Herman Van Rompuy called in December 2012 for the euro area to be given a 'limited fiscal capacity' was at odds with the new intergovernmentalism. That the heads of state or government have thus far showed little enthusiasm for this proposal is not. Periodic calls to give the Commission veto powers over national taxation and expend-iture decisions have proved less workable still.

If the post-Maastricht political economy appears to be unmalleable then what of the problems of political representation that have emerged during the last two decades? One possibility here is that national governments and civil societies could forge new links that lead to more representative policy-making on Europe. There is little evidence to suggest that the first of these scenarios is underway. Social movements are becoming more, rather than less, diffuse and unwieldy, as evidenced by the Occupy Movement with its lack of hierarchical structures and reluctance to engage with policy-makers. As Bickerton remarks in chapter 2, a characteristic of political conflict within member states is that much of the mobilization that takes place is directed at political procedures and institutions themselves. This is obviously a feature of populist movements and parties but it is also characteristic of political opposition in general. Though often forgotten in studies of political conflict in Europe, the theme of political corruption is omnipresent across Europe and leaves many people with a sentiment of disenchantment mixed in with a fatalism that nothing can be done to change the status quo. As Perry Anderson baldly put it, 'Europe is ill' (Anderson 2014: 3; Mény 2012).

Attempts by national governments to bridge the representational divide over European issues have thus far fallen flat. Ireland's National Forum for Europe was one of the more innovative initiatives in this regard. Launched in the wake of Ireland's 'no' vote against the Lisbon Treaty in 2001, the National Forum brought together national and European politicians with members of civil society to discuss Ireland's place in Europe. Having arguably raised the level of public debate in Ireland on European issues, the National Forum was closed by the Irish government in 2009. The official reason given was that the government wanted to reassert the role of Parliament on this issue. The unofficial reason was that the Forum disagreed with the government's deci-sion to hold a second referendum on the Lisbon Treaty. Attempts to engage with civil society from Brussels have been even less successful. The so-called participatory turn in EU policy-making could yet bear fruit but initiatives such as Plan D for Democracy, Dialogue and Debate have served only to illustrate the difficulties of establishing a European public sphere (Kohler-Koch 2009). More disappointing still was the Convention on the Future of Europe, which promised a more participatory approach to treaty revision but contributed to an agreement that proved hopelessly out of touch with public sentiment in some member states.

More robust mechanisms for parliamentary accountability are another possi-bility for addressing the crisis of representation that defines the post-Maastricht period. From a new intergovernmentalist perspective, making governments more accountable to national Parliaments would not necessarily make a difference. There has been no shortage of efforts in the post-Maastricht period to involve national Parliaments in EU policy-making. The problem, rather, is that levels of trust in elected officials are low in a number of member states and declining in the light of the global financial crisis.[3] Economic recovery could make a difference here but public detachment from domestic politics reflects broader societal shifts in the post-Maastricht period. There is little reason to expect these shifts to be reversed in the coming years, with the result that national Parliaments are unlikely to unlock the crisis of representation in Europe in the absence of significant constitutional change on a member state by member state basis. It is worth adding that in those instances of pan-European national parliamentary mobilization that currently exist and aim to hold EU institutions more accountable, national parliamentarians have tended to reproduce the same problems identified by the new intergovernmentalism. Their deliberations appear as ends in themselves and they relate to one another very much as national officials do, in other words, in technocratic and policy-specialized ways (Fasone 2012). Their relationship to their own domestic publics is also very distant as little of what goes on in the form of inter-parliamentary cooperation is known to the public.

Some scholars put their hopes for parliamentary accountability in the EP (Hix 2008) but the new intergovernmentalism gives pause for thought on this point, as indicated above in the discussion of inter-parliamentary cooperation in Europe. The picture of the EU legislature that emerges from this volume is that of a pragmatic competence maximizer rather than a staunch defender of democratic checks and balances. That the two roles do not necessarily go together can be seen from the controversy over the appointment of Jean-Claude Juncker as President of the Commission in 2014. Under the Lisbon Treaty, the Parliament was given an enhanced role in the nomination procedure for this post by requiring the European Council to take account of the elections of the EP when proposing a new Commission president. The main European political parties adopted a maximalist interpretation of this provision by putting forward so-called *Spitzenkandidaten* in advance of the May 2014 EP election and, thereafter, rallying around the European People Party's candidate Jean-Claude Juncker. Defenders of this strategy see it as enhancing the Commission's democratic accountability but this view is difficult to defend given the European People Party's poor showing in May 2014, the low turnout for this election and the willingness of the other parties to put partisan concerns to one side rather than see the European Council overlook the Spitzenkandidaten in choosing the Commission president designate.

---

[3] In the EU as a whole, the percentage of Eurobarometer respondents who tend not to trust their national Parliaments rose from 52 per cent in November 2003 to 69 per cent a decade later. In Greece, this figure rose from 43 per cent to 86 per cent over the same period.

EU heads of state or governments, having been wrong footed by the EP in the process, moved rapidly to rein in the Juncker presidency by agreeing a strategic agenda for the lifetime of this administration and committing to review the process for appointing future Commission presidents.

If these measures speak to the new intergovernmentalism, a situation in which Jean-Claude Juncker embarked on an integrationist agenda along traditional lines would call for a rethink on our part about what supranationalist institutions want. At the time of Juncker's appointment there was considerable scaremongering in the British press about the former Luxembourg Prime Minister being a hard-line federalist (e.g. Popham 2014). In truth, Juncker's track record as President of the Eurogroup and the longest-serving member of the European Council suggests that he is more of a new intergovernmentalist at heart. As such, a proactive Juncker presidency, aimed at closer collaboration with the European Council but avoiding large-scale integrationist initiatives would be consistent with our diagnosis.

Barring unforeseen changes to the European political economy or an unexpected resurgence in participatory or parliamentary democracy, the post-Maastricht period is likely to persist unless national governments either return to the Community method or choose to decelerate the process of integration by other means. The analysis presented in this volume holds out little hope for the Community method in its pre-Maastricht incarnation. Nor does it see any reason why national governments' commitment to deliberation and consensus-building and delegation to *de novo* bodies might wane. Unforeseen shocks that disturb this status quo are always a possibility, of course. One such shock would be a crisis of accountability in *de novo* bodies. A major public crisis of confidence in the performance or governance of a *de novo* body could prompt a rethink here about EU member states' preferences for bespoke institutional arrangements. Another shock would be a major backlash against European integration within the political mainstream. Euro-scepticism is a feature of the post-Maastricht period, of course, but so too is the marginalization of Euro-sceptic groups from the political mainstream. This could change, of course, as evidenced by the strong showing of Euro-sceptic parties in a number of member states in the 2014 EP elections. Should this trend continue or should the rise of Euro-sceptic parties encourage mainstream political parties in a sufficient number of member states to reconsider their attitudes towards European integration, then the long period of integration that followed the ratification of the Maastricht Treaty could come to an abrupt end.

A final question to consider here is whether a geo-political shock could cause EU member states to return to more conventional modes of integration. At the time of writing, Ukraine finds itself in a state of *de facto* civil war between a pro-Western government that is looking to the EU and pro-Russia forces that appear to be backed by the Putin administration in Russia. How the

EU will respond to this fast-moving situation remains to be seen but it shows no signs thus far of paving the way for a more centralized approach to the CFSP. This is to be expected. The two decades following Maastricht saw no shortage of foreign policy crises, from 9/11 to the Iraq War and the Georgian–Ossetian conflict. Only some of these situations encouraged an intensification of cooperation between EU member states in the foreign policy sphere and none led to a more supranational approach.

Conclusion

The new intergovernmentalism refers to an enduring and entrenched form of European integration that has come to characterize the post-Maastricht period as a whole. What characterizes this form of integration is a paradox, namely that an unprecedented expansion in the activity of the EU coincides with a definitive shift away from the further empowerment of traditional supranational institutions. The EU has never been busier and more expansive in its activities and yet it has never been further away from becoming a fully fledged supranational system of policy-making, never mind a European state. This capacity to move forwards and backwards at the same time is at the heart of the new intergovernmentalism and is the source of much confusion about the trajectory of contemporary European integration for both citizens and scholars.

By spelling out the integration paradox and detailing the nature of the EU in the post-Maastricht period, this volume hopes to contribute in some way to demystifying the present-day EU. Its curious combination of strength and weakness stems from the transformations that have taken place across European societies over a number of decades and the manner in which these transformations in domestic politics have been expressed at the pan-European level. As governments have converged in their beliefs about the necessity of closer pan-European cooperation, national publics have become increasingly sceptical about the merits of 'ever closer union'. This gap between governments and peoples has created an unprecedented opportunity for expanding the activities of the EU, but it has also been a powerful constraint on the manner in which integration has taken place. In considering the distinctive characteristics of the new intergovernmentalist EU, we are seeing in a concentrated form the problems of political trust and representation that have been the hallmark of the last two decades of political life in Europe. European integration is less a transcendence of domestic politics than an expression of some of its most troubling features.

References

Adler-Nissen, R. (2008) 'Behind the Scenes of Differentiated Integration: Circumventing National Opt-outs in Justice and Home Affairs', *Journal of European Public Policy*, 16 (1): 62–80.

Allen, D. (2005) 'The United Kingdom: A Europeanized Government in a Non-Europeanized Polity', in S. Bulmer and C. Lequesne (eds) *The Member States of the European Union* (Oxford: Oxford University Press), 119–41.

Alter, K. J. (1998) 'Who are the "Masters of the Treaty"?: European Governments and the European Court of Justice', *International Organization*, 52 (1): 121–47.

Alter, K. (2010) *The European Court's Political Power: Selected Essays* (Oxford: Oxford University Press).

Anderson, P. (2014) 'The Italian Disaster', *London Review of Books*, 36 (10): 3–16.

Anderson, S. and Seitz, T. R. (2006) 'European Security and Defense Policy Demystified', *Armed Forces & Society*, 33 (1): 24–42.

Angenendt, S. and Parkes, R. (2009) 'Can Further Nationalisation Facilitate a Common EU Approach to Migration?', *The International Spectator: Italian Journal of International Affairs*, 44 (3): 77–96.

AOK Bundesverband (2008) 'Vorschlag der EU-Kommission vom 02.07.2008 für eine Richtlinie des Europäischen Parlaments und des Rates über die Ausübung der Patientenrechte in der grenzüberschreitenden Gesundheitsversorgung. Stellungnahme des AOK-Bundesverbandes', AOK, 18 August. www.aok-bv.de/imperia/md/aokbv/politik/europa/aok-bv-stellungnahme-rl-vorschlag-patientenrechte-grenz__berschreitend-logo-fassung-180808.pdf [accessed 31 March 2014].

Apeldoorn, B. Van (2000) 'Transnational Class Agency and the European Roundtable of Industrialists', *New Political Economy*, 5 (2): 157–81.

Armstrong, K. (2010) Governing Social Inclusion: Europeanization through Policy Coordination (Oxford and New York: Oxford University Press).

Armstrong, K. A. (2012) 'Pringle has his Chips', EUtopia Law, 27 November 2012. Available at: <http://eutopialaw.com/2012/11/27/pringle-has-his-chips/>.

Armstrong, K. A (2013) 'The New Governance of EU Fiscal Discipline', *Jean Monnet Working Paper*, 29/13.

Armstrong, K. A. and Bulmer, S. (1998) *The Governance of the Single European Market* (Basingstoke: Palgrave Macmillan).

Arnull, A. (1999) *The European Union and its Court of Justice* (Oxford: Oxford University Press).

Arnull, A. (2007) 'Me and My Shadow: The European Court of Justice and the Disintegration of European Union Law', *Fordham International Law Journal*, 31: 1174–211.

Arnull, A. (2012) 'Judicial Activism and the Court of Justice: How Should Academics Respond?', *Maastricht Faculty of Law Working Paper 2012–13*. Available at <http://ssrn.com/abstract=1986817>.

Arnull, A., Barnard, C., Dougan, M., and Spaventa, E. (2011) *A Constitutional Order of States? Essays in EU Law in Honour of Alan Dashwood* (Oxford: Hart Publishing).

Aron, R. (1957) 'Historical Sketch of the Great Debate', in D. Lerner and R. Aron (eds) *France Defeats EDC* (New York: Frederick A. Praeger).

Artis, M. J. and Buti, M. (2000) ' "Close to Balance or in Surplus": A Policy-maker's Guide to the Implementation of the Stability and Growth Pact', *Journal of Common Market Studies*, 38 (4): 563–91.

Aspinwall, M. (2007) 'Government Preferences on European Integration: An Empirical Test of Five Theories', *British Journal of Political Science* 37 (1): 89–114.

Aucante, Y. and Dézé, A. (eds) (2008) *Les systèmes de partis dans les démocraties occidentales: Le modèle du parti cartel en question* (Paris: Presses de Sciences Po).

Auel, K. (2013) 'De-Parliamentarisation Re-Considered: "Representation Without Corresponding Communication" in EU Affairs', Paper presented at the 13th Biennial Conference of the European Union Studies Association, Baltimore, 9–11 May.

Auel, K. and Hoeing, O. (2015) 'National Parliaments and the Sovereign Debt Crisis', *West European Politics*, 38 (2), forthcoming.

Awesti, A. (2009) 'The Myth of Eurosclerosis: European Integration in the 1970s', *L'Europe en Formation*, 3/4 (353/354): 39–53.

Bache, I. and Flinders, M. (eds) (2004) *Multi-level Governance* (Oxford: Oxford University Press).

Badie, B. and Birnbaum, P. (1979) *Sociologie de l'État* (Paris: Grasset).

Baker, E. and Harding, C. (2009) 'From Past Imperfect to Future Perfect? A Longitudinal Study of the Third Pillar', *European Law Review*, 34 (1): 25–54.

Ball, T. (ed.) (2003) *The Federalist with Letters of 'Brutus'* (Cambridge: Cambridge University Press).

Balzacq, T. (2008) 'The Policy Tools of Securitization: Information Exchange, EU Foreign and Interior Policies', *Journal of Common Market Studies*, 46 (1): 75–100.

Barnard, C. (2001) 'Fitting the Remaining Pieces into the Goods and Persons Jigsaw', *European Law Review*, 26 (1): 35–59.

Barnard, C. (2012) 'A Proportionate Response to Proportionality in the Field of Collective Action', *European Law Review*, 37: 117–35.

Barnard, C. and Scott, J. (2002) *The Law of the Single European Market: Unpacking the Premises* (Oxford: Hart).

Basel Committee on Banking Supervision (BCBS) (2010a) *Basel III: A Global Regulatory Framework for More Resilient Banks and Banking Systems*. Basel: BCBS.

Basel Committee on Banking Supervision (BCBS) (2010b) *Basel III: International framework for Liquidity Risk Measurement, Standards and Monitoring*. Basel: BCBS.

Batora, J. (2013) 'The "Mitraileuse Effect": The EEAS as an Interstitial Organization and the Dynamics of Innovation in Diplomacy', *Journal of Common Market Studies*, 51 (4): 598–613.

Beach, D. (2012) 'A Stronger, More Supranational Union', in H. Zimmermann and A. Dür (eds) *Key Controversies in European Integration* (Basingstoke: Palgrave Macmillan), 49–56.

Becker, U. (2011) *The Changing Political Economies of Small West European Countries* (Amsterdam: University of Amsterdam Press).

Beetham, D. (1987) *Bureaucracy* (Milton Keynes: Open University Press).

Begg, D., De Grauwe, P., Giavazzi, F., Uhlig, H., and Wyplosz, C. (1999) *'The ECB: Safe at Any Speed?' Monitoring the European Central Bank, No. 1* (London: CEPR).

Bengoetxea, J. (1993) *The Legal Reasoning of the European Court of Justice: Towards a European Jurisprudence* (Oxford: Clarendon Press).

Bermann, G. A. (1994) 'Subsidiarity and the European Community', in P. M. Lutzeler (ed.) *Europe After Maastricht: American and European Perspectives* (Oxford: Berghahn Books).

Bertoncini, Y. and Kreilinger V., (2012) 'Seminar on the Community Method. Elements of Synthesis', BEPA/Notre Europe, Paris, <http://ec.europa.eu/bepa/pdf/seminars/synthesemethodecommunautaire_mai2012.pdf> [accessed on 28 March 2014].

Bickerton, C. J. (2008) 'A Union of Disenchantment', *Le Monde Diplomatique*, July.

Bickerton, C. J. (2011a) 'Europe's neo-Madisonians: Rethinking the Legitimacy of Limited Power in a Multi-Level Polity', *Political Studies*, 59 (3): 659–73.

Bickerton, C. J. (2011b) 'Towards a Social Theory of EU Foreign and Security Policy', *Journal of Common Market Studies*, 49 (1): 171–90.

Bickerton, C. J. (2012) *European Integration: From Nation-States to Member States* (Oxford: Oxford University Press).

Bickerton, C. J. and Invernizzi, C. (2014) 'The Ironies of European Democracy', Le Monde Diplomatique, June 5. <http://mondediplo.com/blogs/the-ironies-of-european-democracy> [accessed 12 February 2015].

Bieling, H. J. (2003) 'Social Forces in the Making of the New European Economy: The Case of Financial Market Integration', *New Political Economy*, 8 (2): 203–23.

Bini Smaghi, L. (2009) 'A Single EU Seat in the International Monetary Fund?', in K. E. Jørgensen (ed.) *The European Union in International Organizations* (London: Routledge), 61–79.

Birnbaum, P. (1977) *Les Sommets de l'État: Essai sur l'élite du pouvoir en France* (Paris: Seuil).

Bloomberg News (2013) 'Draghi says Bank Resolution Plan may be too Cumbersome', 17 December, <http://www.bloomberg.com/news/2013-12-16/draghi-says-european-bank-resolution-plan-may-be-too-cumbersome.html> [accessed on 28 March 2014].

Blyth, M. (2001) 'The Transformation of the Swedish Model: Economic Ideas, Distributional Conflict and Institutional Change', *World Politics*, 54 (1):1–26.

Bohman, J. (1998) 'Survey Article: The Coming of Age of Deliberative Democracy', *Journal of Political Philosophy*, 6 (4): 400–25.

Boswell, C., Geddes, A., and Scholten, P. (2011) 'The Role of Narratives in Migration Policy-Making: A Research Framework', *British Journal of Politics and International Relations*, 13: 1–11.

Bradley, K. S. C. (1992) 'Comitology and the Law: Through a Glass, Darkly', *Common Market Law Review*, 29 (4): 693–721.

References

Bradley, K. S. C. (2011) 'Powers and Procedures in the EU Constitution: Legal Bases and The Court', in P. Craig and G. De Búrca (eds) *The Evolution of EU Law* (Oxford: Oxford University Press).

Brady, H. E. and Collier, D. (2010) *Rethinking Social Inquiry: Diverse Tools, Shared Standards* (Plymouth: Rowman & Littlefield).

Brandsma, G. J. (2013) *Controlling Comitology: Accountability in a Multi-Level System* (Basingstoke: Palgrave Macmillan).

Bresser-Pereira, L. C. (2004) *Democracy and Public Management Reform: Building the Republican State* (New York: Oxford University Press).

Buckley, J. and Howarth, D. (2010) 'Internal Market Gesture Politics? Explaining the EU's Response to the Financial Crisis', *Journal of Common Market Studies Annual Review*, 48 (1): 19–41.

Bull, H. (1977) *The Anarchical Society: A Study of Order in World Politics* (Basingstoke: Palgrave Macmillan).

Bulmer, S. (1983) 'Domestic Politics and European Community Policy-Making', *Journal of Common Market Studies*, 21 (4): 349–64.

Bulmer, S. (1996) 'The European Council and the Council of the European Union: shapers of a European confederation', *The Journal of Federalism*, 26 (4): 17–42.

Bulmer, S. (2012) 'Governing the Lisbon Strategy: Uncertain Governance in Turbulent Times', in P. Copeland and D. Papadimitriou (eds) *The EU's Lisbon Strategy: Evaluating Success, Understanding Failure* (Basingstoke: Palgrave Macmillan), 29–49.

Bulmer, S. (2014) 'Germany and the Euro-Zone Crisis: Between Hegemony and Domestic Politics', *West European Politics*, 37 (6): 1244–63.

Bulmer, S. and Lequesne, C. (eds) (2013) *The Member States of the European Union, Second Edition* (Oxford: Oxford University Press).

Bulmer, S. and Paterson, W. (1987) *The Federal Republic of Germany and the European Community* (London: Allen & Unwin).

Bulmer, S. and Wessels, W. (1987) *The European Council. Decision-making in European Politics* (Basingstoke: Macmillan).

Bundesbank (2003) 'Statement by the Executive Board of the Deutsche Bundesbank on the draft EU Constitution and the Stability and Growth Pact', Frankfurt am Main, 10 December.

Bures, O. (2012) 'Informal Counterterrorism Arrangements in Europe: Beauty by Variety or Duplicity by Abundance?', *Cooperation and Conflict*, 47 (4): 495–518.

Burley, A. M. and Mattli, W. (1993) 'Europe before the Court: a Political Theory of Legal Integration', *International Organization*, 47 (1): 41–76.

Burns, C. (2013) 'Consensus and Compromise Become Ordinary—But at What Cost? A Critical Analysis of the Impact of the Changing Norms of Codecision upon European Parliament Committees', *Journal of European Public Policy*, 20 (7): 988–1005.

Burns, C., Rasmussen, A., and Reh, C. (2013) 'Legislative Co-decision and its Impact on the Political System of the European Union', *European Journal of Public Policy*, 20 (7): 941–52.

Busuioc, M. (2009) 'Accountability, Control and Independence: The Case of European Agencies', *European Law Journal*, 15 (5): 599–615.

Busuioc, M. (2011) 'European Agencies and their Boards. Too much Board, too little monitoring', paper presented at the EUSA twelfth biennial international conference, 3–5 March, Boston.

Busuioc, M. and Groenleer, M. (2011) 'Beyond Design—The Evolution of Europol and Eurojust', *Amsterdam Centre for European Law and Governance Research Paper*, No. 2011–03: 1–33.

Cafruny, A. W. and Ryner, J. M. (2009) 'Critical Political Economy', in A. Wiener and T. Dietz (eds) *European Integration Theory*, 2nd edn (Oxford: Oxford University Press).

Callaghan, H. and Höpner, M. (2005) 'European Integration and the Clash of Capitalisms: Political Cleavages over Takeover Liberalization', *Comparative European Politics*, 3 (3): 307–32.

Cappelletti, M., Secombe, M., and Weiler, J. (eds) (1986) *Integration Through Law: Europe and the American Federal Experience* (Berlin: Walter de Gruyter).

Cardwell, P. J. (2013) 'On Ring-Fencing the Common Foreign and Security Policy in the Legal Order of the European Union', *Northern Ireland Legal Quarterly*, 64: 443–63.

Carrera, S. and Guild, E. (2008) 'The French Presidency's European Pact on Immigration and Asylum: Intergovernmentalism vs. Europeanisation? Security vs. Rights?', *CEPS Policy Brief*, No. 170. <http://www.ceps.eu/book/french-presidency's-european-pact-immigration-and-asylum-intergovernmentalism-vs-europeanisatio> [accessed on 12 February 2015].

Carrera, S. and Guild, E. (2012) 'Does the Stockholm Programme matter? The Struggles over Ownership of AFSJ Multiannual Programming', *CEPS Paper on Liberty and Security in Europe*, No. 51. <http://www.ceps.eu/book/does-stockholm-programme-matter-struggles-over-ownership-afsj-multiannual-programming> [accessed on 12 February 2015].

Cerny, P. (2010) *Rethinking World Politics: A Theory of Transnational Neopluralism* (Oxford: Oxford University Press).

Chalmers, D. (2012) 'The European Court of Justice is now Little More than a Rubber Stamp for the EU', available from: <http://blogs.lse.ac.uk/europpblog>.

Chalmers, D., Davies, G., and Monti, G. (2010) *European Union Law: Cases and Materials* (Cambridge: Cambridge University Press).

Chamon, M. (2011) 'EU Agencies between Meroni and Romano or the Devil and the Deep Blue Sea', *Common Market Law Review*, 48 (4):1055–75.

Chang, M. and Monar J. (eds) (2013) *The European Commission in the Post-Lisbon Era of Crises: Between Political Leadership and Policy Management* (Brussels: Peter Lang).

Checkel, J. T. (2003) ' "Going Native" in Europe?', *Comparative Political Studies*, 36 (1–2): 209–31.

Christensen, J. G. (1981) 'Blurring the International-Domestic Politics Distinction: Danish Representation at EC Negotiations', *Scandinavian Political Studies*, 4 (3): 191–208.

Christiansen, T. (1997) 'Tensions of European Governance: Politicized Bureaucracy and Multiple Accountability in the European Commission', *Journal of European Public Policy*, 4 (1): 73–90.

Christiansen, T. and Dobbels, M. (2012) 'Comitology and Delegated Acts after Lisbon: How the European Parliament lost the Implementation Game', *European Integration Online Papers* (EIoP), 16 (13): 1–23.

Christiansen, T. and Neuhold, C. (2013) 'Informal Politics in the EU', *Journal of Common Market Studies*, 51 (6): 1196–206.

Christiansen, T. and Reh, C. (2009) *Constitutionalizing the European Union* (Basingstoke: Palgrave Macmillan).

Christiansen, T. and Vanhoonacker, S. (2008) 'At a Critical Juncture? Change and Continuity in the Institutional Development of the Council Secretariat', *West European Politics*, 31 (4): 751–70.

Christoffersen, P. (2011) 'The Creation of the European External Action Service: Challenges and Opportunities', Lecture given at Maastricht University, 17 February 2011 (Maastricht Monnet Paper Series No. 3), Maastricht Centre for European Governance.

Cichowski, R. (2004) 'Women's Rights, the European Court, and Supranational Constitutionalism', *Law & Society Review*, 38 (3): 489–512.

Cichowski, R. A. (2007) *The European Court and Civil Society: Litigation, Mobilization and Governance* (Cambridge: Cambridge University Press).

Cini, M. and McGowan, L. (2009) *Competition Policy in the European Union*, 2nd edn (Basingstoke: Palgrave Macmillan).

Clift, B. and Woll, C. (2013) *Economic Patriotism in Open Economies* (London: Routledge).

Cocks, P. (1980) 'Towards a Marxist Theory of European Integration', *International Organization*, 34 (1): 1–40.

Coen, D. and Thatcher, M. (2008) 'Network Governance and Multi-Level Delegation: European Networks of Regulatory Agencies', *Journal of Public Policy*, 28 (1): 49–71.

Commission of the European Communities (1999) 'Financial Services: Implementing the Framework for Financial Markets: Action Plan, Communication from the Commission to the Council and European Parliament', Brussels, 11 May.

Commission of the European Communities (2001a) 'European Governance: A White Paper', COM(2001) 428 final, 25 July.

Commission of the European Communities (2004) 'Communication from the Commission. Follow-up to the High Level Reflection Process on Patient Mobility and Healthcare Developments in the European Union', COM(2004) 301 final, Brussels, 20 April. <http://eur-lex.europa.eu/legal-content/EN/TXT/PDF/?uri=CELEX:52004DC0301&from=EN> [accessed 31 March 2014].

Commission of the European Communities (2008) 'EMU@10: Successes and Challenges after 10 years of Economic and Monetary Union', European Economy 2/2008 (Luxembourg: Office for the Official Publications of the European Communities).

Commission of the European Communities (2010a) 'Reinforcing Economic Policy Coordination', COM(2010) 250 final, Brussels, 12 May.

Commission of the European Communities (2010b) 'Proposal for a Directive.../.../EU of the European Parliament and of the Council on Directive on Deposit Guarantee Schemes [recast], COM(2010) 369, SEC(2010) 834, SEC(2010) 835, Brussels, 12 July. <http://ec.europa.eu/internal_market/bank/docs/guarantee/20100712_proposal_en.pdf> [accessed on 28 March 2014].

Commission of the European Communities (2010c) 'Communication The EU Internal Security Strategy in Action: Five Steps Towards a more secure Europe', Brussels, COM (2010) 673 final, 22 November.

Commission of the European Communities (2011a) 'Proposal for a Directive on the Access to the Activity of Credit Institutions and the Prudential Supervision of Credit Institutions and Investment Firms', 2011/453/EC, Brussels, 20 July.

Commission of the European Communities (2011b) 'Proposal for a Regulation on Prudential Requirements for Credit Institutions and Investment Firms', 2011/452/EC, Brussels, 20 July.

Commission of the European Communities (2012a) 'Proposal for a Council Regulation Conferring Specific Tasks on the European Central Bank Concerning Policies Relating to the Prudential Supervision of Credit Institutions', COM(2012) 511 final, Brussels, 12 September.

Commission of the European Communities (2012b) 'Proposal for a Regulation of the European Parliament and of the Council establishing a European Supervisory Authority (European Banking Authority) as Regards its Interaction with Council Regulation (EU) No... /... Conferring Specific Tasks on the European Central Bank Concerning Policies Relating to the Prudential Supervision of Credit Institution', COM(2012) 512 final, Brussels, 12 September.

Commission of the European Communities (2012c) 'Communication from the Commission to the European Parliament and the Council: A Roadmap Towards a Banking Union', COM(2012) 510 final, Brussels, 12 September.

Commission of the European Communities (2012d) 'Proposal for a Directive Establishing a Framework for the Recovery and Resolution of Credit Institutions and Investment Firms and Amending', COM(2012) 280/3, Brussels.

Commission of the European Communities (2012e) 'Bank Recovery and Resolution Proposal: Frequently Asked Questions', MEMO/12/416, Brussels, 6 June. <http://europa.eu/rapid/press-release_MEMO-12-416_en.htm?locale=en%27> [accessed on 28 March 2014].

Commission of the European Communities (2012f) 'A Blueprint for a Deep and Genuine EMU–Launching a European Debate', COM(2012) 777 final/2, Brussels, 30 November.

Commission of the European Communities (2013) 'Proposal for a Single Resolution Mechanism', IP/13/674, Brussels, 10 July. <http://europa.eu/rapid/press-release_IP-13-674_en.htm> [accessed on 28 March 2014].

Committee of Wise Men (2000) 'Initial Report of the Committee of Wise Men on the regulation of securities markets', Brussels. <http://ec.europa.eu/internal_market/securities/docs/lamfalussy/wisemen/initial-report-wise-men_en.pdf> [accessed on 28 March 2014].

Conant, L. (2002) *Justice Contained. Law and Politics in the European Union* (Ithaca, NY: Cornell University Press).

Conant, L. (2007) 'Review Article: The Politics of Legal Integration', *Journal of Common Market Studies*, 45 (s1): 45–66.

Conceição-Heldt, E. d. (2011) 'Variation in EU Member States' Preferences and the Commission's Discretion in the Doha Round', *Journal of European Public Policy*, 18 (3): 403–19.

Conway, G. (2012) *The Limits of Legal Reasoning and the European Court of Justice* (New York: Cambridge University Press).

Coombes, D. (1970) *Politics and Bureaucracy in the European Community* (London: George Allen & Unwin).

Cooper, I. (2014) 'Parliamentary Oversight of the Fiscal Compact: On the Creation of the "Article 13" Interparliamentary Conference', Paper presented at the UACES Conference, September, Cork.

Corbett, R., Jacobs, F. and Shackleton, M. (2011) *The European Parliament*, 8th edn (London: John Harper).

Cornish, P. and Edwards, G. (2001) 'Identifying the Development of an EU "Strategic Culture"', *International Affairs*, 77 (3): 587–603.

Costa, O. (2014) 'Que peut le Parlement européen', *Pouvoirs n° 149—La gouvernance européenne* (April): 77–89.

Costa, O., Dehousse, R., and Trakalova, A. (2011) 'Codecision and "Early Agreements": An Improvement or a Subversion of The Legislative Procedure?', *Studies and Research 84*, Notre Europe [accessed on 29 May 2012].

Costello, R. and Thomson, R. (2013) 'The Distribution of Power Among EU Institutions: Who Wins Under Codecision and Why?', *Journal of European Public Policy*, 20 (7): 1025–39, p. 23.

Council of the European Union (1999) 'Presidency Conclusions: Tampere European Council', 15 and 16 October.

Council of the European Union (2006) 'Council Conclusions on Common Values and Principles in European Union Health Systems. 2006/C 146/01', Brussels: Council of the European Union, 22 June. <http://eur-lex.europa.eu/LexUriServ/LexUriServ.do?uri=OJ:C:2006:146:0001:0003:EN:PDF> [accessed 31 March 2014].

Council of the European Union (2008) 'European Pact on Immigration and Asylum', Brussels, 24 September.

Council of the European Union (2010) 'European Pact to Combat International Drug Trafficking—Disrupting Cocaine and Heroin Routes', 3018th JHA Council meeting, Luxembourg, 3 June.

Council of the European Union (2011) 'European Pact Against Synthetic Drugs', 3121st JHA Council meeting, Luxembourg, 27 and 28 October.

Council of the European Union (2013) 'Council Regulation (EU) No 1053/2013 Establishing an Evaluation and Monitoring Mechanism to Verify the Application of the Schengen acquis and Repealing the Decision of the Executive Committee of 16 September 1998 setting up a Standing Committee on the Evaluation and Implementation of Schengen', Brussels, 7 October.

Cowles, M. G., Caporaso, J. A., and Risse, T. (eds) (2001) *Transforming Europe: Europeanisation and Domestic Change* (Ithaca, NY: Cornell University Press).

Craig, P. (2008) 'The Role of the European Parliament under the Lisbon Treaty', in: S. Griller and J. Ziller (eds) *The Lisbon Treaty. EU Constitutionalism without a Constitutional Treaty* (Vienna/New York: Springer), 109–34.

Craig, P. (2012) *EU Administrative Law* (Oxford: Oxford University Press).

Craig, P. (2013) 'Pringle and Use of EU Institutions Outside the EU Legal Framework: Foundations, Procedure and Substance', *European Constitutional Law Review*, 9: 263–84.

Craig, P. and De Búrca, G. (2011) *EU Law: Text, Cases, and Materials* (Oxford: Oxford University Press).

Cram, L. (1994) 'The European Commission as a Multi-Organisation: Social Policy and IT Policy in the EU', *Journal of European Public Policy*, 1 (2): 195–217.

Crawford, J. (2006) *The Creation of States in International Law* (Oxford: Oxford University Press).

Cross, M. (2007) 'An EU Homeland Security? Sovereignty vs. Supranational Order', *European Security*, 16 (1): 79–97.

Cross, M. D. (2011) *Security Integration in Europe: How Knowledge-based Networks are Transforming the European Union* (Michigan, MI: The University of Michigan Press).

Crouch, C. (1993) *Industrial Relations and European State Traditions* (Oxford: Oxford University Press).

Crouch, C. (2004) *Post-Democracy* (Cambridge: Polity).

Crouch, C. (2009) 'Privatized Keynesianism: An Unacknowledged Policy Regime', *British Journal of Politics and International Relations*, 11 (3): 382–99.

Crum, B. (2006) 'Parliamentarization of the CFSP Through Informal Institution-making? The Fifth European Parliament and the EU High Representative', *Journal of European Public Policy*, 13 (3): 383–401.

Crum, B. (2012) 'The European Parliament as a Driving Force in Informal Institution-building: The Hard Case of the EP's relation with the High Representative for the CFSP', in T. Christiansen and C. Neuhold (eds) *International Handbook on Informal Governance* (Cheltenham: Edward Elgar), 354–73.

Crum, B. (2013) 'Saving the Euro at the Cost of Democracy?', *Journal of Common Market Studies*, 51 (4): 614–30.

Cullen, H. and Charlesworth, A. (1999) 'Diplomacy by Other Means: The Use of Legal Basis Litigation as a Political Strategy by the European Parliament and Member States', *Common Market Law Review*, 36 (6): 1243–70.

Curtin, D. (2007) 'Transparency, Audiences and the Evolving Role of the EU Council of Ministers', in J. E. Fossum and P. Schlesinger (eds) *The European Union and the Public Sphere. A Communicative Space in the Making* (London: Routledge), 246–58.

Curtin, D. (2014) 'Challenging Executive Dominance in European Democracy', *Modern Law Review*, 77: 1–32.

Dangerfield, G. (1935) *The Strange Death of Liberal England 1910–1914* (New York: Perigee Books).

Darling, A. (2009) 'Letter to Miroslav Kalousek, Czech Finance Minister', HM Treasury, 3 March.

Davies, G. (2012) 'Activism Relocated: The Self-Restraint of the European Court of Justice in its National Context', *Journal of European Public Policy*, 19 (1): 76–91.

Dawson, M. (2011) *New Governance and the Transformation of European Law: Coordinating EU Social Law and Policy* (Cambridge: Cambridge University Press).

Dawson, M. (2012) 'The Political Face of Judicial Activism: Europe's Law–Politics Imbalance', Maastricht Faculty of Law Working Paper No. 2012–1. Available at SSRN: <http://ssrn.com/abstract=1984636 or http://dx.doi.org/10.2139/ssrn.1984636>.

Dawson, M., de Witte, B., and Muir, E. (2013) *Judicial Activism at the European Court of Justice* (Cheltenham: Edward Elgar).

Dawson, M. and de Witte, F. (2013) 'Constitutional Balance in the EU after the Euro-crisis', *The Modern Law Review*, 76 (5): 817–44.

De Búrca, G. (1998) 'The principle of subsidiarity and the Court of Justice as an Institutional Actor', *Journal of Common Market Studies*, 36 (2): 217–35.

De Búrca, G. (2010) 'European Court of Justice and the International Legal Order after Kadi', *Harvard International Law Journal*, 51: 1–49.

De Búrca, G. (2013) 'After the EU Charter of Fundamental Rights: The Court of Justice as a Human Rights Adjudicator', *Maastricht Journal of European and Comparative Law*, 20 (2): 168–84.

De Búrca, G. and Weiler, J. H. H. (2001) *The European Court of Justice* (Oxford: Oxford University Press).

De Búrca, G. and Weiler, J. H. H. (2011) *The Worlds of European Constitutionalism* (Cambridge: Cambridge University Press).

de Haan, J., Eijffinger, S., and Waller, S. (2005) *The European Central Bank: Credibility, Transparency, and Centralization* (Cambridge, MA: MIT Press Books).

de la Rosa, S. (2012) 'The Directive on Cross-border Healthcare or the Art of Codifying Complex Case Law', *Common Market Law Review*, 49 (1): 15–46.

De Larosière Group (2009) 'The High Level Group on Financial Supervision in the EU', Brussels, 25 February.

De Schoutheete, P. (2002) 'The European Council', in J. Peterson and M. Shackleton (eds) *The Institutions of the European Union*, 1st edn (Oxford: Oxford University Press), 21–46.

de Waele, H. (2010) 'Role of the European Court of Justice in the Integration Process: A Contemporary and Normative Assessment', *Hanse Law Review*, 6: 3–26.

De Wilde, P. (2011) 'No Polity for Old Politics? A Framework for Analysing the Politicization of European Integration', *Journal of European Integration*, 33 (5): 559–75.

De Wilde, P. and Zürn, M. (2012) 'Can the Politicization of European Integration be Reversed?', *Journal of Common Market Studies*, 50 (1): 137–53.

De Witte, B. (2011a) 'Direct Effect, Primacy and the Nature of the Legal Order', in P. Craig and G. De Búrca (eds) *The Evolution of EU Law* (Oxford: Oxford University Press).

De Witte, B. (2011b) 'The European Treaty Amendment for the Creation of a Financial Stability Mechanism', 1–8 June.

De la Porte, C. and Nanz, P. (2004) 'The OMC—A Deliberative-Democratic Mode of Governance? The Cases of Employment and Pensions', *Journal of European Public Policy*, 11 (2): 267–88.

De la Porte, C. and Pochet, P. (2004) 'The European Employment Strategy: Existing Research and Remaining Questions', *Journal of European Social Policy*, 14 (1): 71–8.

De Zwaan, J. W. (2011) 'The New Governance of Justice and Home Affairs: Towards Further Supranationalism', in S. Wolff, F. Goudappel, and J. W. De Zwaan (eds) *Freedom, Security and Justice After Lisbon and Stockholm* (The Hague: TMC Asser Press), 7–26.

Dehousse, R. (1994) 'From Community to Union', in R. Dehousse (ed.) *Europe after Maastricht: An Ever Closer Union?* (Munich: Law Books in Europe).

Dehousse, R. (1998) *The European Court of Justice: The Politics of Judicial Integration* (Basingstoke: Palgrave Macmillan).

Dehousse, R. (ed.) (2011a) *The 'Community Method': Obstinate or Obsolete?* (Basingstoke: Palgrave Macmillan).

Dehousse, R. (2011b) 'Conclusion: Obstinate or Obsolete?', in R. Dehousse (ed.) *The 'Community Method': Obstinate or Obsolete?* (Basingstoke: Palgrave Macmillan), 199–204.

Dehousse, R. (2013) 'The Politics of Delegation in the European Union', *Les Cahiers Européens de Sciences Po*, 4/2013.

Della Salla, V. (1997) 'Hollowing Out and Hardening the State: European Integration and the Italian Economy', *West European Politics*, 20 (1): 14–33.

Delors, J. (1993) 'Address by Jacques Delors, President of the Commission, to the European Parliament on the Occasion of The Investiture Debate of the new Commission', Strasbourg, 10 February (Brussels: European Commission).

Den Boer, M., Hillerbrand, C., and Nölke, A. (2008) 'Legitimacy under pressure: the European web of counter-terrorism networks', *Journal of Common Market Studies*, 46 (1): 101–24.

Denza, E. (2002) *The Intergovernmental Pillars of the European Union* (Oxford: Oxford University Press).

Deroose, S., Hodson, D., and Kuhlmann, J. (2008) 'The Broad Economic Policy Guidelines: Before and After the Re-launch of the Lisbon Strategy' *Journal of Common Market Studies*, 46 (4): 827–48.

Detterbeck, K. (2005) 'Cartel Parties in Western Europe?', *Party Politics*, 11 (2): 173–91.

Deubner, C. (2013) 'The Difficult Role of Parliaments in the Reformed Governance of the European Economic and Monetary Union', Foundation for European Progressive Studies, Brussels, 19: 1–66.

Deutsch, K. (1953) *Nationalism and Social Communication* (Cambridge, MA: MIT Press).

Deutsch, K. W. (1963) 'Supranational Organizations in the 1960s', *Journal of Common Market Studies*, 1(3): 212–18.

Deutsch, K., Burrell, D., Kann, R., Lee, M., Lichterman, M., Lindgren, R., Loewenheim, F., and Wagenen, R. (1958) *Political Community and the North Atlantic Area* (New York: Charles Scribner's Sons).

Diez, T. (1999) 'Speaking "Europe": the Politics of Integration Discourse', *Journal of European Public Policy*, 6 (4): 598–613.

Dimitrakopoulos, D.G. (2008) 'Collective Leadership in Leaderless Europe: a Sceptical View', in J. Hayward (ed.) *Leaderless Europe* (Oxford: Oxford University Press).

Dinan, D. (2004) *Europe Recast: a History of the European Union* (Basingstoke: Palgrave Macmillan).

Draghi, M. (2011) 'Hearing before the Plenary of the European Parliament on the Occasion of the Adoption of the Resolution on the ECB's 2010 Annual Report', Brussels, 1 December.

Draghi, M. (2012a) 'Introductory Statement at the Hearing of the Committee on Economic and Monetary Affairs of the European Parliament', Brussels, 17 December.

Draghi, M. (2012b) 'Building the Bridge to a Stable European Economy: Speech by Mario Draghi, President of the ECB, at The Annual Event "Day of the German Industries" Organized by the Federation of German Industries', Berlin, 25 September.

Draghi, M. (2012c) 'The Future of The Euro: Stability Through Change', *Die Zeit*, 29 August.

Draghi, M. (2013) 'Europe's pursuit of 'a more perfect Union'', Speech at the Harvard Kennedy School, Cambridge (USA), 9 October.

Duisenberg, W. (1998) 'The international role of the euro', Berlin, 22 October.

Duisenberg, W. (1999a) 'The role of the Central Bank in the United Europe', Warsaw, 4 May.

Duisenberg, W. (1999b) 'The European Project and the Challenges of the Future', Speech at the Edmond Israel Foundation, 11 November.

Duisenberg, W. (2001) Press Conference, 11 April (Frankfurt am Main: ECB).

Duisenberg, W. (2002) 'Some Remarks on the Euro in a US context', Council on Foreign Relations, New York, 19 April.

Duisenberg, W. (2003) 'Letter to the President of the Convention Regarding the Draft Constitutional Treaty', 8 May (Frankfurt am Main: ECB).

Duke, S. (2009) 'Providing for European-Level Diplomacy After Lisbon: The Case of the European External Action Service', *The Hague Journal of Diplomacy*, 4: 211–33.

Duke, S. (2013) 'The European External Action Service and Public Diplomacy', *Discussion Papers in Diplomacy*, No. 127, Clingendael: Netherlands Institute of International Relations.

Dunleavy, P. (1991) *Democracy, Bureaucracy and Public Choice* (Hemel Hempstead: Harvester Wheatsheaf).

Dunleavy, P. and O'Leary, B. (1987) *Theories of the State: The Politics of Liberal Democracy* (Basingstoke: Palgrave).

Dür A. and Elsig, M. (2011) 'Principals, Agents and the European Union's Foreign Economic Policies', *Journal of European Public Policy*, 18 (3): 323–38.

Durand, G. (2013) 'Mitterrand, Maastricht et Moi', *Charles*, 5: 9–15.

Duverger, M. (1951) *Les Partis Politiques* (Paris: Armand Colin).

Dyson, K. and Featherstone, K. (1996) 'Italy and EMU as a "Vincolo Esterno": Empowering the Technocrats, Transforming the State', *Southern European Society and Politics*, 1 (2): 272–99.

Dyson, K. and Sepos, A. (2010) 'Differentiation as Design Principle and as Tool in the Political Management of European Integration', in K. Dyson and A. Sepos (eds) *Which Europe? The Politics of Differentiated Integration* (Basingstoke: Palgrave Macmillan), 3–38.

Eeckhout, P. (2004) *EU External Relations Law* (Oxford: Oxford University Press).

Egeberg, M. (2012) 'Experiments in Supranational Institution-Building: the European Commission as a Laboratory', *Journal of European Public Policy*, 19 (6): 939–50.

Egeberg, M. and Heskestad, A. (2010) 'The Denationalization of Cabinets in the European Commission', *Journal of Common Market Studies*, 48 (4): 775–86.

Egeberg, M. and Trondal, J. (2011) 'EU-Level Agencies: New Executive Centre Formation or Vehicles for National Control', *Journal of European Public Policy*, 18 (6): 868–87.

Ehlermann, C.-D. (1975) 'Applying the New Budgetary Procedure for the First Time', *Common Market Law Review*, 12: 325–43.

Eiselt, I. and Slominski, P. (2006) 'Sub-Constitutional Engineering: Negotiation, Content and Legal Value of Interinstitutional Agreements in the EU', *European Law Journal*, 12 (2): 209–25.

Eiselt, I., Pollak, J. and Slominski, P. (2007) 'Codifying Temporary Stability? The Role of Interinstitutional Agreements in Budgetary Politics', *European Law Journal*, 13 (1): 75–91.

Ekengren, M. (2002) *The Time of European Governance* (Manchester: Manchester University Press).

El-Enany, N. and Thielemann E., (2011) 'The impact of EU asylum policy on national asylum regimes', in S. Wolff, F. Goudappel, and J. de Zwaan (eds) *Freedom, Security and Justice after Lisbon and Stockholm* (The Hague: TMC Asser Press).

Ellinas, A. A. and Suleiman, E. N. (2011) 'Supranationalism in a Transnational Bureaucracy: the Case of the European Commission', *Journal of Common Market Studies*, 49 (5): 923–47.

Elster, J. (1977) 'Ulysses and the Sirens: A theory of imperfect rationality', *Social Science Information*, 16 (5): 469–526.

Euro Area Summit (2012) *Statement*, Brussels, 29 June 2012, <http://www.consilium. europa.eu/uedocs/cms_data/docs/pressdata/en/ec/131359.pdf>.

European Central Bank (ECB) (1999) *Monthly Bulletin—June 1999* (Frankfurt am Main: ECB).

European Central Bank (ECB) (2001) 'Annual Report—2000' (Frankfurt am Main: ECB).

European Central Bank (ECB) (2002) 'Statement of the Governing Council on the Stability and Growth Pact', Press Release, 24 October (Frankfurt am Main: ECB).

European Central Bank (ECB) (2005a) 'The Lisbon Strategy—Five Years On', Monthly Bulletin 07/05 (Frankfurt am Main: ECB).

European Central Bank (ECB) (2005b) 'TARGET Annual Report' (Frankfurt am Main: ECB).

European Central Bank (ECB) (2005c) 'Statement of the Governing Council on the ECOFIN Council's Report on Improving the Implementation of the Stability and Growth Pact', Press Release, 21 March (Frankfurt am Main: ECB).

European Central Bank (ECB) (2008) Monthly Bulletin (10th Anniversary of the ECB), May (Frankfurt am Main: ECB).

European Central Bank (ECB) (2010) 'Reinforcing Economic Governance in the Euro Area' (Frankfurt am Main: ECB).

European Central Bank (ECB) (2012) 'Opinion of the European Central Bank of 29 November 2012 on a proposal for a directive establishing a framework for recovery and resolution of credit institutions and investment firms', CON/2012/99, Frankfurt, 29 November. <http://www.ecb.europa.eu/ecb/legal/pdf/en_con_2012_99_f_sign. pdf> [accessed on 28 March 2014].

European Council (1999) *Presidency Conclusions*, SN 300/99, Helsinki, 10–11 December 1999.

European Council (2002) *Presidency Conclusions*, 13463/02, Seville, 21–2 June 2002.

European Council (2003) *Presidency Conclusions*, 5381/04 POLGEN 2, Brussels, 12–13 December 2003.

European Council (2007) *Presidency Conclusions*, 16616/1/07 REV 1, Brussels 14 December.

European Council (2010) The Stockholm Programme—An Open and Secure Europe Serving and Protecting Citizens (2010/C 115/01). Official Journal of the European Union C 115/1, 4.5.2010.

European Council (2012) 'Council Agrees Position on Single Supervisory Mechanism', 13 December, 17739/12, PRESSE 528, Brussels. <http://www.consilium.europa.eu/ uedocs/cms_data/docs/pressdata/en/ecofin/134265.pdf> [accessed on 28 March 2014].

European Parliament (2005) 'Resolution on the Institutional Aspects of the European External Action Service', Brussels, 26 May 2005, published in the Official Journal of the EU, C 117E/233, 18 May 2006.

European Parliament (2009) 'Activity Report', 1 May 2004 to 13 July 2009 (6th parliamentary term). <http://www.statewatch.org/news/2009/sep/ep-activity-report-2004-2009.pdf>.

European Parliament (2010) 'EU Foreign Service: EP Links Budget Approval to Agreement on EEAS organisation, Press Release of the European Parliament', 16 April. <http://www.europarl.europa.eu/sides/getDoc.do?pubRef=-//EP//NONSGML+IM-PRESS +20100416IPR72928+0+DOC+PDF+V0//EN&language=DE>.

European Parliament (2012) 'EU Medicines, Environment And Food Safety Agencies Fail Budget Discharge Test', Press Release, 17 March. <http://www.europarl.europa. eu/news/en/news-room/content/20120327IPR41993/html/EU-medicines-environ ment-and-food-safety-agencies-fail-budget-discharge-test>.

European Voice (2014) 'Business as Usual is not an Option', 28 May.

Evans, P. B., Rueschemeyer, D., and Skocpol, T. (eds) (1985) *Bringing the State Back In* (Cambridge: Cambridge University Press).

Fabbrini, S. (2013) 'Intergovernmentalism and Its Limits: Assessing the European Union's Answer to the Euro Crisis', *Comparative Political Studies*, 20 (10): 1–27.

Fabry, M. (2010) *Recognizing States: International Society and the Establishment of New States Since 1776* (Oxford: Oxford University Press).

Falkner, G. (2002) 'EU Treaty Reform as a Three-level Process: Introduction', *Journal of European Public Policy*, 9 (1): 1–11.

Farrell, A. M. (2005) 'The Emergence of EU Governance in Public Health: The Case of Blood Policy and Regulation', in M. Steffen (ed.) *Health Governance in Europe: Issues, Challenges, and Theories* (London: Routledge).

Farrell, H. and Héritier, A. (2003) 'Formal and Informal Institutions Under Codecision : Continuous Constitution-Building in Europe', *Governance*, 16 (4): 577–600.

Fasone, C. (2012) 'Interparliamentary Cooperation and Democratic Representation in the European Union', in S. Kröger and D. Friedrich (eds) *The Challenge of Democratic Representation in the European Union* (Basingstoke: Palgrave Macmillan).

Ferran, E. (2004) *Building an EU Securities Market* (Cambridge: Cambridge University Press).

Fioretos, O. (2009) 'The Regulation of Transnational Corporate Identity in Europe', *Comparative Political Studies*, 42 (9): 1167–92.

Fletcher, M. (2003) 'EU Governance Techniques in the Creation of a Common European Policy on Immigration and Asylum', *European Public Law*, 9 (4): 533–62.

Fligstein, N. (2008) *Euroclash: The EU, European Identity, and the Future of Europe* (Oxford: Oxford University Press).

Fligstein, N. and McNichol, J. (1998) 'The Institutional Terrain of the European Union', in W. Sandholtz and A. Stone Sweet (eds) *European Integration and Supranational Governance* (Oxford: Oxford University Press), 59–91.

Føllesdal, A. and Hix, S. (2006) 'Why there is a Democratic Deficit in the EU: A Response to Majone and Moravcsik', *Journal of Common Market Studies*, 44 (3): 533–62.

Foucault, M. (1991) 'Governmentality', in G. Buchell, C. Gordon, and P. Miller (eds) *The Foucault Effect: Studies in Governmentality, with Two Lectures by and an Interview with Michel Foucault* (Chicago, IL: University of Chicago Press).

Fouilleux, E., De Maillard, J., and Smith, A. (2005) 'Technical or Political? The Working Groups of the EU Council of Ministers', *Journal of European Public Policy*, 12 (4): 609–23.

Frankel, J. A. and Rose, A. K. (1998) 'The Endogenity of the Optimum Currency Area Criteria', *The Economic Journal*, 108 (449): 1009–25.

Franzese Jr, R. J. (1999) 'Partially Independent Central Banks, Politically Responsive Governments, and Inflation', *American Journal of Political Science*, 43 (3): 681–706.

Gamble, A. (1988) *The Free Economy and the Strong State: The Politics of Thatcherism* (Basingstoke: Palgrave Macmillan).

Gamble, A. (2014) *A Crisis Without End? The Unravelling of Western Prosperity* (Basingstoke: Palgrave).

Garrett, G. (1995) 'The Politics of Legal Integration in the European Union', *International Organization*, 49, 171–81.

Garrett, G., and Weingast, B. R. (1991) *Ideas, Interests and Institutions: Constructing the EC's Internal Market* (University of California, Center for German and European Studies).

Genieys, W. (2008) *L'élite des politiques de l'État* (Paris: Presses de Sciences Po).

Genieys, W. (2010) *The New Custodians of the State: The Programmatic Elites in French Society* (New Brunswick, NJ: Transaction).

Genieys, W. (2011) *Sociologie Politique des Élites* (Paris: Armand Colin).

Geraats, P., Giavazzi, F., and Wyplosz, C. (2008) 'Monitoring the European Central Bank: Transparency and Governance' (London: Centre for European Policy Research).

Germond, B. and Smith, M. E. (2009) 'Re-thinking European Security Interests and the CSDP: Explaining the EU's Anti-piracy operation', *Contemporary Security Policy*, 30 (3): 573–93.

Giles, C. and Parker, G. (2011) 'Osborne Urges Eurozone to "get a grip"', *Financial Times*, 20 July.

GKV Spitzenverband (2007) 'Potsdamer Erklärung der Gesetzlichen Krankenversicherung. Erklärung anlässlich der gemeinsamen Konferenz von GKV und BMG "Die soziale Dimension im Binnenmarkt—Zukunftsperspektiven der Krankenversorgung in Europa"', 15/16 January. <http://www.aok-bv.de/imperia/md/aokbv/politik/europa/spik_potsdamererkl__rung_europakonferenz_15_160107.pdf> [accessed 31 March 2014].

Glencross, A. (2014) *The Politics of European Integration: Political Union or a House Divided?* (Oxford: Wiley).

Gocaj, L. and Meunier, S. (2013) 'Time Will Tell: The EFSF, the ESM, and the Euro Crisis', *Journal of European Integration*, 35 (1): 239–54.

Goebel, R. (2006) 'Court of Justice Oversight Over the European Central Bank: Delimiting the ECB's Constitutional Autonomy and Independence in the Olaf Judgment', *Fordham International Law Journal*, 29: 600–54.

Goetz, K. H. and Meyer-Sahling, J.-H. (2009) 'Political Time in the EU: Dimensions, Perspectives, Theories', *Journal of European Public Policy*, 16 (2): 180–201.

Goetze, S. and Rittberger, B. (2012) 'A Matter of Habit? The Sociological Foundations of Empowering the European Parliament', *Comparative European Politics*, 8 (1): 37–54.

Goldstein, J. and Keohane, R. O. (eds) (1993) *Ideas and Foreign Policy: Beliefs, Institutions, and Political Change* (Ithaca, New York: Cornell University Press).

Goldthorpe, J. (1987) 'Problems of Political Economy after the Postwar Period', in C. S. Maier (ed.) *Changing Boundaries of the Political: Essays on the Evolving Balance between State and Society, Public and Private in Europe* (Cambridge: Cambridge University Press).

Gough, J. (2004) 'Changing Scale as Changing Class Relations: Variety and Contradictions in the Politics of Scale', *Political Geography*, 18 (6): 669–96.

Gourevitch, P. (1986) *Politics in Hard Times: Comparative Responses to International Economic Crises* (Ithaca, NY: Cornell University Press).

Granger, M.-P. (2005) 'The Future of Europe: Judicial Interference and Preferences', *Comparative European Politics*, 3 (2): 155–79.

Green, C. (2009) 'An Intellectual History of Judicial Activism', *Emory Law Journal*, 58 (5): 1195–264.

Greer, S. L. (2013) 'Avoiding Another Directive: The Unstable Politics of European Union Cross-border Health Care Law', *Health Economics, Policy and Law*, 8 (4): 415–21.

Greer, S. L. and Rauscher, S. (2011) 'When Does Market-Making Make Markets? EU Health Services Policy at Work in the United Kingdom and Germany', *Journal of Common Market Studies*, 49 (4): 797–822.

Greve, M. F. and Jørgensen, K. E. (2002) 'Treaty Reform as Constitutional Politics—a Longitudinal View', *Journal of European Public Policy*, 9(1): 54–75.

Grimmel, A. (2010) 'Judicial Interpretation or Judicial Activism? The Legacy of Rationalism in the Studies of the European Court of Justice', *Centre for European Studies Working Paper Series*, 176.

Groen, A. and Christiansen, T. (2015) 'National Parliaments in the European Union: Conceptual Choices in the EU's Constitutional Debate', in C. Hefftler et al. (eds) *The Palgrave Handbook on National Parliaments and the European Union* (Basingstoke: Palgrave Macmillan).

Gros, D. and Piedrafita, S. (2014) 'Common Misconceptions About the European Parliament Elections', CEPS Commentary, 23 May. <http://www.ceps.be/book/common-misconceptions-about-european-parliamentary-elections>.

Grosche, G. and Puetter, U. (2008) 'Preparing the Economic and Financial Committee and the Economic Policy Committee for enlargement', *Journal of European Integration*, 30 (4): 529–45.

Guiraudon, V. (2001) 'European Integration and Migration policy: Vertical Policy-making as Venue-shopping', *Journal of Common Market Studies*, 38 (2): 251–71.

Haas, E. B. (1961) 'International Integration: the European and the Universal Process', *International Organization*, 15 (3): 366–392.

Haas, E. B. (1964) 'Technocracy, Pluralism, and the New Europe', in S. Graubard (ed.) *A New Europe?* (Boston: Houghton Mifflin).

Haas, E. B. (1968) *The Uniting of Europe: Politics, Social and Economic Forces, 1950–1957*, 2nd edn (Stanford, CA: Stanford University Press).

Haas, E. B. (1990) *When Knowledge Is Power* (Berkeley: University of California Press).

Haas, E. B. (2004) *The Uniting of Europe. Political, Social and Economic forces, 1950–1957* (Stanford, CA: Stanford University Press).

Habermas, J. (2011) 'Europe's Post-democratic Era', *Guardian*, 10 November.

Hagemann, S. and Høyland, B. (2008) 'Parties in the Council?', *Journal of European Public Policy*, 15 (8): 1205–21.

Hall, P. (2007) 'The Evolution of Varieties of Capitalism in Europe', in B. Hancké, M. Rhodes, and M. Thatcher (eds) *Beyond Varieties of Capitalism: Conflict, Contradictions, and Complementarities in the European Economy* (Oxford: Oxford University Press).

Hall, P. A. and Soskice, D. (2001) 'An Introduction to Varieties of Capitalism', in P. A. Hall and D. Soskice (eds) *Varieties of Capitalism: The Institutional Foundations of Comparative Advantage* (Oxford: Oxford University Press), 1–68.

Hameiri, S. (2013) 'Theorising Regions Through Changes in Statehood: Rethinking the Theory and Method of Comparative Regionalism', *Review of International Studies*, 39 (2): 313–35.

Hancher, L. and Sauter, W. (2010) 'One Step Beyond? From Sodemare to Docmorris: The EU's Freedom of Establishment Case Law Concerning Healthcare', *Common Market Law Review*, 47 (1): 117–46.

Hardie, I. and Howarth, D. (2013) *Market-Based Banking and the International Financial Crisis* (Oxford: Oxford University Press).

Hartley, T. (1996) 'The European Court, Judicial Objectivity and the Constitution of the European Union', *Law Quarterly Review*, 112: 95–109.

Harvey, D. (2007) *A Brief History of Neoliberalism* (Oxford: Oxford University Press).

Hatzopoulos, V. (2002) 'Killing National Health and Insurance Systems but Healing Patients? The European Market for Health Care Services after the Judgments of the ECJ in Vanbraekel and Peerbooms', *Common Market Law Review*, 39 (4): 683–729.

Hayes-Renshaw, F. and Wallace, H. (2006) *The Council of Ministers* (Basingstoke: Palgrave-Macmillan).

Hayward, J. (ed.) (2008) *Leaderless Europe* (Oxford: Oxford University Press).

Hegel, G. W. (1991) *The Philosophy of Right* (Cambridge: Cambridge University Press).

Heidenreich, M. (2009) 'The Open Method of Coordination: a Pathway to the Gradual Transformation of National Employment and Welfare Regimes?', in M. Heidenreich and J. Zeitlin (eds) *Changing European Employment and Welfare Regimes: The Influence of the Open Method of Coordination on National Reforms* (London: Routledge), 10–36.

Heijer, den M. (2011) *Europe and Extraterritorial Asylum*, PhD Leiden University, Leiden.

Heisenberg, D. and Richmond, A. (2002) 'Supranational Institution-building in the European Union: a Comparison of the European Court of Justice and the European Central Bank', *Journal of European Public Policy*, 9 (2): 201–18.

Helleiner, E., Pagliari, S., and Zimmerman, H. (2010) *Global Finance in Crisis* (London: Routledge).

Hennessy, A. (2008) 'Economic Interests and the Construction of a European Single Pension Market', *British Journal of Politics & International Relations*, 10 (1): 105–28.

Héritier, A. (1996) 'The Accomodation of Diversity in European policy-making and Its Outcomes: Regulatory Policy as a Patchwork', *Journal of European Public Policy*, 3 (2): 149–76.

Héritier, A. (1999) *Policy-Making and Diversity in Europe: Escape from Deadlock* (Cambridge: Cambridge University Press).

Héritier, A. (2007) *Explaining Institutional Change in Europe* (Oxford: Oxford University Press).

Héritier, A. and Rhodes, M. (2010) *New Modes of Governance in Europe: Governing in the Shadow of Hierarchy* (Basingstoke: Palgrave Macmillan).

Hirst, N. (2013) 'EU Summit to Focus on Digital Economy', *European Voice*, 17 October.

Hix, S. (2002) 'Constitutional Agenda-setting Through Discretion in Rule Interpretation: Why the European Parliament won at Amsterdam', *British Journal of Political Science*, 32 (2): 259–80.

Hix, S. (2008) 'Why the EU needs (Left–Right) Politics? Policy Reform and Accountability are Impossible without It', *Notre Europe Policy Paper*, 19.

Hix, S. and Høyland, B. (2011) *The Political System of the European Union*, 3rd edn (Basingstoke: Palgrave Macmillan).

Hix, S. and Høylund, B. (2013) 'Empowerment of the European Parliament', *Annual Review of Political Science*, 16: 171–89.

Hix, S., Kreppel, A., and Noury, A. (2003) 'The Party System in the European Parliament: Collusive or Competitive?', *Journal of Common Market Studies*, 41: 309–31.

Hix, S., Noury, A., and Roland, G. (2006) 'Dimensions of Politics in the European Parliament', *American Journal of Political Science*, 50 (2): 494–520.

Hobsbawm, E. (1975) *The Age of Capital 1848–1875* (London: Abacus).

Hobsbawm, E. (1987) *The Age of Empire 1875–1914* (London: Abacus).

Hodson, D. (2009) 'EMU and Political Union: What, if Anything, Have we Learned from the Euro's First Decade?', *Journal of European Public Policy*, 16 (4): 508–26.

Hodson, D. (2011a) *Governing the Euro Area in Good Times and Bad* (Oxford: Oxford University Press).

Hodson, D. (2011b) 'The Eurozone in 2010', *Journal of Common Market Studies Annual Review*, 49 (1): 331–50.

Hodson, D. (2012) 'The Eurozone in 2011', *Journal of Common Market Studies*, 50 (2): 178–94.

Hodson, D. (2013) 'The Little Engine That Wouldn't: Supranational Entrepreneurship and the Barroso Commission', *Journal of European Integration*, 35 (3): 301–14.

Hodson, D. and Maher, I. (2001) 'The Open Method as a New Mode of Governance: The Case of Soft Economic Policy Co-ordination' *Journal of Common Market Studies*, 39 (4): 719–46.

Hodson, D. and Puetter, U. (2013) 'The European Union and the Economic Crisis', in M. Cini and N. Pérez-Solórzano Borragán (eds) *European Union Politics*, 4th *edn* (Oxford: Oxford University Press), 367–79.

Hoffmann, S. (1966) 'Obstinate or Obsolete? The Fate of the Nation State and the Case of Western Europe', *Daedalus*, 95 (3): 862–915.

Hoffmann, S. (1982) 'Reflections on the Nation-State in Western Europe Today', *Journal of Common Market Studies*, 21 (1): 21–38.

Hoffmann, S. (1995) *The European Sisyphus: Essays on Europe, 1964–1994* (Boulder. CO: Westview).

Hoffmann, S. (2000) 'Towards a Common Foreign and Security Policy?', *Journal of Common Market Studies*, 38 (2): 189–98.

Hofmann, H. and Morini. A. (2012) 'Constitutional Aspects of the Pluralisation of the EU Executive through "Agentification"', *European Law Review*, 36: 419–43.

Holzinger, K. and Schimmelfennig, F. (2012) 'Differentiated Integration in the European Union: Many Concepts, Sparse Theory, Few Data', *Journal of European Public Policy*, 19 (2): 292–305.

Hood, C. (2013) *The Blame Game: Spin, Bureaucracy and Self-Preservation in Government* (Princeton, NJ: Princeton University Press).

Hooghe, L. (2005) 'Many Roads Lead To International Norms, But Few Via International Socialization: A Case Study of the European Commission', *International Organization*, 59 (4): 861–98.

Hooghe, L. (2012) 'Images of Europe: How Commission Officials Conceive Their Institution's Role', *Journal of Common Market Studies*, 50 (1): 87–111.

Hooghe, L. and Marks, G. (2008) 'A Postfunctionalist Theory of European Integration: From Permissive Consensus to Constraining Dissensus', *British Journal of Political Science*, 39: 1–23.

Horsley, T. (2012) 'Subsidiarity and the European Court of Justice: Missing Pieces in the Subsidiarity Jigsaw?', *Journal of Common Market Studies*, 50(2): 267–82.

Horsley, T. (2013) 'Reflections on the Role of the Court of Justice as the "Motor" of European Integration: Legal limits to Judicial Lawmaking', *Common Market Law Review*, 50(4): 931–64.

Hoskyns, C. (1996) *Integrating Gender: Women, Law and Politics in the European Union* (London: Verso).

House of Commons (2010) 'European Scrutiny Committee - Fifteenth Report'.

House of Lords (2011) 'Implementing the Stockholm Programme: home affairs. Report with Evidence', European Union Committee, 9th Report of Session 2010–2011. <http://www.publications.parliament.uk/pa/ld201011/ldselect/ldeucom/90/90.pdf> [accessed on 30 March 2014].

Howarth, D. and Loedel, P. (2005) *The European Central Bank, 2nd edn* (Basingstoke: Palgrave).

Howarth, D. and Quaglia, L. (2013a) 'Banking on Stability: The Political Economy of New Capital Requirements in the European Union', *Journal of European Integration*, 35 (3): 333–46.

Howarth, D. and Quaglia, L. (2013b) 'Banking Union as Holy Grail: Rebuilding the Single Market in Financial Services, Stabilizing Europe's Banks and "Completing" Economic and Monetary Union', *Journal of Common Market Studies*, 51 (1): 103–23.

Howarth, D. and Quaglia, L. (2014) 'The Steep Road to Banking Union: Constructing the European Union's New Recovery and Resolution Rules', *Journal of Common Market Studies*, 52 (1): 125–40.

Howorth, J. (2004) 'Discourse, ideas, and epistemic communities in European security and defence policy', *West European Politics*, 27 (2): 211–34.

Howorth, J. (2010) 'The Political and Security Committee: A Case Study in "Supranational Intergovernmentalism"', *Les Cahiers Européens de Sciences Po*, 1: 1–25.

Howorth, J. (2011) 'Decision-making in Security and Defence Policy: Towards Supranational Intergovernmentalism?', *KFG Working Paper Series*, 25.

Howorth, J. and Menon, A. (2009) 'Still Not Pushing Back: Why the European Union is Not Balancing the United States', *Journal of Conflict Resolution*, 53 (5): 727–44.

Hunt, J. (2007) 'The End of Judicial Constitutionalisation?', *Croatian Yearbook of European Law and Policy*, 3: 135–55.

Hunt, J. and Shaw, J. (2009) 'Fairy Tale of Luxembourg? Reflections on Law and Legal Scholarship in European Integration', in D. Phinnemore and A. Warleigh-Lack (eds) *Reflections on European Integration: 50 Years of the Treaty of Rome* (Basingstoke: Palgrave Macmillan).

Ikenberry, G. J. (1992) 'Salvaging the G-7', *Foreign Affairs*, 72: 132–9.

Incerti, M. (2014) 'Never Mind the Spitzenkandidaten: It's all about Politics', CEPS Commentary, 6 June 2014. <http://www.ceps.be/book/never-mind-spitzenkandidaten-it%E2%80%99s-all-about-politics>.

Issing, O. (1999) 'Europe: Common Money—Political Union?', Frankfurt, 20 September (Frankfurt am Main: ECB).

Itzcovich, G. (2012) 'Legal Order, Legal Pluralism, Fundamental Principles: Europe and its Law in Three Concepts', *European Law Journal*, 18: 358–84.

Jabko, N. (2006) *Playing the Market: A Political Strategy for Uniting Europe, 1985–2005* (Ithaca, NY: Cornell University Press).

Jachtenfuchs, M. (1997) 'Democracy and Governance in the European Union', *European Integration Online Papers*, 1 (2).

Jachtenfuchs, M. (2001) 'The Governance Approach to European Integration', *Journal of Common Market Studies*, 39 (2): 245–64.

Jachtenfuchs, M. (2005) 'The Monopoly of Legitimate Force: Denationalization, or Business as Usual?', in S. Leibfried and M. Zurn (eds) *Transformations of the State?* (Cambridge: Cambridge University Press).

Jacobs, F. (2014) 'EU Agencies and the European Parliament', in M. Everson, C. Monda, and E. Vos (eds) *European Agencies in Between Institutions and Member States* (Alphen aan den Rijn: Kluwer).

Jacobsson, K. (2004) 'Soft Regulation and the Subtle Transformation of States: the Case of EU Employment Policy', *Journal of European Social Policy*, 14 (4): 355–70.

Joint Statement (2012) Joint Statement of the European Parliament, the Council of the EU and the European Commission on Decentralised Agencies, 19 July, <http://europa.eu/agencies/documents/joint_statement_and_common_approach_2012_en.pdf>.

Judge, D. and Earnshaw, D. (2009) *The European Parliament*, 2nd edn (Basingstoke: Palgrave).

Juncker, J. C. (2014) 'A New Start for Europe: My Agenda for Jobs, Growth, Fairness and Democratic Change—Political Guidelines for the Next European Commission' (Brussels: European Commission).

Juncos, A. and Pomorska, K. (2006) 'Playing the Brussels Game: Strategic Socialisation in CFSP Council Working Groups', *European Integration online Papers*, 10 (11).

Juncos, A. and Pomorska, K. (2011) 'Invisible and Unaccountable? National Representatives and Council Officials in EU Foreign Policy', *Journal of European Public Policy*, 18 (8): 1096–114.

Juncos, A. and Reynolds, C. (2007) 'The Political and Security Committee: Governing in the Shadow', *European Foreign Affairs Review*, 12 (2): 127–47.

Jupille, J. (2004) *Procedural Politics: Issues, Influence, and Institutional Choice in the European Union* (New York: Cambridge University Press).

Kahler, M. and Lake, D. (2009) 'Economic Integration and Global Governance: Why So Little Supranationalism?', in W. Mattli and N. Woods (eds) *The Politics of Global Regulation* (Princeton, NJ: Princeton University Press).

Kaiser, W. (2007) *Christian Democracy and the Origins of European Union* (Cambridge: Cambridge University Press).

Kaiser, W. (2008) 'History meets Politics: Overcoming Interdisciplinary Volapük in Research on the EU', *Journal of European Public Policy*, 15 (2): 300–13.

Kaldor, M. (2003) 'The Idea of Global Civil Society', *International Affairs*, 73 (3): 583–93.

Kaldor, M. and Selchow, S. (2013) 'The "Bubbling Up" of Subterranean Politics in Europe', *Journal of Civil Society*, 9 (1): 78–99.

Kapstein, E. B. (1992) 'Between Power and Purpose: Central Bankers and the Politics of Regulatory Convergence', *International Organization*, 46 (1): 265–87.

Kassim, H. and Le Gales, P. (2010) 'Exploring Governance in a Multi-level Polity: A Policy Instruments Approach', *West European Politics*, 33 (1): 1–21.

Kassim, H., Peterson, J., Bauer, M. W., Connolly, S., Dehousse, R., Hooghe, L., and Thompson, A. (2013) *The European Commission of the Twenty First Century* (Oxford: Oxford University Press).

Katz, R. and Mair, P. (1995) 'Changing Models of Party Organization and Party Democracy: The Emergence of the Cartel Party', *Party Politics*, 1 (1): 5–28.

Katz, R. and Mair, P. (2009) 'The Cartel Party Thesis: A Restatement', *Perspectives on Politics*, 7 (4): 753–66.

Katzenstein, P. (ed.) (1997) *Tamed Power: Germany in Europe* (London: Cornell University Press).

Kaunert, C. (2010) 'Towards Supranational Governance in EU Counter-Terrorism', *Central European Journal of International Security & Security Studies*, 4 (1): 1–32.

Kaunert, C., Léonard, S., and Occhipinti, J. (2013) 'Agency Governance in the Area of Freedom, Security and Justice', *Perspectives on European Politics and Society*, 14 (3): 273–84.

Keating, D. (2013) 'Commission to Clarify State Aid Rules for Energy', *European Voice* (17 October): 5.

Keating, M. (2013) *Rescaling the European State: The Making of Territory and the Rise of the Meso* (Oxford: Oxford University Press).

Kelemen, D. (2002) 'The Politics of "Eurocratic" Structure and the New European Agencies', *West European Politics*, 25 (4): 93–118.

Kelemen, D. (2011) *Eurolegalism: The Transformation of Law and Regulation in the European Union* (Cambridge, MA: Harvard University Press).

Kelemen, R. D. and Majone, G. (2012) 'Managing Europeanization: the European Agencies', in J. Peterson and M. Shackleton (eds) *The Institutions of the European Union*, 3rd edn (Oxford: Oxford University Press).

Kelemen, R. D. and Schmidt, S. (2012) 'Introduction—the European Court of Justice and Legal Integration: Perpetual Momentum?', *Journal of European Public Policy*, 19 (1): 1–7.

Keohane, R. O. and Hoffmann, S. (1991) 'Institutional Change in Europe in the 1980s', in R. O. Keohane and S. Hoffmann (eds) *The New European Community: Decision-making and Institutional Change* (Boulder, CO: Westview Press), 1–39.

Kietz, D. and Maurer, A. (2007) 'The European Parliament in Treaty Reform: Predefining IGCs through Interinstitutional Agreements', *European Law Journal*, 13 (1): 20–46.

Kirchheimer, O. (1966) 'The Catch-All Party', in J. LaPalombara and M. Weiner (eds) *Political Parties and Political Development* (Princeton, NJ: Princeton University Press).

Kitschelt, H. (2000) 'Citizens, Politicians and Party Cartellization: Political Representation and State Failure in Post-Industrial Democracies', *European Journal of Political Research*, 37 (2): 149–79.

Kloka, M. (2013) 'Business as Usual? Negotiation Dynamics and Legislative Performance in the Council of the European Union after the Eastern Enlargement', unpublished PhD dissertation, Bremen International Graduate School of Social Sciences.

Kochenov, D. and Plender, R. (2012) 'EU Citizenship: From an Incipient Form to an Incipient Substance? The Discovery of the Treaty Text', *European Law Review*, 37 (4): 369–96.

Kohler, M. (2014) 'European Governance and the European Parliament: From Talking Shop to Legislative Powerhouse', *Journal of Common Market Studies*, 52 (3): 600–15.

Kohler-Koch, B. (2009) 'The Three Worlds of European Civil Society: What Role for Civil Society for What Kind of Europe?', *Policy and Society*, 28 (1): 47–57.

Kohler-Koch, B. and Rittberger, B. (2006) 'The "Governance Turn" in EU Studies', *Journal of Common Market Studies*, 44 (1): 27–49.

Kokott, J. and Sobotta, C. (2012) 'The Kadi Case–Constitutional Core Values and International Law–Finding the Balance?', *European Journal of International Law*, 23 (4): 1015–24.

König, T. (2008) 'Why Do Member States Empower the European Parliament?', *Journal of European Public Policy*, 15(2): 167–88.

Koopmans, T. (1996) 'Judicial Decision-making', in A. Campbell and M. Voyatsi (eds) *Legal Reasoning and Judicial Interpretation of European Law (Essays in Honour of Lord Mackenzie-Stuart)* (Michigan: Trenton Publishing).

Kostadinova, V. (2013) 'The European Commission and the Configuration of International European Union Border Controls: Direct and Indirect Contribution', *Journal of Common Market Studies*, 51 (2): 264–80.

Krajewski, M. (2010) 'Grenzüberschreitende Patientenmobilität in Europa zwischen negativer und positiver Integration der Gesundheitssysteme', *Europarecht*, 45 (2): 165–87.

Krastev, I. (2007) 'The Strange Death of the Liberal Consensus', *Journal of Democracy*, 18 (4): 56–63.

Krastev, I. (2012) 'A Fraying Union?', *Journal of Democracy*, 23 (4): 23–30.

Kratsa-Tsagaropoulou, R., Vidal-Quadras, A., and Rothe, M. (2009). Activity Report 1 May 2004 to 13 July 2009, 6th Parliamentary Term of the delegations to the Conciliation Committee, PE427.162v01-00. Available at <http://ec.europa.eu/codecision/statistics/index_en.htm> [accessed 4 June 2012].

Kreher, A. (1997) 'Agencies in the European Community—A Step Towards Administrative Integration in Europe', *Journal of European Public Policy*, 4 (2): 225–45.

Kriesi, H., Grande, E., Lachat, R., Dolezal, M., Bornshier, S., and Frey, T. (2008) *West European Politics in the Age of Globalization* (Cambridge: Cambridge University Press).

Krisch, N. (2008) 'The Open Architecture of European Human Rights Law', *Modern Law Review*, 17: 183–216.

Krouwel, A. (2012) *Party Transformations in European Democracies* (New York: State University of New York Press).

Kumm, M. (2006) 'Beyond Golf Clubs and the Judicialization of Politics: Why Europe has a Constitution Properly So Called', *The American Journal of Comparative Law*, 54: 505–30.

Kydland, F. E. and Prescott, E. C. (1977) 'Rules Rather than Discretion: The Inconsistency of Optimal Plans', *The Journal of Political Economy*, 85 (3): 473–91.

Labayle, M. (2013) 'The New Commission's Role in Freedom, Security and Justice in the Post-Lisbon Context. New Era or Missed Opportunity?', in M. Chang and J. Monar (eds) *The European Commission in the Post-Lisbon Era of Crises: Between Political Leadership and Policy Management* (Brussels: Peter Lang).

Lahr, J. (ed.) (2002) *The Diaries of Kenneth Tynan* (London: Bloomsbury).

Lascoumes, P. and Le Gales, P. (2007) 'Introduction: Understanding Public Policy through Its Instruments—From the Nature of Instruments to the Sociology of Public Policy Instrumentation', *Governance*, 20: 1–21.

Lash, S. and Urry, J. (1987) *The End of Organized Capitalism* (Cambridge: Polity).

Lasser, M. (2009) *Judicial Transformations: The Rights Revolution in the Courts of Europe* (Oxford: Oxford University Press).

Lavenex, S. (2010) 'Justice and Home Affairs, Communitarization with Hesitation', in H. Wallace, M. A. Pollack, and A. R. Young (eds) *Policy-Making in the European Union*, 6th edn (Oxford: Oxford University Press), 457–80.

Lavenex, S. and Wallace, W. (2005) 'Justice and Home Affairs', in H. Wallace, W. Wallace, and M. Pollack (eds) *Policy-Making in the European Union*, 5th edn (Oxford: Oxford Press University), 457–80.

Lavenex, S., Lehmkuhl, D., and Wichmann, N. (2009) 'Modes of External Governance: a Cross-National and Cross-Sectoral Comparison', *Journal of European Public Policy*, 16 (6): 813–33.

Le Galès, P. (2014) 'States in Europe: Uncaging Societies and the Limits to the Infrastructural Power', *Socio-Economic Review*, 12 (1): 131–52.

Leca, J. (2009) '"The Empire Strikes Back!" An Uncanny View of the European Union. Part II—Empire, Federation or What?', *Government and Opposition*, 45 (2): 208–93.

Lefevre, S. (2004) 'Interpretative Communications and the Implementation of Community Law at National Level', *European Law Review*, 29: 808–22.

Lefkofridi, Z. and Schmitter, P. C. (2014) 'Transcending or Descending? European Integration in Times of Crisis', *European Political Science Review*, First View article, 1–20.

Lenaerts, K. (2010) 'The Contribution of the European Court of Justice to the Area of Freedom, Security and Justice', *International and Comparative Law Quarterly*, 59 (2): 255–301.

Lenaerts, K. (2011) ' "Civis Europaeus Sum": From the Cross-border Link to the Status of Citizen of the Union', *Online Journal on the Free Movement of Workers in the European Union*, 3: 6–18.

Lenaerts, K. (2013) 'The Principle of Democracy in the Case Law of the European Court of Justice', *International and Comparative Law Quarterly*, 62 (2): 271–315.

Leuffen, D., Rittberger, B., and Schimmelfennig, F. (2012) *Differentiated Integration: Explaining Variation in the European Union* (Basingstoke: Palgrave Macmillan).

Levitt, B. and March, J. G. (1988) 'Organizational Learning', *Annual Review of Sociology*, 14: 319–40.

Lewis, J. (2005) 'The Janus Face of Brussels: Socialization and Everyday Decision Making in the European Union', *International Organization*, 59 (4): 937–71.

Lindberg, L. N. (1965) 'Decision Making and Integration in the European Community', *International Organization*, 19 (1): 56–80.

Lindberg, L. N. and Scheingold, S. A. (eds) (1970) *Regional Integration: Theory and Research* (Cambridge, MA: Harvard University Press).

Lipset, M. and Rokkan, S. (1990) [1967] 'Cleavage Structures, Party Systems and Voter Alignments', in P. Mair (ed.) *The West European Party System* (Oxford: Oxford University Press).

Lipset, M. and Rokkan, S. (1967) *Party Systems and Voter Alignments: Cross-National Perspectives* (New York: Free Press).

Lock, T. (2011) 'Walking on a Tightrope: The Draft ECHR Accession Agreement and the Autonomy of the EU Legal Order', *Common Market Law Review*, 48: 1025–54.

Lopatin, E. (2013) 'The Changing Position of the European Parliament on Irregular Migration and Asylum under Co-decision', *Journal of Common Market Studies*, 51 (4): 740–55.

Loughlin, J. (2009) 'The "Hybrid" State: Reconfiguring Territorial Governance in Western Europe', *Perspectives on European Politics and Society*, 10 (1): 51–68.

MacCormick, N. (1999) *Questioning Sovereignty: Law, State, and Nation in the European Commonwealth* (Oxford: Oxford University Press).

Maduro, L. M. P. (2010) 'How Constitutional can the European Union be? The Tension Between Intergovernmentalism and Constitutionalism in the European Union', New York University Jean Monnet Working Paper 5/04. Available at SSRN: <http://ssrn.com/abstract=1576145> or <http://dx.doi.org/10.2139/ssrn.1576145>.

Magnette, P. (2000) *L'Europe, L'État et la Démocratie: Le Souverain Apprivoisé* (Brussels: Complexe).

Maier, C. S. (1981) ' "Fictitious Bonds...of Wealth and Law": on the Theory and practice of Interest Representation', in S. Berger (ed.) *Organizing Interests in Western Europe: Pluralism, corporatism, and the transformation of politics* (Cambridge: Cambridge University Press).

Mair, P. (2007) 'Political Opposition and the European Union', *Government and Opposition*, 42 (1): 1–17.

Mair, P. (2008) 'The Challenge to Party Government', *West European Politics*, 31 (1–2): 211–34.

Majone, G. (1994) 'The Rise of the Regulatory State in Europe', *West European Politics*, 17 (3): 77–101.

Majone, G. (ed.) (1996) *Regulating Europe* (London: Routledge).

Majone, G. (2005) *Dilemmas of European Integration: The Ambiguities and Pitfalls of Integration by Stealth* (Oxford: Oxford University Press).

Majone, G. (2009) *Europe As the Would-be World Power: Europe at Fifty* (Cambridge: Cambridge University Press).

Malecki, M. (2012) 'Do ECJ Judges all Speak with the Same Voice? Evidence of Divergent Preferences from the Judgments of Chambers', *Journal of European Public Policy*, 19 (1): 59–75.

Malloch-Brown, M. (2011) *The Unfinished Global Revolution: The Limits of Nations and the Pursuit of a New Politics* (London: Allen Lane).

Malmström, Cecilia (2010) Speech at the European Day for Border Guards, 25 May, Warsaw.

Mancini, G. F. (1989) 'The Making of a Constitution for Europe', *Common Market Law Review*, 26 (4): 595–614.

Mancini, G. F. and Keeling, D. T. (1994a) 'Language, Culture and Politics in the Life of the European Court of Justice', *Columbia Journal of European Law*, 1: 397.

Mancini, G. F., and Keeling D. T. (1994b) 'Democracy and the European Court of Justice', *The Modern Law Review*, 57 (2): 175–90.

Mandel, E. (1967) 'International Capitalism and 'Supra-Nationality'', *Socialist Register*, 4: 27–41.

Manin, B. (1997) *The Principles of Representative Government* (Cambridge: Cambridge University Press).

Manzano, G. (2001) 'Is There any Value-Added in the ASEAN Surveillance Process?', *ASEAN Economic Bulletin*, 18 (1): 94–102.

Marks, G. and Steenbergen, M. R. (eds) (2004) *European Integration and Political Conflict* (Cambridge: Cambridge University Press).

Marks, G., Hooghe, L., and Blank, K. (1996) 'European Integration from the 1980s: State-Centric v. Multi-level Governance', *Journal of Common Market Studies*, 34 (3): 341–78.

Martinsen, D. S. (2005) 'Towards an Internal Health Market with the European Court', *West European Politics*, 28 (5): 1035–56.

Martinsen, D. S. and Falkner, G. (2011) 'Social Policy: Problem-Solving Gaps, Partial Exits, and Court-Decision Traps', in G. Falkner (ed.) *The EU's Decision Traps* (New York: Oxford University Press), 128–44.

Martinsen, D. S. and Vrangbaek, K. (2008) 'The Europeanization of Health Care Governance: Implementing the Market Imperatives of Europe', *Public Administration*, 86 (1): 169–84.

Mattli, W. and Stone Sweet, A. (2012) 'Regional Integration and the Evolution of the European Polity: On the Fiftieth Anniversary of the Journal of Common Market Studies', *Journal of Common Market Studies*, 50 (1): 1–17.

Mattli, W. and Slaughter, A. M. (1995) 'Law and Politics in the European Union: a Reply to Garrett', *International Organization*, 49: 183–90.

Mattli, W. and Slaughter, A. M. (1998) 'Revisiting the European Court of Justice', *International Organization*, 52 (1): 177–209.

Maurer, A., Kietz, D., and Völkel, C. (2005) 'Interinstitutional Agreements in the CFSP: Parliamentarisation Through the Back Door', *European Foreign Affairs Review*, 10 (2): 175–95.

Mayntz, R. (ed.) (2012) *Crisis and Control: Institutional Change in Financial Market Regulation* (Cologne: Max Planck Institute for the Study of Societies).

Mazower, M. (1998) *Dark Continent: Europe's Twentieth Century* (London: Vintage).

Mazower, M. (2012) *Governing the World: The History of an Idea* (London: Penguin).

McCown, M. (2003) 'The European Parliament before the Bench: ECJ Precedent and EP Litigation Strategies', *Journal of European Public Policy*, 10(6): 974–95.

McNamara, K. (1998) *The Currency of Ideas: Monetary Politics in the European Union* (Ithaca, NY: Cornell University Press).

Mearsheimer, J. (1995) 'Back to the Future? Instability in Europe After the Cold War', *International Security*, 15 (1): 5–56.

Mégle, A. (2014) 'The Origin of EU Authority In Criminal Matters: A Sociology of Legal Experts in European Policy-making', *Journal of European Public Policy*, 21: 230–47.

Mendes, J. (2011) *Participation in EU Rule-making: A Rights-based Approach* (New York: Oxford University Press).

Menon, A. (2008) *Europe: The State of the Union* (London: Atlantic Books).

Mény, Y. (2012) 'Conclusion: A Voyage to the Unknown', *Journal of Common Market Studies*, 50(1): 154–64.

Mérand, F. (2008) *European Defence Policy: Beyond the Nation-State* (Oxford: Oxford University Press).

Mersch, Y. (2013) 'The European Banking Union—First Steps on a Long March', Speech at the Finanzplatztag, 27 February.

Meyer, C. O. (2005) 'Convergence Towards a European Strategic Culture? A Constructivist Framework for Explaining Changing Norms', *European Journal of International Relations*, 11 (4): 523–49.

Middelaar, L. Van (2013) *The Passage to Europe: How a Continent Became a Union* (New Haven, CT: Yale University Press).

Migdal, J. (1988) *Strong Societies and Weak States: State-Society Relations and State Capabilities in the Third World* (Princeton, NJ: Princeton University Press).

Migdal, J. (1997) 'Studying the State', in M. I. Lichback and A. S. Zuckerman (eds) *Comparative Politics: Rationality, Culture and Structure* (Cambridge: Cambridge University Press).

Milward, A. (1992) *The European Rescue of the Nation State* (London: Routledge).

Ministry of Finance Japan (1999) 'Joint Press Statement: The Meeting Between Minister Strauss-Kahn and Minister Miyazawa', Frankfurt, January 15. <http://warp.ndl.go.jp/info:ndljp/pid/1022127/www.mof.go.jp/english/if/e1e065.htm>.

Monar, J. (2011) 'Deviations from and Alternatives to the Community Method in Justice and Home Affairs', in R. Dehousse (ed.) *The Community Method, Obstinate or Obsolete?* (Basingstoke: Palgrave).

Monar, J. (2013) 'Justice and Home Affairs', *Journal of Common Market Studies*, 51 (Annual Review): 124–38.

Monti, G. (2007) *EC Competition Law* (Cambridge: Cambridge University Press).

Morano-Foadi, S. and Andreadakis, S. (2011) 'Reflections on the Architecture of the EU after the Treaty of Lisbon: The European Judicial Approach to Fundamental Rights', *European Law Journal*, 17 (5): 595–610.

Moravcsik, A. (1991) 'Negotiating the Single European Act: National Interests and Conventional Statecraft in the European Community', *International Organization*, 45 (1): 19–56.

Moravcsik, A. (1993) 'Preferences and Power in the European Community: a liberal intergovernmentalist approach', *Journal of Common Market Studies*, 31 (4): 473–524.

Moravcsik, A. (1994) 'Why the European Union Strengthens the State: Domestic Politics and International Cooperation', Centre for European Studies Working Paper, #5, Harvard.

Moravcsik, A. (1997) 'Taking Preferences Seriously: A Liberal Theory of International Politics', *International Organization*, 51 (4): 513–53.

Moravcsik, A. (1998) *The Choice for Europe: Social Purpose and State Power from Messina to Maastricht* (Ithaca, NY: Cornell University Press).

Moravcsik, A. (1999a) 'A New Statecraft? Supranational Entrepreneurs and International Cooperation', *International Organization*, 53 (2): 267–306.

Moravcsik, A. (1999b) 'Is something rotten in the state of Denmark? Constructivism and European integration', *Journal of European Public Policy*, 6 (4): 669–81.

Moravcsik, A. (2002) 'In Defence of the 'Democratic Deficit': Reassessing Legitimacy in the European Union', *Journal of Common Market Studies*, 40 (4): 603–24.

Moravcsik, A. (2005) 'The European Constitutional Compromise and the neofunctionalist legacy', *Journal of Public Policy*, 12 (2): 349–86.

Moravcsik, A. (2006) 'What Can we Learn from the Collapse of the Constitutional Project?', *Politische Vierteljahresschrift*, 47 (2): 219–41.

Moravcsik, A. (2008) 'The European Constitutional Settlement', *World Economy*, 31 (1): 158–83.

Moravcsik, A. (2010) 'The Old Governance: Informal Institutions in the EU', New York University Workshop, 'Rule-Making in the EU and Global Governance', 5 May.

Moravcsik, A. (2012) 'Europe after the Crisis: How to Sustain a Common Currency', *Foreign Affairs*, 91 (3): 54–68.

Moravcsik, A. and Nicolaïdis, N. (1999) 'Explaining the Treaty of Amsterdam: Interests, Influence, Institutions', *Journal of Common Market Studies*, 37 (1): 59–85.

Moravcsik, A. and Schimmelfennig, F. (2009) 'Liberal Intergovernmentalism', in A. Wiener and T. Diez (eds) *European Integration Theory* (Oxford: Oxford University Press), 67–87.

Moschella, M., and Tsingou, E. (eds) (2013) *Great Expectations, Slow Transformations: Incremental Change in Financial Governance* (Colchester: ECPR Press).

Mügge, D. (2006) 'Reordering the Marketplace: Competition Politics in European Finance', *Journal of Common Market Studies*, 44 (5): 991–1022.

Mügge, D. (2010) *Widen the Market, Narrow the Competition: Banker Interests and the Making of a European Capital Market* (Colchester: ECPR Press).

Munchau, W. (2005) 'Barroso's Misguided Priorities', *Financial Times* (UK edn), 7 February, 17.

Murithi, T. (2008) 'The African Union's Evolving Role in Peace Operations: The African Union Mission in Burundi, the African Union Mission in Sudan and the African Union Mission in Somalia', *African Security Studies*, 17 (1): 69–82.

Musgrave, R. (1959) *The Theory of Public Finance: A Study of Public Economy* (New York: McGraw-Hill).

Naurin, D. and Rasmussen, A. (eds) (2011) 'Linking Inter- and Intra-institutional Change in the European Union', special issue, *West European Politics*, 34 (1): 1–17.

Neill, P. (1995) 'The European Court of Justice: A Case Study in Judicial Activism', European Policy Forum, Frankfurter Institut, August.

Nettl, J. (1968) 'The State as a Conceptual Variable', *World Politics*, 20 (4): 559–92.

Nic Shuibhne, N. (2009) 'A Court with a Court? Is it time to Rebuild the Court of Justice?', *European Law Review*, 34: 173–4.

Niemann, A. (2006) *Explaining Decisions in the European Union* (Cambridge: Cambridge University Press).

Niemann, A. (2006) 'Explaining Visa, Asylum and Immigration Policy Treaty revision: Insights from a Revised Neofunctionalist Framework', ConWEB Papers, No. 1/2006, 1–45.

Niemann, A. (2013) 'EU External Trade and the Treaty of Lisbon: A Revised Neofunctionalist Approach', *Journal of Contemporary European Research*, 9 (4): 633–58.

Niemann, A. and Huigens, J. (2011) 'The European Union's Role in the G8: a Principal-Agent Perspective', *Journal of European Public Policy*, 18 (3): 420–42.

Noël, E. (1994) 'A New Institutional Balance?', in R. Dehousse (ed.) *Europe After Maastricht: An Ever Closer Union?* (Munich: Law Books in Europe).

Norman, P. (2008) *Plumbers and Visionaries: Securities Settlement and Europe's Financial Market* (London: John Wiley & Sons).

Norman, P. and Barber, T. (1998) 'ECB, Bonn in Clash on Euro', *Financial Times*, 23 October.

Novak, S. (2013) 'The Silence of Ministers: Consensus and Blame Avoidance in the Council of the European Union', *Journal of Common Market Studies*, 51 (6): 1091–107.

Nugent, N. (1992) 'The Deepening and Widening of the European Community: Recent Progress, Maastricht and Beyond', *Journal of Common Market Studies*, 30 (3): 311–28.

Nugent, N. (2001) *The European Commission* (Basingstoke: Palgrave Macmillan).

Nyikos, S. A. (2006) 'Strategic Interaction among Courts within the Preliminary Reference Process – Stage 1: National Court Preemptive Opinions', *European Journal of Political Research*, 45 (4): 527–50.

Obholzer, L. and Reh, C. (2012) 'How to Negotiate Under Codecision in the EU', *CEPS Policy Brief*, 270, Brussels, <http://www.ceps.eu/book/how-negotiate-under-co-deci sion-eu-reforming-trilogues-and-first-reading-agreements>.

Obholzer, L., Frantescu, D., Hagemann, S., and Hix, S. (2012) 'Mid-Term Evaluation of the 2009–14 European Parliament: Legislative Activity and Decision-Making Dynamics', *CEPS Special Report*, 23 July, <http://www.ceps.be/book/mid-term-evaluation-2009-14-european-parliament-legislative-activity-and-decision-making-dynamics>.

Offe, C. (1985) *Disorganized Capitalism: Contemporary Transformations of Work and Politics* (Cambridge, MA: The MIT Press).

Offe, C. (1996) 'Bindings, Shackles, Breaks: On Self-Limitation Strategies', in C. Offe *Modernity and the State: East, West* (Cambridge, MA: The MIT Press).

Offe, C. (2013) 'Europe Entrapped', *European Law Journal*, 19 (5): 595–611.

Olson, M. (1982) *The Rise and Decline of Nations: Economic Growth, Stagflation and Social Rigidities* (New Haven, CT: Yale University Press).

Osland, Kari M. (2004) 'The EU Police Mission in Bosnia and Herzegovina', *International Peacekeeping*, 11 (3): 544–60.

Ost, D. (2005) *The Defeat of Solidarity: Anger and Politics in Postcommunist Europe* (Ithaca, NY: Cornell University Press).

Ost, F. (1990) 'Jupiter, Hercule, Hermès. Quel modèle pour un droit post-moderne?', *Le Journal des Procès*, 179: 14–20.

Padoa-Schioppa, T. (1999) 'EMU and Banking Supervision', Lecture at the London School of Economics, Financial Markets Group, 24 February.

Padoa-Schioppa, T. (2000) *The Road to Monetary Union in Europe: the Emperor, the Kings, and the Genies* (Oxford: Oxford University Press).

Papadopoulos, Y. (2013) *Democracy in Crisis? Politics, Governance and Policy* (Basingstoke: Palgrave Macmillan).

Pape, Robert A. (2005) 'Soft Balancing Against the United States', *International Security*, 30 (1): 7–45.

Parker, O. (2013) *Cosmopolitan Government in Europe: Citizens and Entrepreneurs in Postnational Politics* (London: Routledge).

Paul, T. V. (2005) 'Soft Balancing in the Age of U.S. Primacy', *International Security*, 30 (1): 46–71.

Peers, S. (2011) *EU Justice and Home Affairs Law* (Oxford: Oxford University Press).

Peers, S. (2013) 'Towards a New Form of EU Law? The Use of EU Institutions in Treaties Between Member States', *European Constitutional Law Review*, 9: 37–72.

Pescatore, P. (1983) 'The Doctrine of Direct Effect: An Infant Disease of Community Law', *European Law Review*, 8: 155–77.

Peters, G. (1992) 'Bureaucratic Politics and the Institutions of the European Community', in A. M. Sbragia (ed.) *Euro-Politics: Institutions and Policymaking in the New European Community* (Washington DC: Brookings Institution Press), 75–122.

Peterson, J. (1995) 'Decision-Making in the European Union: Towards a Framework for Analysis', *Journal of European Public Policy*, 2 (1): 69–93.

Peterson, J. (1999) 'The Santer Era: the European Commission in Normative, Historical and Theoretical Perspective', *Journal of European Public Policy*, 6 (1): 46–65.

Peterson, J. (2006) 'The College of Commissioners', in J. Peterson and M. Shackleton (eds) *The Institutions of the European Union*, 2nd edn (Oxford: Oxford University Press).

Peterson, J. (2008) 'Enlargement, Reform and the European Commission. Weathering a Perfect Storm?', *Journal of European Public Policy*, 15 (5): 761–80.

Peterson, J. (2012) 'The College of Commissioners', in J. Peterson and M. Shackleton (eds) *The Institutions of the European Union*, 3rd edn (Oxford: Oxford University Press).

Peterson, J. and Shackleton, M. (eds) (2012) *The Institutions of the European Union*, 3rd edn (Oxford: Oxford University Press).

Petkova, B. and Dumbrovsky, T. (2011) 'Structural Changes and Decision-making at the European Court of Justice after the Eastern Enlargement', Paper presented at the EUSA conference, Boston.

Pierson, P. (1996) 'The Path to European Integration: A Historical Institutionalist Perspective', *Comparative Political Studies*, 29 (2): 123–63.

Pierson, P. (2004) *Politics in Time: History, Institutions and Social Analysis* (Princeton, NJ: Princeton University Press).

Piris, J.-C. (2012) *The Future of Europe: Towards a Two-Speed EU?* (Cambridge: Cambridge University Press).

Pizzorno, A. (1981) 'Interests and Parties in Pluralism', in S. Berger (ed.) *Organizing Interests in Western Europe* (Cambridge: Cambridge University Press).

Plender, R. (1976) 'An Incipient Form of European Citizenship', in F. G. Jacobs (ed.) *European Law and the Individual* (Amsterdam: Elsevier).

Poggi, G. (1990) *The State: Its Nature, Development and Prospects* (Cambridge: Polity).

Pollack, M. A. (1999) 'Delegation, Agency and Agenda Setting in the Treaty of Amsterdam', *European Integration online Papers* (EIoP) 3(6).

Pollack, M. A. (2003) 'Control Mechanism or Deliberative Democracy: Two Images of Comitology', *Comparative Political Studies*, 36 (1/2): 125–55.

Pollack, M. A. (2003) *The Engines of European Integration Delegation, Agency, and Agenda Setting in the EU* (Oxford: Oxford University Press).

Pollak, J. and Slominski, P. (2009) 'Experimentalist but not Accountable Governance? The Role of Frontex in Managing the EU's External Borders', *West European Politics*, 32 (5): 904–24.

Pop, V. (2014) 'EU Leaders Decline to Endorse Juncker', *EU Observer*, 28 May 2014. <http://euobserver.com/eu-elections/124401>.

Popham, P. (2014) 'Jean-Claude Juncker: The Face of Federalism', *The Independent*, 6 June.

Posen, B. R. (2006) 'European Union Security and Defense Policy: A Response to Unipolarity?', *Security Studies*, 1/2: 149–86.

Posner, E. (2005) 'Sources of Institutional Change: The Supranational Origins of Europe's New Stock Markets', *World Politics*, 58: 1–40.

Posner, E. and Véron, N. (2010) 'The EU and Financial Regulation: Power Without Purpose?', *Journal of European Public Policy*, 17 (3): 400–15.

Prechal, S. (2013) Interview with Sachal Prechal—Part 2 Cooperation with National Judges, Embedding the Internal Market and Transparency at the CJEU, <http://europeanlawblog.eu/?p=2118>.

Puchala, D. (1971) 'Of Blind Men, Elephants and International Integration', *Journal of Common Market Studies*, 10 (3): 267–84.

Puetter, U. (2004) 'Governing Informally: The Role of the Eurogroup in EMU and the Stability and Growth Pact', *Journal of European Public Policy*, 11 (5): 854–70.

Puetter, U. (2006) *The Eurogroup: How a Secretive Circle of Finance Ministers Shapes European Economic Governance* (Manchester: Manchester University Press).

Puetter, U. (2011) 'Consolidating Europe's New Intergovernmentalism: European Council and Council Leadership in Economic Governance and CFSP under the Lisbon Treaty'. Paper presented at the UACES conference 'The Lisbon Treaty Evaluated', London, 31 January–1 February.

Puetter, U. (2012) 'Europe's Deliberative Intergovernmentalism—the Role of the Council and European Council in EU Economic Governance', *Journal of European Public Policy*, 19 (2): 161–78.

Puetter, U. (2014) *European Council and the Council. New Intergovernmentalism and Institutional Change* (Oxford: Oxford University Press).

Puntscher Riekmann, S. (2007) 'The Cocoon of Power: Democratic Implications of Interinstitutional Agreements', *European Law Journal*, 13 (1): 4–19.

Putnam, R. D. (1988) 'Diplomacy and Domestic Politics: The Logic of Two-level Games', *International Organization*, 42 (3): 427–60.

Quaglia, L. (2007) 'The Politics of Financial Service Regulation and Supervision Reform in the European Union', *European Journal of Political Research*, 46 (2): 269–90.

Quaglia, L. (2008) 'Committee Governance in the Financial Sector in the European Union', *Journal of European Integration*, 30 (3): 565–80.

Quaglia, L. (2009) 'Political Science and the Cinderellas of Economic and Monetary Union: Payments Services and Clearing and Settlement of Securities', *Journal of European Public Policy*, 16 (4): 623–39.

Quaglia, L. (2010a) 'Completing the Single Market in Financial Services: The Politics of Competing Advocacy Coalitions', *Journal of European Public Policy*, 17 (7): 1007–22.

Quaglia, L. (2010b) *Governing Financial Services in the European Union* (London: Routledge).

Radaelli, C. M. (2003) 'The Code of Conduct Against Harmful Tax Competition: Open Method of Coordination In Disguise?', *Public Administration*, 81 (3): 513–31.

Rasmussen, A. (2012) 'Twenty Years of Co-Decision Since Maastricht: Inter- and Intrainstitutional Implications', *Journal of European Integration*, 34 (7): 735–51.

Rasmussen, A. and Shackleton, M. (2005) 'The Scope for Action of the European Parliament Negotiators in the Legislative Process: Lessons of the Past and for the Future', paper presented at the 9th Biennial International Conference of the European Union Studies Association (EUSA), Austin, 31 March–2 April.

Rasmussen, H. (1986) *On Law and Policy in the European Court of Justice: A Comparative Study in Judicial Policymaking* (Dordrecht: Martinus Nijhoff).

Raube, K. (2012) 'The European External Action Service and the European Parliament', *The Hague Journal of Diplomacy*, 7: 65–80.

Raunio, T. (2012) 'The European Parliament', in E. Jones, A. Menon, and S. Weatherill (eds) *The Oxford Handbook of the European Union* (Oxford: Oxford University Press), 365–79.

Reh, C., Héritier, A., Bressanelli, E., and Koop, C. (2013) 'The Informal Politics of Legislation: Explaining Secluded Decision Making in the European Union', *Comparative Political Studies*, 46 (9): 1112–42.

References

Reus-Smit, C. (1999) *The Moral Purpose of the State: Culture, Social Identity and Institutional Rationality in International Relations* (Princeton, NJ: Princeton University Press).

Rhinard, M. (2010) *Framing Europe: the Policy Shaping Strategies of the European Commission* (Dordrecht: Republic of Letters Publishing).

Richardson, J. (2006) 'Policy-making in the EU: Interests, Ideas and Garbage Cans of Primeval Soup', in J. Richardson (ed.) *European Union; Power and Policy-Making* (Abingdon: Routledge).

Rijken, C. (2010) 'Re-Balancing Security and Justice: Protection of Fundamental Rights in Police and Judicial Cooperation in Criminal Matters', *Common Market Law Review*, 47: 1455–92.

Rijpma, J. (2014) 'Institutions and Agencies: Government and Governance after Lisbon', in D. Acosta and C. Murphy (eds) *EU Security and Justice Law; After Lisbon and Stockholm* (Oxford: Hart).

Ripoll Servent, A. (2012) 'Playing the Co-Decision Game? Rules' Changes and Institutional Adaptation at the LIBE Committee', *Journal of European Integration*, 34 (1): 55–73.

Ripoll Servent, A. (2013) 'Holding the European Parliament Responsible: Policy Shift in the Data Retention Directive from Consultation to Codecision', *Journal of European Public Policy*, 20 (7): 972–87.

Ripoll Servent, A. and Trauner, F. (2014) 'Do Supranational EU Institutions Make a Difference? EU Asylum Law Before and After "Communitarization"', *Journal of European Public Policy*, 21 (8): 1142–62.

Risse, T. and Kleine, M. (2010) 'Deliberation in Negotiations', *Journal of European Public Policy*, 17 (5): 708–26.

Rittberger, B. (2012) 'Institutionalizing Representative Democracy in the European Union: The Case of the European Parliament', *Journal of Common Market Studies*, 50 (1): 18–37.

Rittberger, B. and Schimmelfennig, F. (2006) 'Explaining the Constitutionalization of the European Union', *Journal of European Public Policy*, 13(8): 1148–67.

Rittberger, B. and Wonka, A. (2011) 'Introduction: Agency Governance in the European Union', *Journal of European Public Policy*, 18 (6): 780–9.

Roberts, A. (2010) *The Logic of Discipline: Global Capitalism and the Architecture of Government* (New York: Oxford University Press).

Rooduijn, M., de Lange, S., and van der Brug, W. (2012) 'A Populist Zeitgeist? Programmatic Contagion by Populist Parties in Western Europe', *Party Politics*, 20 (4): 563–75.

Rosamond, B. (1999) 'Discourses of Globalization and the Social Construction of European Identities', *Journal of European Public Policy*, 6 (4): 652–68.

Rosamond, B. (2007) 'The Political Sciences of European Integration: Disciplinary History and EU Studies', in K. E. Jørgensen, M. Pollack, and B. Rosamond (eds) *Handbook of European Union Politics* (London: Sage), 7–30.

Rosamond, B. (2013) 'Theorizing the European Union After Integration Theory', in M. Cini and N. Pérez-Solórzano Borragan (eds) *European Union Politics*, 4th edn (Oxford: Oxford University Press).

Ross, G. (1995) *Jacques Delors and European Integration* (Oxford: Polity).

Ross, M. G. and Borgmann-Prebil, Y. (2010) *Promoting Solidarity in the European Union* (Oxford: Oxford University Press).

Röttinger, M. (2010) 'Interinstitutionelle Vereinbarungen und Geschäftsordnungen als Gratwanderung zwischen praeter und contra Primärrecht', in D. Kietz, P. Slominski, A. Maurer, and S. Puntscher Riekmann (eds) *Interinstitutionelle Vereinbarungen in der Europäischen Union; Wegbereiter der Verfassungsentwicklung* (Baden-Baden: Nomos), 297–311.

Ruiter, R. de and Neuhold, C. (2012) 'The Winner Takes it all? The Implications of the Lisbon Treaty for the EP's Legislative Role in Co-Decision', in F. Laursen (ed.) *The EU's Lisbon Treaty. Institutional Choices and Implementation* (Farnham, Surrey: Ashgate), 103–18.

Runciman, D. (2006) *The Politics of Good Intentions: History, Fear and Hypocrisy in the New World Order* (Oxford: Princeton University Press).

Ryner, M. (2012) 'Financial Crisis, Orthodoxy and Heterodoxy in the Production of Knowledge about the EU', *Millennium: Journal of International Studies*, 40 (3): 647–73.

Sabatier, P. and Jenkins-Smith, H. (eds) (1993) *Policy Change and Learning: An Advocacy Coalition Approach* (Boulder, CO: Westview Press).

Sabel, C. F. and Gerstenberg, O. (2010) 'Constitutionalising an Overlapping Consensus: the ECJ and the Emergence of a Coordinate Constitutional Order', *European Law Journal*, 16: 511–50.

Sabel, C. F. and Simon, W. H. (2003) 'Destabilization Rights: How Public Law Litigation Succeeds', *Harvard Law Review*, 117: 1016.

Sabel, C. F. and Zeitlin, J. (2008) 'Learning from Difference: The New Architecture of Experimentalist Governance in the EU', *European Law Journal*, 14 (3): 271–327.

Sack, D. (2012) 'Europeanization Through Law, Compliance, and Party Differences— The ECJ's 'Rüffert' Judgment (C-346/06) and Amendments to Public Procurement Laws in German Federal States', *Journal of European Integration*, 34 (3): 241–60.

Sandholtz, W. (1998) 'The Emergence of a Supranational Telecommunications Regime. European Integration and Supranational Governance', in W. Sandholtz and A. Stone Sweet (eds) *European Integration and Supranational Governance* (Oxford: Oxford University Press), 134–64.

Sandholtz, W. and Stone Sweet, A. (1997) 'European Integration and Supranational Governance', *Journal of European Public Policy*, 4 (3): 297–317.

Sandholtz, W. and Stone Sweet, A. (eds) (1998) *European Integration and Supranational Governance* (Oxford: Oxford University Press).

Sandholtz, W. and Stone Sweet, A. (2012) 'New-Functionalism and Supranational Governance', in E. Jones, A. Menon, and S. Weatherill (eds) *Oxford Handbook on the European Union* (Oxford: Oxford University Press), 18–33.

Saurugger, S. and Terpan, F. (2014) 'La cour de justice au cœur de la gouvernance européenne', *Pouvoirs*, 149: 59–75.

Sauter, W. (2009) 'The Proposed Patients' Rights Directive and the Reform of (Cross-Border) Healthcare in the European Union', *Legal Issues of Economic Integration*, 36 (2): 109–31.

Sbragia, A. (1994) 'From "Nation-State" to "Member State": The Evolution of the European Community', in P. Lutzeler (ed.) *Europe After Maastricht: American and European Perspectives* (Oxford: Berghahn Books).

Scharpf, F. (1987) *Crisis and Choice in European Social Democracy* (Ithaca, NY: Cornell University Press).

Scharpf, F. (1999) *Governing in Europe: Effective and Democratic?* (Oxford: Oxford University Press).

Scharpf, F. (2009) 'Legitimacy in the Multilevel European Polity', *European Political Science Review*, 1(2): 173–204.

Scharpf, F. (2011) 'The JDT Model: Context and Extensions', in G. Falkner (ed.) *The EU's Decision Traps* (New York: Oxford University Press).

Scharpf, F. (2012) 'Perpetual Momentum: Directed and Unconstrained?', *Journal of European Public Policy*, 19 (1): 127–39.

Schimmelfennig, F. (2001) 'The Community Trap. Liberal Norms, Rhetorical Action, and the Eastern Enlargement of the European Union', *International Organization*, 55 (1): 47–80.

Schimmelfennig, F. (2014) 'European Integration in the Euro Crisis: The Limits of Postfunctionalism', *Journal of European Integration*, 36 (3): 321–37.

Schimmelfennig, F. and Sedelmeier, U. (eds) (2005) *The Europeanization of Central and Eastern Europe* (Ithaca, NY: Cornell University Press).

Schmidt, S. K. (2000) 'Only an Agenda Setter? The European Commission's Power over the Council of Ministers', *European Union Politics*, 1 (1): 37–61.

Schmidt, S. K. (2004) 'The European Commission's Powers in Shaping European Policies', in D. G. Dimitrakopoulos (ed.) *The Changing European Commission* (Manchester: Manchester University Press).

Schmidt, S. K. (2011a) 'Law-Making in the Shadow of Judicial Politics', in R. Dehousse (ed.) *The 'Community Method': Obstinate or Obsolete?* (Basingstoke: Palgrave Macmillan).

Schmidt, S. K. (2011b) 'Overcoming the Joint-Decision Trap in Single-Market Legislation: The Interplay between Judicial and Legislative Politics', in G. Falkner (ed.) *The EU's Decision Traps* (New York: Oxford University Press).

Schmidt, V. (1996) *From State to Market? The Transformation of French Business and Government* (Cambridge: Cambridge University Press).

Schmidt, V. (2006) *Democracy in Europe: The EU and National Polities* (Oxford: Oxford University Press).

Schmidt, V. (2009) 'European Political Economy: Labour Out, State Back In, Firm to the Fore', in K. Goetz, P. Mair, and G. Smith (eds) *European Politics: Pasts, Presents and Futures* (London: Routledge).

Schmitter, P. C. (1971) 'A Revised Theory of Regional Integration', in L. N. Lindberg and S. A. Scheingold (eds) *Regional Integration: Theory and Research* (Cambridge, MA: Harvard University Press), 232–64.

Schmitter, P. C. (1974) 'Still the Century of Corporatism?', *The Review of Politics*, 36 (1): 85–131.

Schmitter, P. C. (2004) 'Neo-Neofunctionalism', in T. Diez, and A. Wiener (eds) *European Integration Theory* (Oxford: Oxford University Press), 45–75.

Schmitter, P. C. (2008) 'The Changing Politics of Organized Interests', *West European Politics*, 31 (1–2): 195–210.

Schoenmaker, D. (2012) 'Banking union: Where We're Going Wrong', in T. Beck (ed.) *Banking Union for Europe: Risks and Challenges* (London: CEPR), 95–102.

Schoenmaker, D. (2013) *Governance of International Banking* (Oxford: Oxford University Press).

Schoenmaker, D. and Wagner, W. (2011) 'The Impact of Cross-Border Banking on Financial Stability', Duisenberg School of Finance-Tinbergen Institute Discussion Paper T1-054/DSF 18.

Scholten, M. (2010) 'What if the European Parliament says "No"?: The Strength of the European Parliament's Discharge Power', Utrecht University School of Law Working Paper.

Schout, A. (2009) 'Organizational Learning in the EU's Multi-level Governance System', *Journal of European Public Policy*, 16 (8): 1124–44.

Schout, A. and Wolff, S. (2011) 'The "Paradox of Lisbon": Supranationalism-Intergovernmentalism as an Administrative Concept', in F. Laursen (ed.) *The EU's Lisbon Treaty* (Aldershot: Ashgate).

Schulte, B. (2009) 'Pflegepolitik im Wandel: Europäische Perspektiven'. Vortrag auf der Diskussionsverantstaltung 'Pflegepolitik im Wandel' der Gesellschaft für Sozialen Fortschritt Köln und des Deutschen Zentrums für Altersfragen Berlin, 6 May. <http://www.sozialerfortschritt.de/wp-content/uploads/2009/05/Schulte_09_05_06.pdf> [accessed 31 March 2014].

Schulz, M. (2012) Inaugural speech by Martin Schulz following his election as President of the European Parliament, 17 January 2012, <http://www.europarl.europa.eu/former_ep_presidents/president-schulz/en/press/press_release_speeches/speeches/sp-2012/sp-2012-january/html/inaugural-speech-by-martin-schulz-following-his-election-as-president-of-the-european-parliament> [accessed 12 February 2015].

Scott, J. (2009) 'REACH: Combining Harmonisation with Dynamism in the Regulation of Chemicals', in J. Scott (ed.) *Environmental Protection: European Law and Governance* (Oxford: Oxford University Press).

Scott, J. and Trubek, D. M. (2002) 'Mind The Gap: Law and New Approaches to Governance in the European Union', *European Law Journal*, 8(1): 1–18.

Scottish Nationalist Party (2014) *Scotland's Future—Your Guide to an Independent Scotland* (Edinburgh: The Scottish Government).

Sebag, G. (2012) 'New President Schulz calls for EP Seat at Summit Table', *Europolitics*, 17 January, <www.europolitics.info/new-president-schulz-calls-for-ep-seat-at-summit-table-art323479-32.html>.

Shackleton, M. (2012) 'The European Parliament', in J. Peterson and M. Shackleton (eds) *The Institutions of the European Union*, 3rd edn (Oxford: Oxford University Press), 124–47.

Shaw, J. and More, G. (1995) *The New Legal Dynamics of European Union* (Oxford: Clarendon Press).

Short, P. (2013) *Mitterrand: A Study in Ambiguity* (London: Bodley Head).

Slominski, P. (2013) 'The Power of Legal Norms in the EU's External Border Control', *International Migration*, 51 (6): 41–53.

Smith, M. E. (1998) 'Rules, Transgovernmentalism, and the Expansion of European Political Cooperation', in W. Sandholtz and A. Stone Sweet (eds) *European Integration and Supranational Governance* (Oxford: Oxford University Press), 304–44.

Smith, M. E. (2001) 'The Quest for Coherence: Institutional Dilemmas of External Action from Maastricht to Amsterdam', in A. Stone Sweet, W. Sandholtz, and N. Fligstein (eds) *The Institutionalization of Europe* (Oxford: Oxford University Press), 171–93.

Smith, M. E. (2003) *Europe's Foreign and Security Policy: The Institutionalization of Cooperation* (Cambridge: Cambridge University Press).

Smith, M. E. (2011) 'A Liberal Grand Strategy in a Realist World? Power, Purpose, and the EU's Changing Global Role', *Journal of European Public Policy*, 18 (2): 144–63.

Smith, M. E. (2013) 'The European External Action Service and the Security-Development Nexus: Organising for Effectiveness or Incoherence?', *Journal of European Public Policy*, 20 (9): 1299–315.

Smith, M. E. (2014) 'The Case for an EU Maritime Capability as a Priority for the CSDP', paper prepared for delivery at the CSDP Strategy Workshop, Maastricht University (31 January).

Solana, J. (2003) *A Secure Europe in a Better World: European Security Strategy* (Brussels: EU Institute for Security Studies).

Solanke, I. (2011) 'Stop the ECJ? An Empirical Analysis of Activism at the Court', *European Law Journal*, 17: 764–84.

Spaventa, E. (2007) *Free Movement of Persons in the EU: Barriers to Movement in their Constitutional Context* (The Hague: Kluwer).

Stacey, J. and Rittberger, B. (2003) 'Dynamics of Formal and Informal Institutional Change in the EU', *Journal of European Public Policy*, 10 (6): 858–83.

Stark, J. (2008) 'Does the Euro Area Need an Economic Government?', statement delivered at the HEC European Executive Campus, Brussels, 22 January.

Stasavage, D. (2007) 'Polarization and Publicity: Rethinking the Benefits of Deliberative Democracy', *Journal of Politics*, 69 (1): 59–72.

Stein, E. (1981) 'Lawyers, Judges, and the Making of a Transnational Constitution', *American Journal of International Law*, 75: 1–27.

Stoker, G. (1995) 'Introduction', in G. Stoker and D. Marsh (eds) *Theory and Methods in Political Science* (Basingstoke: Macmillan).

Stokes, S. C. (1999) 'Political Parties and Democracy', *Annual Review of Political Science*, 2: 243–67.

Stone Sweet, A. (2004) *The Judicial Construction of Europe* (Oxford: Oxford University Press).

Stone Sweet, A. (2010) 'The European Court of Justice and the Judicialization of EU governance', *Living Reviews in EU Governance*, available at <http://europeangovernance.livingreviews.org/Articles/lreg-2010-2/> [accessed 13 July 2014].

Stone Sweet, A. and Caporaso, J. A. (1998) 'From Free Trade to Supranational Polity: The European Court and Integration', in W. Sandholtz and A. Stone Sweet (eds) *European Integration and Supranational Governance* (Oxford: Oxford University Press), 92–133.

Stone Sweet, A. S. and Sandholtz, W. (eds) (1998) *European Integration and Supranational Governance* (New York: Oxford University Press).

Stone Sweet, A., Sandholtz, W., and Fligstein, N. (eds) (2001) *The Institutionalization of Europe* (Oxford: Oxford University Press).

Stone Sweet, A., Sandholtz, W., and Fligstein, N. (2001) 'The Institutionalization of European Space', in A. Stone Sweet, W. Sandholtz, and N. Fligstein (eds) (2001) *The Institutionalization of Europe* (Oxford: Oxford University Press), 1–28.

Stone Sweet, A. and Stranz, K. (2012) 'Rights Adjudication and Constitutional Pluralism in Germany and Europe', *Journal of European Public Policy*, 19 (1): 92–108.

Story, J. and Walter, I. (1997) *Political Economy of Financial Integration in Europe: The Battle of the System* (Manchester: Manchester University Press).

Strange, S. (1997) *Casino Capitalism* (Manchester: Manchester University Press).

Streeck, W. (2009) *Re-Forming Capitalism: Institutional Change in the Germany Political Economy* (Oxford: Oxford University Press).

Streeck, W. (2011) 'A Plan for Growth?', The Current Moment, 9 September, available at: <http://thecurrentmoment.wordpress.com/2011/09/07/a-plan-for-growth/>.

Streeck, W. (2014) 'The SPD under Merkel', The Current Moment, 2 June, available at: <http://thecurrentmoment.wordpress.com/2014/06/02/the-spd-under-merkel/>.

Streeck, W. (2014) *Buying Time: The Delayed Crisis of Democratic Capitalism* (London: Verso).

Suvarierol, S. (2011) 'Everyday Cosmopolitanism in the European Commission', *Journal of European Public Policy*, 18 (2): 181–200.

Taggart, P. and Szcerbiak, A. (2013) 'Coming in from the Cold? Euroscepticism, Government Participation and Party Positions on Europe', *Journal of Common Market Studies*, 51 (1): 17–37.

Tallberg, J. (2000) 'The Anatomy of Autonomy: An Institutional Account of Variation in Supranational Influence', *Journal of Common Market Studies*, 38 (5): 843–64.

Tallberg, J. (2004) *European Governance & Supranational Institutions: Making States Comply* (London: Routledge).

Taylor, S. (2010) 'Reformist at the Centre. Barroso II: A Guide to the New European Commission', *European Voice*, Brussels.

Tilly, C. (1985) 'War Making and State Making as Organized Crime', in Evans et al. (eds) *Bringing the State Back In* (Cambridge: Cambridge University Press), 169–91.

Thatcher, M. (2011) 'The Creation of European Regulatory Agencies and Its Limits: a Comparative Analysis of European Delegation', *Journal of European Public Policy*, 18 (6): 790–809.

Thelen, K. (2004) *How Institutions Evolve: The Political Economy of Skills in Germany, Britain, the United States and Japan* (Cambridge: Cambridge University Press).

Thomson, R. (2008) 'National Actors In International Organizations: The Case of the European Commission', *Comparative Political Studies*, 41 (2): 169–92.

Thomson, R. (2011) *Resolving Controversy in the European Union: Legislative Decision-Making Before and After Enlargement* (Cambridge: Cambridge University Press).

Thym, D. (2011) 'Holding Europe's CFSP/CSDP Executive to Account in the Age of the Lisbon Treaty', *Documento de Trabajo Serie Unión Europea*, 53. Available at: <http://www.idee.ceu.es/Portals/0/Publicaciones/Holding-Europes-CFSP-CSDP-Executive-to-Account-in-the-Age-of-the-Lisbon-Treaty.pdf>.

Tindemans, L. (1976) 'European Union', *Bulletin of the European Communities*, Supplement 1/76 (Brussels: European Commission).

Tömmel, I. (2013) 'The Presidents of the European Commission: Transactional or Transforming Leaders?', *Journal of Common Market Studies*, 51 (4): 789–805.

Trauner, F. and Ripoll Servent, A. (eds) (2014) *Policy Change in the Area of Freedom, Security and Justice: How EU Institutions Matter* (London: Routledge).

Trauner, F. and Wolff, S. (2014) 'The Negotiation and Contestation of EU Migration Policy Instruments: A Research Framework', *European Journal of Migration and Law*, 16 (1): 1–17.

Traynor, I. (2014) 'Jean-Claude Juncker: What is the Trouble with Britain's Bogeyman?', *Guardian*, 20 June, <http://www.theguardian.com/world/2014/jun/20/juncker-mer kel-cameron-britain-eu-european-commission>.

Trichet, J. C. (2004a) 'European Priorities: an ECB Perspective', European Institute, Washington, 23 April.

Trichet, J. C. (2004b) 'European Identity', Maastricht, 10 September.

Trichet, J. C. (2006a) 'Press Conference', 6 June (Frankfurt am Main: ECB).

Trichet, J. C. (2006b) 'Interview with *Yediot Ahronot* conducted by Sefy Hendler', 31 March (Frankfurt am Main: ECB).

Trichet, J. C. (2008) 'Address at the Ceremony to Mark the 10th Anniversary of the European Central Bank and the European System of Central Banks', 2 June (Frankfurt am Main: ECB).

Trichet, J. C. (2009) 'Keynote Address by Jean-Claude Trichet, President of the ECB at the Committee of European Securities Regulators (CESR)', Paris, 23 February (Frankfurt am Main: ECB).

Trichet, J. C. (2010a) 'Interview with *Le Point*', 17 March (Frankfurt am Main: ECB).

Trichet, J. C. (2010b) 'Press Conference', 19 June (Frankfurt am Main: ECB).

Trichet, J. C. (2010c) 'Press Conference', 4 May (Frankfurt am Main: ECB).

Trichet, J. C. (2011a) 'Competitiveness and the smooth functioning of EMU', Lecture at the University of Liège, Liège, 23 February (Frankfurt am Main: ECB).

Trichet, J. C. (2011b) 'Reforming EMU—Time for Bold Decisions', Frankfurt, 18 March (Frankfurt am Main: ECB).

Trichet, J. C. (2011c) 'Building Europe, Building Institutions', Aachen, 2 June (Frankfurt am Main: ECB).

Trichet, J. C. (2011d) 'Interview with *Die Welt* conducted by Jan Dams and Martin Greive', 7 October 2011 (Frankfurt am Main: ECB).

Tridimas, T. (2006) *The General Principles of EU Law* (Oxford: Oxford University Press).

Trubek, D. M. and Mosher, J. S. (2003) 'New Governance, Employment Policy, and the European Social Model', in J. Zeitlin and D. M. Trubek (eds) *Governing Work and Welfare in a New Economy: European and American Experiments* (Oxford: Oxford University Press), 33–58.

Uçarer, E. M. (2013) 'Area of Freedom, Security, and Justice', in M. Cini and N. Perez-Solorzano Barragán (eds) *European Union Politics*, 4th edn (Oxford: Oxford University Press), 281–95.

Usherwood, S. and Startin, N. (2013) 'Euroscepticism as a Persistent Phenomenon', *Journal of Common Market Studies*, 51 (1): 1–16.

Van Apeldoorn, B. (2002) *Transnational Capitalism and the Struggle over European Integration* (London: Routledge).

Van Boetzelaer, K. and Princen, S. (2012) 'The Quest for Co-ordination in European Regulatory Networks', *Journal of European Public Policy*, 50 (5): 819–36.

Van Gerven, W. (2005) *The European Union: a Polity of States and Peoples* (Stanford: Stanford University Press).

Van Middelaar, L. (2013) *The Passage to Europe: How A Continent Became A Union* (London: Yale University Press).

Van Rompuy, H. (2010) 'The Challenges for Europe in A Changing World'. Speech delivered at the College of Europe, European Council press release PCE 34/10, Bruges, 25 February.

Van Rompuy, H. (2012) 'Towards A Genuine Economic and Monetary Union. Report by the President of the European Council' (Brussels: European Council).

Verdun, A. (1999) 'The role of the Delors Committee in the creation of EMU: an Epistemic Community?', *Journal of European Public Policy*, 66 (2): 308–28.

Veron, N. and Wolff, G. (2012) 'From Supervision to Resolution: Next Steps on the Road to European Banking Union', 19 February. <www.bruegel.org/download/parent/771-from-supervision-to-resolution-next-steps-on-the-road-to-european-banking-union/file/1646-from-supervision-to-resolution-next-steps-on-the-road-to-european-banking-union/> [accessed 12 February 2015].

Von Bogdandy, A., Kottmann, M., Antpoehler, C., Dickschen, J., Hentrei, S., and Smrkolj, M. A. (2012) 'Reverse Solange—Protecting the Essence of Fundamental Rights against EU Member States', *Common Market Law Review*, 49 (2): 489–519.

Vos, E. (2014) 'European Agencies and the Composite EU Executive', in M. Everson, C. Monda, and E. Vos (eds) *European Agencies in Between Institutions and Member States* (The Hague: Kluwer).

VoteWatch Europe (2012) Agreeing to Disagree: The Voting Records of the Member States in the Council since 2009, Annual Report Brussels: VoteWatch Europe, July. Available at: <www.votewatch.eu/blog/wp-content/uploads/2012/07/votewatch-annual-report-july-2012-final-7-july.pdf>. [accessed 6 August 2014].

VoteWatch.EU (2011) 'Voting in the 2009-2014 European Parliament: How do MEPs Vote after Lisbon?', Third Report. <www.votewatch.eu/static/research.php> [accessed 12 June 2012].

Walker, N. (2002) 'The Idea of Constitutional Pluralism', *Modern Law Review*, 64: 317–59.

Walker, N. (2008) 'Beyond Boundary Disputes and Basic Grids: Mapping the Global Disorder of Normative Orders', *International Journal of Constitutional Law*, 6: 373–96.

Walker, N., Shaw, J., and Tierney, S. (2011) *Europe's Constitutional Mosaic* (Oxford: Hart).

Wall, S. (2008) *A Stranger in Europe: Britain and the EU from Thatcher to Blair* (Oxford: Oxford University Press).

Wallace, H. (2002) 'The Council: An Institutional Chameleon?', *Governance*, 15(3): 325–44.

Wallace, H. (2010) 'An Institutional Anatomy and Five Policy Modes', in H. Wallace, M. Pollack, and A. Young (eds) *Policy-Making in the European Union* (Oxford: Oxford University Press), 69–104.

Wallace, H., Wallace, W., and Webb, C. (eds) (1977) *Policy-making in the European Community* (London: John Wiley & Sons).

Wallace, W. (1977) 'Walking Backwards Towards Unity', in H. Wallace, W. Wallace, and C. Webb (eds) *Policy-making in the European Communities* (Chichester: John Wiley & Sons), 301–23.

Wallace, W. and Allen, D. (1977) 'Political Cooperation: Procedure as Substitute for Policy', in H. Wallace, W. Wallace, and C. Webb (eds) *Policy-Making in the European Communities* (London: John Wiley & Sons).

Warleigh-Lack, A. and Rosamond, B. (2010) 'Across the EU Studies–New Regionalism Frontier: Invitation to a Dialogue', *Journal of Common Market Studies*, 48 (4): 993–1013.

Wasserfallen, F. (2010) 'The Judiciary as Legislator? How the European Court of Justice Shapes Policy-making in the European Union', *Journal of European Public Policy*, 17 (8): 1128–46.

Weatherill, S. R. (2002) 'Pre-emption, Harmonisation and the Distribution of Competence to Regulate the Internal Market', in C. Barnard and J. Scott (eds) *The Law of the Single European Market, Unpacking the Premises* (Oxford: Hart).

Weatherill, S. R. (2004) 'Competence Creep and Competence Control', *Yearbook of European Law*, 23 (1): 1–55.

Weiler, J. H. H. (1991) 'The Transformation of Europe', *Yale Law Journal*, 100: 2403–83.

Weiler, J. H. H. (1993) 'Journey to an Unknown Destination: A Retrospective and Prospective of the European Court of Justice in the Arena of Political Integration', *Journal of Common Market Studies*, 31 (4): 417–46.

Weiler, J. H. H. (1994) 'A Quiet Revolution: The European Court of Justice and its Interlocutors', *Comparative Political Studies*, 26 (4): 510–34.

Weiler, J. H. H. and Wind, M. (2003) *European Constitutionalism Beyond the State* (Cambridge: Cambridge University Press).

Welteke, E. (2001) 'The Introduction of the Euro as a Historic Event', European American Business Council, Washington, 19 November (Frankfurt am Main: Bundesbank).

Wessels, W. (1991) 'The EC Council: The Community's Decisionmaking Center', in R. O. Keohane and S. Hoffmann (eds) *The New European Community: Decisionmaking and Institutional Change* (Boulder, CO: Westview), 133–54.

Wessels, W. (2006) 'Cleavages, Controversies an Convergence in Europen Union studies', in M. Cini and A. Bourne (eds) *Palgrave Advances in European Union Studies* (Basingstoke: Palgrave Macmillan), 233–46.

Wessels, W. and Traguth, T. (2010) 'Der hauptamtliche Präsident des Europäischen Rates: "Herr" oder "Diener" im Haus Europa?', *Integration*, 33 (4): 297–311.

Wilks, S. (2010) 'Competition Policy: Towards an Economic Constitution?', in H. Wallace, M. Pollack, and A. Young (eds) *Policy-Making in the European Union* (Oxford: Oxford University Press), 133–55.

Williams, A. J. (2004) *EU Human Rights Policies: A Study in Irony* (Oxford: Oxford University Press).

Williams, G. (2005) 'Monomaniacs or Schizophrenics?: Responsible Governance and the EU's Independent Agencies', *Political Studies*, 53 (1): 82–99.

Williamson, J. (1990) 'What Washington Means by Policy Reform', in J. Williamson (ed.) *Latin American Adjustment: How Much has Happened?* (Washington DC: Peterson Institute for International Economics), 5–20.

Wincott, D. (1995) 'Institutional Interaction and European Integration: Towards an Everyday Critique of Liberal Intergovernmentalism', *Journal of Common Market Studies*, 33 (4): 597–609.

Wind, M. (2009) 'Post-National Citizenship in Europe: The EU as a "Welfare Rights Generator"?', *Columbia Journal of European Law*, 15 (2): 239–64.

Wind, M. (2010) 'The Nordics, the EU and the Reluctance Towards Supranational Judicial Review', *Journal of Common Market Studies*, 48 (4): 1039–63.

Winzen, T., Roederer-Rynning, C., and Schimmelfennig, F. (2012) 'Five Decades of Parliamentarization: The Evolution of the EU's Multi-level Parliamentary System', Paper prepared for the 1st General Conference of the ECPR Standing Group on Parliaments, Dublin, 24–27 June.

Wolff, S. (2008) 'Border Management in the Mediterranean: Internal, External and Ethical Challenges', *Cambridge Review of International Affairs*, 21 (2): 253–71.

Wolff, S. (2013) 'Frontex, cache-misère des échecs de la politique migratoire européenne?', *Le Monde*, 22 October.

Wolff, S. and Schout, A. (2013) 'Frontex as Agency: More of the Same?', *Perspectives on European Politics and Society*, 14 (3): 305–24.

Wolff, S. and Mounier, G. (2012) 'A Kaleidoscopic View of the External Dimension of Justice and Home Affairs', *European Foreign Affairs Review*, 17 (5): 143–62.

Wonka, A. and Rittberger, B. (2011) 'Agency Governance in the European Union', *Journal of European Public Policy*, Special Issue, 18 (6): 780–9.

Wood, G. S. (1998) *The Creation of the American Republic 1776–1787* (London: University of Chapel Hill Press).

Wright, V. and Cassese, S. (1996) (eds) *La recomposition de l'État en Europe* (Paris: La Découverte).

Wyplosz, C. (2012) 'Banking Union as a Crisis-management tool', in T. Beck (ed.) *Banking Union for Europe: Risks and Challenges* (London: CEPR), 17–22.

Yee, A. S. (1996) 'The Causal Effects of Ideas on Policies', *International Organization*, 50 (1): 69–108.

Young, A. R. and Peterson, J. (2014) *Parochial Global Europe: 21st Century Politics* (Oxford: Oxford University Press).

Zhelyazkova, A. (2012) 'Complying with EU Directives' Requirements: the Link Between EU Decision-making and the Correct Transposition of EU Provisions', *Journal of European Public Policy*, 20 (5): 702–21.

Ziegler, K. S. (2009) 'Strengthening the Rule of Law, but Fragmenting International Law: The Kadi Decision of the ECJ from the Perspective of Human Rights', *Human Rights Law Review*, 9 (2): 288–305.

Zielonka, J. (2006) *Europe as Empire: The Nature of the Enlarged European Union* (Oxford: Oxford University Press).

Zimmerman, H. (2010) 'Varieties of Global Financial Governance? British and German Approaches to Financial Market Regulation', in E. Helleiner, S. Pagliari, and H. Zimmerman (eds) *Global Finance in Crisis* (London: Routledge), 121–38.

Zürn, M. and Joerges, C. (2005) *Law and Governance in Postnational Europe: Compliance Beyond the Nation-State* (Cambridge: Cambridge University Press).

Index